REVIEW OF BEHAVIOR THERAPY

REVIEW OF BEHAVIOR THERAPY

THEORY AND PRACTICE

VOLUME 12

CYRIL M. FRANKS
*Rutgers—The State University of New Jersey
and the Carrier Foundation, Belle Mead, New Jersey*

G. TERENCE WILSON
Rutgers—The State University of New Jersey

PHILIP C. KENDALL
Temple University

JOHN P. FOREYT
Baylor College of Medicine

THE GUILFORD PRESS
New York   London

© 1990 Cyril M. Franks, G. Terence Wilson, Philip C. Kendall, and John P. Foreyt

Published by The Guilford Press
A Division of Guilford Publications, Inc.
72 Spring Street, New York, NY 10012

All rights reserved

No part of this book may be reproduced, stored in a retrieval system, or transmitted, in any form or by any means, electronic, mechanical, photocopying, microfilming, recording, or otherwise, without written permission from the copyright owners.

Printed in the United States of America

This book is printed on acid-free paper.

Last digit is print number: 9 8 7 6 5 4 3 2 1

Library of Congress Catalog Card No. 76-126864
ISBN 0-89862-752-4
ISSN 0899-3378

I have no data yet. It is a capital mistake to theorize before one has data. Insensibly one begins to twist facts to suit theories, instead of theories to suit facts.

> SHERLOCK HOLMES, Esq.
> *A Scandal in Bohemia*

PREFACE

Every book and every series has its own, unique, developmental history, and it is appropriate at this time to review briefly the progress of events over the past two decades that lead from Volume 1, which appeared in early 1973 under the editorship of Cyril M. Franks and G. Terence Wilson, to Volume 12, almost two decades later, changed in title, authorship, format, and content—but unchanged in basic purpose.

> Vastly more books and articles are appearing and, unfortunately, quantity is accelerating at a far greater rate than quality, so that the chore of sifting, selecting and appraising becomes prodigious. Few clinicians, or even research workers for that matter, have time to explore the whole range of the behavior therapy literature in the depth that is required to do justice to this onerous task and there would appear to be a need for some conveniently integrated distillation of this vast literature together with appropriate commentaries to place the many developments in perspective. And in so doing, continuity would seem to be another cogent desideratum so that readers can assess for themselves what seems to be happening from year to year. (Volume 1, 1973, p. vii)

In starting this new series, we viewed ourselves as observers who chronicle and comment upon the changing scene in behavior therapy from year to year rather than as self-appointed arbitrators. To accomplish this process, we reprinted some 40 to 50 articles each year, divided into ten sections and accompanied by appropriate commentary. Each year the number of pages devoted to reprinted articles remained more or less constant. The same could not be said about our commentaries, which grew increasingly wordy until, by Volume 7, commentaries and articles occupied approximately the same number of pages. What to do about it? We could have reduced the number of reprinted articles or we could have severely curbed our urge to comment. Informal surveys and feedback from readers suggested that since, for the most part, the articles were reprinted from readily available journals, it was the commentaries themselves that were the most valuable.

So, commencing with Volume 8, which appeared in 1982, a spanking new *Annual Review of Behavior Therapy* emerged, changed in virtually every aspect other than the title and the two founding authors—note the change in wording from "editors" to "authors." There was even a new cover design and a new publisher. Instead of reprinting articles, the entire Review was devoted to commentary. Instead of ten sections, there were now eight detailed review chapters, each dealing with a selected facet of behavior therapy. Instead of two editors commenting upon ten sections, there were now four authors, each responsible for the same two subject areas from year to year—thereby maintaining the unique continuity that differentiated our series from virtually all other serial publications in this field. Why four authors rather than two? Because it was too much for the founding editors to provide comprehensive and up-to-date yearly commentaries upon every aspect of behavior therapy at the level of scholarship that was indicated. It was at this stage that Philip C. Kendall and Kelly D. Brownell came aboard. The division of labor was as follows: Franks (Overview; Children and Adolescents); Wilson (Fear Reduction and Anxiety; Clinical Issues); Kendall (Assessment and Methodology; Cognitive Processes); Brownell (Behavioral Medicine; Addictive Disorders).

Two volumes later, it had become increasingly evident that, if our aim is to draw searching attention to new developments of substance, the behavior therapy literature does not warrant intensive appraisal on an annual basis. It was therefore decided, commencing with Volume 10, to publish the review on a biennial basis—thereby necessitating a slight change in title. It became the *Review of Behavior Therapy: Theory and Practice*.

Volume 11 brought with it another major change. Kelly Brownell, our coauthor of Volumes 8–10, reluctantly withdrew from the series in order to concentrate on other commitments. Although regretting this loss, especially Kelly's expertise in the areas of addictive disorders and behavioral medicine, we were fortunate enough to have John P. Foreyt as his replacement, covering the same two areas.

Now, with the completion of Volume 12, we are beginning to wonder if there is still a need for our series in its present format. In cost–benefit terms, is the expenditure of considerable time and energy by the four of us warranted in terms of the possible contribution of the final product to behavior therapy at large and to our potential readership, in particular? Could the series be better continued in some other

PREFACE

form and, if so, what? We plan to give some hard thinking to these and related issues.

All that remains is to offer the following acknowledgments:

CMF, as always, thanks Bonnie Emery, Carol Martin, and Sue Wright for their friendly smiles and ready willingness to carry out all sorts of manuscript-related secretarial chores in a prompt and gracious manner. But most of all, there is his wife and colleague, Violet, whose love, loyalty, and shared professional activities over the years make it all worthwhile.

GTW thanks Barbara Honig for help in typing his chapters and Elaine Wilson and Michael Sayette for their useful comments. Preparation of his chapters was facilitated by National Institute on Alcoholic Abuse and Alcoholism Grant No. AA00259-19.

PCK thanks Beatrice Smith and Gloria Basmajian for their cooperative, competent, and prompt efforts; the Department of Psychology for its support of the Child and Adolescent Anxieties Disorders Clinic and related research; Frances Sessa and Tamar Chanksy for helpful comments and bibliographic assistance; all his graduate students and colleagues for sharing in the pleasures of learning; and last, but far from least, his sons, Mark P. and Reed H., and his wife, Sue, for their "intellectual and emotional support and the teases that keep one's perspective." Preparation of his chapters was facilitated by support from National Institute of Mental Health Grant No. 1 R01 MH44042-01A1.

JPF warmly acknowledges the helpful comments of Jennifer Cousins, G. Ken Goodrick, and Scott Raynaud for helpful comments on draft versions of his two chapters. Preparation of these chapters was facilitated by support from National Heart, Lung and Blood Institute Grant No. R01-HL-33954-05. Thanks are also due to Jacki McCoy for her secretarial assistance.

It has been a pleasure to see this series evolve over the years and we hope that our readers feel likewise.

Cyril M. Franks
G. Terence Wilson
Philip C. Kendall
John P. Foreyt

CONTENTS

1. BEHAVIOR THERAPY: AN OVERVIEW 1
CYRIL M. FRANKS
- Introduction *1*
- Professional and Paraprofessional Training in Behavior Therapy *9*
- Issues in Compliance and Noncompliance *14*
- Mental Retardation and the Deinstitutionalization Process *18*
- From Institution to Community *27*
- Consumer Behavior, Business, and Industry *32*
- Crime and Delinquency *35*
- Behavior Therapy and the Aging Process *39*
- Conclusions *42*

2. BEHAVIORAL ASSESSMENT AND METHODOLOGY 44
PHILIP C. KENDALL
- Assessment *44*
- Methodology *60*

3. FEAR REDUCTION METHODS AND THE TREATMENT OF ANXIETY DISORDERS 72
G. TERENCE WILSON
- Theories of Anxiety and Behavior Change *73*
- Specific Anxiety Disorders *86*

4. COGNITIVE PROCESSES AND PROCEDURES IN BEHAVIOR THERAPY 103
PHILIP C. KENDALL
- Depression: Cognitive Theory and Therapy *104*
- Rational-Emotive Therapy *111*
- Anxiety *120*

Conduct-Disordered Youth	126
Attributions	131
Stress Inoculation	133
Social Problem Solving	135

5. BEHAVIORAL MEDICINE — 138
JOHN P. FOREYT

Introduction	138
Health Status of the United States	140
Trends in Heart Disease Research and Control	143
RIP: Type A Behavior Pattern	158
Trends in Cancer Research and Control	162
AIDS	166
Behavioral Medicine at the Worksite	171
Status of Potentially Promising Research Techniques	174
Education and Training Trends in Health Psychology	176

6. THE ADDICTIVE DISORDERS — 178
JOHN P. FOREYT

Introduction	178
Obesity	178
Tobacco Use	200
Alcoholism	212

7. BEHAVIOR THERAPY WITH CHILDREN AND ADOLESCENTS — 225
CYRIL M. FRANKS

Introduction	225
Home and Family in Behavior Therapy	228
Behavioral Parent Training	235
Autism and Behavior Therapy	244
Child Abuse and Neglect	248
Behavior Modification and Education	254
Behavior Modification and the Education of the Atypical Child	265
Conclusions	270

8. CLINICAL ISSUES AND STRATEGIES IN THE PRACTICE OF BEHAVIOR THERAPY — 271
G. TERENCE WILSON

Commonalities among Psychological Therapies	272
Treatment Outcome: The Patient's Right to Effective Therapy	290

Biobehavioral Approaches: Combining Behavior Therapy with Pharmacotherapy — 292
Integrating Research and Practice — 295
Models of Training — 298
Conclusions — 300

REFERENCES — 303
AUTHOR INDEX — 355
SUBJECT INDEX — 372

REVIEW OF BEHAVIOR THERAPY

CHAPTER

1

BEHAVIOR THERAPY: AN OVERVIEW

CYRIL M. FRANKS

INTRODUCTION

Much has happened since Kazdin's (1978) *History of Behavior Modification*. And yet, in another sense, surprisingly little has occurred. The "me too" struggle for a precarious foothold in the mental health mêlée has long since come and gone along with the chauvinistic "I am better than you" stage that soon followed. Subsequent eras of territorial expansion, technique innovation, and increasingly sophisticated methodology, so well documented by Kazdin a decade ago, are now history. Behavior therapists, firmly established on the mental health scene, can now take time out to reflect upon accomplishments and implications for the future. We seem to have reached a plateau characterized largely by theoretical and practical routine. On the more positive side, the closing decade brought with it two encouraging developments.

When the Association for Advancement of Behavior Therapy (AABT) came into being in 1966, the name of the organization, modeled after the British and American Associations for the Advancement of Science, pointed to the directions in which behavior therapists wished to go. Our primary concern was with the advancement of behavior therapy as a scientific discipline rather than the inauguration of a guild. Unfortunately, time and tide mandated otherwise, and it is clinical, technical, and professional matters that now take precedence. This may not necessarily be undesirable other than from my personal perspective (Franks, 1987c). These trends reflect the interests of the AABT and related organizations, and it is this impetus that determines the directions of movements within behavior therapy. It is surely no coincidence that until recently the only text of substance within behavior therapy to deal exclusively and extensively with conceptual and related issues was written by a philosopher rather than a psychologist (Erwin, 1978). The first encouraging development reflects an organized return to these founding principles by a small group of conceptually committed AABT members. The second development, less clearly articulated, is evidenced by a shift from a simplistic S-R model to a nonlinear, mulitcausal, but methodologically rigorous perspective within an ecologically oriented framework (Martens & Witt, 1988).

The first development is long overdue. Handbooks of private practice (e.g., Kaplan, 1986) receive more attention than scholarly texts, and the writing on the wall is further underscored by the recent decision of the AABT's Board of Directors to develop a professional qualification geared exclusively toward practice (Russo, 1987).

For Skinner (1986) the common remedy for both these professional ills and the ailments of daily life is straightforward. All that is needed is a revitalized application of time-proven principles derived from the experimental analysis of behavior. For Lazarus (1988, 1989d) the partial remedy lies in the planful application of systematic eclecticism within behavior therapy. Other behavior therapists and applied behavior analysts are less certain. As Deitz (1987) notes in his call for a return to behavior theory, as applied behavior analysis becomes predominantly dedicated to problem solving, theory becomes increasingly neglected.

It was such concerns that led the call for a new section within the AABT devoted exclusively to the theoretical and conceptual underpinnings of professionalism (Rosenfarb, 1987; Haas, Rosenfarb, & Hayes, 1988). The links among philosophy, theory, data, and conceptual issues, on the one hand, and practical application, on the other, were once considered vital. It is only within the past two decades or so that the trend otherwise has become increasingly evident (Ross, 1985).

Although this new special interest group is unlikely to change the direction of mainstream behavior therapy significantly, this is not an isolated phenomenon and books dealing exclusively with conceptual matters are beginning to emerge. Although of limited appeal to the practitioner, Eysenck and Martin's (1987) edited text is a step in the right direction, a spirited attempt to underscore the sometimes overlooked notion that behavior therapy is an approach rather than a varigated mass of treatment strategies (Martin, 1989). Three major themes emerge. First, Skinner's radical behaviorism is correctly placed in perspective as a science of behavior that does have a place for events that are not directly observable. Second, genetic and individual differences are given due weight. Third, Pavlovian conditioning is reevaluated and placed in perspective.

Eelen and Fontaine (1986) urge us to go beyond an outmoded conditioning model to one that leans primarily upon the findings of cognitive and social psychology, but as Rescorla (1988) points out, dramatic expansions in knowledge of the associative processes underlying Pavlovian conditioning have taken place in the last 20 years. In a closely reasoned argument, Rescorla successfully demolishes the prevailing impression that Pavlovian conditioning is an obsolete technical field that is intellectually stagnant. Cognitive science, neuroscience, and Pavlovian conditioning have points of contact that interface favorably with modern behavior therapy.

In 1983 I organized and moderated a symposium for the Second World Congress on Behavior Therapy dealing with the related issue of the paradigmatic status of behavior therapy. In a closely related publication, Fishman, Rotgers, and Franks (1988) used a Kuhnian (1970) based philosophy of science model to examine the contributions of prominent behavior therapists grouped along various dimensions of this "paradigm" concept.

In this text, Krasner's (1988) opening sociocultural commentary is followed by Eysenck's (1988) neobehaviorist classical conditioning model and Rachlin's (1988) defense of molar behaviorism. Erwin (1988) argues conservatively for the investigation of cognitive approaches by the application of rigorous methodology, Kendall and Bacon's (1988) more middle-of-the-road cognitivism emphasizes the roles of cognitive factors in the genesis of emotional and behavioral disturbances, and Woolfolk (1988), the most "liberal," tries to place such inferential and phenomenonological concepts as "identity," "self," and "freedom" within the behavioral bailiwick. Although primarily a conventional social learning theorist, Rotgers (1988) attempts to integrate conditioning-based cognitive theories within the traditional behavior therapy domain. Staats's (1988) integration is more broad, no less than a linking of both conditioning and cognitive models of behavior therapy with general psychology across a spectrum ranging from neuropsychology and intelligence to group processes. Fishman's (1988) new paradigm attempts to replace the positivism of early behavior therapy with his version of social constructionism. In contrast to the more usual identification of social constructionism with a hermeneutic, qualitative approach, Fishman retains the behavioral science characteristics of behavior therapy. Finally, Schwartz (1988) presents what is perhaps the broadest perspective of all, proposing that theory and practice in behavior therapy be viewed as a subclass of general systems theory. It would seem that continuity and commonality as well as diversity underlie the continuum of paradigms that exist in behavior therapy today. In appraising these matters, our aim was not to advocate one paradigm over another but to articulate the strengths and weaknesses of each and to encourage discussion, surely one raison d'être for the foundation of the Special Interest Group referred to above.

There is no shortage of conceptual issues to explore. For example, what does eclecticism devoid of any conceptual base have to recommend it? (see Branch, 1987). Despite decades of discussion and the fairly recent appearance of what is probably behaviorism's best current advocate (Zuriff, 1985), there is still little agreement about the nature and role of behaviorism within the behavior therapy domain. Similar conclusions apply to current discussion of the role of cognitivism in behavior therapy and the claim of cognitive behavior therapists that this reflects a paradigm shift within the domain of behavior therapy, a matter to which we have had occasion to refer repeatedly in previous volumes in this series. Here, too, there are contrasting points of view. For example, Schnaitter (1987) argues cogently that behaviorism and cognitivism are not alternative theoretical positions addressing a single set of phenomena. An objective of behaviorism is to establish relationships between behavior and the context of its occurrence. One objective of cognitivism is to establish the design of internal machinery such that functioning organisms are capable of behaving in context. Conversely, this may be contrasted with Beidel and Turner's (1986) suggestion that "rather than cognitive-behavior therapy, perhaps cognitive behavior (the same words, but minus the -) is a more appropriate term to describe these new approaches to changing behavior," a sentiment I share.

At least in some circles, increasing dissatisfaction is expressed with respect to both the conceptual and methodological underpinnings of behavior therapy, a situation not unlike that which confronted physics earlier in this century. From the Renaissance to the late 19th century, physics advanced steadily under the benevolent domination of the then prevailing notions of physical causality, notions that vanished with the advent of Einstein (Russo & Budd, 1987). The recognition that multicausal, nonlinear theories are necessary in the study of contemporary disease processes reflects a similar evolution. In much the same vein, Russo and Budd fault traditional applied behavioral analysis and an operant technology that has remained essentially unchanged for over a decade, a methodology that does not lend itself well to the study of multiple contemporaneous stimuli.

Over the years I have drawn attention to the need for nonlinear thinking within behavior therapy, in this series (e.g., Franks, 1985, 1987a) and elsewhere (e.g., Franks, 1987c). The work of Wahler and his colleagues (e.g., Wahler & Hann, 1986), referred to often in this series, provides an excellent example in this respect. When confronted with the many observed discontinuities between the behavior of conduct-problem children and the short-term environmental contingencies operating in family interactions, Wahler seeks empirical explanation through a broader analysis of situational events.

Goldiamond (1984) uses the term "linear" for those cases in which the referred behavior is considered to be a function of variables that a particular explanatory system assigned to the referent as its exclusive domain, such as its conditioning history or maintaining variables. The term "nonlinear" is applied when the referred behavior is also controlled, at least to some extent, by alternative behaviors as well as being directly and functionally related to the more immediate events. Thus, linear analysis pertains primarily to topical interventions in which treatments are defined by the presenting problems and addressed directly toward these areas (see Russo & Budd, 1987). Nonlinear analysis refers to the use of both topical and systemic interventions, initiated by the presenting problems but addressed toward different behavior–contingency systems. Both linear and nonlinear analyses are useful and legitimate forms of inquiry, depending on the controlling variables. In most instances, both are necessary if the operant paradigm is to be expanded to deal constructively with the many issues prevailing in contemporary society. A similar rationale can be extended to behavior therapy at large.

Locke (1986) grapples with the methodological problems involved in the generalization from laboratory to field settings. Laboratory tasks are not realistic and conclusions rarely generalize to the field. What is needed is the identification of the essential features of the field that need to be replicated in the laboratory, a matter of induction rather than deduction. Unfortunately, Locke is less than clear in his distinctions between laboratory studies, field studies, and field settings, and the appropriate methodology, either deductive or inductive, to apply. What Locke does do, however, is to draw attention to the need to reconsider such issues in the light of contemporary behavior therapy and its expanded sociocultural domain.

In what may become a seminal contribution to the behavior therapy literature, Delprato (1987) offers a nonlinear approach that cuts across and yet integrates several closely related areas. He terms this approach "developmental interactionism," a formulation that takes into account the principles of traditional conditioning and learning theory while recognizing their limitations. Thus, developmental interactionism as presented by Delprato is "a relatively recent outgrowth of several confluent movements, including hereditary × environment interactionism, the integrated-field perspective, evolutionary thinking, Schneirla's comparative-developmental psychology, behavioral embryology, life-span developmental psychology, retreats from reductionism, and the systems approach." Development is viewed as an interactive process in which organism and environment are both active participants.

Consistent with the above proposal, there is a revival of interest in Kantor's (1959) much neglected interbehavioral psychology. For years, Kantor has been misunderstood, perhaps in part because of his premature insistence that behavioral theory and therapy could be as scientific as the physical sciences and that behaviorism was a necessary first but far from final step. Kantor, not a well-known figure in psychology despite his productivity, was an outspoken critic of metaphysical dualism. In its place, Kantor offered a monistic behavioral field theory with an organismic focus upon mutual and simultaneous interactions between organism and environment. For Kantor, psychology's subject matter is the holistic and naturalistic coordination of the entire organism. There is no artificial and exclusively linear one-to-one relationship between simulus and response. In their informed discussion of interbehavioral psychology and its implications for contemporary behavior therapy, Ruben (1986) and an edited text by Ruben and Delprato (1987) underscore Kantor's point that a holistic perspective does not have to be at the expense of a return to fuzzy thinking.

À propos of fuzzy thinking, at one time I was impressed with systems theory and its promise for behavior therapy. Then disenchantment set in. It is difficult, if not virtually impossible at this time, to extract objective and testable formulations from the world of systems theory. Part of the problem is that "systems" therapies are only tenuously based on general systems theory, itself not very rigorous. To add to the confusion, there are many different systems theories. Thus, enticing as the notion sounds in principle to those who seek a holistic and nonlinear approach to behavior therapy, systems theory has little to offer at this stage other than as an alternative paradigm against which the usefulness of behavior therapy can be tested.

Behavior therapists have long been concerned with the maintenance of ethical standards. For example, Browne and Mahoney (1984) raise the issue of whether sports psychologists should spend more time applying their expertise to social and personal issues of a more serious or disabling nature rather than to the issues customarily found in such settings. However, while behavioral researchers have developed considerable expertise in examining the circumstances surrounding the effectiveness of their technology, limited attention has been given to the manner in which the use of these technologies affects the influencing agent. How does such technology affect the user, asks Kipnis (1987). Does it humanize, dehumanize, or have no effect on those who apply technologies that cause significant changes in others? The suggestion is made that the use of behavioral technology can produce changes in the values, beliefs, and behavior of practitioner and subject. These changes could include denigration of the target and even a rejection of democratic systems of control. There is an obvious need, argues Kipnis, to establish ethical safeguards for the users as well as the targets of behavioral technology.

For Neef, Iwata, and Page (1986), the issue is not so much the efficacy of ethical absolutes as the resolution of conflicts between the ability of science to benefit society and the values that dictate concern for the individual. Consider, for example, the three usual criteria for the protection of research subjects: informed consent, determination of the cost-benefit ratio, and validation by external professional peers. These are no simple matters. In 1975 Davison and Stuart proposed that the securing of consent involves a hierarchy of protection according to the level of benefit, risk, validation, status of the procedure to be used, and the degree to which the person is in a position to provide informed consent freely. The degree of consent ranges from 1, indicating that acceptable consent can be verbal, to 10, indicating that consent must be witnessed and approved by independent review. For example, if the procedure offers high potential benefit to the subject, is well established, involves a low level of risk, and consent that is free from coercion, then only level 1, verbal consent, is required. At the other extreme, if the procedure offers low potential benefit to the subject and high potential benefit to society, is experimental, and involves a high degree of risk, then a much greater degree of consent is required (level 10).

Wolpe's (1986) chronicle of old and new sources of misinformation from outside and within behavior therapy continues unabated. He is correct in his lamentations. Behavior therapy is still seen in many nonbehavioral circles as a handmaiden to be called on for resolution of minor problems. Wolpe does not say what to do about this. Todd and Morris (1983) are likewise concerned with misconception and miseducation within behavior therapy, but they take the wise precaution of collecting data before reporting apprehensions. It is their contention, substantiated by a survey of relevant textbooks, that currently used introductions to social, cognitive, personality, and developmental psychology misrepresent both the content and the spirit of applied behavior analysis. Although their sample is admittedly small, it is sufficient for their allegations to be taken seriously. Their proposed solutions include improved presentation by behavior analysts together with a vigorous campaign to educate authors and publishers with respect to the errors of their ways and possible steps toward remediation.

Closely related to the image of behavior therapy in the professional literature are the attitudes toward behavior therapy among various student and lay populations. The negative perspective of the lay community seems attributable in large part to the erroneous impression that behavior modification offers a threat to personal endeavor and hence to society as a whole. The misgivings of the student and professional community are more complex. In 1979 Turkat, Harris, and Forehand conducted a questionnaire survey of undergraduate attitudes toward behavior modification. The students tended to view behavior modification as appropriate for target groups such as prisoners and retardates but inappropriate for homosexuals, normal children, those with marital problems, and other more "innocent" populations. According to Turkat and his colleagues, people tend to view behavior modification as more appropriate when applied to a stigmatized target group. It is also suggested that the extent to which individuals view behavior modification negatively depends on how accurate their perceptions are with respect to what constitutes behavior modification.

Boivin, Sweell, and Scott (1986) used a modified version of this questionnaire to evaluate attitudes toward behavior modification among four student populations likely to differ from each other in their feelings with respect to the target groups specified in the survey statements. The population surveyed consisted of inmate students at a state prison, students at a private Christian Liberal Arts college, students at a large state university, and students of criminal justice. Once again, the principal finding was that the extent to which all groups viewed behavior modification as ethical or appropriate depended not only upon how the student concerned viewed behavior modification in general (e.g., its threat to human freedom) but also upon the nature of the target population. If it is important to have an informed public, it is also important to know about prevailing feelings with respect to the population to whom the behavior modification is being applied.

Finally, as further comment upon attitudes toward behavior therapy, we take up once again the hoary issue of where behavioral psychologists take their troubles. In 1971 Lazarus aroused a minor furor when he reported certain anecdotal "findings." According to Lazarus, behavior therapists tend to consult nonbehavioral therapists when they have problems. In a more objective national survey of two APA divisions, Norcross and Prochaska (1984) arrived at similar findings. So it seems that Lazarus was not so far off the mark after all. Watkins, Campbell, Lopez, and Himmell (1987) reanalyzed data from a national survey of 716 counseling psychologists to determine the incidence, duration, and theoretical orientations of behavior therapists' personal psychotherapists. Once again, their findings indicate that a significant number of APA's Division 17 members who identify their primary theoretical orientation as behavioral report having received treatment largely from nonbehavioral practitioners. Noting that psychodynamic therapists were by far the most likely to have received treatment from therapists of a similar persuasion, it is suggested that behavior therapists who provide therapy training are not inclined to "enculturate" their students as vigorously as do therapists from other persuasions.

One final brief comment. In Volume 11, I had occasion to note an unfortunate tendency to think in terms either of neuropsychology for behavior therapists or behavior therapy for neuropsychologists rather than a behavioral approach to problems in neuropsychology. Little has happened in the interim to encourage a more favorable summing up. For example, Hartlage's (1986) "The Future of Behavioral Neuropsychology" pinpoints two emerging trends, neither of which involves such an integration. One involves an increasing focus on the behavioral facets of neuropsychological functioning (see also Wedding, 1986) and the other pertains to the neurobehavioral, potentially neurotoxic, effects of substances commonly found in the environment. As with Wedding, Horton, and Webster's (1987) otherwise impressive *Neuropsychology Handbook*, behavioral neuropsychology, as I view the term, still seems to be given short shrift.

PROFESSIONAL AND PARAPROFESSIONAL TRAINING IN BEHAVIOR THERAPY

Systematic training in behavior therapy is carried out primarily in doctoral programs in clinical psychology. To ascertain prevailing orientations in leading programs in this country, Nevid, Lavi, and Primavera (1986) conducted a cluster analysis of reported training orientations in 96 doctoral programs. Although most programs reported multiple orientations, the predominant cluster is described by

Nevid et al. as eclectic cognitive-behavioral. Three other clusters of significant but lesser emphasis were also present: broad spectrum behavioral; psychoanalytic-humanistic; and a heterogeneous grouping that represented widely varying patterns of identification. Based on this analysis, the authors suggest that eclecticism and cognitive-behavioral approaches are likely to grow in importance as new graduates of programs that emphasize these orientations enter the field.

In a follow-up study, Nevid et al. (1987) report the results of a principal components analysis of these data. The two principal components that emerged clearly contrasted, on the one hand, behavioral versus psychodynamic approaches and, on the other hand, humanistic versus conditioning approaches. The factor score plots revealed clear separation among the various programs indentified with either behavioral or psychoanalytic/humanistic approaches. However, the majority of training programs tended to cluster around the midpoints on both dimensions, which the authors interpret as an indication of multiple approaches in training.

An ongoing controversy in many doctoral programs pertains to the requirement that students receive some form of personal therapy as an integral component of their training. Historically, however, it has been the psychoanalytically oriented programs that have insisted on personal therapy as a necessary prerequisite for competent clinical practice. It is argued by those who recommend personal therapy in analytic training that numerous benefits will acrrue. These include enhanced sensitivity and awareness, more effective technical skills, increased confidence in the validity of the theoretical model, and, finally, reduced personal symptomatology on the part of the therapist, leading toward more effective therapy.

As McNamara (1986) notes, given the strong positions that have been articulated, the empirical evidence is surprisingly limited. In 1978, apparently the last time this issue was systematically addressed, Parloff, Waskow, and Wolfe (1978) concluded that the contributions of personal psychotherapy to the enhancement of the therapist's usefulness "remains undemonstrated."

Understandably, in view of its association with the dynamic model, behavior therapists have been reluctant to involve their students in personal therapy activities. Yet, as Williams and Long (1983) observe, personal therapy conducted within a behavioral framework does not have to have an intrapsychic focus. The use of behavioral knowledge and skills for the more effective management of personal problems can be a useful device for dealing effectively with lifestyle concerns that can readily transfer to patient intervention.

No longer is it suggested that behavior therapists are less interested in relationship factors, a position inadvertently invited by simplistic behavior therapists in earlier years. Behavior therapists seek to establish relationship competencies pertaining to specific outcome goals rather than vague concepts such as growth (Edelstein, 1985). No longer is the therapeutic relationship viewed as a nonspecific treatment factor that cannot be systematically investigated in its own right. Despite this affirmation, there is still a paucity of evidence, theoretical direction, or practical guidelines to help behavioral practitioners to develop positive treatment relationships.

To assess the behavior therapist's perceptions of the client and vice versa, Bennun, Hahlweg, Schindler, and Langlotz (1986) devised two 41-item adjective checklists. The instruments were used first with a German sample and then cross-validated with an English population of hospitalized and outpatient psychiatric patients receiving behavior therapy for various disorders. Regardless of setting, clear associations between both patient and therapist perceptions of each other and treatment outcome emerged. Training in behavior therapy needs to include further attention to interpersonal and relationship factors. In this respect, Bennun et al. note that when behavior therapists are compared with individuals professing other orientations, behavior therapists tend to be more empathetic than psychoanalysts and more emotionally supportive than either Gestalt or psychoanalytically oriented therapists.

McNamara's (1986) self-management program of personal intervention, required as one of the components of the doctoral training program in the Behavior Therapy Treatment sequence at Ohio University, provides a splendid illustration of these principles in application. First, students are instructed to select a personal behavior, habit, cognition, or emotional response that they wish to modify, preferably, a problem of potential relevence to their clinical careers. Then they are given extensive self-recording and self-management reading lists followed by appropriate demonstration. Although no control or long-term outcome data are reported, short-term benefits remain generally positive. Most important, students become clients and, despite obvious limiting factors, are able to gain some perspective with respect to that role. What is not known is the extent to which students who undergo this experience become better therapists as a consequence.

Most use of microcomputers by behavior therapists is geared toward necessary but tedious chores, such as report writing and information management. Lambert's (1987a, 1987b) pioneering innovations are more exciting. Through sophisticated simulation techniques, the computer's superior logic and branching capabilities are applied to the difficult task of training behavioral assessors and therapists. In one report, Lambert (1987a) shows how the case of a computer-simulated 32-year-old man with anxiety can be used as an aid to more traditional behavioral training. In principles, 42 separate pieces of information gleaned from eight assessment areas can be used to form diagnostic impressions and selection of treatment strategies. Following problem resolution, the user may use the program to conduct posttreatment assessment. The program can be tailored to specific training needs and terminated or modified at will.

According to Lambert, this simulation is an accurate representation of clinical decision-making processes in contemporary behavior therapy. However, as Lambert cautions, even the best of simulation training cannot substitute for direct work with real patients. Therapy simulations represent restricted and necessarily contrived situations. To facilitate and enrich training, Lambert, Intrieri, and Hollandsworth (1986) have also developed a sophisticated computerized reference retrieval system for behavior therapists confronted with a vast array of literature. How effective this adjunctive device is depends on the vitality of the training program within which it is imbedded.

Behavioral training of nonbehavioral professionals and paraprofessionals necessitates somewhat different goals and strategies. As noted in Volume 11, by far the most sophisticated behavioral training for nurses has been carried out by Milne and associates in the United Kingdom. In his latest book (Milne, 1986), the focus extends to parents and teachers. For Milne, the primary concerns are with the systemic nature of the triadic relationship among supervisor, mediator, and trainee and the need to overcome constraints imposed on the training relationship by the system.

A related concern is the assessment of staff knowledge about behavior modification. In Volume 10 we reported a 50-item multiple-choice procedure for assessing how well residential setting respondents understood the application of behavior modification principles (O'dell, Tarler-Benlolo, & Flynn, 1979). Furtkamp, Gifford, and Schiers (1982) have since developed two considerably shorter parallel forms of the same test. Virtually nothing was known about relationships between test scores, staff performance, and changes in the children being trained until Sturmey, Newton, Milne, and Burdett (1987) reported encouraging findings based upon large samples of mental health and teacher behavior modification trainees in multiple settings. As the authors caution, knowledge of either principles or applicability is not necessarily synonymous with performance. Furthermore, according to Milne (1986), scores and measures of ability to carry out a functional behavioral analysis of a videotape is demonstrably superior to any questionnaire measure in the prediction of actual staff skills.

The national emphasis on deinstitutionalization leads to proportionately more severe behavior disorders in those who remain. Thus, the need for effective treatment of such individuals becomes a matter of even greater urgency and the roles of paraprofessionals assumes even greater importance than hitherto. Poorly trained direct care workers having frequent contact with residents could make matters even worse. Unintentionally, the staff may be reinforcing undesirable behaviors.

In Reid and Schepis's (1986) behavioral supervision model, the first step defines performance areas in terms of observable and accountable work outputs or behaviors. The second step, monitoring, refers to the systematic collection of objective data about staff performance. In the third step, the staff are instructed in their respective job responsibilities, using the behavioral definitions established in step 1 to ensure that these responsibilities are clearly delineated. The fourth step, the provision of behavioral consequences, consists of the use of supervisor arranged events and items contingent on identified staff behavior. The final step, evaluation or review, is used to determine whether the supervisory procedures are actually producing the desired effects. As noted, such matters as outcome evaluation, extension to other work areas, and enhanced cost–benefit efficiency await further study. So far, the approach has been demonstrated effective only for restricted duties at a particular time rather than the entire set of job responsibilities.

Finally, I draw attention to a timely ecological analysis of staff training in residential settings by Landesman-Dwyer and Knowles (1987). Every residential setting has its own ambience. Everyday operations are related in one way or another to external political, financial, and social realities, all subject to change. Thus, staff performance reflects a complex pattern influenced directly and indirectly by the surrounding social environment, the personal characteristics of the staff, and available training facilities. Within this context, evaluation of staff performance prior to implementation of any paraprofessional training program is essential, followed closely by immediate and long-term outcome assessment of any training that is instituted. In so doing, Landesman-Dwyer and Knowles assume that effectiveness of staff training programs is a function of how well matched their content is to the actual and perceived needs of the staff concerned. Additionally, the ability to benefit from particular training methods is a function of individual staff characteristics. This emphasis on the total environment from both subjective and objective perspectives is a far cry from traditional behavior modification.

ISSUES IN COMPLIANCE AND NONCOMPLIANCE

The study of compliance is still in the stage of specific rather than general principles. The literature is long on homilies and short on general principles. To take but one example, Black and his associates offer excellent practical guidance for pharmacists seeking to exert positive influences on their clients when it comes to taking medication (Black, Aller, Madonna, & Skinner-Smith, 1983; Black, Madonna, Skinner-Smith, & Blinde, 1983; Black, Madonna, Skinner-Smith, & Thompson-Skinner, 1984). No conceptual schema is presented, perhaps because this is of little or no concern to the commercial aspects of everyday living.

Peck and King (1988), in a somewhat more sophisticated study, draw attention to the fact that many medical practitioners are unaware that their patients are not following the advice given. Most greatly overestimate compliance and many are unable to recognize which patients are noncompliant. Why is it that physicians are so lacking in this awareness? One reason, suggest Peck and King, is that many patients are not even asked if they are following the regimen prescribed. Peck and King's simple suggestions for improvement include involving the patient in decision making to the extent that this is possible, giving volunteering appropriate information, and engaging in a "mutual participation" or "contractual" model. Because patients tend to behave in accordance with their belief systems, it is also necessary at times to influence or otherwise change these beliefs and attitudes.

Ley's (1986, 1988) particular concern is with the controversial role of cognitive factors in compliance. Although the provision of information is not guaranteed to enhance compliance, it seems likely that understanding, recall, and compliance can be meaningfully enhanced by the use of written materials. Unfortunately, compliance-enhancing strategies are often less than optimal. Explanatory booklets are usually written at too high a level of difficulty, and no attempt is made to ensure that the information provided is ever read. Research into the conditions under which increasing understanding effects compliance is needed and exploration of ways in which behavioral strategies may be successfully incorporated into the written materials. Finally, Ley

BEHAVIOR THERAPY: AN OVERVIEW

draws attention to the circumstances under which the relatively inexpensive deployment of cognitive variables should be instituted. It is suggested that cognitive intervention be the strategy of first choice in situations in which the consequences of noncompliance are not likely to be too serious or costly. The more effective and expensive behavioral strategies should be used when the consequences of noncompliance are likely to be serious, cognitive strategies have failed, or under conditions in which cognitive strategies are known to have little chance of success.

To the best of my knowledge, the only other recent book of significance in this area is that of Nehemkis and Gerber (1986). Written for a multidisciplinary audience, this book stresses the multiple determinants of failure to comply with medical regimens and the need to adapt an ideographic approach. Unfortunately, methodological problems are given short shrift and the unwary reader is likely to be more impressed with the level of research in this complex field than is justified by the data. Nevertheless, this book has much to offer. Even with the growing appreciation of multifactorial determinants, the literature is still largely one-dimensional. Single-focus behavioral approaches, argues Gerber (1986), tend to be simple-minded in their neglect of more subtle and indirect influences. For example, a critical aspect of patienthood frequently ignored is quality of life, a variable particularly likely to influence compliant behavior in cases of chronic illness. When Barofsky (1978) examined the relationship between quality of life and compliance in cancer patients who discontinued treatment, one-third declared that nonparticipation was due to the adverse effects of the treatment on their daily lives. Research techniques that focus on specific short-time parameters would probably fail to detect the life consequences of compliance and noncompliance with the proposed intervention. In the Gerber and Nehemkis book (1986), the focus is upon how becoming more compliant with medical recommendations can affect the patient's life and how knowledge can improve the physician's interactions with the chronically ill patient.

Turk, Salovey, and Litt (1988) discuss the circumstances under which cognitive–behavioral strategies are likely to bring about lasting change. Three conditions need to be met: the patient has to accept the therapeutic objectives because of their expected values to them rather than their worth to the health care provider; the patient must learn to attribute ultimate success or failure to his or her own behavior; and, finally, the patient has to believe that he or she is competent to carry out the self-care regimen prescribed. Behavioral approaches that fail to take into account the phenomenological experience of the patient are of limited utility. A strictly operant model is doomed to failure if it does not take into account meaningful existential issues for which there are generally no facile answers. However, again, this is easier said than done, and we are still left very much in the air as to what to do about it.

As a parting shot, Cummings and Nehemkis (1986) draw attention to society's role in the development of noncompliance. Numerous shortcomings serve to reinforce noncompliance. Among these are legal shackles, the structure of our health care institutions, and a compensation system that sometimes inadvertently removes the financial incentive to get well in a hurry. Within this context, deinstitutionalization may have brought about more harm than good. Many mentally disturbed persons end up on the streets, preyed upon by criminals, deteriorating physically, and thereby becoming the objects of attention from the criminal justice system. Many fail to comply with prescribed medication regimens either because they dislike the side effects or because they lack insight into the fact that they are ill. For other patients, there are strong financial or social incentives for seeking to return to the hospital if at all possible. When a patient role inside the institution becomes more attractive than a worker role within the community, patienthood can easily become addictive. For those who get some secondary gain from the sick role, for whatever reason, noncompliance can be the ticket of admission. Wittingly or otherwise, lawyers reinforce this pattern. The patient's lawyer is motivated to obtain maximum financial benefit for the client even if this means maximizing the associated pain and disability. Significant improvement by compliance with the treatment program could result in financial disadvantage. Thus, the hapless patient is torn between the desire to feel better and the realization that this could result in adverse financial consequences.

Virtually all compliance research suffers from major methodological problems (Levy, 1986). Definitions of social support lack consistency, clarity, and operational specificity, and current research reflects this lack of direction (Cameron & Best, 1987). A comprehensive, theoretical model, so far conspicuously lacking, could provide a framework for thinking about how specific interventions might be woven together synergistically. There is a need for standardization of interventions and their examination in relation to both change processes and context. Instead of asking "What is the effect of this maneuver?" it is necessary to ask the more sophisticated question "What is the effect of this maneuver, when offered to this type of person, in this kind of context?" Finally, there is a need for more sophisticated outcome evaluation that takes into account both the roles of the individual components and their interactions. Heiby and Carlson's (1986) health compliance (HC) model includes both external, situational antecedents and consequences of compliant behavior and internal or organismic variables. For compliance to be maintained, argue Heiby and Carlson, it is necessary to provide a prompt for the target behavior, determine that the behavior is followed by reinforcing rather than punishing sequences, and ascertain that individual perceptions, beliefs, and attitudes facilitate the effects of the antecedent and consequence variables. Numerous subtypes of compliance can be predicted from their model. For example, individuals with deficient self-reinforcement skills may be more susceptible to noncompliance to a regimen with delayed benefits than will individuals with adequate self-reinforcement skills. As Heiby and Carlson note, the effectiveness of their model remains to be determined. Nevertheless, the proposed model offers promise of a much needed integration in the area of health compliance (see also Heiby, Onorato, & Sato, in press, cited in Heiby & Carlson, 1986, p. 148).

Finally, I draw attention to one of the more sophisticated models of compliance. For Leventhal and Cameron (1987), even more important than the level of noncompliance is the large variation in compliance across different treatment regimens and the smaller but still significant variation within any given regimen. This suggests that noncompliance is a multifaceted problem that is influenced by the characteristics of the disease, the treatment regimen and setting, and the relevant personality characteristics of the individuals concerned. Perhaps for these reasons, approaches effective under one set of circumstances may be unpredictably less effective in another setting.

What this means is that current theories offer limited guides to compliance research. Given this situation, Leventhal and Cameron first summarize current endeavors, highlighting contributions and deficiencies. In the second phase of their paper, they propose a way to integrate the major theories into an overall system. According to Leventhal and Cameron, most compliance studies are guided by one of five major orientations: biomedical, social learning, rational belief theories, a communication approach, or self-regulative systems theory. Each views noncompliance from a different perspective and hence arrives at a different resolution of the problem. Each offers its own strengths and weaknesses. As far as behavioral approaches are concerned, the most salient empirical deficit seems to be a demonstrable failure to maintain long-term changes. In addition, by focusing on the development of multifaceted programs aimed at reinforcing desired behaviors, they fail to identify the specific social cognitive, and motivational processes underlying change.

For reasons not hard to discern, Leventhal's three-stage self-regulation model of illness is the favorite (Leventhal, Nerenz, & Steele, 1984). The three stages are as follows: (1) the cognitive representation of the health threat (e.g., perceived identity, potential causes, and possible consequences); (2) action plan or coping, in which a plan of action is formulated and begun; and (3) appraisal, in which specific criteria are utilized to gauge success, with perceptions of insufficient progress leading to appropriate modifications of the representation or coping plans. Suggestions are made for integrating the biomedical, behavioral, and rational decision models into the framework, and special attention is given to the processes whereby the psychological system is affected by the social institutions, cultural values, expectations, and norms of the surrounding environment.

MENTAL RETARDATION AND THE DEINSTITUTIONALIZATION PROCESS

A decade or so earlier, most behavioral interventions in the area of mental retardation stemmed either from experimental psychology or traditional S-R learning theory. The main thrust in behavior therapy with the mentally retarded now lies in the development of nonlinear but experimentally rigorous, multidimensional, ecological perspectives (e.g., Barrett, 1986).

The extent to which these changes percede or follow attitudinal changes in the public at large is difficult to determine at this time. What is more probable is that the relationships between public sentiment and professional management are based upon reciprocal influences and feedback. Even more certain is that preconceived notions about mental retardation and institutional care are still too often based on stereotypes and inadequate information. Many strategies have been deployed within residential care facilities to counteract these preconceptions and misconceptions. One such strategy is the institutional tour, admittedly one small component in a complex situation, but, nevertheless, something that is relatively easy to implement. According to Gottlieb (1975), depending on how the tour is designed and implemented, institutional tours tend to change attitudes positively toward institutions but negatively toward clients.

To shed light on these matters, Carsrud et al. (1984) examined the effects of tours conducted in a large public residential facility for the mentally retarded located in rural Texas. It was argued that the last clients visited would be the most potent influences on subsequent attitudes. The subjects consisted of 56 psychology students enrolled at a large public university. Of these, 35 completed an inclass pretour attitudinal test. Subjects had no prior experience of either residential facilities or mentally retarded individuals, or course material on mental retardation. Tours were conducted 4 weeks before course completion. Thirty-five subjects completed a pretest 1 week prior to the tour and 2 preceding weeks of lectures on mental retardation. The dependent measures were pretour and posttour semantic differential scales assessing attitudes regarding mentally retarded children, adults, ward attendants, and the residential facility. High- and low-functioning clients consisted of adults and children, thereby allowing the student tour groups to see a variety of clients and age ranges.

The high–high configured tour group visited training workshops with mildly mentally retarded clients, followed by visits by classrooms with mildly mentally retarded ambulatory clients. The high–low tour first visited classrooms for mildly mentally retarded clients. Then they saw profoundly mentally retarded nonambulatory clients in their classrooms. The low–high group took the reverse of the high–low tour. The low–low tour visited profoundly mentally retarded clients training in their living units. Next, they saw a different class of nonambulatory, profoundly mentally retarded clients.

This study has obvious limitations. The "public" consisted of a small group of psychology students in one university and only one institution was visited. No attempt was made to determine how lasting these attitudes were or how they were modified over time. Nevertheless, within these constraints, it would seem that tours can have positive effects on attitudes regarding mentally retarded adults and children in residential settings, provided that they are structured in ways to counter preexisting negative stereotypes. Most important, the present findings fail to support still prevailing impressions that institutional tours of this nature are more likely to influence prevailing attitudes regarding specific institutions rather than feelings about mental retardation at large. Although mentally retarded clients still tend to be rated more negatively than their settings, appropriate tour configurations can have beneficial effects on subsequent attitudes. It would seem that it is the enjoyment of the contact (high-functioning clients), rather than its extent, that is more likely to induce positive attitude changes regarding clients. Finally, it would seem that tours that are most effective in changing attitudes regarding clients are not necessarily the same as those that bring about attitude changes regarding staff and settings.

Attitudes regarding institutionalized mental retardates are closely related to prevailing trends toward deinstitutionalization. Deinstitutionalization and normalization are probably among the more controversial and emotionally charged issues in mental retardation at this time. As Landesman and Butterfield (1987) observe, normalization is an ideology of human service based on the proposition that it is necessary to increase access to culturally typical activities and settings to enhance the overall quality of life. The places where people live, learn, work, and play should facilitate rather than restrict involvement in the mainstream of society to the maximum possible extent. It would seem to be a logical corollary of this premise that the development of community-based living arrangements for mentally retarded individuals is generally preferable to institutionalization for other than the more severely disturbed or otherwise impaired. Curiously enough, however, or perhaps not so curiously, this remains an area of heated debate among psychologists, some of whom are among the chief advocates of normalization and deinstitutionalization, whereas others are vocal critics.

More heat than light seems to have been generated in this highly charged area, and the literature is replete with speculation and position papers rather than data. Landesman and Butterfield draw attention to three chronic problems. First, there is no standard terminology or nomenclature for describing and evaluating residential environments. Second, such studies as are available tend to be seriously flawed in design. Third, "quality of life" is a multidimensional and value-labeled concept; multiple perspectives and multiple outcome measures are essential.

It is still not possible to provide other than limited and provisional answers to such major questions as "Should there be any institutionals at all?," "For what individuals and under what circumstances is normalization attainable or desirable?," and "Under what circumstances is institutionalization unavoidable and for whom?" Even within one type of residential care, significant variation can occur across individual facilities. Resident experiences are related in little understood ways to differential treatment by staff and individual differences in resident responsivity. Nevertheless, it seems fairly certain that, given appropriate support systems, most profoundly retarded individuals, even those with severe behavior or health problems, can progress favorably in settings other than large, traditional institutions.

Recognizing that most effort has gone toward the rehabilitation of the less severely handicapped, O'Neill, Brown, Gordon, and Schonhorn (1985) conducted a longitudinal study of changes in activity patterns and skills of severely and profoundly mentally retarded, multiply handicapped residents as they moved from large total care institutions to community living. Twenty-seven individuals were evaluated just before leaving the institution, 3 months after exit, and 9 months later. Some 192 nondisabled individuals who had participated in various research projects at the Institute for Rehabilitation Medicine at New York University served as a reference group.

Based on weekly activity and skill data, it would seem that these individuals can benefit from entering a community residential program under certain circumstances. With respect to activity patterns, the disabled participants had a more constricted tempo in daily activity than members of the nondisabled reference group. They tended to participate less in home and community life and to have lower levels of social contact, mobility, and independence in functioning, all of which is understandable. What is encouraging is that, following deinstitutionalization, the disabled group became significantly more like the reference group. Normalization of daily activities is not an all-or-nothing outcome; behavior change occurs gradually.

In terms of skills enhancement, the answer is less clear. All participants in the O'Neill et al. study showed higher levels of skill in at least one area after deinstitutionalization but not in all. An especially important area of significant improvement was expressive communication. It would seem that institutional environments suppress the emergence of certain skills more than others in ways that may vary from facility to facility, a finding that highlights one of the major problems with this study. Institutional and community staff may be using individual rather uniform standards when reporting residents' skills and activities.

Most investigators utilize global assessments to measure the impact of community-based placements upon mentally handicapped individuals transferred from traditional institutional settings. Although a more difficult undertaking, continuous observation of each subject offers many advantages. In this respect, Felce, deKock, and Repp's (1986) well-designed study, which combines the more customary indirect global measures with direct continuous observation of each subject, is exemplary. In addition to examining the effects of transfer to small community homes on the behavioral functioning of severely mentally handicapped adults, staff activities were also measured in terms of both providing opportunities for engaging in activity and consequating client behavior. Two comparisons were made: between a group of clients in a small home and a comparable group within various institutions and between the latter group upon entering the institution and after moving to a small home.

The observed improvements were attributed to the allocation of staff to small groups of clients, to a readily accessible, maternally enriched environment, to job specification and to staff training. Unfortunately, their study did not permit evaluation of the specific contributions of these factors. Clients showed increased functioning, particularly in the areas of domestic activity and staff interaction. These benefits seemed to be independent of age, years of institutionalization, or degree of impairment.

The problems involved in generalization from laboratory to field settings have already been noted. The assumptions that behavior observed in everyday living inevitably has a laboratory counterpart and that it is possible to extrapolate fairly directly from laboratory to the natural environment ignore the fact that every behavioral act has meaning only within context. As early as 1977, Brooks and Baumeister offered this warning, but it is only now that their caveat is beginning to be taken seriously. Extrapolation to real-life only becomes meaningful when there is clear demonstration of precisely how it is that such tasks are related to the real world. Mental retardation is a social as well as genetic and laboratory phenomenon. IQ-based definitions, argue Brooks and Baumeister, are of value for administrative and initial screening purposes but little more. As an alternative, these authors suggest that categorization measures be devised in terms of the social criteria used to define poor adaptation to living. Although somewhat extreme, this perspective has much to recommend it if it facilitates the infusion of ecological validity into the experimental psychology of mental retardation.

The deinstitutionalization movement has led to a host of promising behavioral procedures both for implementing alternative living arrangements and their evaluation. Unfortunately, neither the advent of demonstrably useful strategies nor legal advances has led to significant community acceptance. Chadsey-Rusch and Rusch (1986) explain why this is so. Societies such as ours have established customs, laws, or moral codes that determine "normative" behavior. These norms set the standards by which individuals are being judged. From this perspective, mentally retarded adults frequently display behaviors that do not "fit" community expectations and, consequently, are either ostracized or, what is perhaps worse, ignored. Individuals who display severe behavior disorders are especially likely to be excluded from mainstream community activities. It is Chadsey-Rusch and Rusch's premise that all mentally retarded individuals are capable of being involved in habilitation programs involving integration into the community. (They deliberately use the term "habilitation" rather than rehabilitation for obvious reasons: most of these individuals have never had any experience of community living.)

Within this context, Rusch, Chadsey-Rusch, White, and Gifford (1985) define community integration as "the process of uniting handicapped and nonhandicapped individuals as equal members jointly participating in recreational, residential and employment settings." An integrated community is further defined as a cohesive network of people and resources linked together by common expectations and shared interests. Equally important for Chadsey-Rusch and Rusch is the need to define what is meant by an "habilitation program." Such a definition depends upon diagnosis. If the diagnosis is in terms of mental illness, then the treatment tends to be psychiatrically oriented; if the diagnosis is mental retardation, the treatment is usually educationally oriented. In their discussion of habilitation programs, Chadsey-Rusch and Rusch focus upon educationally relevant treatment programming.

Even though environmental events (antecedents and consequences) play major roles in maintaining a particular variable, Voeltz and Evans (1983) stress the equal importance of behavioral interrelationships. Relevant operants may be maintained solely by chains or clusters of behaviors displayed by the individual in addition to stimuli emanating from the external environment. The study of multiple rather than single behaviors is emphasized together with the recognition and changes in one behavior are going to affect others. Some habilitation behaviors may be more important to teach than others, especially if the acquisition of target behaviors leads to multiple behavior improvements. Because mentally retarded persons are slow to learn new behaviors, it is important that habilitation specialists become adept at selecting these target behaviors that are most likely to result in multiple positive effects on other behaviors. To date, most research has focused upon eliminating maladaptive behaviors and noting the collateral effects of these procedures on other behaviors. Relatively little research has been conducted on the effects of teaching habilitative and more adaptive behaviors and then noting the effects on maladaptive behaviors.

The concept of setting or context is central to behavioral ecological theory. If the goal of habilitation is community integration, then community settings or contexts need to be carefully assessed to discover what Thurman (1977) calls ecological congruencies. According to Thurman, ecological congruence occurs when an individual's behavior is in harmony with the social norms of the environmental context. With mentally retarded persons, ecological incongruence occurs whenever behaviors that vary significantly from the established social norms are displayed or whenever the individuals concerned lack the particular skills necessary to function or perform adequately within these different contexts. Ecological congruence facilitates both the expression of maximum competence by the individual and his or her acceptance within the community. Thurman is careful to stress that congruence does not necessarily imply "normal" so much as a maximal adaptation to the environment, an adaptation that incorporates both maximal expression and maximal acceptance, or at least tolerance.

The reforms of the 1970s (see *Wyatt v. Stickney*, 1972) established the presumed minimal requirements for safe and humane living environments for mentally retarded individuals. As a consequence, most living environments for mentally retarded persons now provide for basic life support and humane care. Issues of health and safety are no longer of major concern. Unfortunately, as Jones, Lattimore, Ulicny, and Risley (1986) stated, despite sweeping reforms, other than improvements in physical conditions, many environmental features remain essentially unchanged. The emphasis is still upon the promotion of ongoing health care and minimizing or preventing harm rather than encouraging client development. For the sake of client safety and facilitation of ability to provide care and supervision, or so it is rationalized, opportunities for clients to explore and interact with the environment are minimized. When interaction between staff and clients does occur, it is characterized by staff performance of activities for the clients rather than encouragement of independent behavior or interventions to terminate episodes of undesirable behavior.

Meaningful engagement, argue Jones et al., is the basis for learning adaptive behavior. Adaptation occurs in response to interaction with the environment. Additionally, appropriate engagement provides a context for teaching. By appropriately consequating engagements, staff may teach clients to differentiate appropriate and inappropriate behaviors. Finally, appropriate engagement is important because it is inversely related to inappropriate engagement. When clients are not engaged in appropriate behavior, they are doing nothing or engaging in undesirable behavior.

Jones et al. provide suggestions for environmental programming. Their basic premise is that behavior is controlled by the environment in which it occurs and that it may be modified by systematic manipulation of environmental determinants. The ultimate goal in such programming is the elimination of the need for specialized environmental arrangements even for those with severe behavior disorders. By this token, treatment success is gauged in terms of the ability of these individuals to succeed and function effectively in the natural environment.

Largely as a consequence of this radical change in direction, the vocational outlook for individuals with mental retardation has improved dramatically within the past decade. The below minimum wage, center-based, sheltered-employment training that seemed so forward-looking in the early 1970s has given place to a variety of industry-based, cost–benefit employment options within the more real-world of the 1980s. The evidence to date, reviewed by Shafer (1987), suggests that effective, competitive employment services must attend not only to the workplace but also to the residential, recreational, and other behavioral domains that are interconnected with employment and the circumstances surrounding employment. Additionally, these services must attend to the development of effective and appropriate social survival skills and not simply to vocational task performance. Finally, perhaps most important of all, competitive employment service delivery must be longitudinal, providing support services as needed long after job placement has been made. Mentally retarded workers must be able to interact effectively with co-workers, supervisors, and, in some cases, customers. Teaching social skills within the context of productivity needs to become one of the primary tasks confronting those involved in the vocational habilitation of mentally retarded workers (Salzberg, Likins, McConaughy, & Lignugaris-Kraft, 1986).

To learn more about the reasons why mentally retarded workers are terminated, Salzberg, Lignugaris-Kraft, and McCuller (1988) reviewed relevant studies published over the past 35 years. Reasons for job loss among mentally retarded workers seem to be broadly distributed across both social and nonsocial domains, including such job responsibility factors as attendance and punctuality: task production factors, such as inadequate quality and quantity of work: task-related social skill deficits, such as not following instructions or responding appropriately to criticism; and personal–social inadequacies, such as inappropriate dress or bizarre behavior. Unfortunately, it is easier to construct appropriate job profiles and identify the range of reasons for job failure than to teach the repertoires necessary to ensure job maintenance. Individuals are responsible in various ways, to various degrees, and under various circumstances. Eventually, idealize Salzberg et al., behavioral job retention profiles will become available for the description of minimal skill thresholds for various jobs. After placement training might then proceed with those skills for which individuals do not exhibit minimal competencies.

As a first step in this process, Salzberg, Agran, and Lignugaris-Kraft (1986) obtained opinions from employers offering different types of jobs about behaviors considered important. These behaviors were then analyzed within three clusters: nonsocial production-related behaviors, task-related social behaviors, and personal–social behaviors. The respondents were competitive employment supervisors of janitors, dishwashers, maids, food service workers, or kitchen helpers.

Judgments about importance seemed to depend on the extent to which specific behaviors were related to work productivity. Whereas work productivity seems to be the prime concern, social behaviors are also critical to employment success, particularly those behaviors that are directly related to work productivity. Although hardly surprising, the documentation of these findings could lead to the provision of a generically applicable employment preparation curriculum for mentally handicapped individuals. First, as Salzberg, et al. suggest, skills could be sequenced in terms of their importance to the specific job being targeted for a particular client. Second, behaviors thought to be the most important might be further prioritized by their frequency of occurrence for that job. Behaviors that are least important and least frequently required for a particular job could be trained last. In this way, a set of viable training guidelines could be generated.

One complex skill that seems to be characteristic of success for mentally handicapped workers is that of appropriate job initiative, the recognition that something needs to be done and attending to it even though it is not an explicitly assigned responsibility. As McCuller, Salzberg, and Lignugaris-Kraft (1987) observe, establishing a single job initiative response is relatively straightforward. It simply requires that the response be reinforced in the presence of the intended discriminative stimulus and not reinforced, or even punished, in the absence of that stimulus. However, the development of a repertoire of job initiative responses is much more complex. The individual concerned must first learn how to discriminate when something needs to be done. Then he or she must learn to respond by performing the appropriate response. The necessary conditional discriminations and responses for job initiative are notoriously laborious to teach, especially if later ones require as much time and effort as earlier ones (McCuller et al., 1987).

FROM INSTITUTION TO COMMUNITY

The trend toward deinstitutionalization notwithstanding, there is still a valued place for the residential treatment facility. Both the new journal *Behavioral Residential Treatment* and a recently edited text by Fuoco and Christian (1986) make the point in many ways that comprehensive residential treatment programs are complex interactive systems. Their many components need to be specified, quantified, and monitored. Probably the most significant publication in this area to date is Paul's (1986) edited text, *Assessment in Residential Treatment Settings: Principles and Methods to Support Cost-Effective Quality*, second only to Paul and Lentz's (1977) monumental study of milieu versus social learning residential programs (reviewed in detail in this series). In the first phase of a five-part study of alternative research methods for use in the evaluation of residential care facilities, the proposed methodology is expensive and time-consuming, a highly quantified, statistical approach to multiple direct observation and analysis. The present volume sets the stage for the four phases that follow. In tune with the times, Paul's work goes beyond the patient as an individual to the patient as an individual within a series of complex social systems.

Within this context, a brief commentary by Boudewyns and Fry (1986), a kind of postscript to Paul and Lentz's monumental epic, is of interest. Paul and Lentz, it will be recalled, concluded that their token-economy-based social learning theory program was the treatment of choice for chronic mental patients. In 1977 it was Boudewyns's convinced belief that 5 years hence such treatment programs would be commonplace within residential facilities of the kind with which Paul dealt. A decade later he followed up this assumption. Of 150 VA centers having psychology services, only 20 reported a token economy program of any kind. Only ten of these 20 medical centers had social learning programs similar to that developed by Paul and Lentz.

Boudewyns and Fry speculate that one such reason for this regrettable state of affairs is that token economies require most staff effort at the lowest level of the nursing hierarchy and that staff resistance is thereby encountered. Additionally, nurses trained to help and care for patients rather than to teach patients to care for themselves may reject token economies as punitive and unappealing. Similarly, administrators may develop resistance because of their concerns that patients may be deprived and, furthermore, that they are going to be accused of mistreatment by families, service organizations, and the public at large. Such objections are hardly novel. If, then, we are going to think either in terms of token economies as originally proposed by Paul or the sweeping innovations suggested in his latest volume, it is clear that further research should evaluate the cost-effectiveness of residential programs and methods for reducing resistance.

According to Ferguson and Cullari (1983), this failure to accept and implement behavior modification programs within residential facilities is due primarily to three factors: incorrect or inconsistent implementation programs by direct care staff members, the failure of behavior analysts to attend to the behavioral dynamics of organizational change and the related inherent conservatism of institutional systems, and the utilization by behavioral analysts of overly simplistic conceptualization and intervention strategies. According to Emerson and Emerson (1987), based upon the notion that staff members do not possess the necessary skills, the customary response to this situation has been the investment of limited staff resources in training programs. This overlooks other possible determinants. Poor performance may be related, for example, to unclear or inconsistent performance expectations, lack of adequate feedback, and the subsequent failure to consequate staff behaviors appropriately.

Thinking along these lines, Emerson and Emerson conducted a small sample, possibly nonrepresentative, self-administered questionnaire survey of all personnel directly involved in patient care within a medium-sized North American institution for persons with mental retardation or psychiatric disabilities. Two major misconceptions emerged, namely, that behavioral methods were useful primarily for bringing about changes in specific subroups and that effective implementation required total control over all relevant contingencies. When Solomon (1983) surveyed a large metropolitan area, she uncovered much resistance to the establishment of group homes for troubled adolescents. As part of a more lengthy door-to-door interview program, interviewees were asked to respond to a complex question geared toward elucidating their feelings about having various groups of people living together in a home in their neighborhood. The possible establishment of a group home for troubled adolescents was not well received, with only alcoholics and drug addicts eliciting slightly greater opposition. The reasons voiced tended to be the usual ones: disturbed young people make the neighborhood more dangerous, they are annoying, and they do not belong in a family neighborhood.

Regardless of prevailing negative sentiment, the establishment of community residences is probably critical. Many important life skills cannot be taught efectively in institutions. Unfortunately, despite the seemingly obvious advantages of community-based group homes, prospective neighbors continue to voice concerns, such as those indicated above, in addition to fears about declining property values and increasing taxes to subsidize these facilities. Thus, the stage is set for community rejection rather than acceptance. As McClannahan et al. (1987) note, it is essential to introduce and assess strategies for defusing these various pockets of resistance as they arise. At every step, the program developers' decisions and ensuing public behavior will have an impact upon the community's receptiveness to a new group home. Whereas specifics depend upon the situation, certain general principles apply. In the experience of McClannahan et al. individualized combinations of high-and low-profile approaches geared toward the community concerned are usually the most functional neighborhood entry strategies. Decisions in favor of low-profile entry are appropriate only if the group home has a legal right to be in the neighborhood. At some point, low-profile approaches always achieve a high profile and appropriate strategies have to be prepared well beforehand but always considering modification as circumstances dictate. Large group meetings (e.g., with block associations or town councils) should be avoided whenever possible. Whatever the strategy, failure to assess community resources and reactions could result in community backlash.

For coping with such complicated problems as inadequate housing, substandard education, crime, disease and unemployment, organized community self-help is essential. This relies largely on the use of locally available resources and self-directed change to create and implement situations. As Seekins, Mathews, and Fawcett (1984) note, a critical element in the facilitation of self-help efforts is the development of indigenous leadership and local decision making. Although grass-root, self-help organizations can provide the opportunity for problem sharing and identification and proposals for resolution, members of such groups are often unfamiliar with the rules of discussion that contribute to effective meetings. This can result in low levels of participation. It is therefore important to train individuals in the basic principles of group leadership and decision-facilitating skills. Although procedural guides are available, few are directed toward members of low-income groups. For many such individuals, Robert's rules are complicated, difficult to master, or beyond the experience of community residents.

The study by Seekins et al. is the only one to evaluate the effectiveness of such guides in assisting members of low-income community groups acquire the apposite new skills. Two members of a neighborhood service center served as trainees. The effects of a behaviorally based textbook and training procedure designed to teach effective chairing of meetings were analyzed. Measures were collected during regularly scheduled meetings dealing with chairperson performance, member participation, and the closing of discussion topics. Despite the lack of adequate follow-up, ratings by expert judges of the overall performances of both trainees were encouraging. The use of specified chairperson activities increased after training and more decisions were made. Social validation, in terms of trainee ratings of general satisfaction with the training program, was equally encouraging. What is not known is the extent to which this procedure improved the decision making effectiveness and problem prevention value of the self-help groups concerned.

In a disquieting article by Barber, Barber, and Clark (1983), a sharp distinction is drawn between community group homes that are "community-oriented" and those that are merely "community-based." Community-oriented treatment programs parallel standards of the community in which they exist rather than functioning as a neighborhood mini-institution. A community-oriented treatment program is achieved not simply by the mere fact of placing houseparents or sponsors in a spacious home within the community. What is required, argue Barber et al., is that the live-in staff be professionally trained in appropriate treatment modalities and that they have the authority to conduct treatment that, in their estimation, is in the best interest of the client. The typical deinstitutionalized chronic patient receives instead "a patch-work quilt of services provided by overworked social workers, psychologists, mental health workers, and psychiatrists through weekly visits or therapy sessions." It is their contention that, even when community-based, such an institutional approach is rarely effective or adequately responsive to client needs.

One highly successful community-oriented residential treatment approach, reported in detail in this series, is that of the teaching-family model (Phillips, Phillips, Fixsen, & Wolf, 1974). The original Achievement Place home of 1967 evolved into the over 150 group homes, which are now operating under the eight regional training sites of the National Teaching-Family Association within the United States. The focus of the article by Barber et al. is the Vermont home in which this treatment model was first adapted to serve mentally ill adults rather than the court-adjudicated, predelinquent youths for whom it was originally evolved. From 1979 to 1981, two of the three authors served as the "life-skills teaching couple" for the six adult men and women who lived with them at any one time. They were also responsible for conducting follow-ups with those who left the home for reintegration into the community. Referrals for this voluntary program were received from the state hospital and the local community mental health agency. Regrettably, the treatment center was closed 2 years after its beginning. On the surface, the authors found it difficult to understand why this closing took place, and it was not until a detailed investigation was conducted that some leads were provided. It gradually became apparent that the behavioral orientation of the life-skills teachers and the more traditional orientation of many of the administrators and psychiatrists at the county's mental health center, which served as a sponsor, were in serious conflict. The usual canards were paraded—that the observed changes were simply a reduction in psychotic symptomatology and that the "diseases" were not being treated. The view was expressed that these clients were sick individuals who could benefit only from long-term psychotherapy, trust, and personality development, a perspective that was at painfully obvious variance with the active teaching therapy program instituted by the authors to bring about more appropriate repertoires for their clients.

Many strategies were deliberately adopted to bring about the demise of the group home in its present form. For example, mandatory attendance of all six clients at the center's psychodynamically oriented day treatment program was instituted, thereby marking the end of the group homes' treatment planning autonomy and the beginning of even more acrimonious clashes between the center staff and the authors. The fact that the behavioral treatment program brought about dramatic and rapid improvements merely served to add fuel to the conflict. With the wisdom of hindsight, the authors sadly comment that they might have got further had they "shaped" the ideas of their opponents rather than "casting them aside with a disgusting glance or curt remark." Instead, the situation became increasingly polarized and eventually one of the center psychiatrists refused to approve any more referrals to the group home. The center administrators also threatened the state with closure of the home unless they could convert it to their own treatment and program philosophy. The state's response was to withdraw funds from the center and the little facility folded.

What the authors learned from this experience and from similar failures elsewhere is that the concept of "community orientation" is easily voiced but more difficult to implement. In Vermont the program failure was not because of some all-too-common neighborhood "uprising" at the prospect of having sick people on their doorstep or because the program was ineffective. Rather, the failure was the result of a community-oriented program being plunged into a conceptually alien institutionally oriented system without adequate planning.

With the vantage of hindsight, the authors offer three prescriptions: (1) develop community responsibility and organizational involvement in the program; (2) ensure that the host organization adopts a treatment model appropriate to the needs of the client; and (3) maintain clear organizational and staff accountability.

Finally, attention is drawn to a useful, if rather general, overview by Gesten and Jason (1987) of efforts by psychologists and others to enhance the well-being of various groups and communities in our society, their main thrust is ecological. The creation or modification of social systems—as with the evaluation of long-term impacts dealing with more limited interventions—requires longitudinal program commitment to settings and issues in addition to concentration upon organizational issues. A broadly similar perspective is adopted by Geller (1986) in his discussion of ecological, systems-level approaches to the prevention of such environmental concerns as crowding, pollution, poverty, and energy problems. Programs need to be interdisciplinary, reciprocally based as far as behavior and environment are concerned, maximizing the use of naturally occurring contingencies, and they must involve the development of communication networks between government, industry, and all levels of the community. Although this is clearly a formidable proposal that is easier to advocate than implement, it is certainly in tune with these changing times in behavior therapy.

CONSUMER BEHAVIOR, BUSINESS, AND INDUSTRY

In Volume 11 I drew attention to encouraging new developments in behavioral economics. These included the advent of the Society for the Advancement of Behavioral Economics and the emergence of two major textbooks. Skinner noted the parallel between ratio schedules of reinforcement studies in the laboratory and piece-rate wages and commission selling more than 36 years earlier (see Green & Kagel, 1987), but it was not until the 1980s that any systematic attempt was made to develop a relationship between economic and psychological theory in general, let alone between economics and behavior therapy. As Green and Kagel remind us, the reasons for this lack of integration are not hard to discern. Economists traditionally use macrodata, compiled for large populations and related to aggregate economic variables, whereas experimental psychologists have tended to use data generated by fewer subjects relating more to the behavior of the individual. It is only during the past decade that economists have begun to enter the laboratory and psychologists to incorporate economic theory into their experimental designs. This led to the birth of behavioral economics, a field so new that Green and Kagel suggest that attempts to define this new domain rigorously would be premature. Fortunately, this has not stopped them from launching a promising new series upon the receptive waters of the academic and professional community. *Advances in Behavioral Economics* is intended to provide a transdisciplinary forum for research, theory, and practice.

A relatively undeveloped region in this sea of behavioral economics coheres around the nature of ethical behavior in organizations and its relationship to the decision-making process. By and large, there is a dearth of research and the available literature is largely descriptive. Recognizing these limitations, Bommer, Gratto, Gravander, and Tuttle (1987) propose a first-level attempt to identify the factors that influence implicit and explicit managerial decisions to act ethically or otherwise. These include the social environment of the decision maker, government and legal environments, professional environments, work environments, personal environments, and the personal attributes of the individuals concerned. As Bommer et al. correctly observe, this proposal is primarily a blueprint for the future. What is needed now is a series of empirical studies of specific decision-making situations pertinent to ethical issues.

Consumer behavior, in which the decision-making process has generally been neglected, is rapidly becoming an area of significance. Volume 20 of the long-established *European Journal of Marketing* devotes an entire issue to this theme. The able and prolific editor, Foxall, a determined user of radical behaviorism, makes his position clear from the onset (e.g., Foxall, 1986c). The radical behaviorist does not avoid theory as long as it is couched in terms similar to those in which the observations are described, but there is no place for mental, neural, or conceptual expectations of behavior that appeal primarily to events taking place at some other level of abstraction. By contrast, uncritical cognitivism, a bête noire for Foxall, attributes behavior to intrapersonal causes, especially those assumed to be innate, and this precludes the investigation of other determinants of action. With Skinner, Foxall views research that ensues from this line of thought as a largely wasted endeavor based upon "explanatory fictions."

Consumer research, argues Foxall (1984), has traditionally been characterized by this cognitively dominated perspective based upon abstract unobservables. Consumer researchers have adopted cognitively based inner-state explanations to the virtual exclusion of all others. Recognizing this situation, Foxall calls for the generation of alternative, radical behavioral models of conservative behavior (Foxall, 1986a, 1986b, 1986c). To be fair, it should be placed on record that Foxall's allegiance to radical behaviorism does not prevent his recognition of the need to explore alternatives. General attitudes are poor predictors of specific behaviors even when an adequate number of intervening variables have been included. Verhallen and van Raaij (1986) cite three studies to illustrate the application of a cost-benefit behavioral model in the study of consumer behavior. In the first, Verhallen and Robben (1984) evaluated gift giving and receiving. They found that the perception of behavioral costs (time, subjective feelings, and physical) to the giver by the receiver influences the evaluation of the gifts. When receiving a gift, the evaluation is affected by a perception of costs incurred; in giving, the giver does not expect the receiver to value the gift more highly merely because costs have been incurred. Thus, it is necessary to broaden the notion of price-quality relationships to include cost-value variables. In the second study, Verhallen and DeNooij (1982) showed how housewives differ in the way they trade off differences in price, distance, assortment, and quality of stores in their daily shopping. These trade-offs were then related to sociodemographic characteristics, such as family size, income, and availability of a car. In a third study, Pieters and Verhallen (in press) use a longitudinal design to investigate household participation in a waste separation project. Throughout, their intent is not so much to submit a fully fledged, testable model of consumer behavior as to develop a comprehensive way of organizing and understanding consumer behavior from a cost-benefit behavioral perspective. For both Foxall and Verhallen, a radical operant behavioral perspective lends itself well to the comprehensive understanding of consumer behavior more effectively than does either a classical conditioning approach (see Lennon, 1984) or traditional cognitive explanation alone (see Foxall, 1985).

As far as industry is concerned, behavior analysis and organizational behavior management (OBM) are now the order of the day. While gratifying, I must confess to a twinge of uneasiness upon reading the well-meant appeals to "hustle" that are beginning to emerge. For example, Bailey (1988), a scholarly and respected leader in the applied behavior analysis community, offers an editorial in the pages of the *Journal of Applied Behavioral Analysis* in which consultants are urged to translate the attention-getting buzzwords of their nonbehavioral colleagues into behavioral terms to "sell" behavioral analysis to industry. If this is the price of victory in the marketplace, it could be high. In the long run, data derived from real-life investigations are likely to be more efficacious than slogans, no matter how well intended. Consider, for example, the examination by Fellner and Sulzer-Azaroff (1984) of goal setting as a promising strategy for improving performance in industrial settings.

Mining is a particularly hazardous occupation and a significant amount of behavior research has been directed toward changing unsafe environmental conditions. Unfortunately, most behavioral safety research to date has reported only relatively brief intervention periods. A notable exception is offered by Fox, Hopkins, and Anger (1987) in which miners were given tokens for not having accidents or injuries for specified periods of time. What is remarkable about this program is that, in addition to the clearly discernible short-term benefits, the treatments were kept in effect for 11 and 12 years, respectively, in the two mines studied without return to baseline levels of injuries. At least as encouraging, from management's point of view, is the fact that cost reductions due to these benefits far exceeded the cost of operating the token economy. Maintenance programs are as important as the initial behavioral training itself (Hopkins, Conard, & Smith, 1986). At least in this context, it is not necessary to think in terms of either engineering- or technology-oriented approaches to occupational safety or behavioral approaches.

CRIME AND DELINQUENCY

Every time I write this section, I either begin or end by drawing attention to the fact that no new behavioral theory of crime or delinquency seems to have surfaced. This year is no exception. If anything, second thoughts are beginning to arise in areas that were once thought to be established bastions of progress. The Achievement Place Teaching-Family Model, referred to favorably in an earlier section of this overview, is a case in point. Studies have repeatedly shown positive during-treatment effects on behavior, and there are currently some 215 such homes in the United States. Now, however, the founding mothers and fathers are taking a cold, hard look at what they have created and are having second thoughts that they are honest enough to share with us. Let them speak for themselves.

> Two decades ago, when we began this research, we hoped to develop a short-term treatment program that would be a permanent "cure" for all our youths. We clearly have not accomplished this. Although the Model appears differentially effective during treatment in affecting delinquent behavior and social skills, the posttreatment behaviors of Teaching Family youths approximate those of non-Teaching Family group-home

youths. . . . Both Teaching Family and comparison youths exhibit less delinquent behavior after treatment than before, but both groups still remain well above national norms, on an average, in their levels of offending. (Wolf, Braukmann, & Ramp, 1987, p. 348)

Recognizing that the above outcome reflects both current technological limitations and possibly the limited skills of the investigators (which I find hard to believe), Wolf et al. suggest that these deficits also point to a failure to appreciate more long-term problems. A more realistic approach might involve what they call "extended supportive environments," a relatively permanent arrangement of socioenvironmental conditions to provide ongoing support for the desired behavior.

The disorders of many delinquent youths appear less like the circumscribed and modest problems of childhood and more like complex developmental disabilities, such as retardation, autism, and cerebral palsy. Just as lifelong supportive arrangements are essential for individuals with these disorders rather than short-term interventions, so it is with delinquency. In making this point, Wolf et al. are careful to remind their readers that investigators should continue their search for profound permanent changes that can take place without the need for extended environmental modification. Wolf *et al.* it should be noted, are not the only ones to arrive at the grim conclusion that, to date, there has not been any clear and convincing demonstration of effective strategies for coping with the problems of either antisocial children or adults (see Morris & Braukmann, 1987; Wilson & Herrnstein, 1985). Behaviorally based group homes were once thought to offer a differential long-term positive impact that would carry over into the youth's posttreatment environments. As noted, subsequent research showed that this assumption is incorrect despite initial promise and modest, but significant, successes (see also Braukmann & Wolf, 1987).

Long-term supportive family treatment programs led by carefully selected parents backed up with appropriate training, consultation, financial support, and monitoring similar to that provided for teaching parents in group homes is one possibility. A parent team might provide treatment in their own home for one youth carefully matched to the family's strengths and other characteristics. The youth selected could have the benefit of an adequate family throughout the high-risk years of adolescence and beyond, and perhaps throughout life.

This is not such a far-fetched notion as it might seem and encouraging data are beginning to accrue (see Bank, Patterson, & Reid, 1987), but as Wolf et al. recognize, long-term supportive family treatment will not work for everyone and alternatives need to be developed. Long-term supportive family treatment, for example, is not likely to be appropriate as a first-stage intervention for youths considered dangerous to themselves or to others.

Despite innumerable negative or equivocal findings, parole officers still remain committed to programs that are essentially the same today as they were a century ago. The notion that most offenders are "sick" and in need of a "cure" still prevails, and most probation agencies remain committed to bringing about change through traditional clinical processes; if intrapsychic deficiencies are the primary culprits, then the probation officer's accountability falls by the wayside (Cohn, 1987).

The infrequent use of behavior modification procedures in probation work flies in the face of the data. Studies repeatedly provide evidence of its beneficial impact. For example, Wood, Green, and Bry (1982) show that, in comparison with matched controls, behavior modification training for juvenile probation officers significantly improves both knowledge and competence.

Remington and Remington (1987) separate out the basic issues. Does behavioral training for probation officers lead to increased application in the working environment? Does the competent use of these methods result in desirable changes in client behavior? With the notable exception of Jesness, Allison, McCormick, Wedge, and Young (1975), most studies confound these two questions.

Remington and Remington (1987) draw attention to serious methodological deficits and suggest the necessary corrections. Training courses that are to short cannot provide sufficient detail or practice. Even with more lengthy programs, training officers find difficulty in accepting procedures that run counter to the traditional probation case work model. In this respect, support from superiors and colleagues becomes essential, and such support is usually lacking. How to bring this about is not discussed in detail by the authors.

Although literature reviews dealing with the treatment of criminal behavior generally cite social learning theory as the most successful approach (e.g., Gendreau & Ross, 1979), few show how this theory is to be applied. Of the recent attempts to meet this deficit, Stumphauzer's (1986) treatment manual, geared primarily toward those not well versed in behavior therapy, is possibly one of the more effective.

Burchard and Burchard's (1987) collection of original empirical studies and critiques by Jesness and Leitenberg are much more satisfying. If dramatic decline in delinquency is not yet attainable, it does seem that early prevention is more promising than later treatment at this time. This sourcebook goes a long way to bringing home this important message, but perhaps the event of the year, as far as the behavior therapy of crime and delinquency is concerned, is the appearance of Morris and Braukmann's (1987) 600-page handbook of application, research, and concept. Morris, Braukmann, and their team of outstanding contributors offer a comprehensive appraisal of the field marred only by a tendency to empahsize more radical behavioral approaches at the expense of social learning theory and more cognitively oriented interventions, but this is a minor limitation. Successes and failures are placed in perspective with an eye to present needs and future potential. Commitment to empiricism by knowledgeable investigators versed in behavioral methodology, commitment to early prevention, and an ecological, interdisciplinary perspective would all seem to be essential prerequisites for progress. A recurrent theme seems to be that the best of what is known is not going somehow to find its way into widespread practice automatically (see also Paine, Bellamy, & Wilcox, 1984). Regrettably or otherwise, rewards for researchers are typically for creating new knowledge rather than for its transfer to the public arena (Fawcett, Seekins, & Braukmann, 1981).

In the concluding section, the focus is upon professional issues. Sheldon (1987) offers helpful guidelines for therapists. The use of motivational programs to increase appropriate behaviors should be viewed with particular caution. At least in the United States, the courts have not taken favorably to motivational systems based upon an initial deprivation of basic rights, which then have to be "won" back. Thus, therapists are advised to find idiosyncratic reinforcers geared toward individual problems and situations that do not involve the initial withdrawal of basic rights.

Finally, Burchard (1987a) draws once again upon his Vermont experience to stress the need for behavior therapists to focus upon social and political contingencies. In so doing, it is necessary to distinguish between therapeutic and sociopolitical contingencies. Typically, therapeutic contingencies are designed by behavior therapists to facilitate adaptive functioning, whereas sociopolitical contingencies are established primarily by administrators and legislators. Sociopolitical contingencies may or may not be in accord with behavioral principles and behavior therapists have to recognize that this is so if only because such contingencies are critical to the role of the therapist in the prevention of delinquent behavior (Burchard, 1987b).

As behavior therapists, the role of psychologists in the sociopolitical arena is inevitably limited. It also seems to be increasingly evident that the impact of "traditional" behavior therapy is beginning to wane. What was forward-looking in the 1960s is passé in the emerging '90s. As noted in this chapter, behavior therapists are now thinking in terms of systems rather than exclusively individual or even group approaches and of a methodology that combines behavioral discipline with the flexibility of a nonlinear, ecologically oriented interactive model. This encouraging trend is exemplified in the work of O'Donnell and his associates in the area of juvenile delinquency. Although the individual is by no means neglected, the emphasis is on the generation of new and potentially therapeutic social networks for the development of diversion programs as alternatives for youths who would otherwise be processed in a court of law and neighborhood programs for high-risk potential delinquents. Most important, O'Donnell's sensitivity to the need for innovative thinking is not at the expense of behavioral rigor (O'Donnell, 1987; O'Donnell, Manos, & Chesney-Lind, 1987).

BEHAVIOR THERAPY AND THE AGING PROCESS

Treatment of the developmentally delayed has shifted from a medical to a behavioral model. Because many elderly persons have significant health problems, this is unlikely to occur in geriatric care. What is needed, argue Burgio and Burgio (1986), is coexistence characterized by collaboration between behavior therapists and members of the medical and allied professions. The bottom line, however, is the number of new students entering the field. Unfortunately, the variables controlling entry into behavioral gerontology are different from those that govern admission to other clinical behavioral areas. For example, it is generally rewarding to teach new skills to a handicapped child, skills that can remain in evidence for a lifetime and result in positive outcomes visible to all. By contrast, the life expectancy of an elderly person is more limited and therapists are likely to see a decrement in relearning skills that have taken many months to establish. Such experiences may discourage new students either from entering or remaining in the field.

Most behavioral techniques with the elderly are applied *to* rather than *with* people (Meunier, 1988). Thus, in only three of the 29 behavioral geriatric studies reviewed by O'Donohue, Fisher, and Krasner (1986) were the clients significantly involved in the determination of treatment goals and target behaviors. For the most part, younger professionals choose the clients, their problems, and how the problems should be resolved. One reason why elderly patients tend not to be consulted is that usually they are not the real clients. In most cases, either the caregiving facility, the government, or some financially responsible individual is the *real* client. Those who hold the purse strings are consulted very closely before treatment is commenced.

Mosher-Ashley (1987) critically reviewed some 151 studies pertaining to behavioral gerontology. Each was examined for variations in behavioral methodology across three categories: observation, assessment, and intervention. Serious methodological deficits were encountered at all stages and in all areas. For understandable if not acceptable reasons, the focus of these studies was the institutionalized subject. Investigators who fail to include staff members in both the design and the conduct of the project are also faulted by Mosher-Ashley. Finally, she draws attention to the tendency to perpetuate passivity and helplessness in the institutionalized elderly and the failure to consult the individuals directly concerned with respect to the target behaviors to be modified. In the 1975 volume of this series, Bandura advised readers that, to gain public respect and confidence, behavior therapists would do well to do things with and for people rather than to them, a maxim even more timely now than when it was first offered.

Behavioral interventions with and for people rather than to them is very much part of the tactics recommended by Amaral (1986) for enhancing compliance in the older adult. With Gray (1983), she advocates improved communication as a first step toward patient–care provider collaboration. First, the patient is educated with respect to pertinent disease processes to minimize the attribution of health problems to old age per se. Second, the patient is helped to identify various facets of the suggested rehabilitative regimen with which he or she may be less likely to comply. Alternative plans are then discussed and implemented to the extent that this is feasible. Finally patient and care provider must come to an agreement with respect to goals and thereby establish a working partnership. Unfortunately, once again, all of this is easier said than done.

On the surface it would seem axiomatic that social relationships influence psychological well-being. By far the most frequently cited study relating mental and physical health to social support is a 9-year follow-up of residents of Alameda County by Berkman and Syme (1979). Persons with fewer social ties suffered mortality rates averaging 2.6 times higher than those who reported greater social support. Yet, as Carstensen (1986) cautions, although most social interactions are probably beneficial, exclusive focus on rates of interaction rather than their nature may limit appreciation of the complexities involved. As far as the elderly are concerned, there is little evidence that increasing the frequency of social interactions is necessarily advantageous. Interestingly, in his sample of elderly women, Rook (1984) found that negative social interactions had more influence on well-being than positive social interactions, a finding confirmed independently by Carstensen and Erickson (1986) in a study to be discussed shortly.

Few individuals are more knowledgeable than Baltes and her team with respect to the social ecology of institutions for the aged. Well-controlled studies demonstrate consistently that contingencies differ for dependent and independent behaviors in such individuals. For example, dependent self-care behaviors of elderly residents in nursing homes are followed by the complementary supportive reactions of social partners; independent self-care behaviors are only rarely affiliated with such external social contingencies. In general, there is a tendency to perpetuate a passive and helpless role and to exclude patients from any form of active participation.

Proceeding from the assumption that it is desirable to enhance and optimize functioning as well as offering care, Baltes and her associates suggest that the most pertinent question to ask is not "How can we change dependent self-care behaviors?" but rather "How can we change the environment so that the instrumental character or function of dependent self-care behavior in the elderly, namely securing social contact, is taken over by a different, socially acceptable behavior?" Staff and social partners need to be shown how to provide social contact in a continuous and immediate fashion following behavior other than independent self-care (e.g., Baltes, Kindermann, Reisenzein, & Schmid, 1987).

Carstensen and Erickson (1986) provide a splendid example of the subtle issues involved in the experimental investigation of strategies for enhancing the social environment of the institutionalized elderly. Over the past decade or so, numerous studies have demonstrated that simple strategies such as the provision of refreshment to nursing home residents, produces an increase in social interactions. However, what type of interaction the intervention brings about is unknown. Using a group reversal design, Carstensen and Erickson investigated the social validity of serving food during a social hour, commonly reported to facilitate social interactions among nursing home residents. Rates of interaction were measured, and the vocal content of the interactions were recorded and coded by blind raters. Rates of interaction more than doubled during the treatment phases, with vocal behavior accounting for the bulk of the increase. No evidence was found to support the assumption that increases in rates of interaction were accompanied by concomitant changes in the number of positive vocalizations. Not only did ineffective interactions (communications largely incoherent or nonsensical in content or not responded to by the person to whom the interaction was directed) account for the bulk of the proportional increase in vocal behavior, but rates of more appropriate behaviors actually declined during the treatment phases. Thus, although the provision of refreshments increased the number of resident-to-resident interactions in the activity area, it would be erroneous to assume that this produced a similar improvement in the quality of the social environment.

Finally, I draw brief attention to the relationship between staff attitudes and behavior toward the elderly in residential facilities. To explore this area, Kahana and Kiyak (1984) examined the relationships between staff attitudes and behavior in nursing homes for the elderly in Detroit and Seattle. Completion of a specially constructed attitude questionnaire was followed by repeated observations directed toward ten staff-patient interactional categories. Factor analyses of the ensuing data yielded no significant relationship between actual and intended behavior. Staff members who were less likely to stereotype older persons and more likely to see them as individuals did exhibit more positive parenting behavior and affect toward their clients. However, these attitudes were unrelated to the likelihood of treating the elderly as equals. At least as far as the populations studied by these investigators are concerned, intended behavior does not predict observed behavior as well as stereotypes do. Additional potentially relevant variables that await investigation include organizational demands on the staff, the characteristics of the older people, and the total structure of the institution. Attitudes of staff responsible for the implementation of behavioral programs toward the process of data collection itself also need to be taken into account (Bays & King, 1988).

CONCLUSIONS

Once again, this chapter emphasizes general issues rather than specific studies. As new technologies emerge, behavior therapy continues to expand into domains unheard of less than a decade earlier. Sometimes the expansion is more apparent than real, a matter of words rather than substance (as with the much touted new discipline of behavioral neuropsychology; e.g., see Hartlage, 1986, 1987; Wedding, 1986). Sometimes the impetus for expansion comes from disciplines other than behavior therapy. For example, the heightened sensitivity to legal and ethical problems arising out of certain behavior modification procedures was spearheaded by members of the judiciary professions and their counterparts in various legislative and regulatory agencies (Herr, 1984, 1987).

All of this is probably secondary to the conceptual strivings noted in the introduction to this chapter, in particular the partial return to theoretical and philosophical concerns in addition to more practical matters and the shift from linear to multicausal models. Whether individual behavior therapists are able to span the technological/ conceptual spectrum and incorporate this diversity into their personal *Weltanschauung* is a matter that only the future can decide. It may be that, in the long run, integration at this level is impossible for either the individual or behavior therapy at large.

Be this speculation as it may, what is certain is that at this time behavior therapy is in the mainstream of psychotherapy research and practice. As each year goes by, the president of the AABT presents his or her recipe for confronting the challenges and opportunities facing behavior therapy (e.g., Agras, 1987; Ross, 1985). That these leaders harmoniously disagree about needs and solutions is yet another measure of the vitality of contemporary behavior therapy. If the diverse opinions of mental health professionals and historians of psychology, on the one hand, and the proliferation of behavioral organizations and behaviorally oriented scholarly journals, on the other hand, are valid measures, then behavior therapy is indeed alive and well (Wyatt, Hawkins, & Davis, 1986).

CHAPTER

2

BEHAVIORAL ASSESSMENT AND METHODOLOGY

PHILIP C. KENDALL

ASSESSMENT

One fact that may or may not be distressing to those active in behavioral therapy is that the counting of the frequency of specific behaviors—the heart of behavioral assessment—has declined dramatically and significantly over recent years. I noted the beginning of this trend in an earlier volume of this series (Kendall, 1987), and Adams (1989), in his review of that book, noted also that self-report scales and/or inventories were apparently replacing the more traditionally behavioral approach of frequency counting. This volume of the *Review of Behavior Therapy* again notes the decline of frequency counts and the increase in inventory/scale development.

One piece of data confirming the impression of a precipitous drop-off in the frequency counting of behavior in its naturally occurring environment is taken from recent issues of the *Journal of Psychopathology and Behavioral Assessment.* A scanning of the articles published in 1988 revealed that one-half of the articles that were assessment focused, as opposed to disorder- or treatment-focused, for example, addressed very traditional objective inventories. Several studies dealt with the Minnesota Multiphasic Personality Inventory (MMPI) and the Million Clinical Multiaxial Inventory (MCMI), whereas others dealt with the State–Trait Anxiety Inventory, the Cognitive–Somatic Anxiety Questionnaire, and the Profile of Mood States (POMS). However, only one article addressed issues directly linked to behavioral assessment, for instance, testing the significance of interobserver agreement measures (Faraone & Dorfman, 1988). Frequency counts are becoming rare, potential collectors' items.

True, the *Journal of Psychopathology and Behavioral Assessment* is only one journal, and many other journals are available for publication of behavioral assessment information. However, the observation of a downward trend in the recording of the naturally occurring frequency of target behaviors is perhaps most clear-cut in a journal that specifically appeals to assessment within the behavioral tradition. It appears that the time, cost, and other attendant difficulties associated with behavioral frequency counting has eventually had the negative effect of reducing its use. Add to this the field's acceptance of other data sources and there is limited rationale for continued expenditures to achieve frequency recordings.

When one looks to other journals for evidence of trends within the area of assessment, it is clear that we are in an age of scale development. The following list is intended to document my observation: Fetal Health Locus of Control (Labs & Wurtele, 1986), Measure of Irrational Belief (Malouf & Schutte, 1986), Automatic Thoughts Questionnaire—Revised (Kendall, Howard, & Hays, 1989), Child Abuse Potential Inventory (Milner, Gold, & Wimberley, 1986), Parent Opinion Questionnaire (Azar & Rohrbeck, 1986), Eating Attitudes Test and Eating Disorders Inventory (Gross, Rosen, Leitenberg, & Willmuth, 1986), Inventory of Interpersonal Problems (Horowitz, Rosenberg, Baer, Ureno, & Villasenor, 1988), Beck Anxiety Inventory (Beck, Epstein, Brown, & Steer, 1988), Inventory of Positive Automatic Thoughts (Ingram & Wisnicki, 1988), Cognitive Status Examination (Barrett & Gleser, 1987), Inventory to Diagnose Depression (Zimmerman & Coryell, 1987), Children's Beliefs about Parental Divorce Scale (Kurdek & Berg, 1987), Adolescent Perceived Events Scale (Compas, Davis, Forsythe, & Wagner, 1987), Crisis Call Outcome Rating Scale (Bonneson & Hartsough, 1987), Modified Scale for Suicidal Ideation (Miller, Norman, Bishop, & Dow, 1986), Problem Inventory for Adolescent Girls (Ward & McFall, 1986), Modifiers and Perceived Stress Scale (Linn, 1986), and Anxious Self-Statements Questionnaire (Kendall & Hollon, 1989). It seems apparent that scale development is occurring at a high frequency. Not all scales or scale developers hold to behavioral or cognitive–behavioral principles; thus, the trend may be beyond behavioral limits as well as pertinent to those within them.

A closer look at a few select scales is worthwhile. Our society has experienced marked changes in the structure of the family. Indeed, the family is in transition, with several of the once stable institutions being rethought, such as marriage, sexuality, child rearing, and family organization (Skolnick & Skolnick, 1989). Behavioral psychology specifically, and clinical psychology in general, like many of the mental health professions, has witnessed a marked increase in treatments focused on the family (family therapy) but a distressingly small degree of research effort directed toward the assessment and study of family factors in psychological adjustment. As is true of certain other theories in psychology, there are books and articles available about family therapy but an unacceptably limited number of research investigations. The absence of acceptable measures has contributed to the limited amount of research. In an effort to overcome existing limitations, Roehling and Robin (1986) report on the development and validation of a Family Beliefs Inventory (FBI) to assess unreasonable beliefs regarding parent–adolescent relationships.

The FBI is a self-report measure of parent–adolescent conflict, separate forms for parents and for adolescents. The topics assessed regarding parental beliefs concerned ruination, obedience, perfectionism, malicious intent, self-blame, and approval. The adolescent version of the FBI assessed beliefs regarding ruination, unfairness, autonomy, and approval. The researchers compared the responses of 30 distressed and 30 nondistressed families, with the result indicating that beliefs do contribute to the distressed condition; that is, on several of the specific beliefs assessed by the FBI, adolescents and fathers, but not mothers, held unreasonable beliefs. For example, fathers in distressed families held unrealistic beliefs regarding demands for flawless, obedient behavior, worries about negative consequences of too much autonomy, and personalization of the adolescent's motives for rebelliousness. As Roehling and Robin point out, distressed adolescents, in a complementary fashion, were more concerned about the injustice and adverse consequences of too much parental restriction. These results suggest that distorted beliefs held by family members may be contributory to family distress. Moreover, the findings are consistent with speculations regarding the role of cognitive factors in family adjustment.

Other measures, although not developed during the period of the present review, continued to receive research attention. For example, teacher ratings of children's self-control (Kendall & Wilcox, 1979; Humphrey, 1982) were replicated and extended, with the data again supporting a strong relationship between ratings of self-control and adjustment (Work, Hightower, Fantuzzo, & Rohrbeck, 1987).

The one behavioral observation system that seems to have passed the test of time, as well as issues of reliability and validity, is the Marital Interaction Coding System (MICS; Hops, Wills, Patterson, &

Weiss, 1972; see also earlier discussion in this series, Kendall, 1987). Accepting the assumption that direct observation of behaviors among spouses is important in assessing marital functioning, Floyd, O'Farrell, and Goldberg (1987) evaluated the relationship between MICS data and data from the Communication Skills Test (CST; Floyd & Markman, 1984). Couples engaged in a 10-minute problem resolution task discussion of a moderately severe marital problem that was videotaped. Coders then applied both coding systems to the tapes.

The results indicated that although both systems are intending to measure aspects of interpersonal communication, the MICS and CST are not interchangeable measures. Indeed, the authors reported finding less agreement across the codings than they had anticipated. One area where this lack of agreement is potentially troublesome is in regard to the often found and oft-mentioned difference between distressed and nondistressed couples, that is, distressed couples reciprocate rates of negative behavior. What was reported by Floyd et al. was that the two different systems led to two different findings. The MICS results indicated that spouses reciprocated positive (but not negative) behaviors, whereas results based on the CST indicated that spouses reciprocated rates of negative (but not positive) behaviors. Similarly, it was found that CST negative behaviors and MICS positive behaviors were those that discriminated distessed and nondistressed couples in the Floyd et al. study. Floyd et al. discuss these results in relation to the treatment outcome literature and suggest that the inconsistency in the effects of marital therapy on communication patterns of couples may result, in part, from the insensitivity of the measures used. The CST, in their study, was described as more sensitive to spouses' negative communications and may be more sensitive to the identification of treatment produced gains. Analyses of marital interactions have proved illuminating and continued efforts seem worthwhile. However, I would not want to hone in on detailed codes at the cost of losing sight of the big picture—gaining a better understanding of the processes of marital dissatisfaction and developing more effective interventions. A strength of behavioral assessment has been its link to therapy.

Psychophysiological Assessments

Although it would be unfair to argue that psychophysiological assessments have been unhelpful in the measurement of psychological disorders, it may be true in some cases that physiological recordings have not fulfilled their initial promise. In the assessment of sexual arousal there are concerns about the meaningfulness of physiological recordings, whereas in the anxiety disorders physiological assessments (with adults) have shown continued promise.

Pedophilic sexual arousal is often linked to crimes of sexual offense toward minors. Sex offenders with a history of aggressive sexual behavior toward minors have been studied using physiological recording devices, most typically the penile plethysmograph. As noted in Volume 10 of this series, there have been studies that suggest that the measurement device, although offering the desirable features of brass nob technology, may be subject to falsification. Recently, Hall, Proctor, and Nelson (1988) recorded the penile erection of 122 inmates in response to nondeviant and pedophilic audiotapes. Eighty percent of the subjects were able to voluntarily and completely inhibit their sexual arousal, a finding that calls into question the validity of the physiological device as a true measure of arousal. Also, the relationship of the physiological measures to outside sexual offense criteria was weak. The authors suggest that caution is appropriate in the interpretation of physiological measures among sex offenders. What may have been operating in this, and possibly other, studies is that the cognitive activity of the subjects can be controlled by the subjects and thereby moderate the arousal that is recorded by the physiological device. Although the device itself is not at fault as a measure, the organism's ability to produce false-negative responses via cognitive modulation of arousal renders the assessment methods less than optimally useful.

In contrast, psychophysiological responses have been helpful in differentiating among certain anxiety disorders. For example, Lang (1985) suggested that differential visceral reactivity across anxiety disorders might uncover different patterns of S-R organization. Using psychophysiological indices of heart rate and skin conductance, Cook, Melamed, Cuthbert, McNeil, and Lang (1988) have subjects follow tape recorded scripts to prompt imaginal experiences. Subjects had different anxiety disorder diagnoses. The results suggested that phobic imagery produced significantly larger heart rate and skin conductance increases than control imagery. Also, the effects were of greater magnitude for simple phobics, followed by social phobics, followed by agoraphobics (see also Turner, Beidel, & Larkin, 1986). The utility of psychophysiological indices seem determined by the type of psychopathology under investigation.

Research with anxiety-disordered youth has proceeded at a slower rate than that with adult clients, but the present state of affairs regarding psychophysiological recordings seems to be one of relative disinterest. Although used infrequently, the following types of measures have been taken in studies of children and adolescents: electromyography, cardiovascular activity, and electrodermal activity. Children present particular problems in psychophysiological assessment in refusing to stay stationary or in refusing to wear the required equipment (Johnson & Melamed, 1979). Often no meaningful correlations are found between measures of heart rate and other self-reports or observer ratings of anxiety. Heart rate measures have been found to be affected by other emotions and by motoric and perceptual activity (Werry, 1986; Wells & Virtulano, 1984). In general, children tend to show idiosyncratic patterns of psychophysiological response, and these measures may be influenced by expectancy effects (Werry, 1986). In addition, differences across developmental stages may undermine the identification of meaningful relationships; certainly, one of the main areas of natural developmental change taking place during late childhood and adolescence involves physical maturation.

Anxiety and Depression: Focus on Assessment

A great deal of attention has been paid to the disorders labeled depression and anxiety. Regarding depression, there have been advances in descriptions of the symptom picture as well as a better understanding of the pharmacotherapy and psychological therapy for this disorder. Similarly, anxiety has been the focus of important research (see Barlow, 1988). Why then, has so much less attention been paid to the relation between anxiety and depression?

In *Anxiety and Depression: Distinctive and Overlapping Features* (Kendall & Watson, 1989), the question of the relation between the two emotional states of distress is addressed directly (a separate volume, edited by Maser, on the comorbidity of anxiety and depression is planned for the near future). Topics in Kendall and Watson's volume include theoretical perspectives, assessment methods, variations in the precursors and concomitants of the disorders, as well as consideration of various treatments for anxiety and/or depression. For our present purposes, we will give closer examination to the assessment of the related constructs.

L. Clark (1989) opens her discussion of the differential diagnosis of anxiety and depression by laying out the puzzle and potential solutions: Do anxiety and depression (1) exist as points along a single dimension? (2) share a common underlying diathesis? (3) share phenomenology but differ in time of onset (anxiety turning to depression when it is without relief)? (4) each represent a set of heterogeneous disorders? (5) exist as conceptually and empirically distinguishable constructs? Her examination of the material related to questions of the differentiation of anxiety and depression led Clark (1989) to conclude that "at every level from mood state to diagnostic entity, substantial overlap exists between anxiety and depression" (p. 121). Mood and symptom ratings often correlate 0.4–0.5, single anxious–depressed factors emerge from factor analytic studies, ratings of diagnosed cases show evidence of symptoms of both disorders, and family and drug treatment studies show overlap as well. Nevertheless, Clark was also able to identify meaningful distinctions. The 0.4–0.5 correlation may be evidence of independence of the two states. Cases with one or the other disorder tend to show a dominant symptom picture for one but not both disorders; panic, autonomic arousal, and avoidance appear often as distinct from loss of interest, pessimism, psychomotor retardation, and suicidal behavior. Gotlib and Cane (1989) would add excessive worry and muscle tension to the list of symptoms specific to anxiety and poor appetite to the list of symptoms specific to depression.

The most often used instruments for the assessment of emotional states such as anxiety and depression are self-report questionnaires. In a review of the major self-reports instruments of anxiety, depression, and both depression and anxiety, Gotlib and Cane (1989) drew the conclusion that existing self-reports do not discriminate between anxiety and depression. (For a review of assessments of depression for children and adolescents, see Kendall, Cantwell, & Kazdin, 1989; Carey, Faulstich, Gresham, Ruggiero, & Enyart, 1987.) However, given the existence of overlapping symptomatology, one would necessarily expect that assessment instruments would overlap. An instrument that assesses anxiety (or depression) and does not correlate with depression (or anxiety) would, in Gotlib and Cane's view, be suspect. As was true in the conclusions of other writers, the overlap in the two disorders should not be forced away, denied, or considered an annoyance. Rather, the data may simply be pointing to the existence of a condition that involves the presence of both anxious and depressive symptomatology.

Given our present focus on assessment, it is worth noting that certain scales were reviewed more favorably than others. The Beck Depression Inventory (BDI) was considered one of the most satisfactory self-rating instruments for assessing severity of depression (see also Kendall, Hollon, Beck, Hammen, & Ingram, 1987). The MMPI D scale and the Zung Self-Rating Depression Scale were also given adequate endorsement. It should be noted, however, that the MMPI has just undergone an extensive revision that may alter aspects of the normative data base and, subsequently, interpretation of the depression scale. It is true that the original MMPI will be maintained within the MMPI-2, but the presence of additional items and the results of subsequent analyses may produce a modified, and potentially more predictive, scale to assess level of depression (see Butcher, Dahlstrom, Graham, & Tellegen, 1989).

When considering assessments of anxiety the Taylor Manifest Anxiety Scale (TMAS), the Zung Self-Rating Anxiety Scale, the State–Trait Anxiety Inventory (STAI), and the S-R Inventory of General Trait Anxiousness (S-R GTA) were reviewed. Evidence concerning the TMAS is somewhat dated, and there is a somewhat limited literature on the Zung scale. The STAI has an extensive literature, much of which supports (in adults) a distinction between state and trait anxiety. Only partial support was said to exist for the multidimensional measure of trait anxiety (S-R GTA), with the interpersonal and physical danger dimension seeming to be most promising (see also Kendall, 1977).

It is probably true that the BDI is one of the most often used/cited psychological assessment devices in the literature. It spans professional affiliations, decades of use, and has been found useful in studying both basic psychopathology and the effects of clinical interventions. Beck, Epstein, Brown, and Steer (1988) reported on the psychometric characteristics of an anxiety assessment instrument, the Beck Anxiety Inventory (BAI). The 21-item BAI was designed to assess self-reported severity of anxiety in psychiatric populations. Data indicated an internal consistency coefficient of 0.92, a 1-week test–retest reliability of 0.75, and the ability to discriminate anxious from nonanxious groups. Given the present and growing interest in the comorbidity of anxiety and depression, it should be noted that the BAI was moderately related to clinicians' ratings of client anxiety (0.51) but not significantly related to ratings of depression (0.25). Also, a along these lines it is worth noting that the BAI's ability to discriminate between anxious and nonanxious clients was actually a comparison of anxious and depressed clients. The BAI serves therefore as a self-report instrument that has, at the outset, the apparent ability to separate anxious and depressive difficulties. However, because anxiety and depression can arguably be said to correlate in nature, it is not surprising that the BAI correlated 0.48 with the BDI. As Beck et al. noted, however, the BDI-BAI correlation is perhaps inflated by method variance; both are self-reports, whereas the correlations to the clinician ratings examined relationships across measures and may be underestimates of agreement.

Beck et al. suggest that the BAI is superior to other measures of anxiety, such as the STAI, because the BAI offers a built-in discrimination between anxiety and depression. Certainly, in clinical studies or tests of theory in which a separation of anxiety and depression is sought, the BAI may be a promising scale. If anxiety and depression are indeed overlapping constructs, a separation of them may be an unnatural force fitting to diagnostic systems. It is possible that, given the repeated evidence to support a strong overlap between anxiety and depression, the diagnostic system needs modification to include a disorder the symptoms of which are a combination of anxiety and depression—negative affect disorder (Watson & Kendall, 1989).

As for the scales that are intending to assess both anxiety and depression, Gotlib and Cane (1989) reviewed the Costello–Comrey Scales, the Millon Clinical Multiaxial Inventory, the Multiple Affect Adjective Checklist, the Symptom Checklist 90, and the Profile of Mood States. The Costello–Comrey scales were developed with a methodology that sought to select items that would differentiate the two affective states; yet the separate anxiety and depression dimensions correlate in the typical 0.4–0.6 range. The MCMI offers separate anxiety and depression scales, but, as Gotlib and Cane (1989) noted, they were reported to correlate 0.92. Also, a response bias may influence reporting because all but a few items are keyed false. The adjective checklist approach has been criticized because the depression items assess only the mood portion of depression (and not the vegetative or cognitive dysfunction; Hammen, 1981), and Gotlib and Cane (1989) suggested that the MAACL might be more appropriately used to assess positive and negative affect. None of the scales purporting to assess anxiety and depression are routinely endorsed as adequate.

In their conclusions section Gotlib and Cane (1989) suggest that when one is trying to discriminate between anxiety and depression, the BDI and Center for Epidemiological Studies Depression Scale for depression and the STAI-State and Zung Self-Rating Anxiety Scale for anxiety were the endorsed inventories. Other situations may call for consideration of other issues and therefore use of an alternate measure. With respect to development of new assessment instruments, Gotlib and Cane (1989) agreed with Watson and Kendall (1989a, 1989b) that because negative affect is evident in both anxiety and depression, whereas only depression evidences a lack of positive affect, measures seeking to discriminate the two disorders might place a greater emphasis on this distinctive feature. An important suggestion that Gotlib and Cane saved for the end of their chapter deserves attention; that is, where one is trying to separate anxiety and depression, self-reports have tended to assess how the respondent feels. It may be useful to assess why the person feels the way he or she does. As seen in an analysis of the cognitive information processing factors separating anxiety and depression (Kendall & Ingram, 1989), depressives, but (typically) no anxious subjects, show a distinct attributional pattern. Such attributional difference might be assessed by asking "Why do you feel the way you do?" The results may indeed help to discriminate anxious from depressive conditions.

Two recent studies addressed the attributional differences between depressed and anxious adults, another examined depressed youth, and another examined the role of hopelessness as a differentiation. A brief examination of these studies and their outcomes will help shed light on a potentially important distinction between the otherwise somewhat similar emotional disorders.

In one study (Riskind, Castellon, & Beck, 1989), clients dysfunctional thought records were analyzed using the Content Analysis of Verbatim Explanations (CAVE) technique. The clients were diagnosed either unipolar major depression or generalized anxiety disorder. The CAVE procedure involves judges reading and rating the described attributions for negative events. Judges look for phrases (i.e., the reason is, because, as a result of) that indicate causal explanations. Riskind et al. reported some overlap in attributional styles for the depressed and anxious groups but also found that, related to attributions for negative events, the depressed group had higher scores than the generalized anxiety group. These findings are consistent with earlier reports using an attributional style questionnaire (Raps, Peterson, Reinhard, Abramson, & Seligman, 1982).

Heimberg and his colleagues (1989) also conducted a test of the attributional specificity question. Using scores on a modified Attributional Style Questionnaire, normal controls were compared with patients with dysthymic disorder, agoraphobia, panic disorder, and social phobia. Based on attributional styles for negative events (internal, global, stable), depressives were different from normals and from some of the anxiety disorders. Specifically, depressives did not differ from social phobics or agoraphobic cases. In other words, dysthymic clients exhibited helpless attributions for negative outcomes, but so did the social phobics and agoraphobics. Moreover, several of the anxious clients did not score depressed on an independent measure of depression (BDI), suggesting that nondepressed anxious clients had attributional patterns similar to those seen in depressed clients. These data would suggest an attributional style that is associated with depression but not entirely specific to it. These results are different from those reported in an earlier study by Heimberg's group (Heimberg, Vermilyea, Dodge, Becker, & Barlow, 1987), and may be, in part, the result of the type of depressed clients studied: dysthymia may differ attributionally from major depressive disorder. Before conclusions are drawn regarding the specificity of attributional styles to a specific disorder, any unwanted differences in the disorders in question must first be addressed.

McCauley, Mitchell, Burke, and Moss (1988) examined the self-reports of depressed youth and compared them with those on youth with other psychiatric conditions. The depressed children endorsed significantly lower self-esteem, more hopelessness, a more external locus of control, and a more depressive attributional style than nondepressed children. McCauley et al. concluded that the depressive thinking style found in depressed adults (negative view of the self and the future) could also be seen in depressed children and adolescents. The attributional style seen in depressed youth consisted of positive events seen as due to external and unstable factors. Rather than seeing negative events as due to internal stable factors, their attributional style was different for the positive attributions. Also, it is interesting to note that developmental factors entered into the results. Older depressed children endorsed more of the "depressed style" of thinking than did the younger subjects.

Hopelessness is a concept that emerged from the cognitive theory of depression. Depressed clients are said to hold, among other beliefs, a negative view of the future (Beck, 1967). Is such a sense of hopelessness specific to depression, or does it appear in anxiety disorders? Beck, Riskind, Brown, and Steer (1988) compared scores on the hopelessness scale of subjects diagnosed as either major depression, generalized anxiety disorder, or mixed (nonaffective, nonanxiety) disorder. This later group served as a control condition. The findings were supportive of the content specificity hypothesis; mean hopelessness scores were not only higher for the depressed versus other groups, but there were also more meaningful relationships between hopelessness and clinical ratings of depression than ratings of anxiety.

The results of several studies suggest that the tendency to attribute the causes of negative outcomes to internal, stable, and general factors is linked to depression. Whether this characterization is specific to depression has created some confusing results. When the subjects are diagnosed major depressive disorder, the results seem to support the theory. When the cases are less depressed or when there are subtypes of comparison disorders (subgroups of anxiety), then the data are not as clearly supportive of the specificity hypothesis. As noted, studies of subjects'/clients' current affective state and their corresponding attributional statements about the causes of their affective state may be a worthwhile approach to the testing of the specificity of cognitive features in the emotional disorders.

Cognitive Assessments

Measures that are designed to assess various features of cognitive involvement in psychopathology and therapy have been described in other portions of this and earlier volumes of this series. Indeed, this section is not intended as a complete review of the recent work in this important area. Rather, a few measures will be mentioned and a recent review of the area will be summarized.

One of the more widely used self-statement measures, the Automatic Thoughts Questionnaire (ATQ; Hollon & Kendall, 1980), is a self-report scale containing 30 items to which the subject responds by indicating the frequency that they have had the listed thoughts. Subjects are asked to report for the period of the prior week. All of the 30 items are negative, and depressed persons are routinely found to have higher scores, indicating a greater frequency of negative thoughts. Two studies have appeared to address the question of the potential added benefit of positive thoughts in the ability of the ATQ to discriminate groups. Ingram and Wisnicki (1988) reported the development of a positive ATQ and Kendall, Howard, and Hays (1989) reported the development of a revised ATQ (ATQ-R) that includes positive items.

Ingram and Wisnicki (1988) reported two studies focusing on the assessment of positive cognition. In the first study, subjects helped to produce 30 positive items and a large pool of subjects completed inventories to assess their thoughts (ATQ and the positive items) and level of depression (BDI). Each of the positive thoughts reliably discriminated between depressed and nondepressed subject groups (using BDI scores as a cutoff). Interestingly, the correlation between the positive and negative automatic thoughts was 0.29, indicating that the scales assessing positive and negative thinking are not a simple bipolar representation of one continuum. Rather, the presence of negative thinking and the absence of positive thinking seem to separately discriminate depressive from nondepressive individuals. In their second study, the authors took a closer look at positive and negative thinking. Building from the idea that negative and positive thinking may show different relationship patterns to dysfunction (see Kendall,

1984), Ingram and Wisnicki (1988) found three groups: (1) depressed, with BDI scores over 20, being treated for depression, and having a family history of disorder, (2) mildly depressed, with BDI scores over 12, but no current treatment or family history, and (3)a control group randomly selected from subjects with BDI scores below 9. Results indicated that the depressed subjects endorsed significantly fewer positive thoughts than the mildly depressed subjects and that both the depressed and mildly depressed groups endorsed more negative thoughts than the control group. It may be the case, as Ingram and Wisnicki noted, that decreases in positive cognition may be associated not only with depression but also with the severity of depression. Further, the scale used by Ingram and Wisnicki, the ATQ-P, seems to be a viable instrument for further investigation of the role of positive cognition in psychopathology.

The ATQ-R (Kendall, Howard, & Hays, 1989) was developed by an item selection process similar to that used in the original ATQ, but with the intent to pull positive self-statements that could help discriminate depressed from nondepressed cases. The inclusion of positive items produced a scale that had greater discriminant validity; the addition of the positive items to the 30 negative automatic thoughts added to the predictive accuracy of the test. As expected, depressives were less likely to endorse the positive items. Depressive cases, both psychometrically defined and clinically diagnosed, showed the same pattern. As a result, Kendall, Howard, and Hays (1989) recommend use of self-statement inventories that can tap positive as well as negative thinking, such as the ATQ-R, for assessing the automatic thinking of emotionally distressed individuals.

To assess cognitive content associated with anxiety, two scales have received attention: (1) the Social Interaction Self-Statement Inventory (SISST; Glass, Merluzzi, Biever, & Larsen, 1982) and (2) the Anxious Self-Statements Questionnaire (ASSQ; Kendall & Hollon, 1989). Dodge, Hope, Heimberg, and Becker (1988) assessed cognitive content using the SISST and a thought listing procedure, along with other assessments of anxiety and depression. The scores on the negative self-talk portion of the scale, but not the positive items, were related to measures of anxiety and depression. SISST and thought listing data were meaningfully related to each other, suggesting that, in this instance, the two methods of assessment did not produce divergent information. Additional support for the utility of the SISST in discriminating groups was also reported by Dodge et al. who found that the negative subscale on the SISST separated those social phobics whose primary distress involved social interactions from those whose fears were more associated with public speaking. The importance of negative thinking in the understanding of the role of cognitive content in psychopathology has been underscored (e.g., Kendall, 1984) and is considered further in the following section.

Thought listing and self-statement inventories were not found to produce similar data in a study of test anxiety reported by Arnkoff and Smith (1988). They reported that an inventory of negative thoughts was meaningfully related to levels of test anxiety and performance, whereas the thought listing assessment did not differentiate among subjects. Also, it was the negative thoughts that were the most strongly related to performance.

The ASSQ (Kendall & Hollon, 1989) is an instrument that parallels the ATQ (ATQ-R) with item content reflecting anxious emotional distress. The items were cross-validated on a separate sample of psychometrically defined subjects and factor analyzed. A stressful situation produced elevated anxious self-talk (on the ASSQ), as expected, and the scale may be useful to assess variations in anxious thinking as well as changes that are the result of therapeutic intervention. To date, there have been relatively few data regarding the specificity of self-talk to discrete emotional conditions. One would suspect, given the natural overlap between anxiety and depression, that the self-statement inventories that assess anxious and depressotypic self-talk would also show overlap and meaningful correlations. Potentially exciting results, such as the possibility that the positive and negative items can separate the groups, await empirical tests.

D. A. Clark (1988a) provides a comprehensive review of the literature dealing with the validity of measures of cognition, and it is the purpose of the present commentary to highlight some of his major conclusions as well as areas in need of further investigation and clarification. Clark's analysis divides the measurement of cognition according to the methods of assessment used (after Kendall & Hollon, 1981): recording, production, sampling, and endorsement methods. Clark addresses the content validity, the ability to separate groups, the concurrent validity, the sensitivity to treatment effects, the accessibility of cognition, and the agreements across methods of measurement. The conclusions drawn by Clark are based on empirical reports and are reasonable. For example, although no one method is consistently superior to all others, inventories have received the greatest research support. More work is needed in the development of the alternative assessment approaches. Instruments such as the ATQ and SISST were found to have been able to separate groups of adjusted and maladjusted subjects, to be sensitive to treatment effects, and had convergent validity with other measures. Consistent with our earlier discussion of the need for studies of the specificity of cognitive assessments to certain psychopathologies, Clark concludes that discriminant validity (specificity) had not yet been established.

Assessing Positive and Negative Thinking: Contributions to an Understanding of Emotional Psychopathology

Recent theory and research have placed a great deal of emphasis on the role of cognitive functioning in the origin, maintenance, and treatment of emotional distress, with the study of depression and anxiety being the primary targets. The presence of negative thoughts, an aspect of the negative bias in depressed cases, was described by Beck (1967) in his early contributions. Negative automatic thoughts have been assessed, typically using the ATQ (Hollon & Kendall, 1980; Hollon, Kendall, & Lumry, 1986), and treatments have been found to produce reductions in negative automatic thinking. The popular press, in contrast, often refers to cognitive therapy in a manner paralleling the older notion of the power of positive thinking. In an earlier volume in this series (Kendall, 1984), I suggested that the power of nonnegative thinking was a more parsimonious description.

Schwartz and Garamoni (1986, 1989) outlined and described a model that employs the presence and absence of positive and negative thinking in a ratio format. Their model, referred to as the "states of mind" (SOM) model, describes an information-processing system built on the ratios of positive to negative thinking across various types and levels of psychological distress. According to the SOM model, five distinct states are conceptualized within intrapersonal communication (self-talk): positive dialogue, internal dialogue of conflict, negative dialogue, positive monologue, and negative monologue. The central variable (as noted in Schwartz & Michelson, 1987) for defining an SOM is the ratio of positive cognitions to total positive plus negative cognitions. The specific ratio set points and score ranges for each SOM are presented in Table 2-1. Using as guides the set points described in Table 2-1, the positive monologue is positively balanced but contains enough negative thought to remain realistic. The negative dialogue contains an abundance of negative thinking and is associated with moderate psychopathology. The internal dialogue of conflict contains equal positive and negative thinking and is linked to mild forms of psychopathology. The positive monologue is dominated by positive thinking and is not seen as optimal, indeed, certain pathologies may

TABLE 2-1. Theoretical States of Mind[a]

State of mind	Quotient [pos./(pos. + neg.)]	Range	Related disorders
Positive monologue	<0.69	(0.69–1.0)	Mania, hypomania, narcissism
Positive dialogue	0.618	(0.56–0.68)	(Psychological health)
Internal dialogue of conflict	0.500	(0.45–0.55)	Mild anxiety/depression, obsessive traits
Negative dialogue	0.382	(0.32–0.44)	Moderate anxiety/depression
Negative monologue	<0.31	(0.31–0)	Severe anxiety/depression

[a]Proposed by Schwartz and Garamoni (1986, 1989).

be linked to excessive and unrealistic positive thinking (e.g., hypomania, hysterical patterns). The negative monologue is dominated by negative thinking and reflects severe distress, such as panic and profound depression.

Several studies have now performed analyses of the SOM model, and Schwartz and Garamoni (1989) have provided a review of the reports. For the present time, we will look at two research reports addressing the SOM model. Schwartz and Michelson (1987) examined outcome data from the treatment of agoraphobic clients and found that at pretreatment agoraphobics evidence a negative dialogue. However, at midtreatment and posttreatment they had a positive dialogue and a moderate positive dialogue at follow-up. These data offer strong support for the model and, given that the SOM changes were associated with demonstrated improvements, suggest that changes in SOM can help to track therapeutic gain.

Kendall, Howard, and Hays (1989) examined the ratio of positive and negative thinking in psychometrically defined and clinical cases of depression. Psychometrically defined cases of hypomania were also examined. The ATQ-R was used to assess not only the frequency of negative automatic thinking but also that of positive thought. The proportions obtained by these researchers supported the notion of the healthy internal dialogue being a positive dialogue (0.62). Also, using a clinically depressed psychiatric inpatient sample, the findings were again supportive: a more negative dialogue for the more severely depressed sample. In addition to supporting the SOM model, the Kendall et al. report provided evidence for the value of the ATQ-R as a predictor of depression. Present space limitations prevent a detailed review of all of the studies that have produced data relevant to the question of the balance of positive and negative thinking in adjustment. The interested reader is referred to Schwartz and Garamoni (1986, 1989).

METHODOLOGY

Meta Analysis

It has been more than a decade since the methods of meta analysis were introduced as a means to assess the overall and relative effects of psychological interventions. For historical reference, readers are referred to the seminal treatise by Smith and Glass (1977) and to the two special issues of research journals that addressed the methodology (i.e., *Journal of Consulting and Clinical Psychology*, 1983, *51*, 4-75, and *Clinical Psychology Review*, 1985, 5). As readers of earlier volumes of this series know, meta analysis has been described and evaluated (Kendall, 1985a; Wilson, 1987a). More recent work with meta analysis includes evaluations of the effects of cognitive therapy for depression, the effects of various forms of therapy for depression, the effects of paradoxical interventions, and the effects of therapy for children and adolescents.

Cognitive (cognitive–behavioral) therapy for depression, after Beck, has been evaluated in many outcome trials. Dobson's (1989) meta-analytic review identified and included 28 studies that met his criteria: all studies from January 1976 to December 1987 either known to the author or published in any of the major journals. For a study to be included it had to involve an evaluation of cognitive therapy for depression (either explicit reference to the Beck et al. treatment manual (Beck, Rush, Shaw, & Emery, 1979) or a description of treatment procedures consistent with the manual and explicit reference to Beck's work. Also, the study had to have targeted depression as the focal problem and used the BDI as an index of outcome.

When examining the average effect size for cognitive therapy versus waiting list or no-treatment controls, the findings indicated that the average cognitive therapy client did better than 98% of the control subjects (based on ten studies). When comparing effect sizes for cognitive therapy with a more behavioral therapy, the average cognitive therapy client had an outcome superior to 67% of the behavior therapy clients (based on nine studies). Lastly, when compared with medications, the effect sizes indicated that the cognitive therapy client did better than 70% of the pharmacotherapy patients (based on eight studies). Seven other studies made comparisons to alternate forms of intervention not listed thus far and the results were consistent: the effect size indicated that the average cognitive therapy client did better than 70% of the other psychotherapy clients. Dobson (1989) concluded, "On the basis of the results presented here, it appears to be a reliable conclusion that, as assessed by changes in the BDI, cognitive therapy is more effective than nothing at all, behavior therapy, or pharmacotherapy in the treatment of clinical depression" (p. 417).

Clinical significance, discussed later in this chapter, has emerged as a concern to therapy outcome researchers. In Volume 10 of this series (Kendall, 1985a) I suggested that meta-analytic procedures could be employed to test the clinical significance of outcomes. Using BDI scores from psychotherapies for depression, Nietzel and associates made an intriguing set of meta-analytic normative comparisons (Nietzel, Russell, Hemmings, & Gretter, 1987). Nietzel et al. sought to answer the question, "How similar is the posttherapy adjustment of depressed adults to that of nondepressed adults?" (p. 156). If patients after treatment are indistinguishable from those individuals in a normative group, then the treatments can be said to have produced clinically meaningful changes (Kendall & Grove, 1988). Nietzel et al. offered "a guarded 'yes'" as their answer to the question (p. 159), but went on to offer some qualifications. For instance, depending on the criteria chosen, the effects are more or less impressive. If one selects a change that brings patients to within two standard deviations from the mean, then it will be easier to make claims of clinical significance compared with a one standard deviation criterion. Because there are cutoff scores recommended for differentiating nondepressed from dysphoric and depressed cases using the BDI (see Kendall, Hollon, Beck, Hammen, & Ingram, 1987), these scores might serve as the criteria. Nietzel et al. state a reasonable and rational conclusion: "Psychotherapy for symptoms of unipolar depression produces moderately significant clinical outcomes whose strength is relative to the criterion utilized" (p. 160).

Dobson's review offers an encouraging summary of the results of studies showing cognitive (cognitive–behavioral) therapy to be useful in the remediation of depression. In addition, Nietzel et al.'s study suggests that the effects are clinically meaningful as well. It should be noted, perhaps as a methodological weakness, that both reports were based solely upon subject's self-reports to the BDI. The sole reliance on the BDI as the index of change provided the much needed consistency across the many studies reviewed but nevertheless restricts the conclusions that can be drawn. I was pleased to see that both Dobson and Nietzel et al. recognized this limitation. Indeed, although Dobson's conclusions are reasonable, they are based solely on changes on the BDI. For several reasons, sole reliance on the BDI could be troublesome. First, self-reports may be responsive to unwanted influences and are, in general, considered less impressive than observed behavioral changes. Second, the BDI is often readministered at individual sessions as subjects go through cognitive therapy and this procedural influence may create an expectation that scores change. Third, the BDI, although a useful and recommended measure for the assessment of depression, is more a measure of the symptoms of depression than a diagnostic instrument. Thus, the conclusions regarding the positive effects of cognitive therapy based on the Dobson study are in reference to reduced self-reported symptomatology of depression. These potential reservations aside, the Dobson and Nietzel et al. reports support the beneficial gains produced by psychotherapy and the Dobson report, like the cumulative non-meta-analytic reviews before it, offers a rational and enthusiastic document encouraging continued use and evaluation of cognitive (cognitive–behavioral) therapy for depression.

Paradoxical interventions have received limited professional attention; yet, as most parents can attest, there are many instances in their interactions with the offspring when straightforward requests go unheeded but where paradox works. Noncompliance, in the extreme, may be of clinical significance, but mild or moderate noncompliance is certainly within the normal range of youth behavior. To get children to comply, parents have naturally tried a wide range of strategies. When asking a child to finish his or her sandwich, a parent might make dessert contingent upon completion, threaten the child, or place a potential punishment as linked to continued noncompliance. Other parents might apply paradox and say simply and with a smile, "You can't eat that *whole* sandwich, no way. Only big kids can eat a whole sandwich. I bet you can't eat it all," only to find that the child responds with, "Oh yeah," smiling back, "I can too," and proceeds to eat it all. Such paradoxical interventions have been popularly labeled reverse psychology.

Shoham-Salomon and Rosenthal (1987) identified 12 studies using a paradoxical intervention and conducted a meta-analytic evaluation of the outcomes. The overall effect size of paradoxical intervention was significant and similar to the effect sizes reported as outcomes from meta analyses of other forms of intervention. This result suggests that, based on the studies reviewed and for the disorders in question (e.g., insomnia, procrastination, phobia), paradoxical interventions are of average therapeutic effectiveness. The authors further examined paradoxical interventions by dividing them into categories. One such category, positive connotation, was reported to be superior. In this type of paradox, the therapist changes the meaning of the symptom for the client. Paradox is both theoretically complex and empirically understudied. Perhaps researchers with a cognitive–behavioral, information-processing slant will be able to untangle the knot of paradoxical interventions.

Applications of the meta-analytic methodology has expanded to the area of child/adolescent interventions. For example, Weisz, Weiss, Alicke, and Klotz (1987) and Dush, Hirt, and Schroeder (1989) have reported meta-analytic studies of the outcomes of various forms of child/adolescent intervention. A closer look at the Weisz et al. study reveals generally favorable outcomes.

Following Casey and Berman's (1985) meta analysis of treatment outcomes for children younger than 12 years of age, Weisz et al. enlarged the age group and were able to locate 108 well-designed outcome studies (participants were 4 to 18 years of age). To be included, a study had to have compared a treated group with an untreated or minimally treated control group in which the control group provided little more than attention to the youngsters. The authors reported that across 163 treatment–control comparisons, the mean effect size was 0.79. Such a result indicates that the average treated youngster would emerge at the 79th percentile of those not treated. This effect size was then compared with that reported in other studies (e.g., 0.71 in Casey & Berman, 1985; 0.93 in Shapiro & Shapiro, 1982). When age level of the subjects was examined, it was found that children improved more than adolescents. When therapist experience was examined, there were meaningful effects only for the paraprofessionals/graduate students. These more novice therapists were more effective with younger than older children. Professional therapists were about equally effective with younger and older clients (Weisz et al., 1987).

Unlike some interpretations of the findings of meta analyses of adult therapies (that all forms of therapy seem to produce comparable effect sizes), the findings with 4- to 18-year-olds supported the superiority of behavioral over nonbehavioral methods. Moreover, this finding was similar across ages of clients, types of client problems, and therapist experience. Weisz et al. (1987) note, however, that there are relatively few controlled studies of nonbehavioral methods, such as those approaches that may take longer and focus less on observable behaviors as goals. Weisz et al. rightfully recommend that the burden of proof rests on those who argue that alternate treatments (nonbehavioral) are superior. Claims of effectiveness and/or relative superiority require empirical testing, and the superiority of behavioral over nonbehavioral approaches, at present, seems the reasonable conclusion. This conclusion has pertinence in making sense of the Dush et al. review.

Dush et al. (1989) reported a meta analysis of self-statement modification studies. Forty-eight studies were examined, only those studies that treated children with behavior disorders of clinically significant severity were included. The average effect size produced, according to Dush et al., was 0.47, a score that is generally within the range of psychotherapy performance. Returning to the Weisz et al. (1987) conclusion, it would be worth further study to evaluate the presence or absence of behavioral procedures within the studies labeled self-statement modification. Because I have been a contributor to this literature myself (e.g., Kendall & Braswell, 1985), I have witnessed large variations in the "application" of a treatment that focuses on self-statement modification. Some form of quantification and coding of these differences might help to further isolate those more successful from the less successful outcomes. An argument I have made elsewhere and one I believe still holds is that cognitive training alone is not the preferred intervention, cognitive training should be an added portion of a basically behavioral treatment. Weisz et al. found behavioral programs to be superior to nonbehavioral ones. Maintaining the demonstrated efficiencies of the behavioral treatments is an essential part of the strength of a cognitive–behavioral intervention.

Age of the client can be an important indicator of other factors that may moderate treatment outcome; thus, it would seem prudent to assess treatment outcome relative to age groupings. Dush et al. conducted such a test and reported that, although not linear, age did influence outcome. Children 11 years of age and older did tend to show more improvement than younger children. Although these findings are not fully consistent with the initial theory behind self-statement modification, they do underscore the potentially important role of cognitive ability (which improves with age) in the use of cognitive and/or cognitive–behavioral interventions with children/adolescents.

Clinically Significant Change

And just what is "clinically significant" change? We are all comfortable using and making sense of the phrase statistically significant, but what are the meanings attached to significant clinical change? Several separate papers, published at different times and in different places, have included suggestions about how to measure and/or test for clinically significant change (e.g., Jacobson, Follette, & Revenstorf, 1984; Kazdin, 1977; Kendall & Norton-Ford, 1982; Wolf, 1978) and, more recently, under the guest editorship of Neil Jacobson, the journal *Behavioral Assessment* ran a special issue on the topic of defining clinically significant change. In the pages that follow, several approaches to defining clinically significance are examined and some of the related commentaries are discussed.

Four approaches to the definition of clinical significance can be identified (see Jacobson, 1988): (1) the use of statistical criteria, (2) the use of norms (normal ranges) for comparisons, (3) the use of specific criteria for specific disorders, and (4) the use of functional analysis.

The primary proponents of the use of statistical criteria have been Jacobson and his colleagues (Jacobson et al., 1984; Jacobson & Revenstorf, 1988). In their 1988 paper, the authors summarized their proposal: "the operationalized recovery for an individual subject as a posttest score that was more likely to belong in the functional than in the dysfunctional population on the variable of interest" (p. 134). They went further, stating: "The cut-off point, which is the point at which the subject is equally likely to be a member of either functional or dysfunctional distributions, is simple to calculate when the distributions are normal and the variances of functional and dysfunctional populations are equal" (p. 134).

When the variances of the two populations are not equal, the formula provided by Jacobson et al. (1984) is:

$$C = \frac{s_0 M_1 + s_1 M_0}{s_0 + s_1}$$

where s_0 is the normative sample standard deviation, s_1 is the dysfunctional sample standard deviation, M_0 is the mean of the normative population, and M_1 is the mean of the dysfunctional population. When norms are unavailable, Jacobson et al. proposed the criterion that for a client to have shown clinically significant change he or she "must end up two standard deviations (in the direction of functionability) beyond the mean of the dysfunctional population by the time that therapy is over" (p. 135).

In addition, Jacobson et al. proposed that the magnitude of change due to therapy be sufficient that it was unlikely ($p < .05$) to have resulted from measurement error. They offered the reliable change (RC) index as a metric for therapeutic effects. RC is calculated (after Christensen & Mendoza, 1986) by dividing the absolute magnitude of change by the standard error of the change score (posttest minus pretest). Jacobson and Revenstorf (1988) point out that when

RC exceeds 1.96, it is unlikely ($p < .05$) that the magnitude of change could be an artifact of unreliable measurement.

Data gathered on a large sample of individuals—norms—have been proposed by Kendall and colleagues (e.g., Kendall & Grove, 1988; Kendall & Norton-Ford, 1982) as a means to assess clinical significance. For example, when focusing on the "convincingness" of outcome data, one could take the perspective that, to be effective, an intervention must produce gains that are significant and "convincing" in that the interventions produced changes that materially improved the client's functioning—once troubled and disordered clients are, after treatment, not distinguishable from a meaningful and representative nondisturbed reference group. In this manner, normative data are used for comparisons of the functioning of treated clients, hence, normative comparisons (Kendall & Grove, 1988).

In describing the potential uses of normative comparisons, Kendall and Grove (1988) used self-report scales, behavioral assessments, and rating scales are examples of norm-based evaluations of clinical significance. Nietzel and Trull (1988) adapted the normative comparison approach and applied it in a sophisticated manner using meta-analytic technology. Although these and other authors endorse normative comparisons, they also point to several issues that impinge on the use of norms. For example, what group will constitute those whose data are considered normal? If depression is the disorder under inquiry, then will those in the population who are depressed be included among the normative sample that provides the data for the "distribution of acceptance." If depressed persons in the population are excluded, would that not inflate the criterion "nondistinguishable from a normative population"? What about the notion that some patients who seek therapy may, initially, not score outside the normative range on the target measures (Saunders, Howard, & Newman, 1988)? The example Saunders et al. used is a good one. What about a person who seeks marital therapy for a sexual difficulty but who otherwise scores as adjusted of measures of marital adjustment? Certainly, the measures chosen for use in normative comparisons would need to consider the sample and whether the scores are outside the normative range at the outset. Nevertheless, when different norms are used, the results of tests of clinical significance would vary. Hollon and Flick (1988) recommend that the best way of realizing the goal is to compare treated samples with purely normative data on the indices of interest, but these authors go on to ask who would be deleted from such a normative sample. The recommended solution, consistent with the notion above, is that the normative sample would not systematically exclude cases (depressed persons in the present example) but would keep them in the normative sample to the same extent as they exist in the population at large. Epidemiological investigations would be needed for proper implementation of this approach.

Another issue concerns the accuracy of the estimates of normative ranges of acceptable adjustment. In addition, when a comparison is stated as trying to produce client gains that leaves them indistinguishable from nondisturbed samples, are we not seeking to confirm the null hypothesis? These and related issues concerning the use of normative comparisons are given fuller explication in several articles (e.g., Jacobson, 1988; Hollon & Flick, 1988; Kendall & Grove, 1988, Nietzel & Trull, 1988; Saunders et al., 1988).

A third method for assessing clinical significance is the recommendation that specific criteria be used for specific disorders. As Jacobson (1988) pointed out, this approach is exemplified by the suggestions of Blanchard and Schwarz (1988) who, when considering clinical significance in the context of behavioral medicine, provided illustrations of degrees of meaningful change that vary across disorders. The authors discuss hypertension, obesity, smoking, headache, and irritable bowel syndrome. In the case of hypertension, for instance, Blanchard and Schwarz (1988) point out that the World Health Organization and most American authorities define hypertension as blood pressure in an adult that exceeds 140 millimeters of mercury (mm Hg) for systolic blood pressure and/or 90 mm Hg for diastolic blood pressure. According to Kaplan (1986; reproduced in Blanchard & Schwarz, 1988), the following ranges of diastolic blood pressure are used in common practice: high normal, 85-89 mm Hg; mild hypertension, 90-104 mm Hg; moderate hypertension, 105-114 mm Hg; severe hypertension, 115 mm Hg.

When one considers what is required for the normalization of blood pressure, there is not uniform agreement. As Blanchard and Schwarz pointed out, to reduce a score to below 90 (to remove the patient from the mild hypertensive category) may reflect a change as small as one or two points, and this may be the result solely of measurement error. Despite these potential drawbacks, specific criteria have been suggested in the behavioral medicine area for definition of clinically meaningful change.

The fourth and last approach to the definition of clinically meaningful change revolves around, although at times not directly, the methods of functional analysis (Baer, 1988b; Hayes & Haas, 1988). For example, Baer states that "if you know why you're changing a behavior, you'll know when you've changed it enough." The main idea here is that the behavior in question has caused someone to complain. When the change in that behavior is of a magnitude that the complaint is no longer relevant, then the degree of change is clinically significant. Altering the antecedent and consequent conditions are a part of the change process.

Resolutions to the question "What is clinically meaningful change?" are not uniformly offered nor recommended. However, the authors of individual proposals and several of the authors of commentaries did find some merit in each of the proposals. Researchers and practitioners will no doubt need to select from the various options according to the particular topic and individual needs in each instance. What can be said about the question and the related discussions is that the field is ready for greater attention to be paid to questions of the "convincingness" of the treatment outcomes that we can produce.

Follow-Ups

A methodological nicety just a few years ago, follow-ups have become essential in most evaluations of psychological interventions, be they prevention, enhancement, or therapeutic. The recent literature has seen several instances of long-term follow-ups. For instance, Blanchard, Andrasik, Guarnieri, Neff, and Rodichok (1987) reported 2-, 3-, and 4-year follow-up on the self-regulatory treatment of chronic headache.

Researchers and clinicians interested in follow-ups of their earlier reported outcomes may be dismayed to discover the low rate with which they can contact former patients. Proactively, it is recommended that at the time of treatment termination one obtains from the client the names and addresses of two other persons who would be likely to be reachable in the event the client has moved. Clients can also be asked to report any address and/or phone number changes to the clinic, but this method has produced limited compliance. Another methodological matter when considering follow-up assessments is the determination of any activities that may have an effect on client reports and taken place since the end of treatment. Did clients seek alternate or additional therapy since the end of the program being evaluated? Cases who report continued success, but who have been involved in more than the one treatment, would produce misrepresentative data. Follow-up surveys would benefit from asking respondents to indicate their involvement in activities that might moderate the data interpretation.

Follow-up studies, such as those in depression, have increasingly assessed relapse, recurrence, and maintenance of gains. These terms are not always easily transmitted from one writer to another, with specific meaning getting lost or diffused in the process. Relapse often refers to a return of the problem. In depression this can mean a return of symptoms within the same episode. Recurrence, in depression research, typically refers to the onset of symptoms in a new episode of depression. The duration of time required to call a second set of symptoms a recurrence as opposed to a relapse has not been clear (e.g., 2 to 6 months). Also determinations of relapse can be made based upon differing criteria. Diagnostic interviews may appear at pretreatment, but are not always included at posttreatment or follow-up intervals. Although there seems to be some consistency, with researchers using BDI scores to determine relapse, even the cutoff scores on the BDI can vary and, as a result, integrating data from various studies can become increasingly difficult. On how many consecutive weeks must a client show BDI scores above a criterion to qualify as a relapse?

As noted above, the activities of the clients during the posttreatment interval are important when attempting to study relapse. Did, for instance, clients seek a form of maintenance therapy? Lastly, calculations of relapse rates will be markedly affected by the initial sample of subjects/clients who are followed. If only those clients who show a positive response to treatment are tracked, relapse will be markedly different than if all subjects are tracked, regardless of their response to the therapy. As the field focuses on the issues of relapse, recurrence, and long-term effects, additional attention must be paid to the operational definitions employed. More than self-report may be necessary for true determinations of relapse/recurrence, and some indication of the stability of the presence/absence of symptoms would also help produce a clearer picture of the outcomes of the psychological therapies being evaluated.

The "No-Cure" Criticism

When researchers and clinicians discuss the outcomes of psychological treatments, the bulk of the content refers to the posttreatment status of once troubled clients. However, our clinical and research methods do provide means for the assessment and evaluation of maintenance and generalization. Why are these topics given relatively little attention? Do our interventions produce "cures" that persist over time and across situations? Does therapy "cure" psychological disorder?

A common definition of cure refers to remedial healing that rids one of an illness or bad habit (cure is not the same as care, which refers to looking after someone with a difficulty that is cureless). Evaluations of psychological therapies have employed various definitions of gain, although unwittingly they have left unanswered the question of cure. If one were to believe that therapy produces changes that are beyond chance, that hold over time, and that spread to related situations, then one would be holding the belief that therapy cures psychological disorders. The "no-cure" criticism is that although we can now offer clients well-reasoned and integrated programs for the treatment of a variety of disordered behaviors, many psychological problems persist and are not cured as a result of current treatments (Kendall, 1989).

In a special series edited by Barry Edelstein (*Behavior Therapy*, 1989, *20*), three authors considered the issues of maintenance and generalization of behavior change. Edelstein (1989) reviewed the animal literature to offer suggestions for how to examine and achieve generalization. He recommended probes as a means to assess the generalization of newly acquired skills. For instance, a behavior that is acquired in one setting may or may not generalize to another setting, and assessing such generalization can be accomplished by exposing the person to the new situation and assessing the newly learned skill (see Kendall, 1981, for a related discussion).

Stokes and Osnes (1989) offered suggestions for gaining generalized behavior change. For example, these authors pointed to the merits of training diversely as a means to achieve generalized change. In other words, if you want the behavior change to generalize, train the behavior in the various situations in which you wish to eventually see it. Stokes and Osnes also recommended that training be accomplished in a nonrigid manner, flexible application of programs was also a recommendation when treatment manuals were examined. Stokes and Osnes (1989) offered several potentially useful suggestions, but their work draws largely from the literature on autistic, retarded, and handicapped children. As I noted elsewhere (Kendall, 1989b), it is likely that the strategies reported by Stokes and Osnes will continue to be beneficial to clients like those in the original studies, but will the strategies themselves generalize to other samples of clients? To bright but detrimentally anxious adults? To depressed adolescents? Strategies that facilitate the generalization of behavior change in one cluster of client types may not be the same set of strategies most optimal for the maintenance and generalization of behavior change among other types of clients.

Jacobson (1989a) considered the marital (couples) therapy literature and noted that although gains are made by clients as a result of the behavioral marital therapies provided, maintenance and generalization do not occur routinely. What may be needed, Jacobson continued, is a longer commitment to treatment on the part of clients, a commitment to checkups, where, with no inference of prior failure, treated clients arrange to meet with their therapist at points past the end of the initial treatment period.

One apparent consistency across the papers by Edelstein, Stokes and Osnes, and Jacobson is the fact that generalization/maintenance does not routinely occur on its own. A second consistency, which itself deserves research attention, is the idea that strategies that make psychological gains more resilient are those that are provided in a less rigid (more flexible, more diverse) manner. As I have argued elsewhere (Kendall, 1989b), it is also the case that psychological therapies do not cure psychological disorders; effects do not automatically maintain and generalize.

Behavioral/cognitive–behavioral therapies do produce gains, but we must acknowledge and accept that there are limitations to these gains. A rational expectation for a therapist (and client) is one that anticipates the alleviation of disturbed psychological states but also anticipates that continued efforts will be required to cope and manage adjustment. One might consider what we provide as psychological therapy as a form of "management skills," in which the client is helped to alleviate distress and taught the skills necessary to manage psychopathology. For example, the anxious person will be able to learn to be less stressed/anxious but will have to continue to employ management skills to remain nondistressed. Arousal will happen, even after treatment, but the arousal should then serve as a cue to engage in the therapy-trained management skills. Chronic disorders may require continual application of management (coping) skills. Research is needed to assess the potential addictive effects to therapy when the provision of therapeutic services includes an explicit acknowledgment of the limits of gains that are to be expected, the need for regular checkups, and the description of the goals of treatment as the teaching of skills that will allow for the management of psychopathology rather than its total elimination.

CHAPTER

3

FEAR REDUCTION METHODS AND THE TREATMENT OF ANXIETY DISORDERS

G. TERENCE WILSON

Throughout this series we have commented on the rich and ever-accelerating behavior therapy literature on the treatment of anxiety disorders and the psychological mechanisms involved in anxiety reduction. DSM-III (American Psychiatric Association, 1980) and later DSM-III-R (American Psychiatric Association, 1987) ushered in an important new era of the greater diagnostic specificity and precision in identifying the anxiety disorders. Not surprisingly, research and clinical practice within behavior therapy followed suit. There is a clear trend toward greater specificity in the assessment and treatment of different problems. This development is consistent with the fundamental tenet of behavior therapy that, optimally, specific treatment methods should be applied to particular problems. Another welcome trend is the increasing focus on biological and psychological mechanisms in the effort to develop more effective treatments and to refine existing theories about anxiety and its modification.

To note that the literature in this area is burgeoning is an understatement. The content of the present chapter is based selectively only on some of the recent literature. Among the more notable recent developments has been the publication of several major books that provide detailed and comprehensive analyses of the field of anxiety disorders. These scholarly and highly informative volumes include Barlow's (1988) *Anxiety and Its Disorders,* Taylor and Arnow's (1988) *The Nature and Treatment of Anxiety Disorders,* Michelson and Ascher's (1987) *Anxiety and Stress Disorders,* and Rachman's (1990)

Fear and Courage. Even more broadly speaking, 1987 marked the publication of the *Journal of Anxiety Disorders.* This specialty journal notwithstanding, articles on cognitive-behavioral analyses of the anxiety disorders continue to appear in the full panoply of relevant psychological and psychiatric journals.

The remainder of this chapter focuses on theoretical issues in anxiety and its reduction and on specific developments within social phobia, generalized anxiety disorder, panic disorder, and agoraphobia.

THEORIES OF ANXIETY AND BEHAVIOR CHANGE

Theoretical analyses of anxiety and anxiety disorders have run the gamut from psychological to biological mechanisms. Psychological theories, for the most part, continue to feature familiar conditioning and cognitive mechanisms. Barlow (1988) provides an excellent summary of less familiar but significant biological conceptions of anxiety and its disorders. In the present chapter I selectively review developments in classical conditioning theory, the exposure principle, self-efficacy theory, and Barlow's (1988) recent formulation of "anxious apprehension."

Classical Conditioning

Classical or Pavlovian conditioning was *the* theoretical foundation on which the early behavior therapy conception of anxiety and its reduction rested, but it has also helped to define the nature of behavior therapy as a whole (Eysenck, 1982; Franks, 1969; Wolpe, 1958)—hence, the importance for contemporary behavior therapists of a timely review of modern Pavlovian conditioning by Rescorla (1988), one of the foremost experts in this field. Rescorla's (1988) message is signaled in the subtitle of his paper, "It's not what you think." The nature of modern classical conditioning is widely misunderstood. To illustrate this sobering state of affairs, Rescorla cites descriptions of classical conditioning from several leading textbooks on introductory, developmental, and abnormal psychology. These descriptions rely upon outdated notions of 20 years ago; they completely misrepresent the current field. It can be argued that Rescorla's point extends to many present-day views about classical conditioning within the behavior therapy literature.

Accounts of behavior therapy still typically portray classical conditioning as the pairing (contiguity) of two stimuli with the result that the originally neutral stimulus (the CS) comes to elicit the response previously produced by the unconditioned stimulus (UCS, US). Rescorla (1988) provides a succinct and compelling summary of research from the past two decades that contradicts this conventional view of classical conditioning. The pairing or contiguity of two stimuli is neither necessary nor sufficient for conditioning to take place. Spring (1988) provides the following illustration:

> Consider two cases in which tone and shock are paired three times. In the first, ten additional tones are presented without shock; in the second, no additional tones appear. The contiguity of tone and shock is equivalent in both instances, but only in the second will conditioning be engendered and the organism be able to predict the occurrence of shock. The crucial ingredient for conditioning is not the contiguity between the two stimuli, but the CS's ability to provide information about the UCS. Moreover, the contiguity of two stimuli is not necessary for conditioning to occur. For example, if shocks never occur in contiguity to tones, the tones will nonetheless become conditioned inhibitors. The animal will learn that tones predict the non-occurrence of shocks. (p. 716)

Classical conditioning is not a reflexive process in which the organism forms an association whenever two events happen to co-occur. Essentially, it is a cognitive process in which the organism learns about relationships among events in its world. To quote Rescorla (1988):

> The organism is better seen as an information seeker using logical and perceptual elations among events, along with its own preconceptions, to form a sophisticated representation of its world. Indeed, in teaching undergraduates, I favor an analogy between animals showing Pavlovian conditioning and scientists identifying the cause of a phenomenon. If one thinks of Pavlovian conditioning as developing between a CS and a US under just those circumstances that would lead a scientist to conclude that the CS causes the US, one has a surprisingly successful heuristic for remembering the facts of what it takes to produce Pavlovian associative learning. (p. 155)

Hugdahl (1987) provides additional support for this view.[1]

---

[1] This cognitive view of classical conditioning is also referred to as signal learning. Baeyens, Crombez, Van den Bergh, and Eelen (1989) argue that signal learning is an important form of classical conditioning but should not be equated with all of classical conditioning. They argue for the role of what they call evaluative conditioning. This form of conditioning does not require that the person be aware of the contingency between the related events, and it is more resistant to extinction. Although the applicability to behavior therapy is unclear, Baeyens et al.'s analysis suggests that it would be prudent to entertain the possibility of more than one kind of classical conditioning. The distinction between the automatic and controlled processing views of classical conditioning makes the same point (e.g., Sherman, Jorenby, & Baker, 1988).

Modern classical conditioning meshes nicely with cognitive social learning theory, which informs contemporary behavior therapy to a much greater degree than outdated versions of classical and operant conditioning (Bandura, 1986). The therapeutic implications vary greatly depending on whether the goal is the breaking of a simple S-R bond or habit versus altering ways in which a person construes both the real and perceived relationships in his or her world. The latter view is the essence of what is now usually referred to as cognitive-behavior therapy.

It is ironic that the dwindling number of critics who chastise current behavior therapists for allegedly abandoning "conditioning theory," and who dismiss the value of cognitive analyses (e.g., Levis, 1988), appear to miss the fundamental change that has taken place in Pavlovian conditioning itself. Conditioning, as psychology, has gone cognitive. An important observation by Rescorla (1988) is relevant to those critics who decry the lost values of the early learning theories:

> Those who study [modern Pavlovian conditioning] are not nearly as imperialistic as the animal learning psychologists of the 1940s and 1950s. In those days, conditioning was more than a learning process. It was the centerpiece for a set of theories intended to explain all behavior. More than that, it represented a way of doing science. Because conditioning came to psychology at a time when psychologists were working out scientific ways of studying behavior, it became bound up with considerable philosophical baggage. It stood not only for an explanation of psychological phenomena but also for a way of doing psychology altogether. One can still see some of the aftereffects of this heritage in the conservative style of introducing new theoretical concepts and in the commitment to elementarism. But Pavlovian conditioning has largely shed its philosophical role. Those who study conditioning have little interest in recapturing all of psychology in the name of behaviorism. (p. 158)

Understanding the radical reconception of Pavlovian conditioning moves the focus to the empirical study of clinically important phenomena and divests behavior therapy of unnecessary and divisive conceptual legacies. It allows serious analyses of similarities and differences between the conditioning view of how organisms learn about the relationships among life events and related conceptual frameworks such as attribution theory.

The Exposure Concept

Exposure treatment, in one form or another, has for some time now been the basis of behavioral treatment of several anxiety disorders. In the wake of the failure of the traditional two-factor theory to account satisfactorily for the maintenance and modification of avoidance behavior, attempts have been made to elevate the concept of exposure into an explanation of treatment effects. The problem, however, is that the exposure concept is only a description of a condition for therapeutic change, a condition that is not always necessary and is often insufficient (De Silva & Rachman, 1981). As emphasized in previous volumes in this series, the exposure concept neither explains the mechanisms responsible for behavior change nor generates sufficiently precise guidelines for the optimal implementation of cognitive–behavioral treatments (Wilson, 1984).

In his theoretical essay on the nature of anxiety and its role in phobia, Williams (1987) is severely critical of the utility of what he dubs the "exposure principle." As Williams (1987) points out, the procedure of exposing individuals to phobic stimuli is predicated on the assumption that such contact, be it direct or indirect, will result in "habituation" or "extinction" of anxiety. There are two problems with this assumption. First, the terms habituation and extinction, as they are commonly used, describe an outcome (reduction in anxiety or avoidance behavior) but do not explain this variable outcome. Second, anxiety itself is accorded a causal role in the regulation of phobic behavior. Yet, anxiety, as discussed below, is a poor predictor of phobic behavior (Bandura, 1986, 1988b).

Williams (1987) notes that stimulus exposure alone does not account for the heterogeneous patterns of outcome within and between procedurally similar or different treatments. At the theoretical level, Williams argues that the notion of stimulus exposure is an inevitably flawed attempt to externalize anxiety and minimize the role of cognitive mediation. As Williams suggests:

> To have meaning and explanatory value, "exposure" must be operationally defined independently of the behavioral changes it is supposed to explain. The concept of "functional exposure" simply begs the question, What makes treatments functional? If exposure is defined in terms of anxiety arousal (or "fear extinction/habituation"), it will suffer from all of the weaknesses of the anxiety theory it sought to replace. Operationally defining exposure without reference to psychological mediators will prove exceedingly difficult, and once the mediators are identified, the concept of exposure becomes superfluous. (p. 173)

At the procedural level, Williams (1987) reiterates the clinically important point that the stimulus exposure concept is an inadequate blueprint for guiding the development and application of maximally efficient treatment methods (Wilson, 1982b). Essentially replicating his own previous studies in this area (Williams, Dooseman, & Kleifield, 1984; Williams, Turner, & Peer, 1985), Williams reports a recent study in which he compared a guided mastery treatment derived from the stimulus exposure model with one based on Bandura's (1986) self-efficacy theory in agoraphobics. The former emphasized prolonged exposure to individualized phobic stimuli; the latter sought to foster a sense of personal mastery via direct behavioral change. Guided mastery proved to be significantly more effective than stimulus exposure in reducing the self-reported anxiety of the agoraphobics. This result was obtained even though the conditions for effective stimulus exposure were carefully met, namely, prolonged exposure, documented arousal of anxiety (which was higher in stimulus exposure than in guided mastery subjects), and exposure to stimuli during treatment that were identical to the stimulus conditions at posttreatment.

Marks (1987) has responded to what he sees as a "farrago of flaws" in Williams's criticisms of the stimulus exposure concept. Most clinicians, Marks contends, would readily concede that attentional mechanisms are important during exposure treatment. Patients should not be distracted and should actively engage in their counterphobic activities to "allow the signal to reach whichever brain structures can process it towards habituation" (p. 189). This is a restatement of Borkovec's (1978) attempt to cope with the problems encountered by the stimulus exposure concept by introducing the notion of "functional exposure" (see Wilson, 1987c, for a discussion of the limitations of functional exposure).

Simply recognizing that environmental information has to get into the brain is a far cry from elucidating the nature of information (and emotion) processing that significantly influences behavior. The complex function of attentional and cognitive encoding processes cannot be trivialized by casting them in simple reductionistic terms. It is also important to note that more is at stake here than agreeing, as Marks does, that patients have to be motivated to engage in exposure. What is at issue is the conceptualization of how the person processes his or her experience before, during, and after engaging in planned exposure.

Marks (1987) also rebuts the criticism that "exposure has difficulty explaining the marked differences between treatments in their average effectiveness, such as the robust advantage of the performance-based in vivo mode of treatment over the imaginal mode" (p. 189). Marks claims, for example, that performance-based exposure is more effective than its imaginal variant because it exposes the patient to more fear cues: "the closer the practice is to the real thing, the better the learning because the transfer gap is less" (p. 189). But explaining generalization of treatment effects requires more than a simple S-R view of stimulus generalization.

A relatively rare experimental analysis of generalization of therapeutic changes in agoraphobia treated with a performance-based method has been reported by Williams, Kinney, and Falbo (1989). The subjects were 27 severe agoraphobics with an average of four distinct areas of fear and behavioral avoidance. These "phobic areas" included such typical agoraphobic fears as driving, supermarket shopping, indoor shopping malls, restaurants, bridges, enclosed spaces, and heights. Williams et al. selectively treated only one or two of each subject's phobias, leaving the remainder untreated to assess any generalization or transfer effects. An additional group of agoraphobics served as a delayed treatment control condition to rule out any effect of mere passage of time or reactive effects of repeated measurement.

The results showed that treated phobias improved significantly more than untreated phobias and untreated phobias improved significantly more than those in control subjects. Addressing the question of the nature of agoraphobia, Williams et al. note that the "extent of therapeutic transfer, and the significant relationship between treatment benefit and transfer benefit, indicate that the various phobias constituting agoraphobia are psychologically cohesive and interrelated to a notable extent" (p. 441). The generalization effects, while clinically significant, were highly variable within and among subjects. The authors argue that the stimulus exposure concept cannot explain the highly idiosyncratic pattern of generalization effects they found: "Exposure has difficulty explaining the variable transfer within and between subjects because pairs of phobias with many overlapping stimulus features often changed to quite different degrees in a subject, whereas phobias with quite dissimilar stimulus features often changed to a similar extent" (p. 441). The authors themselves propose a cognitive or self-efficacy explanation of their findings, which is discussed below.

Self-Efficacy Theory

In the decade plus since Bandura's (1977) original publication, self-efficacy theory has been intensively studied and applied to a remarkably diverse range of psychological and even biological phenomena. Areas of application include substance use and abuse (Condiotti &

Lichtenstein, 1981), depression (Kavanaugh & Wilson, 1989), health behavior (O'Leary, 1985), decision making and organizational management (Wood & Bandura, 1989), sports psychology (Weinberg, Gould, & Jackson, 1979), catecholamine secretion (Bandura, Taylor, Williams, Mefford, & Barchas, 1985), opioid activation (Bandura, Cioffi, Taylor, & Brouillard, 1988), and immune function (O'Leary, 1989). Ironically, although Bandura (1977) introduced the self-efficacy theory to explain the maintenance and modification of phobic anxiety and behavior, the theory has had limited impact on clinicians' views of the nature and treatment of anxiety disorders.

The criticisms of self-efficacy theory within the anxiety field vary. Marks (1987) repeats a frequently voiced objection that self-efficacy is only a correlate or consequence of the reduction of phobic fear and avoidance. This objection ignores the evidence that fear, operationalized as either self-report or autonomic arousal, is at best a weak predictor of phobic avoidance (Bandura, 1988b; Williams, 1987). It also fails to take into consideration several well-controlled studies that have used partial correlation analyses to sort out the causal relationships among self-efficacy, anticipatory anxiety, anticipated anxiety, perceived danger fear arousal, and avoidance behavior. As we discussed in the previous volume in this series, self-efficacy accounts for a substantial amount of variance in phobic behavior when anticipated anxiety is partialed out, whereas the relationship between anticipated anxiety and phobic behavior essentially disappears when perceived self-efficacy is parceled out. This type of analysis provides some of the strongest support to date for the role of perceived efficacy in determining phobic avoidance.

Persistent belief in a view (i.e., that anxiety arousal leads to avoidance behavior) that is widely contradicted by the evidence requires psychological analysis in its own rights. As Bandura (1988b) speculates:

> A possible answer may lie in the force of confirmatory biases in judgments of causality (Nisbett & Ross, 1980). Confirming instances in which anxiety and avoidance occur jointly are likely to remain highly salient, whereas nonconfirming instances in which anxiety and approach behavior occur together, or avoidance occurs without anxiety command less attention. It is not that the nonconfirming instances are any less prevalent. Quite the contrary. People commonly perform activities at lower strengths of perceived self-efficacy despite high anxiety arousal. (p. 93)

A more novel criticism is that self-efficacy provides "no guidance on how to modify (self-efficacy) so that frightening tasks can be executed" (Marks, 1987, p. 194). The ways in which the construct of self-efficacy in particular and the broader cognitive social learning framework within which it must be interpreted provide significant guidelines for the implementation of treatment have been discussed previously (Wilson, 1982b, 1984). The Williams and Zane (1989) paper describes a number of detailed guidelines for performance-based treatment, which derive directly from self-efficacy theory. Although it could be argued that the clinical strategies recommended by Williams and Zane and Wilson need not necessarily follow from self-efficacy theory per se, they clearly derive from the cognitive social learning framework of which self-efficacy is an integral component. Even more to the point, there is nothing in conditioning or the simply descriptive concept of "exposure" that would have led to the use of the treatment strategies or maintenance principles (see the discussion of Ost's [1989] paper below) that are now a common feature of effective cognitive-behavioral therapy (Wilson, 1984).

SELF-EFFICACY AND PANIC

Another reason self-efficacy theory has had limited influence on the treatment of anxiety disorders in general is spelled out by Barlow (1988). As Barlow interprets self-efficacy theory, it is largely restricted to predicting overt avoidance behavior and is only weakly related to self-reported or physiological anxiety arousal and panic. Yet as Barlow points out, anxiety states (generalized anxiety and panic disorder) are the most commonly seen clinical disorders. Then there is the recent thinking, which we address later in this chapter, that panic rather than avoidance behavior should be the primary target of treatment of agoraphobia. Any theory that failed to account for anxiety and its relationship to panic would not surprisingly attract little attention from clinicians. However, self-efficacy bids fair to provide a full explanation of the causes and consequences of anxiety, and, if successful, would have pressing relevance to the treatment of clinical anxiety states (Bandura, 1988a, 1988b).[2]

According to Bandura's social cognitive theory[3] (1986, 1988a), self-efficacy is an important determinant not only of behavior, but also motivation and affect. Perceived coping efficacy plays a critical role in

---

[2]Barlow (1988) does note Bandura's (1986) "extension" of self-efficacy to include perceived control over unpredictable events, but Barlow still emphasizes the connection between self-efficacy and behavior.

[3]Bandura (1986) introduced the term "social cognitive theory" as a more recent development of the more familiar "cognitive social learning theory" (Bandura, 1977).

regulating anxiety, namely, affective arousal, which is labeled cognitively as fear or anxiety. To establish that perceived coping efficacy is a cognitive mediator of anxiety arousal, Bandura (1986) and his colleagues conducted a series of studies in which they experimentally induced different levels of coping efficacy and related them to different measures of anxiety. To summarize these studies, the greater the perceived inefficacy, the greater the level of subjective distress, autonomic arousal, and catecholamine secretion. The greater the perceived efficacy, the lower the psychological and biological measures of anxiety (Bandura, 1988b).

Bandura (1988b) has recently expanded on the role of self-efficacy in regulating anxiety arousal. He hypothesizes that anxiety is influenced not only by perceived coping efficacy, but also by "cognitive control self-efficacy." In terms of this analysis, "it is not the sheer frequency of frightful cognitions but rather the strength of perceived self-inefficacy to control their escalation or perseveration that is a major source of anxiety arousal" (p. 89). Or, as Bandura states, "You cannot prevent the birds of worry and care from flying over your head. But you can stop them from building a nest in your head" (p. 89). In addition, perceived coping efficacy can also affect anxiety arousal and action through its influence on perceived personal vulnerability and judgments of risk.

The causal relationships between self-efficacy and exposure to threat were investigated by Ozer and Bandura (1989). They used a mastery modeling program to help women develop coing skills for preventing sexual assaults. Not surprisingly, mastery modeling resulted in enhanced perceived coping and cognitive control self-efficacy, decreased behavioral avoidance, and significantly less anxiety arousal. Of interest here, however, is Ozer and Bandura's detailed analysis of potentially causal mechanisms involved in changes in action, affect, and subjective anxiety.

Use of path analysis revealed that both perceived coping efficacy and cognitive control self-efficacy influenced anxiety arousal and avoidance behavior following the training program. Perceived coping efficacy altered the women's sense of personal vulnerability and estimation of risk, whereas cognitive control self-efficacy reduced intrusive negative thoughts. The relative effects of these two cognitive mediators of action and affect varied in a complex fashion over time. Consistent with previous studies, direct measures of anxiety arousal showed no independent causal contribution to outcome. Summarizing their findings, Ozer and Bandura (1989) liken this "differential linkage of action and thought efficacy to perceived personal vulnerability is in keeping with the distinction drawn by Lazarus and Folkman (1984) between coping strategies that regulate affect and those used to promote adaptive behavior. Being able to turn off scary thoughts does not make one more skilled at fending off assailants. However, mastering self-protective capabilities does reduce one's sense of personal vulnerability."

What is needed now is an analysis of this expanded self-efficacy theory to clinical states, such as generalized anxiety and panic disorder. The evidence, some of it summarized herein, seems to point to an important role of cognitive mediation in both disorders. Self-efficacy theory should provide a potentially powerful means of clarifying the relationship between the cognitive component of these disorders and anxiety arousal. Barlow (1988) has concluded that "reductions in panic and anxiety during exposure-based treatments may be the single most important predictor of successful outcome, outranking even amount of practice between sessions" (p. 430). Experimental analyses, using the statistical techniques employed so successfully in the studies reviewed above, are needed to sort out the relative causal contributions of self-efficacy, anticipated anxiety, and actual anxiety arousal to treatment outcome.

Perceived self-efficacy for controlling panic attacks, and its relationship to avoidance behavior, was investigated by Telch, Brouillard, Telch, Agras, and Taylor (1989). This analysis was part of a broader study that focused on several cognitive dimensions of panic, including anticipated panic and catastrophic appraisal of the consequences of panic.

The results followed a clear and consistent pattern. Compared to patients with little or no avoidance behavior, panic patients with extensive avoidance behavior exaggerated the likelihood of occurrence of panic, engaged in more catastrophic thinking about the consequences of panic, and reported lower self-efficacy for coping with panic. Anticipation of the probability of occurrence of panic was the most powerful correlate of avoidance behavior. Appraisal of the consequences of panic was significantly less predictive of avoidance than anticipated panic (Adler, Craske, Kirshenbaum, & Barlow, 1989, report a similar finding). Similarly, the association between perceived efficacy for coping with panic and avoidance ceased to be significant when the contribution of anticipated panic was partialed out. Telch et al. (1989) conclude that "in the case of agoraphobia, avoidance is more closely linked to panic expectancy than to judgments of personal efficacy to cope with panic" (p. 381). As described earlier in this chapter, several studies have shown that perceived efficacy about engaging in phobic behavior is a stronger predictor of avoidance behavior than anticipated anxiety (Bandura, 1986). Why panic coping efficacy is apparently less effective than coping efficacy as measured in previous studies is unclear.

SELF-EFFICACY AND GENERALIZATION EFFECTS

Support for self-efficacy theory comes from the Williams et al. (1989) study of generalization of therapeutic effects. The results showed that self-efficacy was the best predictor of behavior change in both treated and untreated domains of phobic functioning. Aside from replicating once again the superiority of self-efficacy over self-reported anticipated anxiety and perceived danger, this study also showed that past performance failed to predict the extent of generalization. Williams et al. note that "the fact that self-efficacy judgments were just as predictive of outcome in domains where past performance is quite uninformative as in domains where subjects received treatment, attests to the importance of self-efficacy in regulating action" (p. 441). This is an important finding because several critics have contended that self-efficacy is simply a correlate or consequence of behavior change with no causal properties.

Self-efficacy theory has been less successful in explaining what Rachman (1989) has termed the "return of fear." This phenomenon is defined as the renewal or an extinguished fear response (Craske & Rachman, 1987). Rachman points out that the concept is closely related to, but not identical with, relapse. The latter may have multiple forms and causes; the former does not necessarily entail relapse. The Craske and Rachman study deserved further analysis because the phenomenon challenges the role of self-efficacy in accounting for cognitive and affective responses.

Anxious Apprehension and Affective Therapy

In his scholarly and richly informative book *Anxiety and Its Disorders*, Barlow (1988) outlines a theory of the process, origins, and modification of anxiety or what he terms "anxious apprehension." As background for his theoretical proposals, Barlow offers an up-to-date synopsis of a range of different literatures and theoretical formulations. His summary of current neurobiological theory and the research of emotion researchers, such as Izard (Izard, Kagan, & Zajonc, 1984), introduces both fresh and useful perspectives into the behavior therapy literature.

In contrast to most of the behavior therapy literature, Barlow draws a key distinction between fear and anxiety. Fear is presented as an innate and pure emotion. Anxiety is not a basic emotion. Rather, it is viewed as a "diffuse blend of emotions reflecting interest, anger, and excitement mixed with a primary component of fear" (p. 70). Barlow adopts the term "anxious apprehension" instead of anxiety because "perceptions of unpredictability and lack of control over potentially aversive events contribute a marked apprehension surround the future" (p. 70). Panic is equated with fear. Thus, Barlow distinguishes between panic (or fear) and anxiety. This distinction has both theoretical and practical implications.

The model of anxious apprehension is summarized in Figure 3-1. The process begins when certain external or internal (arousal-based) stimuli elicit negative affect. A biological vulnerability, probably genetically transmitted, predisposes individuals to react this way. Negative affect, Barlow contends,

> is associated with a perceived inability to predict, control, or obtain desired results in upcoming situations or events. This cognitive set,

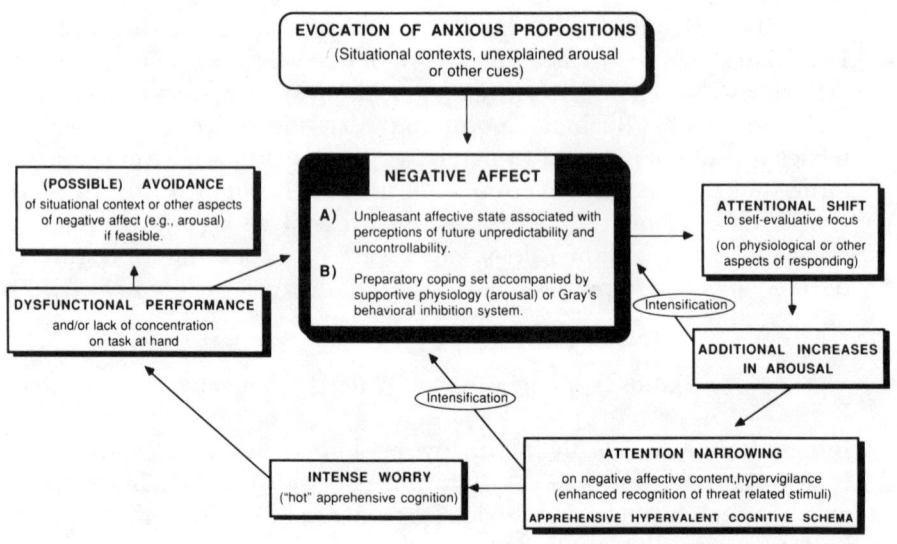

FIG. 3-1.
Barlow's model of anxious apprehension. From *Anxiety and Its Disorders* by D. H. Barlow, 1988, p. 250, New York: Guilford Press. Copyright 1988 by The Guilford Press. Reprinted by permission.

which can be categorized as an apprehensive "hypervalent cognitive schema," leads to (1) a shift in focus of attention from external to internal self-evaluative content, (2) further increases in arousal, (3) narrowing of attention, and (4) hypervigilance regarding sources of apprehension. At sufficient intensity, this process results in disruptions in concentration and performance, and ultimately in avoidance of sources of apprehension if this method of coping is available. (p. 248)

Based on this model of anxiety or anxious apprehension, Barlow (1988) argues that effective treatment must modify certain psychological processes; other processes are helpful but not essential to change. These psychological processes are summarized in Table 3-1 and are the targets of what Barlow describes as "affective therapy."

Barlow's (1988) model is complex, and necessarily so. Any modern theory of anxiety and its modification must involve some type of cognitive–affective mechanism that emphasizes the importance of cognitive appraisal and the concepts of predictability and controllability (Bandura, 1986; Lazarus & Folkman, 1984). The model is thus a far cry from the simplistic classical conditioning formulations of years past. It overlaps heavily with self-efficacy theory in particular and social cognitive theory in general. The core of the model can be said to be perceptions of unpredictability and uncontrollability. These concepts are embraced by perceptions of self-efficacy. Negative self-focus and self-evaluation are a function of low self-efficacy:

> People who believe they can exercise control over potential threats do not conjure up apprehensive cognitions and, therefore, are not perturbed by them. But those who believe they cannot manage potential threats experience high levels of stress. They tend to dwell on their coping deficien-

TABLE 3-1. Components of Affective Therapy

Essential targets for change
   Action tendencies
   A sense of uncontrollability/unpredictability
   Self-focused attention

Helpful but not essential targets for change
   "Hot" apprehensive cognitions
   Hypervalent cognitive schemata and attention narrowing
   Coping skills and social support
   Elevated physiological responding and altered neurobiological functions

---

Note. From *Anxiety and Its Disorders* by D. H. Barlow, 1988, p. 318, New York: Guilford Press. Copyright 1988 by The Guilford Press. Reprinted by permission.

cies and view many aspects of their environment as fraught with danger. Through such inefficacious thought they distress themselves and constrain and impair their level of functioning. (Bandura, 1988b, p. 4)

Negative self-evaluation, in turn, generates physiological arousal in the same negative feedback loop proposed by Barlow (1988).

Barlow (1988) makes the following comments on the similarity between his model and self-efficacy theory:

> If the concept of self-efficacy is altered to include perceptions of abilities to control future unpredictable negative events of any kind, it comes extremely close to what I have proposed as one of the three essential components of affective therapy.[4] . . . It is the development of this sense of control, along with changes in action tendencies and alterations in focus of attention, that may ultimately be the target of all drug and behavioral treatments. (p. 438)

Bandura (1986) predicts that behavioral treatments will be effective to the degree that they enhance self-efficacy; Barlow (1988) states that the same treatments will work to the extent that they reduce anxious apprehension.

SPECIFIC ANXIETY DISORDERS

Historically, both research and practice in behavior therapy focused mainly on simple phobias and agoraphobia. As we noted in Volume 11 of this series, one of the welcome developments in the 1980s has been the increasing attention that has been devoted to other anxiety disorders, such as social phobia, generalized anxiety disorder, and panic disorder. The remainder of the present chapter focuses predominantly on these disorders for reasons other than the breaking of new ground. Advances in the understanding and treatment of social phobia, generalized anxiety disorder, and panic disorder with and without agoraphobia are arguably of greater clinical relevance to the average practitioner than experimental analyses and modification of simple phobias that are probably less likely to cause individuals to seek professional assistance. Furthermore, experimental analyses of these disorders provide rich opportunities for refining existing theoretical models of anxiety and behavior change.

[4]As I have argued, self-efficacy does encompass perceived unpredictability and uncontrollability. Moreover, the theory accommodates all three of Barlow's essential targets for change, not just one.

Social Phobia

As recently as 1985, social phobia was described as the "neglected anxiety disorder" (Liebowitz, Gorman, Fyer, & Klein, 1985). Predictably, following such an invitation to biobehavioral researchers, social phobia has become an important focus of experimental analysis. A handy and up-to-date source of information about social phobia can be found in a special issue of *Clinical Psychology Review* on this disorder (Heimberg, 1989a). This collection of invited papers provides a state-of-the-art summary of what is known about the diagnosis, etiology, explanation, and treatment of social phobia.

The preparedness concept first introduced by Seligman (1971) to explain the nature of primarily simple phobias was later extended by Ohman (1986) to account for social phobias. The hypothesis was that people are biologically prepared to associate fear with certain facial stimuli, particularly the eyes. For example, Marks (1987) has suggested that the concern of social phobics about being watched is an extreme form of normal human sensitivity to eye contact. In a recent test of this reasoning, Merckelbach, Van Hout, Van den Hout, and Mersch (1989) systematically exposed social phobics to normal controls to slides of angry faces, happy faces, or neutral objects. Although the angry face slides elicited greater skin conductance responses and were rated more negatively, the two groups did not differ. The authors argue that their findings are inconsistent with Ohman's (1986) view that social phobias can be explained as the product of phylogenetically prepared conditioning to negative facial cues.[5]

Butler (1989) provides a clear and practical account of the clinical use of specific behavioral and cognitive strategies. Practitioners will welcome her clinical observations and recommendations. Heimberg (1989b) himself has compiled a detailed and comprehensive review of the effectiveness of cognitive and behavioral treatments for social pho-

---

[5] A critical tenet of Seligman's (1971) preparedness concept and its elaboration by Ohman (1986) is that people are biologically prepared, as a result of evolutionary experience, to fear certain classes of stimuli. Proponents of this view have pointed to studies showing that nonprepared but fear relevant stimuli (e.g., a gun) do not produce the same resistance to extinction of a classically conditioned fear response as a prepared stimulus (e.g., a snake). A well-controlled study by Hugdahl and Johnsen (1989) compared a prepared stimulus to one showing a gun pointed directly at the subjects. With this subtle but important modification of the nonprepared, fear-relevant stimulus in the otherwise typical methodology, Hugdahl and Johnsen found no difference between the prepared and nonprepared stimuli. Their findings lend support to an ontogenetic rather than a phylogenetic explanation of fear conditioning.

bia. His conclusion is that a combined cognitive–behavioral treatment program currently appears to be an effective intervention. Nonetheless, enthusiasm for this approach must be tempered by the relatively few controlled studies, most of which contain one or other methodological limitation.

The outcome research on this topic is illustrated by a well-controlled study by Mattick, Peters, and Clarke (1989). This antipodean group compared four treatment conditions: exposure, cognitive restructuring, a combination of exposure and cognitive restructuring, and a waiting list control. Efforts were made to ensure that the cognitive restructuring group did not receive any formal exposure to their phobic stimuli, thereby allowing an uncontaminated comparison. Process measures showed that the integrity of the distinctive treatments was maintained. Within-group analyses showed that the combined and cognitive restructuring alone groups improved significantly on all outcome measures. The exposure only group improved significantly on phobic avoidance but not attitudinal measures. Between-groups analyses revealed that the combined group was superior to exposure only on two measures of phobic fear and avoidance. On the behavioral approach task at posttreatment, the combined and exposure groups were superior to cognitive restructuring. However, at the 3-month follow-up, the exposure group had deteriorated while the cognitive restructuring had improved; the two groups did not differ. Mattick et al. (1989) derived what they called a composite, endstate measure of patients' functioning to assess the clinical as opposed to the statistical significance of treatment effects. The authors conclude that overall, no clinically significant differences were demonstrated, and that the degree of clinical improvement was limited.

Finally, in view of the increasing use of combined behavioral and pharmacological treatments for other anxiety disorders, a summary of pharmacotherapy for social phobia by Levin, Schneier, and Liebowitz (1989) warrants attention. Although benzodiazepines are frequently prescribed for social phobics, Levin et al. (1989) call for caution in their use: "Clinically, we find that social phobic patients can derive significant relief from benzodiazepines but they may abuse them. These drugs should be particularly avoided in social phobic patients with a history of alcohol abuse. In addition, high doses of alprazolam may cause disinhibition and poor social judgment" (p. 136).

A consistent finding has been that phenelzine appears to reduce social anxiety. Nevertheless, the interplay between the drug and behavior appears to be important. Levin et al. (1989) cite evidence indicating that both alprazolam and phenelzine often require 3 to 4 weeks before they affect patients' social functioning. They speculate that this delayed effect may be due to the role of exposure following the drug's initial anxiolytic impact: "After receiving an initial boost in confidence and symptom reduction in the first 4–6 weeks of phenelzine treatment, social phobic patients appear to enter a positive reinforcing cycle. Successful negotiation of previously difficult performance or social situations further boosts confidence and encourages more exposure and learning" (p. 136). As the authors observe, if this proves to be the case, it points strongly to the combined use of medication and cognitive-behavior therapy.

Generalized Anxiety Disorder

Diffuse or generalized anxiety disorder (GAD) is a common clinical problem, and one seen far more frequently by clinicians than the phobic disorders that have received such intensive study in the behavior therapy literature. GAD is especially likely to be encountered in general medical practice. Barlow (1988), citing data from the recent NIMH Epidemiologic Catchment Area study, places the population prevalence of GAD at 4%. The population prevalence of GAD is roughly four times that of panic disorder. In contrast, analyses of patients treated in anxiety clinics indicate that panic disorder is seen far more frequently (Barlow, 1988). It appears that GAD patients only seek specialized psychological or psychiatric care when their somatic symptoms become too severe. The remainder are likely to put up with their "worrying" or see a general medical practitioner.

The most common treatment of GAD has been the use of benzodiazepines. The continued use of these drugs is unsatisfactory, however, due to problems of tolerance and dependence. Their efficacy is also in question. Therapeutic effects appear to be short-lived (Barlow, 1988; Committee on the Review of Medicine, 1980; Taylor & Arnow, 1988). Summarizing the literature on benzodiazepines, Barlow (1988) reaches the following conclusion: "On the basis of these studies, most investigators conclude that these drugs may have some temporary palliative value in reducing anxiety over the short term, but not over the long term. Conventional clinical wisdom suggests prescribing these drugs for a short time during a particularly difficult or stressful situation and then removing the drug very quickly" (p. 588).[6] And even if antide-

---

[6]Barlow (1988) offers a theoretically stimulating and practically important discussion of the hazards of combining benzodiazepines with exposure treatment in the treatment of phobic disorders. The drugs might impair the treatment outcome achieved by exposure

pressants such as imipramine prove to be effective with GAD, as some data indicate, the usual problems of discontinuing medication and sustaining therapeutic effects will remain. Clearly, there is a need for the development of effective psychological treatments.

Most welcome, therefore, has been the recent increase in controlled clinical outcome studies. One of the most carefully studied and promising treatments for GAD is anxiety management, a method developed by Butler and her colleagues at Oxford University. This method, which overlaps with, but which can also be distinguished from the anxiety management training method of Suinn and Richardson (1971), consists of the following components: (1) information about the nature of anxiety and what might be expected from treatment, (2) a cognitive component to help patients identify and respond to specific anxiety-provoking thoughts, (3) distraction and relaxation to cope with anticipatory anxiety, (4) *in vivo* exposure for overcoming avoidance behavior, and (5) a component designed to increase "self-confidence" by identifying the person's strong points, by engaging in rewarding and pleasurable activities, and by paying attention to aspects of life in which the person is functioning relatively well" (p. 536). The treatment program is described in an easy to understand, self-help booklet that the patient follows. Patients played an active role in setting goals, planning homework assignments, and monitoring their progress. This practical and effective treatment manual is available from the Oxford group and should be of considerable benefit to busy practitioners.

The value of this approach with social phobia has been previously demonstrated (Butler, Cullington, Munby, Amies, & Gelder, 1984). In a recent study, Butler, Cullington, Hibbert, Klimes, and Gelder (1987) compared their method of anxiety management with a waiting list control condition (12 weeks) in the treatment of GAD. Forty-five reliably diagnosed patients with GAD were randomly assigned to either the treatment or control conditions. The patients had to have a primary diagnosis of GAD in which the current problem had to have existed for at least 6 months but no longer than 2 years. This criterion excluded patients with chronic anxiety who Butler, Cullington, et al.

---

via physiological as well as psychological mechanisms (e.g., inviting external attributions of behavior change to the drug rather than facilitating self-attribution and thereby inadvertently undermining self-efficacy). Especially in view of the apparent value of including exposure methods in the treatment of GAD as indicated by the Butler, Cullington, et al. (1987) data described later in this chapter, practitioners would do well to be aware of the issues Barlow raises.

(1987) suggest may have greater diagnostic heterogeneity. Patients were also excluded if they met the criteria for phobic, obsessive–compulsive, or major depressive disorder. Treatment lasted an average of 8.7 sessions and was conducted by three experienced clinical psychologists. In addition to patient self-report of anxiety and depression, an independent assessor made "blind" evaluations of treatment outcome.

Active treatment resulted in significant reductions in anxiety and depression at posttreatment compared with the waiting list condition, which showed little change. Subjects in the latter condition showed comparable improvement when they subsequently received the anxiety management treatment. Moreover, therapeutic improvement was maintained at a 6-month follow-up. The clinical significance of these results is reflected in the finding that at posttreatment the anxiety ratings of half of the patients had fallen below the cutoff point that distinguishes a normal from a clinical population on the Leeds Anxiety Scale. Of both practical and theoretical interest is the finding that a subgroup of patients who experienced recurrent panic attacks fared as well as patients with GAD alone. Patients whose anxiety at pretreatment was lower and who were less demoralized responded significantly better than those who were more anxious and demoralized (Butler & Anastasiades, 1988).

The same group of investigators examined the extent to which therapeutic improvement was a function of specific elements within their anxiety management treatment (Butler, Gelder, Hibbert, Cullington, & Klimes, 1987). Clinical interviews and ratings of the patients in their controlled trial, described above, yielded several findings of note. First, the GAD patients were able to identify specific cognitions associated with their anxiety. These cognitions, examples of which were thoughts about dying or collapsing, inability to cope, loss of control, and anxiety itself (e.g., "I may get anxious"), were similar to previous analyses of the thoughts of GAD patients (Beck, Laude, & Bohnert, 1974; Rapee, 1985). Patients with recurrent panic attacks were twice as likely to report thoughts of dying/collapsing, and illness/health than patients who were panic-free. This finding is consistent with Clark's (1986) theory of panic, which holds that panic patients have distinctive, health-related thoughts.

Second, virtually two-thirds of the patients reported avoidance behavior, although none met the criteria for phobic disorder. The pattern of avoidance behavior was diffuse, resembling that of social phobics. This finding, if replicated, is most significant. It contradicts several accounts of GAD in the clinical literature and suggests obvious therapeutic strategies. Butler, Gelder, et al. (1987) state that "avoidance stands out as the feature of our patients' disorder which is reversed by anxiety management. Before treatment patients actively sought to avoid, afterwards they tried to face anxiety-provoking situations, and they reported that this change was beneficial" (p. 521).

Third, patients reported having used techniques, such as distraction, talking to themselves, and relaxation, to cope with their anxiety prior to treatment but with little success. After treatment, these techniques that are a part of anxiety management, were rated as helpful. The authors suggest that the difference lies in the precision and persistence with which the techniques are applied during treatment. Finally, patients rated strategies designed to increase self-confidence (e.g., graded task assignments for resuming social activities) as particularly helpful.

Lindsay, Gamsu, McLaughlin, Hood, and Espie (1987) compared brief cognitive therapy with relaxation training and a waiting list control condition. Both treatments were more effective than the waiting list control but not significantly different from each other. The studies by Butler, Cullington, et al. (1987) and Lindsay et al. (1987) provide strong evidence that treatment can help GAD patients. Lacking a control condition for the so-called nonspecifics of intervention, they cannot, however, tell us whether the specific elements of the treatments are necessarily effective.

A well-controlled study by Blowers, Cobb, and Mathews (1987) compared anxiety management training with both a nondirective counseling treatment and a waiting list control. The patients were similar to those in the Butler, Cullington, et al. (1987) study: "the presence of mild depressive, phobic or obsessional symptoms was acceptable, provided they did not meet other diagnostic criteria, and did not require treatment in their own right; . . . any other diagnosed psychiatric conditions were right" (p. 494). The anxiety management training did differ from the Oxford group's in that it relied solely on brief cognitive and relaxation therapy. The former was a modified version of Beck and Emery's (1985) approach, the latter drawn from Bernstein and Borkovec (1973). The emphasis in anxiety management training was on coping with anxiety; the nondirective treatment, derived from Rogers (1957), focused on understanding anxiety. Tapes of therapy sessions were sampled and assessed to ensure that the two treatments were implemented in a consistent and discriminating manner.

Following 10 weeks of treatment, the anxiety management training was superior to the waiting list control on a variety of measures but not clearly more effective than the nondirective counseling. The same pattern of findings were obtained at a 6-month follow-up of the two active treatments. One of the more striking findings of this study was the high attrition rate, 29 of 66 patients. The attrition rate was equally distributed across the three treatment conditions. The authors also note that the magnitude of their anxiety management training effect was considerably less than that achieved by Butler, Cullington, et al. (1987). The main difference between the two treatment packages was the degree of exposure to anxiety-producing cues. Blowers et al. (1987) explicitly minimized such exposure, whereas the Oxford group featured it in their treatment. Blowers et al. conclude:

> Comparisons of effect size across the various studies discussed here would appear to support a role for exposure, and suggests that in its absence, relaxation and cognitive methods may be only slightly more potent than are relatively non-directive and non-structured methods of psychological counseling. The present results can thus be used to argue for treatment involving a combination of exposure to anxiety-arousing situations, and simultaneous practice in cognitive coping methods. (p. 502)

Two other recent studies have attempted to differentiate specific from nonspecific treatment effects. In the first, mildly to moderately disturbed undergraduate GAD clients received relaxation training (Borkovec et al., 1987). In addition, half received brief cognitive therapy and half nondirective therapy. Both groups showed significant improvement at the end of treatment, with the cognitive therapy condition superior to nondirective therapy. The second study, however, failed to replicate these results (Borkovec & Mathews, 1988).

In the latter study patients with either GAD or panic disorder received 12 sessions of relaxation training. They were also randomly assigned to one of three treatment conditions: cognitive therapy, adapted from Beck and Emery (1985); coping desensitization (imaginal exposure to anxiety-eliciting cues plus relaxation training); and nondirective therapy. The patients were older and more anxious than those in the Borkovec et al. (1987) investigation. There were six GAD and four panic patients in each group.

Results at posttreatment and at 6- and 12-month follow-ups showed that all three treatments produced significant and continuing improvement but did not differ from each other. There were also no differences between GAD and panic patients. These results are consistent with those of Blowers et al. (1987). Borkovec and Mathews (1988) considered different explanations of their failure to find differences among treatments. They reject the view that their treatments were simply less effective than previous studies and suggest that common elements among the treatments might explain the data. For example, patients' ratings of expectancy of improvement at the beginning of treatment correlated strongly with outcome. This raises the likelihood that GAD patients might be responsive to a placebo effect.

Another obvious common element is relaxation training. The methodology used in this study made it impossible to evaluate the independent effects of this component of treatment. Borkovec and Mathews (1988) suggest that relaxation did have significant effects because degree of adherence in practicing the method was related to outcome and because they found that relaxation-induced anxiety was negatively related to outcome. Finally, uncontrolled actions on the part of patients in the control treatment condition may have blurred the procedural differences among the treatments. The difficulties facing all investigators in conducting controlled treatment outcome studies are well illustrated in the authors' following observation: "Two of the most successful nondirective clients in the present study indicated during final sessions that they now realized the importance of confronting their fears and of talking more rationally to themselves when they felt anxious, despite the complete absence of prompting therapist comments or instructions" (p. 882).

Another familiar problem in treatment outcome research is comparing closely related and hence overlapping approaches. Therapeutic labels often mean different procedures to different investigators. Durham and Turvey (1987) compared 16 sessions of cognitive therapy with behavior therapy. In describing the respective methods, the authors state that they

> had the same style but differed in content. The Cognitive Therapy condition (CT) included behavioral techniques when appropriate in the context of the cognitive model of treatment. The Behavior Therapy condition (BT) employed behavioral strategies such as relaxation, distraction and graded exposure, but excluded any attempt to elicit or modify automatic thoughts, thinking errors or maladaptive underlying assumptions. However, it did include the use of positive self-statements and general problem-solving strategies when appropriate. (p. 230)

The two treatments produced equivalent effects at posttreatment, a finding which, in the absence of a no treatment or waiting list control, makes interpretation difficult. Nevertheless, a 6-month follow-up indicated that cognitive therapy was superior to behavior therapy on several measures. Durham and Turvey (1987) caution that at the follow-up virtually no patient was symptom-free and fully one-third and reverted to their pretreatment status.

Comparative studies of the separate and joint effects of cognitive-behavioral methods and different drugs are surprisingly rare. A recent study along these lines was reported by Power, Jerrom, Simpson,

Mitchell, and Swanson (1989). They compared cognitive-behavioral treatment (CBT) with diazepam and a drug placebo. The CBT treatment was based on Beck and Emery (1985) and combined with relaxation training and what the authors refer to as "individual behavioural targets, such as graded exposure . . . where necessary" (p. 5). The results at posttreatment indicated that CBT was more effective than the placebo, not significantly different from diazepam. One of the problems with this study is the brevity of treatment. In CBT patients were seen for only four treatment sessions. It would appear difficult to implement cognitive therapy, relaxation training, and individualized exposure within the course of so few sessions.

CONCLUDING COMMENTS

Treatment outcome research on GAD is still in its early stages. At this point it is possible to conclude that cognitive-behavioral treatment (i.e., a combination of cognitive restructuring à la Beck, coping relaxation, and exposure) helps a majority of patients. The degree of improvement one can expect is uncertain, varying from one study to another. Although helped, many patients still experience anxiety symptoms following therapy. What is encouraging is that the improvement that is achieved at the end of treatment seems to be maintained at follow-up.

We cannot say that cognitive-behavioral treatment has been shown to be significantly more effective than other psychological treatments. Part of the problem here is a familiar one, namely, the difficulty of testing cognitive-behavioral treatment against a credible comparison treatment that does not contain potentially potent cognitive-behavioral components. We do not know whether the roughly similar results obtained thus far are due to these common elements or simply reflected a more general, nonspecific responsiveness to treatment by GAD patients. Comparative treatment trials of cognitive-behavioral and drug therapies, along the lines of the research on agoraphobia and panic disorder, are needed given the extent to which GAD is typically treated with benzodiazepines.

Panic and Agoraphobia

The 1980s saw the emergence of panic as an independent anxiety disorder and the focus of intensive theorizing and research. The rather sudden spotlight of inquiry that has been trained on panic is particularly evident in the cognitive-behavior therapy literature (e.g., Barlow & Cerny, 1988; Rachman & Maser, 1988). Panic has become not only an important disorder in its own right but now is also seen as the basis of agoraphobia. This shift in thinking has led to a reconceptualization of the nature and treatment of agoraphobia. This new look at agoraphobia is summarized by Barlow (1988) as follows:

> My colleagues and I now believe that panic is the central feature of agoraphobia (and panic disorder), and good evidence exists that avoidance behavior is a subsequent complication of initial panic. Of course, avoidance behavior may well become functionally autonomous after a period of time. In addition, the development of strong safety signals or rituals seem to strengthen avoidance behavior even if panic attacks have long since disappeared. Therefore, treating avoidance behaivor will always be necessary. Nevertheless, the primary goal should be the treatment of panic. (p. 428)

Data from the Epidemiologic Catchment Area study indicate that between 2.8% and 5.7% of a random sample of the population meet the criteria for agoraphobia; the prevalence of panic disorder was roughly 1% (Myers et al., 1984). The epidemiological data show that 25% to 50% of agoraphobics do not report panic, a finding that seems inconsistent with the view that agoraphobia is merely the severe end of a continuum of avoidance behavior associated secondarily with primary panic disorder. Clinical reports, however, suggest that very few agoraphobics have not experienced panic attacks (Barlow, 1988). Other experimental findings also challenge the increasingly popular psychiatric view that agoraphobia is a secondary variant of a primary panic disorder. For example, Telch et al. (1989) showed distinct differences between their panic patients with little or no avoidance behavior versus those with extensive avoidance behavior on different cognitive dimensions of panic, even though the two groups were comparable on measures of panic frequency and intensity.

MODELS

The development of a biological model of panic has been heavily influenced by the pioneering research of Klein, Rabkin, and Gorman (1985). According to this view, panic is a direct product of an abnormal neurobiological mechanism. One of the predictions from this neurobiological model is that pharmacotherapy is the optimal, if not necessary, form of treatment of panic. The effects of pharmacotherapy for panic disorder and their implications for the biological model were summarized in Volume 11 of this series (Wilson, 1987a). Barlow (1988) and Rachman and Maser (1988) provide more recent, state-of-the-art analyses of this prediction.

Klein, Ross, and Cohen (1987) have once again asserted that panic causes avoidance behavior and must be treated via pharmacotherapy. In this study, they use path analysis to reanalyze the results from the Zitrin, Klein, and Woerner (1980) and Zitrin, Klein, Woerner, and Ross (1983). This statistical reanalysis, regardless of the sophistication of the statistical technique, reminds one of the misuse of meta analysis to salvage methodologically flawed studies (e.g., Smith, Glass, & Miller, 1980). The two studies in question, although pioneering and heuristic in their time, have been repeatedly and cogently criticized on a number of grounds (see summary of some of these criticisms in Volume 11 of this series; Wilson, 1987b). Barlow (1988) dismisses these studies as "more interesting for their historical contribution . . . than for substantive value at this point" (p. 432). No amount of statistical reworking can remedy the methodological shortcomings of the original studies, only one of which was the absence of an acceptable measure of panic.

The conclusions Klein et al. (1987) draw from their path analysis are highly questionable. They assert that exposure reduces avoidance behavior but not panic. This assertion is reliably contradicted by several studies, as shown below (see also Barlow, 1988; Rachman & Maser, 1988; Telch, Agras, Taylor, Roth, & Gallen, 1985). Current analyses focus not on the obvious (that exposure reduces panic) but on the critical question of how it achieves such an effect. Any conceptual model of panic—neurobiological or psychological—must be able to explain the documented success of both exposure treatment and pharmacotherapy in reducing panic.

Psychological models of panic are comprehensively reviewed and analyzed in Rachman and Maser's (1988) volume on this topic. Of the views that have been proposed, none is better developed than Clark's (1988b) cognitive model, which was discussed in some detail in Volume 11 of this series. Several recent findings are consistent with this model.

A critical tenet of Clark's model (and related cognitive–behavioral models) is that panic is a product of the individual's dysfunctional appraisal of physiological cues. To test this basic hypothesis, Ehlers, Margraf, Roth, Taylor, and Birbaumer (1988) gave panic patients and normal controls false feedback of a sudden increase in their heart rate. Patients who believed the false feedback showed significantly more anxiety and physiological arousal than controls. The two groups did not differ in their accuracy of heart rate perception. These results strongly support the cognitive model by demonstrating that panic patients differ from normals in reacting fearfully to perceived bodily cues. It is the perception of danger rather than the actual physiological cues themselves that causes them to respond with anxiety.

The Ehlers et al. (1988) study is typical of the line of research in which investigators have experimentally provoked anxiety or panic in panic patients in a structured laboratory setting. An important study by Taylor et al. (1986) assessed panic patients' reactions under naturalistic conditions. These researchers monitored the heart rate of panic patients and normal controls round-the-clock for 6 days. Importantly, they were able to separate increased heart rate associated with panic from simple physical activity and to correlate this physiological index of panic with patients' self-reports.

Several significant findings emerged from this informative study. The average increase in heart rate during panic was 38.6 beats per minute; the average duration was 20 minutes. Panics occurred most frequently in the early morning hours. Of particular relevance for the present purpose, however, is the finding that approximately 40% of the panic attacks reported by patients were not associated with any significant change in heart rate. In contrast, numerous instances of heart rate changes that met Taylor et al.'s (1986) criteria for panic were not reported as panic by the patients. The conclusion is inescapable that cardiovascular arousal per se cannot cause panic attacks; the patient's perception or cognitive appraisal of real or imagined bodily changes seems to be a critical factor in panic. (It could be argued that other bodily changes that were not measured could have been the trigger for panic, but the onus is on proponents of such a view to demonstrate it.) These results are consistent with the cognitive model of panic.

Returning to the experimental provocation of panic in the laboratory, Holt and Andrews (1989) compared the reactions of panic patients with those of agoraphobics, social phobics, GAD patients, and controls on three measures of panic: somatic symptoms, subjective anxiety and fear of impending doom, and actual experience of a panic attack. The panic patients did not differ from normal controls on somatic or subjective anxiety in response to provocations such as hyperventilation. Only fears of impending doom differentiated among the groups. Holt and Andrews (1989) conclude that "cognitions appeared to be the only discriminator between panic or nonpanic patients and in this way, the present data best supports a psychophysiological model of panic, a model in which panic is said to result from catastrophic misinterpretation of somatic symptoms of anxiety" (p. 259).

TREATMENT OF ANXIETY DISORDERS

Rachman and Levitt (1988) reanalyzed their data on the experimental induction of panic in claustrophobic subjects to examine the relationship between fear reduction and habituation. Consistent with the thrust of Holt and Andrews's (1989) findings, subjects' cognitions (e.g., "I am going to pass out") was a powerful discriminator between those who did or did not show habituation of fear. The authors note that these results are consistent with Clark's (1988b) cognitive model. In a replication of their research on claustrophobic panic in panic patients, Rachman, Lopatka, and Levitt (1988) once again found that specific cognitions were a hallmark of panic patients' reactions to the provocation of panic. Rachman et al. (1988) did find, however, that unlike their claustrophobic subjects, 25% of their panic patients reported "noncognitive" panics. The import of this finding remains to be followed up. Additional support for the cognitive model of panic comes from Kenardy, Evans, and Oei (1988), who report that negative cognitions preceded panic attacks and conclude that "a panic attack appears to require specific catastrophic cognitions to precipitate panic onset" (p. 482).

Wolpe and Rowan (1988) have criticized the cognitive model and proposed that panic disorder is a product of classical conditioning. As they see it, "the initial panic is an unconditioned response to a bizarre stimulus complex produced by excessive hyperventilation, and panic disorder is the result of contiguous stimuli, especially endogenous stimuli, being conditioned to the elicited anxiety" (p. 441). One of the problems with this model is the striking desynchrony between physiological or endogenous stimuli and experience of panic as shown by Taylor et al. (1986) and others. There is ample evidence to reject a view of panic or anxiety that rests primarily on the automatic coupling of contiguous stimuli without taking into account the cognitive context. In dismissing the cognitive model, Wolpe and Rowan (1988) report uncontrolled data from ten panic patients to argue that catastrophic cognitions follow rather than precede panic attacks. They buttress their view by pointing to Rachman et al.'s (1988) finding that a significant minority of panic patients report noncognitive panics. This observation warrants further experimental analysis.

Wolpe and Rowan (1988) also contend that the failure of simple reassurance or persuasive communication to eliminate panics means that they cannot be cognitively based. This reasoning assumes a simplistic and an unnecessarily limited view of cognition and, as such, does not bear on the merits of the cognitive model. Wolpe and Rowan do not do justice to the more complex and accurate conception of cognition, which forms the basis for cognitive-behavior therapy (e.g.,

Bandura, 1969, 1986; Lazarus & Folkman, 1984). It has long been a cardinal tenet of social learning theory that verbal persuasion is, at best, a weak means of changing cognition or behavior, both of which are altered most effectively modified using performance-based (behavioral) methods.

Seligman (1988) provides a clear and crisp analysis of the strengths and weaknesses of the competing cognitive and Pavlovian conditioning theories of panic. He identifies three main predictions from Clark's (1988b) cognitive model—that panic patients will interpret bodily sensations more negatively than other anxiety disorder patients; that drugs produce panic by producing bodily sensations of panic; and that treatments that change interpretations of bodily sensations will do better than treatments that do not—and points out that a conditioning model would make much the same predictions.

Calling for research to "sharpen the differences, not dull them," Seligman (1988) lays out some differential predictions between the two models. Of particular importance are the following predictions from the cognitive model:

> 1. Cognitive misinterpretation, which is not a mere epiphenomenon of Pavlovian conditioning, is necessary for panic. Panics will occur only when the sensations are perceived and misinterpreted, not on trials in which they are perceived but not catastrophized about. 2. Mere exposure to extinction contingencies will not produce decrements in panic, except insofar as exposure changes misinterpretation for the better. (p. 325)

The Pavlovian model predictions would be the converse of these.

Seligman (1988) also raises some important questions about the ability of the cognitive model to distinguish between rational and irrational, conscious or unconscious processes, or what in a conditioning framework might be called automatic and controlled processes. In this connection, it might be noted that this distinction is drawing the attention of cognitive–behavioral researchers (e.g., Brewin, 1988; D. A. Clark, 1989). Seligman's (1988) lucid analysis of some of the core theoretical issues regarding panic provides a challenging framework for researchers in this important area.

TREATMENT

Excellent analyses of the effects of cognitive–behavioral and pharmacological therapies are to be found in Barlow (1988), Marks and O'Sullivan (1988), Rachman and Maser (1988), and Taylor and Arnow (1988). Suffice it here to comment selectively on a few developments of both theoretical and practical significance.

The results of the Albany study (Barlow, 1988) are of particular note. The core of the cognitive–behavioral treatment that was evaluated in this study consisted of systematic exposure to feared internal sensations. Three experimental treatment groups were formed by adding either progressive relaxation training or cognitive restructuring adapted from Beck (1976), or a combination of the two, to this exposure component. Compared with a waiting list control group, preliminary results showed that the combined treatment was significantly more effective.

The major finding of this study thus far is that this strictly psychological treatment reduced panic attacks virtually to zero. Here we have a striking, but now familiar, refutation of the groundless contentions that pharmacotherapy is necessary to reduce panic attacks and that cognitive–behavioral treatment affects only avoidance behavior. These highly promising results appear to be no fluke. Other investigators are reporting that similar cognitive–behavioral treatments are effective in eliminating panic attacks (e.g., Beck, 1988). The combined treatment tended to produce more improvement than exposure plus cognitive restructuring only or exposure plus progressive relaxation.

The Albany study is noteworthy in another sense. Barlow and Cerny (1988) have published a therapy manual that is based on their systematic development and evaluation of an effective cognitive-behavioral treatment program. The book is a welcome resource to clinicians who treat panic disorder. In a more general sense, the availability of a manual describing a replicable and effective treatment program represents a breakthrough in the psychological therapies. Manuals such as these bridge the vexing gap between research and clinical practice.

The treatment methods of Barlow and Cerny (1988), Beck (1988), and Clark (1988b) all combine some form of exposure to internal, physiological cues and varying degrees of systematic cognitive restructuring. Ost (1988) reports impressive success using only relaxation training. Panic disorder patients received 14 individual sessions of either progressive relaxation or what Ost (1988) calls applied relaxation in which patients learn more actively to cope with specific anxiety-inducing situations. Applied relaxation was superior to progressive relaxation at posttreatment and especially at follow-up (a mean of 19 months). The striking result of this study is not the comparative outcome difference, however. Rather, it is the clinical significance of the outcome; remarkably, all patients treated with applied relaxation were panic-free at both posttreatment and follow-up. Although the study had its methodological limitations, as Ost (1988) is careful to note, they do not undermine these results.

On a practical note, Ost (1989) describes a maintenance program for use in the treatment of all anxiety disorders. His recommendation follows from a review of long-term follow-ups phobic patients treated with behavior therapy. Not only is there a significant relapse rate, but many other improved patients are left with residual anxiety problems. According to Ost (1989), a single session of his maintenance program during therapy and 1.5 to 2 hours of telephone contract over the 6 months following end of treatment combine to produce fewer relapses and even continued improvement in panic and agoraphobic patients. The maintenance program reduces to preparing patients to differentiate between a setback and a relapse and to reinstitute specific coping skills in high-risk situations. For example, one of the instructions given the patient (Ost, 1989) is, "Tell yourself that this is what the therapist said would occur sooner or later, and it's not a catastrophe. It is not a relapse, but a temporary failure to manage a situation that you have managed before" (p. 126). Readers familiar with the substance abuse disorders will recognize this maintenance program as the application of the theoretical framework and specific strategies of Marlatt's (1985) relapse prevention model. In Volume 9 of this series (Wilson, 1984; and before that [Wilson, 1982b]), I pointed out that the well-known Mathews, Gelder, and Johnston (1981) program for treating agoraphobics contained many of the features of Marlatt's relapse prevention model even though these were not emphasized by Mathews et al. (1981). The absence of any reference to Marlatt's (1985) model in Ost's (1989) article is surprising, perhaps indicating an unfortunate lack of communication between workers across different disorders.

CHAPTER

4

COGNITIVE PROCESSES AND PROCEDURES IN BEHAVIOR THERAPY

PHILIP C. KENDALL

Marking time by noting events and activities can help to provide a basis for the observation of trends. When examining cognitive and cognitive-behavioral treatment approaches there are several events that serve to document its current position. For example, consider the conferences that have taken place over the last decade. For each of 5 years, a conference on the clinical applications of cognitive-behavior therapy was held across the United States (coordinated by G. Amundson). Currently, the Institute for Advancement of Human Behavior is sponsoring conferences on advances in the cognitive therapies, and an average of two per year have already taken place. Practitioners and reseachers continue to display strong interest in learning the basic and advanced applications of cognitive and cognitive-behavioral approaches to therapy, and these data provide a basis for the claim that cognitive-behavioral treatments are alive, growing, and healthy. I hasten to add that these treatments are themselves in the process of learning and making the modifications that data and practice dictate.

On the international scene there is again strong evidence of growing academic and practitioner interest in cognitive processes and procedures. The World Congress of Cognitive Therapy, which met at Oxford University in June 1989 (organized by Clark and Salkovskis), had a larger than expected turnout. The earlier congresses, held a few years prior, had fewer than half the attendees who participated at Oxford. True, one must factor in the location of the conference when making interpretations of attendance records (some attendees were no doubt drawn by the academic and other history of the city of Oxford), and less attendance would have resulted had the meeting been held elsewhere, but prior conferences were also in desirable locations. A reasonable hypothesis, therefore, and one that is consistent with the data, is that there continues to be increasing interest in the role of cognitive processes and procedures within psychological therapy on an international level.

DEPRESSION: COGNITIVE THEORY AND THERAPY

Beck's cognitive therapy of depression (see Beck, Rush, Shaw, & Emery, 1979) was a central theme of the recent World Congress on Cognitive Therapy (Oxford, England, June 1989). Research reports of treatment outcome, summary reviews of related theories, empirical studies of cognitive hypotheses, and related convention activities were scattered throughout the four and one-half day event. Beck, in his keynote address to this convention, made several important points and provided contemporary position statements and conclusions regarding his cognitive theory and therapy of depression.

"Cognition does not cause depression." This sentence was the second transparency of Beck's keynote address: It followed his first transparency, which inquired as to the cause of depression. Surprised? Beck did not argue for the model of cognitive primacy, that illogical thinking causes depression. He did, however, argue for and present data to support the notion that in the state of depression individuals show cognitive functions that are biased. Once a person is depressed, a primary aspect of the maintenance of the depression is a function of cognitive processing. For instance, processing involves perception, interpretation, and memory. Some distortion in depression exists in each of these areas of information processing. Cognitive bias in depression, therefore, has strong implications for assessing risk, as well as for understanding relapse and recurrence. Before reviewing some recent work on the effects of cognitive therapy, we first consider the current efforts to examine cognitive vulnerability to depression.

Vulnerability

In a series of papers presented at the World Congress, cognitive vulnerability to depression was given detailed and careful consideration.

These efforts represent an illustration of the present interest in testing theories of cognitive vulnerability to depression. For example, the theme appears in several places in Alloy's (1988) edited volume entitled *Cognitive Processes in Depression*. In Beck's address to the World Congress (Beck, 1989), he stated that cognition is a risk factor (vulnerability) and one of several causes of depression. According to some theories, a person who is vulnerable to depression is one who holds beliefs that are rigid, perfectionistic, and easily engender disappointment and failure. Kuiper and Olinger (1986) propose that excessively rigid and inappropriate rules for guiding one's life constitute a cognitive predisposition or vulnerability to depression (see also Kuiper, Olinger, & MacDonald, 1988). The person carries a bias that facilitates the processing of information in a manner that is consistent with depressogenic negative traits about themselves. As Alloy (1988) concluded, however, the accumulated research to date does not entirely support such a description of cognitive vulnerability. What seems to hold promise (see Hammen, 1985) is the study of the interaction of cognitive predispositions and actual stressful life-events. For instance, individuals who carry dysfunctional attitudes have been found to provide higher estimates of the stress associated with actual and potential life events (Olinger, Kuiper, & Shaw, 1987). I would suggest the need to separate initial depression from a relapse of depression because these two experiences may be different, especially when making prospective predictions.

One effort to improve predictions of depression from cognitive vulnerability factors was reported by Segal and Shaw (1989). In their work, dividing subjects based on their scores on the Dysfunctional Attitudes Scale (DAS) into those with personal concerns versus those with more social concerns proved useful. When the nature of the stress was congruent with the type of dysfunctional attitudes held by the person, then one could more accurately predict relapse. It should be kept in mind that these subjects were depressed clients and the prediction of subsequent depression for these subjects may be different from the prediction of depression for subjects who have yet to experience a first episode.

Teasdale (1989) offered an interesting commentary regarding cognitive vulnerability to depression. In his model, the prediction of depression and the prediction of relapse of depression would not necessarily be the same. Within the already depressed groups, cognitive vulnerability seems to exist; yet, Teasdale was less confident about predictions for those persons who have never experienced a depressive episode. Teasdale (1989) also cautioned that, in vulnerability research, the depressed state influences how subjects think and respond to questionnaires. Being depressed could increase scores on the DAS, for example, just as being in a nondepressed state could reduce DAS scores. Teasdale referred to data by Miranda and Parsons (1988; cited in Teasdale, 1989) that suggested that when a mildly depressed mood comes along, formerly depressed patients show increased DAS scores, whereas never-depressed subjects did not show elevated DAS when in a mildly depressed state.

Splitting subjects into high and low cognitive dysfunction subgroups was reported by Miller, Norman, and Keitner (1989) to untangle the results of a treatment outcome study. High cognitive dysfunction subjects did not respond to medications but did well in response to cognitive-behavior therapy. Low cognitive dysfunction clients did not show a differential response to the two treatments. The high cognitive dysfunction subgroup was younger at their first episode and had a shorter duration of current depressive episode. Also, drug-treated cases had no therapist contact. These factors could moderate the reported effects. Nevertheless, there do seem to be some meaningful differences between subjects whose degree of cognitive dysfunction varies.

Among the consistencies emerging from research on the issue of cognitive vulnerability is the need to consider current emotional state when assessing predispositions and the role of personal assessments of potentially stressful life events. The data to date suggest that cognitive vulnerability is important as a predictor of subsequent depression among those who have already experienced an episode of depression. Among the "never depressed," the evidence is, as yet, not as clear. It is interesting to speculate about the factors that may emerge as predictive of depression among never-depressed individuals. Assessments of cognitive processing styles among key individuals in the person's life/family might prove useful. Among children and adolescents, certainly, the attributional patterns displayed by parents can set the stage for an attributional predisposition. Assessing the attributional dominance in the social context of individuals who have never been depressed may uncover stylistic features that subsequently predispose the individual for an episode of depression. The effects of stress, especially stress as perceived by the individual, also deserves continued attention.

Treatment

Before addressing some of the recent work on the outcomes of cognitive therapy for depression, it is first worthwhile to note that a central strategy for the evaluation of treatment outcome is one that accumulates evidence across a series of studies, with the studies following a preferred sequence. For example, a systematic model for the evaluation of treatment effects would begin with more circumscribed studies, such as single-subject designs, and proceed to comparisons of treated cases to those randomly assigned to waiting lists. Following a demonstration of beneficial effects, one could pursue questions pertaining to the active ingredients within the treatment package. Later, specific components of the treatment can be varied to determine if there are differential effects. Later still, comparisons to other established treatments would follow to examine if the newly established treatment produces effects that are greater than the "best-available treatment" (O'Leary & Borkovec, 1978). It is pleasing to see the relatively systematic approach that has been followed in the evaluation of cognitive therapy for depression. Although we currently have access to a substantial body of evidence supporting the efficacy of the treatment, specific dismantling studies, variations in certain treatment components, and comparisons to alternate treatments (including medications) remain worthy of continued pursuit.

The dismantling approach, or components analysis, typically involves manipulations of identified features of the treatment, such as variations in the use of self-monitoring or pleasant activities scheduling. One facet of the dismantling approach that is unfortunately given too little attention is the question of the effects of variations in the quality of the treatment (see Kendall & Hollon, 1983). Are variations in outcome associated with variations in the adequacy of the implementation (operationalization) of the treatment? One positive aspect of the literature on the cognitive–behavioral treatment of depression is the fairly regular use of a treatment manual to guide clinical intervention. Indeed, in Dobson's (1989) review of the outcomes of cognitive/cognitive–behavioral treatments of depression, every study used a treatment manual. Dobson and Shaw (1988) provide a review of the issues related to the use of treatment manuals in cognitive/cognitive-behavior therapy for depression.

As Dobson and Shaw (1988) described, one of the assumptions behind the manualization of treatment is that therapy could be provided in a precise and replicable manner and open to investigation. Manuals do help to specify the treatment approach and are valuable in treatment outcome studies, but one must guard against rigid adherence to a manual. Dobson and Shaw (1988) noted the need for flexibility in the application of cognitive therapy. Flexible application of a treatment manual is the fiat that I wish to underscore. It is worth noting also that, in a discussion of a series of papers that addressed the maintenance and generalization of behavior change (i.e., Edelstein, 1989; Jacobson, 1989a; Stokes & Osnes, 1989), Kendall (1989b) noted the consistent mention of the need for more flexible (less rigid) application of treatments.

Dobson and Shaw (1988) identified several positive and several less than positive effects of the adherence to manualized treatments. The positive effects are noted first. Clearly, treatment manuals contribute to the internal validity of a study by helping to ensure that a specified set of procedures exist and can be replicated. This positive effect can be seen in two ways: treatment integrity and treatment differentiability. Treatment integrity refers to the extent to which the treatment was applied as stated in the manual. Proper training, supervision, and ongoing monitoring of treatment are necessary for adequate assurance of treatment integrity. Also, methodologically, random checks of audio and/or audiovisual tapes can be conducted to assess and check on treatment integrity. Treatment differentiability refers to the extent to which the treatment can be differentiated from other treatments. In a study reported by DeRubeis, Hollon, Evans, and Bemis (1982), cognitive therapy could be differentiated from interpersonal therapy. In a more recent study of differentiations of therapies, Stiles, Shapiro, and Firth-Cozens (1988) found that, in terms of therapists' verbal response modes, dynamic and cognitive-behavior therapies could be differentiated. Similarly, Wills, Faitler, and Snyder (1987) were able to distinguish behavioral marital therapy and insight-oriented marital therapy, with each administered in a distinct and uncontaminated fashion (see also Collins & Thompson, 1988; Snyder, Wills, & Faitler, 1988). Other positive effects of the manualization of treatment, such as the increased ability to replicate research methods and the facilitation of therapist training were discussed by Dobson and Shaw (1988).

Among the potential disadvantages of treatment manuals identified by Dobson and Shaw (1988) were as follows: (1) the potential suppression of other factors, such as therapist characteristics or relationship features, as important in accounting for outcomes; (2) a diminished ability to study the therapeutic process; (3) overresearching dated approaches (once a manual appears, it may be used even after it has been revised and updated); and (4) the promotion of "schoolism" in the therapy enterprise. Also, the authors noted that manualization focuses on treatment fidelity rather than on the competence of the therapist in applying the treatment. As noted above and argued elsewhere (Kendall & Hollon, 1983), studies of treatment outcome would benefit from a greater focus on the quality of the therapy and the relationship of quality to the variations in observed outcomes. The Cognitive Therapy Scale (see Dobson & Shaw, 1988) is a measure to assess the degree of therapist competence in providing cognitive therapy for depression. Of all the variables that have been identified and studied as potential contributors to treatment outcome, it is shocking to realize the extremely small amount of effort addressing the extremely important issue of the quality of the therapist's provision of treatment.

Rehm's manualized treatment for depression focuses on self-control and has been described as having both cognitive and behavioral features. In somewhat of a dismantling type study, Rehm, Kaslow, and Rabin (1987) treated diagnosed depressed women in groups with the focus of the groups being either cognitive (e.g., modification of self-statements), behavioral (e.g., increasing overt behavior), or a combination of the two. Outcome measures indicated that all treatments were effective, with improvements being comparable on the cognitive and behavioral measures, independent of the focus of the treatment. Stated differently, despite the differences in the targets of therapy, there were no significant differences across therapies on measures of the targets. These findings are consistent with others (e.g., Zeiss, Lewinsohn, & Munoz, 1979) in which the effects of treatments that are focused on one or the other factor (cognitive and behavioral) nevertheless produce gains on both features. As the authors noted, and as is consistent with arguments regarding common principles across versions of psychotherapy, the treatments provided structure, explicit feedback, and evidence of progress for the patients, and these features may be among the active ingredients in cognitive therapy. Additional research, in which these features are manipulated, will help to better understand the factors accounting for positive gains.

A recent report by Beutler and colleagues (1987) provided additional information regarding the effects of cognitive therapy and medications for the treatment of depression. In this particular study, the medication was alprazolam, the treatment was provided in groups, and the subjects were a geriatric sample diagnosed major unipolar depression. Four conditions were compared: alprazolam support, placebo support, cognitive therapy plus placebo support, and cognitive therapy plus alprazolam support. In terms of subjective state and sleep efficiency, the group cognitive therapy was reported superior to nongroup therapy. Interestingly, Beutler et al. (1987) reported no difference between alprazolam and placebo, regardless of the presence of the other intervention. The effects were maintained at follow-up and the subjects in the group cognitive therapy showed lower attrition rates and lower dissatisfaction ratings than subjects in medication-only conditions. Although not all dependent measures showed similar patterns (e.g., Hamilton ratings may have been influenced by the age of the sample), the effects are consistent with the general conclusion that psychological and pharmacological interventions can have therapeutic effects on the depressed elderly. However, consistent with already mentioned caveats, it is not clear from this study that the cognitive therapy is necessarily better than other forms of therapy as the provision of group support could be a portion of the active ingredient in the production of the desired gains. Further investigation, where degree of group support is varied, for instance, would help to clarify this matter.

Other comparative outcomes studies with older adults have examined the merits of bibliotherapy, the use of literary work to help remediate emotional problems. For example, a self-help approach was reported to be helpful in reducing mild depression in geriatric subjects (Scogin, Hamblin, & Beutler, 1987). In a more recent study (Scogin, Jamison, & Gochneaur, 1989), cognitive bibliotherapy and behavioral bibliotherapy were compared with a delayed treatment control for the remediation of mild to moderate depression in older adults. The books were *Control Your Depression* (Lewinsohn, Munoz, Youngren, & Zeiss, 1986) for the behavioral intervention and *Feeling Good* (Burns, 1980) for the cognitive bibliotherapy. Subjects were given 4 weeks to read the assigned book and weekly phone contacts were used to monitor progress. The results of this study indicated that a self-paced bibliotherapy produced gains as assessed by self-rating and observations. Measures of negative automatic thinking (Automatic Thoughts Questionnaire) and pleasant events (Older Adults Pleasant Events Schedule), potentially sensitive to one but not the other treatment, did not result in differential change. As noted earlier, treatment outcome does not appear to be specific to the type of treatment provided. Both cognitive and behavioral treatments produced gains on cognitive and behavioral assessments. Although these results do not suggest that all forms of depression can be effectively treated by means of bibliotherapy, they do support the usefulness of self-paced readings to lift dysphoria and suggest that bibliotherapeutic efforts may be worthwhile as additions to other more traditional forms of clinical therapy.

Unlike the more typical comparisons of cognitive, behavioral, and waiting list treatments, Thompson, Gallagher, and Breckenridge (1987) added a fourth condition to their comparative outcome study of the treatment of elderly depressed clients. A brief psychodynamic treatment was their added intervention. Nonpsychotic adults who were older than 60 years, met Research Diagnostic Criteria, and had Beck Depression Inventory (BDI) scales over 17 and Hamilton ratings of 14 (other criteria also) were randomly assigned to treatment conditions. Sixteen to 20 individual sessions were provided by qualified therapists, with training in the area of the specialized form of treatment. The authors reported that 70% of the treated clients showed significant improvement at posttreatment. Thompson et al. (1987) also reported that the patients who received any of the three active therapies improved beyond the waiting list delayed treatment condition. As before, but in this case adding a brief psychodynamic condition, there appears to be nonspecific improvement effects.

In addition to the application of cognitive/cognitive–behavioral treatments to geriatric clients, adolescent cases have been used to test the applicability of the treatments across the lifespan. For example, Reynolds and Coats (1986) compared a relaxation treatment to a cognitive-behavioral program (ten sessions of small group treatment emphasizing self-control). Subjects were selected using a multiple-gating procedure with two assessments of depression over time. Several criteria were employed to select depressed cases, such as a BDI score over 12. Whereas the mean of the treated cases was about 18, scores as low as 12 might best be described as dysphoric rather than depressed. Indeed, the adolescent subjects in the study were not selected on the basis of a diagnostic interview. The results of this investigation indicated significant improvement produced by both treatments over a waiting list control. Self-reports and clinical ratings indicated improvements. Academic self-concept was also positively affected by the interventions, and the relaxation condition had a positive effect on client anxiety. Overall, consistent with many other reports reviewed at various times in this series, the effects of cognitive and behavioral treatments are not specific to the target focus of the intervention. These findings have been reported for adolescents, young adults, adults, and a geriatric sample.

RATIONAL-EMOTIVE THERAPY

In the four preceding reviews rational–emotive therapy (RET) has received its fair share of attention. In Volume 8, RET discussions included consideration of its relationship to cognitive-behavior therapy, similarities and differences between RET and other cognitive-behavioral approaches, and a look at some of the, albeit rare, empirical research examining RET. Volume 9 considered the various philosophical discourses that appeared and the challenges to the assumptions on which RET is based, whereas Volume 10 considered issues of assessment and a review of some analogue studies of treatment effectiveness. RET was included but was not a major heading or a major source of discussion in Volume 11.

The present review of RET will focus on (1) several chapters in a recent critical appraisal of the theory and therapy of Albert Ellis, entitled *Inside Rational-Emotive Therapy* (Bernard & DiGiuseppe, 1989), (2) an address by Ellis (1989a) to the World Congress on Cognitive Therapy, and (3) some published reports regarding the theory and practice of RET. It continues to be unfortunate that scientifically rigorous evaluations of the effects of RET are few and far between. As noted in Volume 9 (Kendall, 1984), RET, although a seminal and central theoretical and applied system, generates more discussion than research evaluation (see also Rorer, 1989). Indeed, Ellis himself identifies and accepts that research evaluation has not been the strength of RET (Ellis, 1989a).

Ellis's address focused largely on RET's philosophical features—that it is constructivist, not entirely rationalistic. However, the initial portion of Ellis's address (warmly received by the audience) identified several of the early influences on the development of his theory/therapy. He mentioned his psychoanalytic training and his view of its inefficiencies. He described his own young adult efforts to meet women and how he gave himself homework assignments to sit beside single women and talk to them—and he found out that although not all responded as he wished, it wasn't the end of the world. For Ellis the experience of testing his irrational fears helped dramatically to overcome them. What seems to have facilitated his own entrance into adulthood (manhood) also serves as a fundamental component of this theory of behavior change.

Inside RET, Bernard and DiGiuseppe's (1989) contemporary examination of RET begins with a statement of its philosophical foundations (Woolfolk & Sass, 1989) and a related critique (Ziegler, 1989). Ziegler tackles RET as a scientific theory of personality and describes it as low on verifiability and comprehensiveness but gave it high marks on heuristic value, internal consistency, parsimony, and functional significance (i.e., useful in helping people). Ziegler's evaluation and description of RET is consistent with my view of its scientific status—namely, it lacks efforts at verification but remains heuristically potent and functionally significant.

Mahoney, Lyddon, and Alford (1989) provide an interesting evaluation of the adequacy of RET as a theory of psychotherapy. These authors begin by detailing what they identify as the fundamental assertions of RET regarding human change processes: (1) rational

COGNITIVE PROCESSES AND PROCEDURES

supremacy and explicit awareness, (2) argumentation and rationalist interventionism, and (3) "negative" emotions as problems. The assumption of rational supremacy concerns the assertion that rational thought should govern behavioral and emotional processes. Ellis emphasizes the need to make people aware of their irrational thoughts and beliefs, but, as Mahoney et al. (1989) point out, there are limits to rationality. For instance, it may be the case that interpersonal systems are so complex and evanescent that a true rational understanding is not available. Also, humans may be governed by other determinants in addition to rational thought.

As stated in Mahoney et al. (1989), argumentation and rationalist interventionism are hallmarks of RET. The therapist is relied upon to recognize the irrational thinking of the client and actively argue and persuade the client to become a less irrational and more rational being. The emphasis in RET seems to be on prescribing rational particulars (Mahoney et al., 1989): getting clients to use specific self-statements, make thoughts explicit, and accept specific beliefs. As Mahoney et al. (1989) suggest, however, it may be fruitful for a therapist to set the stage for the client to generate for himself or herself instances of understanding of more abstract general principles. I am intrigued by this commentary because it appears remarkably consistent with some data about the effectiveness of other versions of cognitive-behavior therapy. When the therapist serves as a consultant who collaborates with the client to help test experiences in the client's world, the client can come to discover for himself or herself the unwanted guiding rules that interfere with their adjustment. For example, training in conceptual skills was found to be superior to specific skill training, general self-instructions were favored over specific ones, and the collaborative empiricism of cognitive therapy for depression provides for the merits of therapist-guided client discovery. The appeal of a directed discovery approach, as opposed to an argumentative one, is that the level of the client's involvement is likely to be greater with a consultative therapist and involvement is considered a potent predictor of improvement (e.g., Braswell, Kendall, Braith, Carey, & Vye, 1985).

In RET, negative emotional reactions are viewed as problems; such distress is dysfunctional and in need of rational reevaluation. Authors such as Mahoney (1988) have begun to describe adaptive roles for negative emotions. For instance, when an individual's adjustment is being challenged, as cued by the presence of negative arousal, it is a reminder for the use of coping skills. Negative emotions are important in the management of emotional equilibrium. Elsewhere, I have suggested that heightened emotional states, be they positive or negative, are important for the eventual generalization of newly acquired coping skills (Kendall, 1991). For example, a couple in marriage counseling is taught to use a *quid pro quo* arrangement for making equitable decisions. The wife may assert a need for an evening free of responsibilities when she can pursue exercise, whereas the husband may want free time on Sunday afternoon for the pursuit of athletic activity. The couple negotiates rationally in the safe environment of the therapist's office and a fair tit for tat deal is worked out. However, when the spouse is found to be having an affair, rationality and fair discussion are dispensed with as emotional distress takes over. Despite the fact that the couple learned a method of fair discourse and equitable interaction, the emotional challenge of the moment overpowers rational thought. I would not expect the person, at first learning of the fact, to remain fully rational and calm and simply discuss the new situation for a fair arrangement. Intense emotional states reduce the likelihood that cognitive processing and rational planning will be in control. Although it is true that no one would want extreme negative emotional conditions, they do occur and it is therapeutic for clients to learn to adapt their skills to conditions that are emotionally challenging. It is not that negative emotions should be eliminated but that they are to serve as cues for the adaptive use of skills that would otherwise be overtaken by emotional distress.

Ellis (1989b) finds fault with Mahoney et al.'s view that RET is more "rationalist" as opposed to "constructivist." A constructivist position is one that views the person as an active generator of his or her knowing process, sees the human as participatory in human design (humans can deliberately design, choose, and plan parts of their lives), and acknowledges conscious decision making. Ellis's World Congress address (1989a) outlined these and other constructivist premises and illustrated how RET holds constructivist views. RET does involve irrationality, but it is not solely a rationalistic philosophy.

R. Lazarus (1989) discusses the merits and demerits of RET as a theory of emotion. As he noted, it would be stretching things to say that Ellis has presented a fully elaborated theory of emotion. However, R. Lazarus is quick to add that "probably no one has." One criticism of RET offered by R. Lazarus concerns the static nature of the role of beliefs. For Ellis, an individual's irrational beliefs are held, largely fixed, and shape emotional disturbance. However, beliefs may be changing as a result of ongoing activities, input from other persons, or planned intervention. R. Lazarus, like Mahoney et al. (1989), also comments that negative emotions are not per se pathological. R. Lazarus's example concerns depression: this mood state may be acceptable following death of loved ones and is only pathological when its duration is excessive or when its consequences are destructive. Depression following a genuine life stress may only be dysfunctional if the person cannot over time come to accept the new reality. Lazarus's crucial criticism of RET is that it places too harsh an emphasis on the maladaptive nature of negative emotions.

To what degree does the therapeutic relationship contribute to outcome in RET? Garfield (1989) addresses this question, using Ellis himself as the prototype. It is interesting to note that Ellis's style, which is often seen as confrontive, actually includes several relationship building features. For example, Ellis routinely compliments clients when they look good, has an impressive memory for past events in the client's lives, and uses down to earth language, all of which communicate to the patient that Ellis, the therapist, is genuinely interested in them and their lives. Such messages build a strong relationship and, therefore, relationship factors may be contributing to treatment outcome. When the actual number of well-controlled clinical trials is as limited as it is for RET, there is added difficulty in seeking answers to general as well as more fine-tuned questions. As Haaga and Davison (1989) concluded from their comprehensive review of the outcome studies, there are still several important questions that remain unanswered. For example, is there a disorder for which RET is the treatment of choice? What factors predict responsiveness to RET? What proportion of patients achieve clinically significant gains (see also discussion in Chapter 2).

I have elsewhere noted that it seems paradoxical that while RET argues forcefully that absolutistic thinking is maladaptive and disturbing, Ellis and some proponents of RET adhere to its system in absolute terms (absolutistically). For someone who is so much against the "shoulds," it is surprising to see his use of language that is at least as strong and imperative. A. Lazarus (1989a), in a section he entitled "A Note of Personal Irritation," pointed directly to the language of RET (Ellis) and its categorical imperatives. As A. Lazarus noted, Ellis seems to work to avoid the use of the words should, ought, and must. In their place Ellis uses "had better." A. Lazarus's point, one with which I agree, is that "had better" is just as absolutistic, if not more, than should or ought. Indeed, although it apparently was used to convey a preference more than an imperative, it seems to convey more absolutistic demands than the alternative terms. Teaching clients to see their wishes/goals as preferences rather than absolutistic imperatives can prove therapeutically beneficial. However, the language that is used to communicate this concept, should (had better?) also avoid absolutism.

In what I view as a clear strength of *Inside Rational-Emotive Therapy* (Bernard & DiGiuseppe, 1989), the final chapter is a reply to the critics by Ellis himself (Ellis, 1989b). It would be a disservice to try to condense Ellis's lengthy replies and selected quotes in this review. Instead, I refer the reader to the chapter for the specifics. I do wish to note here that Ellis's reply communicates a relatively balanced set of reactions. Ellis himself seems to recognize and accept certain criticisms of his theory and therapy and avoids an overly defensive or self-righteous posture. It was refreshing to read his acknowledgment of the identified weaknesses in his position. Ellis nevertheless does identify statements by the other authors that he feels are inaccurate, dated, or misrepresentative. His commentaries are focused toward clarification of his current position and seem, in good faith, to take into account earlier comments and criticisms. I found it of interest to note that Ellis stated, "The chapters in this book have given me considerable food for thought and made me realize that I *had better* update and revise some of my fundamental aspects and theories of RET" (p. 231, italics added). Although I agree with A. Lazarus (1989a) that the tone of "had better" is somewhat harsh, it is of interest to see that Ellis chides himself in such language.

That Ellis attended to his critics is praiseworthy; that he provided a written update of his position is even more commendable. Accordingly, because of both the seminal nature of RET and Ellis's efforts to provide a 1989 update, I have chosen to reproduce Ellis's (1989b) eight *re*formulations (from pp. 232-233) exactly as he published them.[1]

1. People largely become (or make themselves) emotionally disturbed mainly through their rigid, inflexible, absolutistic, dogmatic philosophies (or irrational beliefs). They have many attributions, inferences, and other false or exaggerated cognitions that are involved with their disturbances; but most of these are derivatives of their absolutistic, unconditional thoughts and would exist more rarely than they do if the dogmas that impel and sustain them were eliminated.

2. What we call our "emotions" have a huge cognitive component (though are not identical with our thoughts). But our cognitions also have a strong emotional component; and cognitions, emotions, and behaviors are rarely, if ever, pure but are interactional, reciprocal, and transactional. They all importantly influence each other.

3. When people become significantly less disturbed they have usually, consciously or unconsciously, made a significant cognitive change, have given up some of their dogmatic musts, have become more flexible in their thinking

---

[1]Reprinted by permission of Academic Press.

about achieving their goals and values, and have begun to accept alternate solutions to their practical and emotional problems instead of rigidly sticking to the "solutions" that they previously held.

4. In terms of therapeutic methods, the most pervasive, far-reaching, and lasting one probably consists of people's making a profound philosophic change, especially their keeping their major preferences and values (their goal orientation to happiness) but surrendering their dogmatic irrational beliefs (notably, their imperatives) that get them into emotional trouble.

5. Probably the best way to help many people make a profound, healthy philosophic change is to show them, with persuasive and educational methods, the precise details of their musturbatory thinking and to teach them the scientific method of thinking skeptically, nonabsolutistically, and flexibly. If people can be helped to change these insistences to strong preferences, they will tend to make themselves significantly less emotionally disturbed.

6. Because musturbatory demands are partially created and importantly reinforced by certain kinds of actions and avoidances (e.g., fear of encountering others is reinforced by continual avoidance of encountering them), many kinds of performance anxiety require counter conditioning actions as well as disputational arguments to overcome performance and social anxiety. Thus, forcing oneself to behave more socially will often help one overcome one's irrational belief that one cannot effectively socialize and that social rejection is terrible.

7. Sometimes actions speak louder than words, especially in psychotherapy. So forcing ourselves to counterattack our fearful actions may be the best way to overcome our irrational fears; and *in vivo* desensitization of a phobia may be more effective than cognitive or imaginal desensitization. Thus, if we keep playing tennis in spite of our horror of failing at it, we may show ourselves that we can improve our game and that we do survive when we fail. By this kind of *in vivo* desensitization we can sometimes actually turn a horrible act into a pleasurable one.

8. Action, even when done in spite of our fears, often leads to skill training. If we are afraid to dance poorly, our terror of doing so will often keep us away from, practicing dancing. But if we force ourselves to engage in dancing, we will often improve at this activity, thereby lose our rational belief that we are likely to fail, and perhaps also undercut our irrational belief that it is horrible to fail and that we are worthless people if we fail.

What Do RET Therapists Think They Are Doing?

Warren and McLellarn (1987), in an article by the title above, reported on the results of an international survey of completers of the Fellow or Associate Fellow program of the Institute for Rational Emotive Therapy. Their questionnaire was mailed to 228 people and 144 were returned (63%). Among the questions that they sought to answer was "How similar to Albert Ellis are most RET therapists in philosophy and practice?" Do RET therapists have the personality characteristics predicted by Ellis? Do RET therapists use a wide variety of interventions or do they mainly use cognitive intervention? Are RET therapists seen by their clients as overly intellectual and emotionally cold? Are there personal hazards associated with practicing RET? What type of assessment procedures do RET therapists use?

The respondents to the survey were, not surprisingly, predominantly (64%) self-declared RET therapists. What is surprising is the fact that only 64% were self-defined RETers. Fully 23% self-defined as cognitive–behavioral (3% behavioral and 1% client centered). Although perhaps surprising, it is pleasing to see that many RET-trained therapists see themselves as cognitive–behavioral.

Respondents were presented with 34 specific in-session treatment techniques and a list of 16 homework assignments and asked to check the ones that they use in therapy and provide an estimate of the percentage of clients with whom the techniques were used. The most frequently used techniques were humor, presentations of RET theory, cognitive rehearsal, unconditional acceptance, strong forceful language, and evaluative and empirical disputation. From among the homework tasks, bibliotherapy, risk taking, relaxation practice, written ABCDE analyses, and shame-attacking exercises were most often prescribed. These results are to be expected given that the sample that was surveyed was a group of graduates of the RET school of thought. The majority of RET practitioners report that they do indeed practice RET. What may be less predictable was the strong behavioral flavor to the lists of most frequently used interventions. On practice, Ellis's empirical disputing, in all likelihood, closely resembles behavioral assignments. The label may be the only difference. Certainly, any use of homework assignments is a behavioral strategy and RET uses many homework tasks. My position has been (and remains) that RET is an intervention that incorporates a focus on changing cognition (i.e., irrational beliefs) and uses cognitive and behavioral procedures to effect change. Accordingly, RET is a form of cognitive–behavioral intervention (Kendall, 1982, 1984).

Two Outcome Studies

Although clearly too soon to predict a trend, the appearance of two outcome studies evaluating RET is a step in the right direction. Emmelkamp, Visser, and Hoekstra (1988) compared a version of RET to exposure *in vivo* in the treatment of obsessive-compulsive disorder, and Warren, McLellarn, and Ponzoha (1988) studied the outcome of variations of RET as a therapy for clients with low self-esteem and related emotional disturbances.

As Emmelkamp et al. (1988) noted, cognitive approaches to the treatment of depression and anxiety have received empirical endorsement, but the evidence regarding cognitive procedures with agoraphobic clients and obsessive-compulsive clients is limited. Furthermore, the particular version of cognitive therapy that is employed with agoraphobic or obsessive-compulsive cases may need modification to optimally address the nature of the target disorder, especially the cognitive aspects of anxiety disorder. Emmelkamp et al. (1988) selected RET as an approach to dispute the irrational beliefs of obsessive-compulsive patients and compared this version of cognitive therapy with an *in vivo* exposure program that already has demonstrated effectiveness. The subjects who received treatment met DSM-III diagnostic criteria for obsessive-compulsive disorder and were approximately 30 years of age on average. The average duration of their target complaint was 6.6 years with a range of 1 to 20 years.

Clients receiving the *in vivo* exposure helped draw up a hierarchical list of the stimuli that triggered avoidance. Items on the hierarchy were practiced *in vivo*. Clients self-imposed response prevention during the exposure trials. In the RET condition, clients were first taught to observe and record their self-talk, followed by the therapist's challenging of the irrational beliefs. Homework assignments were required and therapy included discussion of the assignments and any irrational beliefs linked to them. The results, as described by Emmelkamp et al. (1988), indicated that cognitive therapy had clinically beneficial effects on obsessive-compulsive patients and that these effects, using obsessive-compulsive targets as the dependent variable, were comparable with those produced by the already established *in vivo* exposure treatment. Both treatments also produced a reduction in social anxiety. On an assessment of depression, the cognitive therapy, but not the *in vivo* exposure, led to reductions in depressed mood. Although there are some cautions to be recognized regarding this study—namely, small number of clients, additional treatments sought during the follow-up interval, client-guided (as opposed to therapist-guided) exposure—the results nevertheless suggest that cognitive-behavior therapy, in the form of RET, can have desired effects on the difficult to treat obsessive-compulsive anxiety disorder.

Clients responding to a newspaper article and scoring low in self-esteem were used to compare the effects of what Ellis (1980) has referred to as "elegant RET" to general cognitive-behavior therapy. As readers of this review series will recall, Ellis (1980) has argued that RET and cognitive-behavior therapy are different, with his preferred version of RET being "elegant," and other cognitive–behavioral approaches being inelegant or less preferred (see Kendall, 1982). Relatedly, Ellis hypothesized that elegant, relative to inelegant, treatment would produce differential client gains. Warren et al. (1988) conducted the empirical evaluation of this prediction. The 36 subjects were randomly assigned to either RET, cognitive-behavior therapy, or a waiting list control. Therapy was provided in small groups, for 1½ hours on each of 8 weeks. On all measures (e.g., self-esteem, depression, anxiety, anger), both treatment groups were found to have shown significant improvements over the control group. On measures of self-esteem and self-efficacy, the cognitive-behavior therapy condition resulted in greater gains than those found for the RET clients. Both treatments evidenced maintenance of gains at 6-month follow-up. (Readers interested in the specifics of each of the comparison treatments in the Warren et al. report are referred to p. 30 of the journal article.) The independent variable had integrity, a position based in part on the fact that Ellis himself reviewed the therapy audiotapes. The Warren et al. report supported both cognitive treatments and did not support the idea that an elegant/inelegant variation would produce differential outcomes.

ANXIETY

This review of cognitive processes and procedures has for several years placed greatest emphasis on the cognitive processes and procedures involved in the nature and treatment of depression. Anxiety and its disorders have received separate consideration in other chapters of this series (e.g., Wilson, 1982b, 1985a). In light of the reemergence of anxiety and its disorders as a concept of central importance to cognitive and cognitive–behaviorally oriented researchers and practitioners, some attention will be given to anxiety in this chapter. The interested reader should, without doubt, also examine Chapter 3 (this volume), the Barlow (1988) and Beck and Emery (1985) books, the special issue of *Cognitive Therapy and Research* (Vol. 11, No. 4, 1987), and the special issue of *Behavior Modification* (Vol. 12, 1988), which addresses the nature and treatment of anxiety in children. Moreover, given the increased recognition being given to the fact that anxiety and depression overlap, portions of the present volume (Chapter 2) will examine the distinctive and overlapping features between anxiety and depression (see also Kendall & Watson, 1989).

What are the cognitive features hypothesized to be important in anxiety disorders? What are the data on the development of anxiety disorders, such as the data available from the study of anxiety in children? What do some of the current studies say about cognitive treatments of anxiety disorders? Consideration of these topics, albeit brief, will highlight some of the cognitive processes and procedures being given consideration in the treatment of anxiety. In the discussion that follows I will address material relevant to the three questions noted above.

Cognitive Features of Anxiety

Several aspects of anxiety that can legitimately be labeled cognitive have been hypothesized by various authors. To help clarify the role of the specific features, Ingram and Kendall (1987) and Kendall and Ingram (1987, 1989) proposed that "critical" and "common" features be differentiated. Critical features are those that are specific to a particular disorder, they not only differentiate adaptive from maladaptive functioning; they also differentiate one psychopathology from another. Common features do not differentiate specific disorders but do, more broadly, separate adaptive from maladaptive functioning. The critical versus common features distinction can be applied to the anxiety disorders (Ingram & Kendall, 1987). Use of the common and critical features distinction, along with separate cognitive factors (e.g., schemata, content), can help to unravel the cognitive influences in anxiety disorders.

At the schematic level, anxious individuals seem to be consistent in their misperceptions of environmental demands. Beck and Emery (1985) refer to the schema of anxious individuals as one that is predisposed to see danger, threat, or harm. In panic, for example, the perception of danger is due more to internal than external variables (Clark, 1986, 1988b). Kendall and Ingram (1987) suggest that there may be at least two anxiety-liked schemata. For example, in routine activities the anxious person has an active schema regarding self (danger or threat to the self). The second schema refers to evaluations by others, and is especially sensitive to information concerning how others are evaluating him or her. The "other-evaluative" schema is closely linked to the "threat-to-self" schema but may be functionally different and necessary to improve predictions of behavior in different situations.

At the level of automatic thinking, anxious persons are said to have a disproportionate emphasis on the future. "Automatic negative thinking" is certainly evident in depression (Beck, 1963), whereas it seems that "automatic questioning" is a concern for anxious individuals. The cognitive content of automatic questioning is illustrated here: "What will people think about me?" "Will I do well, or fail?" (Kendall & Ingram, 1987, 1989). Note that these cognitive contents are different from the depressive's self-talk ("No one likes me," "I am a failure"). Distorted self-talk may be common to several psychopathologies, but the specific type/nature of the self-talk (cognitive content) has features that are critical and may separate different disorders. Sarason (1980), for example, has stressed that the content of anxious thought includes task-irrelevant thinking. Depressed clients have task-irrelevant thoughts too, but the content of the task-irrelevant thinking is critical.

At the level of common features, anxiety is linked to heightened self-focused attention, automatic (rather than purposeful) information processing, and reduced cognitive capacity for effective task performance. Although these features are seen in anxiety, they are common to other psychological states of distress as well (see Ingram & Kendall, 1987). What may be extracted from this overview of critical and common cognitive factors in anxiety is the need for research that addresses the nature of cognitive influence for specific disorders. Our knowledge will benefit most, as will our treatment efforts, from data that help to isolate those critical features that demark an anxiety disorder. Due to the natural overlap of anxiety and depression and the related need not to procrustean force away any overlap, study of common features is also important.

Work with Anxious Children

It is easy to recognize the central role of anxiety and its disorders in the study of psychopathology and its treatment. Broad-based behavioral therapy has been most active in the empirical evaluations of anxiety treatments including systematic desensitization (Wolpe, 1973), anxiety management training (Suinn, 1974), stress inoculation (Meichenbaum, 1986), flooding, *in vivo* exposure (Wilson, Chapter 3, this volume; Foa, Rothbaum, & Kozak, 1989), cognitive therapy (Beck & Emery, 1985), relaxation training (Borkovec, 1982), and combinations of these procedures. Wachtel (1977) refers to anxiety as a common core across schools of psychotherapy, with the continuum from behavior therapy to psychoanalysis being concerned with anxiety disorders. What is particularly surprising given the prominence of anxiety within psychological treatment research is the lack of attention until the present (e.g., Kendall, Kane, Howard, & Siqueland, 1989), given to the anxiety disorders of childhood. Important research on the treatment of children's fears and phobias has been conducted and reported (see Morris & Kratochwill, 1983; Ollendick & Cerny, 1981), but these studies were done prior to both the DSM-III system and the field's current want for diagnoses of treated cases. As a result, we do not know if the youth in those earlier studies would or would not receive diagnoses by the present system.

The revised version of DSM-III provides diagnostic criteria for three anxiety disorders of childhood: overanxious disorder (OAD), avoidant disorder, and separation anxiety disorder. The diagnostic criteria overlap in some instances, but the diagnostic system defines the three in different terms. For example, separation anxiety disorder includes the presence for a period of at least 2 weeks, but the primary concern is reactivity to separation or detachment from the attachment adult. Avoidant disorder requires a 6-month duration and focuses on the child's shrinking from contact with others. Lastly, OAD refers to global anxiety, self-consciousness, and future and past concerns (presence of four of seven symptoms) for a period of 6 months.

The availability of specific diagnostic categories for the anxiety disorders of children offers the potential opportunity to uncover which types of treatments are best for which specific anxiety disorders. However, available information suggests that the task will not be that simple. First, OAD occurs at a much higher rate than the other two disorders; Costello et al. (1988) indicated that of 33 cases, 22 were OAD, 8 were avoidant, and 3 were separation anxious. Second, there are developmental factors that can influence the rates of the various diagnoses and potentially interfere with adequate treatment evaluation. Separation anxiety disorder, for instance, is more common among younger children than older youth. The frequency of occurrence/ identification of separation problems will therefore be influenced by the target age range of the children to be studied. Lastly, the issue of comorbidity emerges, with many anxiety-disordered youth receiving multiple diagnoses, including more than one anxiety problem, the presence of diagnosable depression, and occasionally the existence of oppositional problems and attention deficit disorder with hyperactivity.

Strauss, Lease, Last, and Francis (1988) reported data that supported the notion of developmental differences in the nature of anxiety disorders in children. The researchers clustered their subjects into two groups: the younger sample was 5 to 11 years of age and the older group was 12 to 19. Whereas the prevalence of OAD did not differ across these groups, the older children presented with a higher total number of overanxious symptoms and more frequently exhibited a concurrent major depression or simple phobia. Younger children more commonly had coexisting separation anxiety or attention deficit disorders.

The specific issues of comorbidity of the anxiety disorders with depression has received attention in the literature on anxiety disorders in youth (e.g., Finch, Lipovsky, & Casat, 1989). Strauss, Last, Hersen, and Kazdin (1988) examined a sample of 106 children and adolescents referred to an outpatient anxiety disorder clinic for children. Twenty-eight percent of the children with anxiety disorders displayed a concurrent major depression. Those cases with concurrent major depression tended to be older, as was the case in the earlier report by Strauss, Lease, Last, and Francis (1988). It was not clear if any or how many of the cases in this study overlapped with cases in the earlier report. To the extent that overlap existed, one would want to be cautious in viewing the studies as providing replicated evidence. Caution is also needed in light of the fact that multiple disorders (anxiety plus depression) are more likely to be brought to a clinic than are single disorders (anxiety alone). Thus, studies of a clinic sample may suggest an overestimate of the true (in nature) co-occurrence of disorders.

Using test anxiety as the initial criterion, Beidel and Turner (1988) found that 60% of their test-anxious sample met DSM-III criteria for an anxiety disorder. Also of interest, Beidel and Turner (1988) reported that the test-anxious children reported more thoughts than their non-test-anxious peers during a behavioral task. The difference between the groups was the result of the test-anxious children having a higher frequency of negative thoughts, where the test-anxious and non-test-anxious group did not differ in terms of the frequency of positive thoughts.

Rubin and Mills (1988) reported on a series of analyses conducted to study social isolation in children. The results suggested that at least one pattern of social isolation (labeled passive–anxious) was stable across three grade levels and was consistently and concurrently related to peer rejection and internalizing problems. Add to this the finding that passive–anxious isolation in early grades predicted depression (nonclinical level) and isolation in fifth grade. Although limited by the range of ages of the sample, the Rubin and Mills study nevertheless underscores the negative effects of passive–anxious child behavior and points directly toward the need for empirically evaluated treatments to rectify the unwanted social isolation. The unfavorable social status of anxiety disordered youth was also documented in a study reported by Strauss, Lahey, Frick, Frame, and Hynd (1988). The children, 6 to 13 years of age, who received a diagnosis of an anxiety disorder were most likely to fall in the socially neglected category of peer status and, when depression was evident as well, suffered diminished peer popularity.

Although studies of the anxiety disorders in youth are relatively rare, the apparent consistency in the comorbidity of anxiety disorders with other disorders raises important questions about the nature of anxiety disorders and the most effective strategies for treatment. It is interesting to speculate, for example, that one of the natural challenges facing all human beings is the successful adaptation to anxiety-provoking situations and that children who are, early on, unsuccessful at this developmental challenge are stymied in their psychological development, miss other related psychological activities, and perhaps are at greater risk for later psychological maladjustments. Early intervention (both prevention and remediation) is warranted.

Borkovec's Recent Studies

Borkovec and Mathews (1988) conducted a comparison of a nondirective therapy, coping desensitization, and cognitive therapy for adult patients with generalized anxiety disorder and panic disorder. All clients, in addition to the treatment condition noted above, also received relaxation training. The outcomes, assessed at posttreatment and at 6- and 12-month follow-up, indicated that the treatments were effective, but there were no differential results. Neither coping desensitization nor cognitive treatment added anything beyond a nondirective approach or to the relaxation training provided to all clients. It should be noted that each of the treatment conditions did produce desirable gains on the various dependent measures (e.g., self-reports, clinician ratings) and that the amount of change was comparable to that produced in other treatment evaluations. Although these results would appear to suggest that there were no additive effects produced by the three different treatment conditions, an earlier study by the same research group provided evidence to the contrary.

Borkovec, Mathews, Chambers, Ebrahimi, Lytle, and Nelson (1987) reported that cognitive therapy with relaxation was superior to nondirective therapy with relaxation on several questionnaire measures of change. Borkovec and colleagues suggested that, given the two studies, cognitive therapy may make a unique contribution to the outcome of treatment for anxiety disorders when the anxiety is not too severe or chronic. A similar conclusion was reached by Foa and Kozak (1985).

If depression was the disorder of the 1980s, will anxiety emerge as the prime target for research in the 1990s? Behavior therapy has certainly focused on anxiety during its history of treatment outcome research, and it may be that the reemergence of anxiety disorders will provide opportunities for learning more about cognitive-behavior therapy.

CONDUCT-DISORDERED YOUTH

Antisocial behavior in children is a serious and significant social problem that manifests itself in many areas of concern to mental health professionals. For example, 33% to 50% of clinic referrals are associated with conduct-disordered behavior. Add to this the developmental stability of antisocial action: antisocial behavior in children is predictive of adult psychopathology (Kazdin, 1987; Robins, 1966) and the fact that there is transgenerational concordance for antisocial difficulties and one can readily see the severity of the problem facing us.

One feature of conduct disorder that is often seen is impulsive, non-self-controlled behavior. Given the availability of a program designed to reduce impulsivity (Kendall & Braswell, 1985), it would seem reasonable to apply and evaluate such a program. Also, given the evidence to suggest that aberrant, often acting-out youth display deficiencies in interpersonal cognitive problem solving, it is also important to include training in problem-solving skills. In a global sense, the cognitive–behavioral treatments that have been applied to the remediation of difficulties linked to conduct disorder are designed as a match to the nature of the cognitive deficit seen in these children.

Applications of combinations of cognitive and behavioral training to the problems of conduct disordered youth have been examined in recent treatment outcome research. Two studies have been completed and the results are consistent, encouraging, and suggestive of how best to proceed with future clinical interventions. A closer look at each report will now proceed an attempt to draw conclusions.

Cognitive–behavioral problem-solving training was compared with a relationship therapy for the treatment of antisocial child behavior by Kazdin, Esveldt-Dawson, French, and Unis (1987). The children who received treatment in this outcome study were inpatients of a psychiatric facility who ranged in age from 7 to 13 years. Children were diagnosed as having conduct disorder ($n = 32$), attention deficit disorder ($n = 2$), depression ($n = 6$), adjustment disorder ($n = 4$), and other mental disorders ($n = 12$). Sixty-nine percent of the sample received a primary or secondary diagnosis of conduct disorder. Children had been referred for treatment for antisocial behavior and they scored above the 98th percentile on either the aggression or the delinquency scale of the Child Behavior Checklist (CBCL; Achenbach & Edelbrock, 1983). Although some of the diagnoses evidenced other areas in the children's lives that were also troublesome, antisocial/conduct disorder was a major concern for the treated cases. Parent and teacher rating (CBCL) were gathered before and after treatment, as well as at 4-, 8-, and 12-month follow-up. Therapists and children also completed evaluation measures.

The treatment that was provided under the label "problem-solving skills training" consisted of 20 sessions of individually administered treatment. Sessions lasted 45 minutes and took place two to three times per week. The therapy was a combination of the Kendall and Braswell (1985) program for impulse control and the Spivack, Platt, and Shure (1976) program for teaching interpersonal cognitive problem solving. This combination included both cognitive and behavioral treatment techniques that focused on generating alternative solutions, means–ends and consequential thinking, and taking the perspective of others. Children were given models to observe, role play opportunities for practice, corrective feedback, and social rewards to develop and buttress problem-solving skills. The problems to be solved were initially academic in nature, followed by more game-like activities, and subsequently emphasized enacting interpersonal situations. Response–cost was used for errors in the problem-solving steps. Earned chips and chips acquired for completion of homework assignments could be exchanged for small toys and prizes.

Those familiar with the Kendall and Braswell program and the Spivack and Shure approach will recognize them as the program applied and evaluated by Kazdin et al. (1987). The combination of interventions seems appropriate, consistent with the thrust of the original authors, and appropriately labeled cognitive–behavioral. For purposes of evaluation, Kazdin et al. compared the cognitive–behavioral program to a relationship therapy in which the therapist developed a close relationship with the child and focused on helping the child to express feelings. Play materials were available during sessions, and the child and therapist did discuss interpersonal situations related to the child's problem areas. The control condition was treatment contact only. The children met with the therapist for comparable durations, but they did not receive specific cognitive–behavioral problem-solving training or the development of a close interpersonal relationship.

The effects of the treatment program applied by Kazdin et al. (1987) were favorable. Specifically, cognitive–behavioral problem-solving training led to significantly greater changes than the other two conditions (relationship, therapist-contact control). As Kazdin et al. reported, the changes were sustained at 1-year follow-up and were evident at home and at school. Using normative comparisons (Kendall & Grove, 1988; see also discussion of clinical significance, Chapter 2, this volume), Kazdin et al.'s results indicated that the proportion of children who fell within the normative (nonclinic) range for behavior problems was greater for the cognitive–behavioral problem-solving treatment than for the other groups. The improvements were especially marked for the prosocial behavior. It should be noted, however, that the majority of treated cases remained outside the level that was selected to be the criterion for nonclinical deviance. Realism dictates a cautious interpretation of these results: the treatment was not a "cure." However, the results do document that a cognitive–behavioral problem-solving program can effect changes in a seriously disturbed clinic population. As Kazdin et al. noted, these results are consistent with recent studies of impulsive, aggressive, and delinquent youths who show significant improvements following cognitive–behavioral interventions.

The second study addressing the efficacy of cognitive–behavioral programs for children/adolescents with conduct disorder was conducted at the Eastern Pennsylvania Psychiatric Institute in collaboration with Temple University and was reported by Kendall, Reber, McLeer, Epps, and Ronan (1990). The subjects were youth in a psychiatric day-hospital who were diagnosed as conduct disordered (five had concurrent diagnoses of attention deficit disorder with hyperactivity). Children were 7 to 13 years of age, from urban environments, and of minority ethnic origins. A battery of measures was used to evaluate treatment outcome, including behavior rating scales, self-report measures, and task performance. Children were randomly assigned to either the cognitive–behavior therapy or a supportive/psychodynamic therapy (as practiced at the site) in a crossover design. One half of the subjects received the cognitive–behavioral program first, and one half of the subjects were in the supportive/psychodynamic treatments: after completion of the program subjects were crossed over and received the other intervention program. The cognitive–behavioral problem-solving intervention (based on Kendall & Braswell, 1985) was provided in 20 1-hour sessions.

Results of the Kendall et al. project indicated that the cognitive-behavioral treatment led to significant improvements on teacher's blind ratings of self-controlled behavior in the classroom (Self-Control Rating Scale; Kendall & Wilcox, 1979) and improvements in appropriate behavior and adaptive functioning. On both the Self-Control Rating Scale and the prosocial components of the CBCL, the children receiving the cognitive-behavioral training evidenced significant improvements. Using normative comparisons to assess the degree of clinically significant change, the authors reported that the majority of improvements that reached the criterion for clinical significance were produced by the cognitive-behavioral treatment. Like the reported outcome of the Kazdin et al. study, the successfully treated conduct disordered youth evidenced the greatest degree of improvement on the prosocial behaviors. It was not the case that the treatment "cured" the conduct disorder (see Kendall, 1989b; discussion in Chapter 2, this volume) but that the children seemed to learn the skills to engage in more prosocial behavior.

There are several important similarities across the Kendall et al. (1990) and Kazdin et al. (1987) studies. For example, there were methodological consistencies, both used related interventions and similar outcome measures, and both employed normative comparisons to assess clinical significance. The subjects were also similar: diagnosed cases referred to psychiatric facilities. The outcomes of the two studies are also similar and of interest. The emerging consistency is that the treatment produces statistically significant improvements, changes that are beyond chance, on such target measures associated with aggression and antisocial activity, but that the magnitude of the change is not sufficient to claim that the treatment is the antidote for conduct disorder. The more realistic conclusion would be that a treatment has been identified as active in producing desirable gains, but that it is of limited duration relative to that which is needed to effect the kind of change that would be preferred. A related consistency in the results has to do with the emergence of increases in prosocial behavior due to treatment. It may be the case, given the difficulty in changing peer and teacher perceptions of children, that it will take a longer period of time for the newly acquired prosocial skills to have their full impact on those in the child's environment. It may take an especially responsive social environment to notice, accept, and indeed reinforce these prosocial actions for them to be maintained. It is true that we have been humbled by the vicissitudes associated with reprogramming large social environments to encourage and support target behaviors, but that should not distract us from selecting extratherapy environments that are cooperative and including their participation in interventions. With an outside support system to foster and reward the new prosocial skills, the effects of the cognitive–behavioral treatment may be more fully maximized.

A question that has been raised about the outcomes of cognitive-behavior therapies for children concerns the quality of the training that is provided. Specifically, applications have been only minimally successful in achieving a true operationalization of the intervention, whereas others are more successful at implementing the program but experience difficulties associated with the novelty of the approach. The question then is as follows: "Do therapists provide a superior version of the treatment with increased experience?" We are not interested here in the bigger question of the relative potency of paraprofessionals and professionals in the generating of treatment gains. We are, instead, interested in the relationship between the experience of the therapists in providing a manualized cognitive-behavior therapy and the degree of improvement that is produced. Assuming a reasonably solid operationalization of the treatment program (the independent variable has integrity), do therapists improve with experience? The crossover design employed in the Kendall et al. (1990) study allowed for a preliminary examination of this question, and the results proved informative. On the four dependent variables reflecting improvements produced by the cognitive–behavioral treatments, the greater improvement was observed during the therapist's second application of the program; therapists produced greater changes with increased experience. It is worthwhile to note that this effect is not due to limited outcomes in the first administration of the program. The first administration of the program did produce some gains. All therapists, trained mental health professionals, received detailed training in the application of the cognitive-behavioral program that included a treatment manual, a set of training exercises, and weekly 1-hour supervision throughout the conduct of the study. It seems reasonable to suggest that, where gains were made, the magnitude of the effects can be improved with increased therapist experience. One speculation concerns the therapist's ability, acquired with experience, to make opportunistic applications of the cognitive–behavioral problem-solving skills in daily activities. Clinicians reported, and unsystematic checks of audiotapes of the therapy confirmed, that they were increasingly comfortable with the treatment after completing several cases and that the comfort allowed them to become a more involved model and problem solver. This would often translate into the therapist using the problem-solving approach in more informal conversations with the child and in more realistic modeling demonstrations. Although only speculative at this time, it is worth pointing out that it was "involvement" that was the strongest predictor of improvement in an earlier outcome study of the cognitive–behavioral training and it may be that therapist "involvement" is a potent source of outcome as well.

Another question worthy of investigation is the role of affective arousal in the efficacy of treatment. For instance, when children acquire prosocial problem-solving skills in a safe therapeutic environment, they may not have acquired the ability to apply these skills when under conditions of heightened/charged emotionality. In the Kendall et al. (1990) treatment, therapists provided the subjects with opportunities to engage in problem solving when emotionally aroused, although this has not often been a component of other cognitive-behavioral training. Future research in this area should address the influences of affective charge in the ability of successfully treated cases to modulate impulsive and aggressive behavior.

Rival explanations for the observation that treatment effects were greater when provided by more experienced practitioners of the specific treatment are available. For example, such effects could result from the fact that the children who received the second application of the problem-solving therapy were first exposed to the alternate treatments. This and other explanations cannot be ruled out at this time. Nevertheless, if one credits the greater gains to increased therapist experience, then it is interesting to speculate as to why and/or how the experiences translates into effects.

ATTRIBUTIONS

The study of how individuals disambiguate the causes of their own and others behavior has continued to receive widespread attention within the cognitive–behavioral literature. Areas of continued investigation include the nature of cognitive psychopathology in depression, the process of coping (e.g., Compas, Forsythe, & Wagner 1988), and understanding marital interactions (e.g., Fincham & Beach, 1988). To illustrate from the marital interaction arena, Fincham and Beach (1988) tested the attributional differences between distressed and nondistressed married couples. Unlike much of the earlier research that used hypothetical situations as stimuli for subjects attributional judgments, Fincham and Beach employed both actual and hypothetical marital events in testing the attributional hypothesis. In their study, wives in distressed and nondistressed marriages made attributions about both hypothetical and actual marital behaviors. The real versus hypothetical nature of the target behaviors did not affect the attributional results. However, distressed spouses saw their own behavior as more unselfishly motivated and less intentional than the behavior of their spouse. The nondistressed subjects made comparable attributions, both benign, about their own and their partner's behavior. These findings replicate others but also add to the generalizability of the results, for actual as well as hypothetical behaviors, distressed spouses show attributional biases. In a related study, Halford and Sanders (1988) found that distressed couples compared with nondistressed couples engaged in higher levels of partner-referent negative self-talk and lower levels of partner-referent positive self-talk. Moreover, as reported by Camper, Jacobson, Holtzworth-Munroe, and Schmaling (1988), distressed spouses compared with nondistressed spouses viewed negative partner behavior as a global and stable feature and positive partner behavior as less global and stable. Camper et al. also reported that couples engaged in more attributional activity for negative partner behavior than for positive relationship events.

Attributional analyses of health-related behaviors have appeared more frequently in the literature (see Michela & Wood, 1986; Hayes & Hesketh, 1989). In a study by Affleck, Tennen, Croog, and Levine (1987), 287 heart attack victims were interviewed 7 weeks and 8 years after their attack. With certain factors controlled, it was found that patients who identified benefits from their first attack (at 7 weeks) were less likely to have another attack and had lower levels of morbidity 8 years later. Also of interest, attributing the initial heart attack to other people was predictive of reinfarction. As the authors note, other psychological variables (emotional stress, perceived mastery) were not measured and may moderate the reported outcomes. Nevertheless, the findings do have important health-related suggestions that are linked to how an individual makes sense of experiences that occur in his or her life. Blaming others seems unhealthful, seeking to find benefit seems healthful; to the extent that such attributions can be shaped in persons who are not themselves predisposed in the preferred directions is a topic worthy of increased clinical and research attention.

As a risk factor in illness, Peterson (1988) reported that college students with an attributional style that consisted of attributing negative events to stable and global factors experienced more illness days and made more visits to the physician. Also, college students with

COGNITIVE PROCESSES AND PROCEDURES

stable and global attributional styles for negative events reported more unhealthy habits, less confidence to change these habits, and more stressful experiences than did students who attributed negative outcomes to unstable and specific causes.

Attributional processes have been found in several studies to be important in the maintenance of desirable behavior change. For example, Harackiewicz, Sausone, Blair, Epstein and Mauderluik (1987) examined attributions for success and failure and the relationships with maintenance. Subjects were seeking to quit smoking. Some were given nicotine gum, and others were in a self-help condition. Those subjects in an intrinsic self-help group made fewer external attributions for success and remained abstinent longer. Subjects given nicotine gum were superior in initial cessation but were inferior in maintenance. The findings suggest that ex-smokers who make external attributions for their initial ability to stop smoking were more likely to relapse.

Before leaving the topic of individuals' attributions about the causes of behavior, it should be noted that when one strives to separate anxiety and depression (see discussion in Chapter 2, this volume), there appears to be some consistency in the conclusion that depressives are more likely to display attributional biases for negative events, whereas anxiety is less related to dysfunctional attributional processes.

STRESS INOCULATION

Applications and evaluations of stress inoculation (Meichenbaum, 1986) procedures have continued over the years of this review. Many of the applications have expanded the initial focus of the treatment approach, whereas others have provided more rigorous tests of the intervention in areas where it had been applied earlier. For example, Wells, Howard, Nowlin, and Vargas (1988) employed a stress inoculation intervention for patients undergoing surgery (see also Kendall & Epps, 1990). Twenty-four patients scheduled for elective surgery were randomly assigned to either a stress inoculation intervention or a standard hospital instructions control. Dependent measures included assessments of patient anxiety, pain, and postoperative adjustment. Self-report scales were used for anxiety and pain assessments, whereas a nurse provided ratings (blind) of each patient's adjustment during hospitalization. Also, type and dosage of analgesic medication, as well as the number of patient requests for medication, were taken from the patients' medical charts.

The intervention followed the typical stress inoculation approach: an educational phase, a skill acquisition phase, and an application phase. Patients were warned of the anxiety and pain sensations they might feel and were given simplified explanations of psychological theories of emotions and pain. Patients were taught to identify and monitor cognitive and physical cues of stress relations, such as increased heart rate and negative self-statements, and to use deep breathing, muscle relaxation, positive images, and coping self-talk. During the application phase, patients used the skills when experiencing the activation of their anxiety cues. The Wells et al. (1988) project produced results that support the efficacy of stress inoculation. Decreases in state anxiety and a positive impact on the patient's experience of pain were reported. In addition to these data, which were based on self-reports, treated subjects also requested and received significantly fewer analgesics.

One area of expansion for applications of stress inoculation is for coping with severe medical conditions, such as multiple sclerosis (Foley, Bedell, LaRocca, Scheinberg, & Reznikoff, 1987). Multiple sclerosis can have profound psychosocial effects, including disruption to the family, school setting, or work environment, and has untoward effects on family, sexual, and recreational activities. Patients with multiple sclerosis ($n = 40$) were randomly assigned to either a stress inoculation treatment or current available care (control). The stress inoculation procedures included monitoring daily stresses and the associated cognitive, emotional, and behavioral responses. Deep muscle relaxation, an evaluation of cognitive self-statements in response to stress, and identification of cues to use for stress reduction techniques were part of the first four sessions. Sessions 5 and 6 focused on the role playing of how to cope while integrating the use of the strategies. At posttesting the group of patients who had received the cognitive–behavioral stress inoculation program were significantly less depressed, anxious, and distressed than those patients receiving the standard care. Those in the stress inoculation condition were also using more problem-focused coping. It should be noted, however, that not all of the effects held at follow-up (6 months). Nevertheless, Foley et al. (1987) provide data to encourage the greater application of stress inoculation procedures with individuals with medical difficulties.

Jay, Elliott, Katz, and Siegel (1987) examined cognitive–behavioral and pharmacological interventions for children's distress during painful medical procedures. The subjects were leukemia patients between 3½ and 13 years of age whose medical protocol required at least three bone marrow aspirations. Fifty-six subjects completed the study.

Three interventions were applied and compared: (1) cognitive-behavior therapy, consisting of filmed modeling, breathing exercises, positive incentives, imagery/distraction, and behavioral rehearsal (based on a stress inoculation model); (2) medication (Valium); and (3) minimal treatment attention control. As the authors reported, the findings supported the efficacy of the cognitive-behavioral intervention in ameliorating children's distress. Main effects were obtained for behavioral distress, pulse rate scores, and children's self-reported pain. It is of interest to note that the medication treatment, Valium, produced results that were in the positive direction but not as pronounced as the stress inoculation approach and in some cases not significantly better than the minimal treatment attention control.

The application of stress inoculation in hospital settings fits with earlier conceptualizations of hospitalization as a temporary crisis (Auerbach & Kilmann, 1977) and patients as subjects who do not display psychopathology but who, when in crises, require psychological intervention (Kendall & Watson, 1981). It would have been interesting if the Wells et al. research group (1988) had had sufficient numbers of subjects to examine the data for any individual differences in reactions to the stress inoculation procedure. Several individual difference variables have been investigated as moderators of the effects of psychological help in medical settings (e.g., monitors vs. blunters; Miller, Leinbach, & Brody, 1989), and there is need for further investigation of the influences of individual differences on psychological interventions.

SOCIAL PROBLEM SOLVING

Research and clinical application of concepts linked to problem solving continue to remain among the dominant themes in contemporary cognitive-behavior therapy. Books on general applications of problem solving with adults have appeared (e.g., D'Zurilla, 1986), as have more focused books such as the Nezu, Nezu, and Perri (1989) volume addressing problem solving treatments designed specifically for depression. Regarding children and adolescents, there are numerous clinical, educational, and popularized versions of cognitive problem solving. Entire curricula for grades in the elementary school have been developed (see Elias & Clabby, 1989; Weissberg, Caplan, & Bennetto, 1988); more focused problem-solving programs for impulsive, overactive, attention-deficit children (*Stop and Think Workbook*; Kendall, 1989a) and reviews of related work are available (e.g., Pellegrini, 1985; Pellegrini &

Urbain, 1985). The section on treating conduct-disordered youth contains additional discussion of problem-solving treatments with children/adolescents.

For Nezu et al. (1989) social problem solving refers to a process in which people discover, create, and/or identify effective means of coping with stressful life events. Deficits in such problem solving are a vulnerability for subsequent depression, according to these authors, and treatments designed to remediate social problem-solving deficits are recommended to overcome depression. The guiding theory behind problem-solving approaches to treating depression are described in detail in the Nezu et al. book, as are the procedures used for implementing the program. In a recent research investigation, Nezu and Perri (1989) provided a preliminary components analysis of the problem-solving approach. Depressed clients were assigned to either a complete problem-solving therapy condition, an abbreviated treatment condition, or a waiting list control condition. In the complete treatment protocol, the clients were taught an overall problem orientation—a rational view of interpersonal and social problems that involved problem solving as a means of coping—as well as how to (1) define/recognize problems, (2) generate a wide range of alternatives, (3) evaluate the potential consequences of a solution, and (4) implement a plan and monitor and evaluate its outcomes. The abbreviated treatment was not given the initial overall problem-solving orientation. Treatments were provided in groups, over 10 weeks, with each meeting lasting 1½ to 2 hours.

Although several caveats (e.g., reliance on self-reports, restricted sample) required mention, the findings do provide support for the efficacy of a cognitive–behavioral problem-solving treatment for depression. Those subjects in both treatment conditions were significantly less depressed at both posttreatment and follow-up, relative to those in the waiting list condition.

Results of a comparison of qualitative and quantitative assessments of social problem solving indicated that, when seeking to make predictions about child disorders among a large group of nonclinical cases, qualitative scoring offered more than a quantitative approach (Fischler & Kendall, 1988). For example, children whose social problem solutions were judged to be more socially appropriate and more consistent across situations were rated by teachers and parents as better adjusted.

Studying suicidal psychiatric patients, Schotte and Clum (1987) reported that suicidal individuals were deficient in impersonal and interpersonal problem solving, with the interpersonal problem-solving deficits being seen in generating limited alternative solutions

COGNITIVE PROCESSES AND PROCEDURES

to problems and limited anticipation of negative consequences of proposed solutions. The authors linked these findings to other data suggesting that suicidal individuals display cognitive rigidity, an inflexible and restrictive approach to life and life's problems.

The impact of a social problem-solving perspective on assessment and intervention within behavior therapy specifically, and clinical psychology in general, cannot be denied. Different subgroups within our various professional affiliations use slightly different language to refer to social problem solving, but the interest in the topic crosses many boundaries. The interested reader can pursue this line of investigation by checking any of the many articles dealing with interpersonal cognitive problem solving, social problem solving, social competence enhancement, cognitive–behavioral problem solving, and cognitive problem solving. What this area lacks in a consistent title it makes up for with widespread applicability.

CHAPTER

5

BEHAVIORAL MEDICINE

JOHN P. FOREYT

INTRODUCTION

The Society of Behavioral Medicine, an organization of more than 2,300 members, recently revised its definition of behavioral medicine for its bylaws. Article II now reads: "Behavioral medicine is the interdisciplinary field concerned with the development of behavioral and biomedical science, knowledge, and techniques relevant to the understanding of health and illness, and the application of this knowledge and these techniques to prevention, diagnosis, treatment, and rehabilitation" (Society of Behavioral Medicine, 1989, p. 1). Whatever definition used, behavioral medicine continues to be a growing, dynamic field. There have been a number of major gains since the last edition of this series. Among them, Congress has mandated that each of the National Institutes of Health (NIH) National Advisory Councils include behavioral scientists on them (U.S. Department of Health and Human Services, 1989a). These councils advise the institute directors on policy matters and conduct the final reviews of grant applications. Institute directors are also required to report on the status of behavioral research in the NIH biennial report to Congress. The National Science Foundation has been directed by Congress to increase funding for behavioral sciences (American Psychological Association, 1989). At the private level, the American Cancer Society has added an independent peer review study section to evaluate psychosocial and behavioral research proposals.

As in previous volumes of this series, this chapter surveys several topics of importance to the field. The first one highlights the discrepancy between the actual and the perceived health of individuals in the

United States. Despite new data documenting solid gains in the health status of the United States, Americans report increasing dissatisfaction with their own feelings of well-being.

The second topic reviews the trends in heart disease research and control. The National Cholesterol Education Program is having a particularly strong impact in the United States in heightening awareness of cholesterol and stimulating interest in treatment for reduction of high levels. New guidelines for detection, evaluation, and treatment have been published. A number of recent large clinical trials showing the impact of cholesterol-lowering drugs has shifted the trend in research to interventions involving a combination of diet and drugs for long-term control of lipids. Data on nonpharmacological approaches for reducing blood pressure show a similar trend. Stress management strategies, for example, have not provided strong evidence of efficacy in clinical trials. The new Surgeon General's report documents the impressive gains that have been made in smoking cessation programs and prevention approaches and the subsequent decline in smoking-related deaths in some groups.

The Type A behavior pattern, identified during the 1970s as an independent cardiovascular risk factor, is the third topic surveyed. The trend in this area has now turned from investigations of the global Type A construct to components of the behavior pattern.

Fourth are the trends in cancer research and control. Mortality rates continue to increase for some cancers. According to two reviewers, we are losing the war on cancer and treatment efforts have been qualified failures. Progress on smoking and diet with respect to cancer are reviewed.

The number of AIDS cases in the United States now exceeds 100,000. Behavioral research and trends in the AIDS area are the fifth topic covered.

The sixth issue reviewed is the impact that behavioral medicine is having at the worksite. Researchers have tried to reduce the high attrition rates of the early programs by being more creative in their interventions.

An unusual report from the National Academy of Sciences funded by the U.S. Army is the seventh topic covered. The report consists of an evaluation of a number of techniques for enhancing human performance primarily developed outside of mainstream science. A number of the techniques are popular in the behavioral medicine field and several others have potential usefulness. Many of the report's conclusions are surprising and relevant to behavioral researchers and clinicians.

Finally, training guidelines for practitioners in health psychology are summarized. As the field begins to mature, formal criteria for licensure and practice will undoubtedly require adequate preparation in relevant areas. Over the next several years, this topic will continue to grow in importance for all disciplines involved in the behavioral medicine field.

HEALTH STATUS OF THE UNITED STATES

The health status of the United States continues to improve. Americans are healthier and are living longer than ever before. The 12th Annual Report on the Health Status of the Nation (National Center for Health Statistics, 1988) documents these gains. For example, the life expectancy at birth increased for white females from 48.7 years in 1900 to 78.7 years in 1985; it increased for white males from 46.6 years to 71.9 years during the same time period. The increase has been most dramatic for black females, from 33.5 years in 1900 to 73.5 years in 1985. Black males also showed impressive gains, increasing from 32.5 years in 1900 to 65.3 years in 1985.

White females born in 1985 have an 86% chance of surviving to age 65; white males have a 75% chance. Black females also have a 75% chance compared with black males' 58% chance. Black males born in 1900 had only a 19% chance of surviving to age 65 compared with white males' 39% chance.

In 1900 the leading causes of death were tuberculosis, pneumonia, and diarrhea and enteritis. None of these causes is now a major problem in the United States. They have been replaced by diseases of the heart, cancer, and cerebrovascular disease. Figures 5-1 and 5-2 illustrate the shifts in mortality between 1900 and 1985. Major advances in public health practices, medical science, and the resultant aging population seem to account for much of the increase (National Center for Health Statistics, 1988). Most of the causes of premature death, including heart disease, stroke, emphysema, some cancers, and accidental injuries, are to some extent preventable.

Mortality from heart disease began an encouraging decline in females in the 1950s, and in males in the 1960s. Behaviorally, we appear to be taking better care of ourselves, including better control of our blood pressure, diet, and exercise, along with cutting down on smoking (Goldman & Cook, 1984). Medical advances in the treatment of heart problems and increased access to coronary care units also have played a role (National Center for Health Statistics, 1988). Middle-

BEHAVIORAL MEDICINE

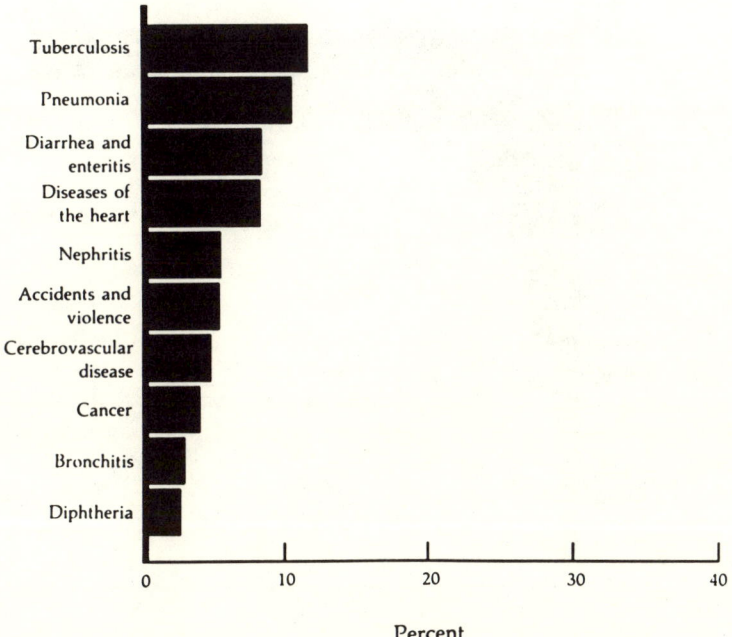

FIG. 5-1.
The ten leading causes of death as a percentage of all deaths: United States, 1900. From *Health, United States, 1987* (DHHS Publication No. PHS 88-1232) by the National Center for Health Statistics, 1988, p. 10, Washington, DC: U.S. Government Printing Office.

aged black males, however, have a 70% higher death rate from heart disease than comparable white males. Middle-aged black females have a 30% higher death rate than comparable white females. Unlike heart disease, lung cancer, the leading cause of cancer deaths in males, continues to increase overall. Among females, mortality from lung cancer has risen dramatically, and now is similar to mortality from breast cancer (U.S. Department of Health and Human Services, 1989b). One optimistic trend is a decline in death rates begun in the early 1980s from lung cancer in males under age 55, presumably reflecting the decreases in cigarette smoking in this group.

From 1945 until 1985, breast cancer was the leading cause of cancer mortality among women. In both the 1970s and 1980s, deaths from breast cancer increased in women over 55 years and decreased slightly in those under 55 years. This slight drop for the younger women may have been due in part to both earlier detection and increased fertility of these women when they were in their 20s (Na-

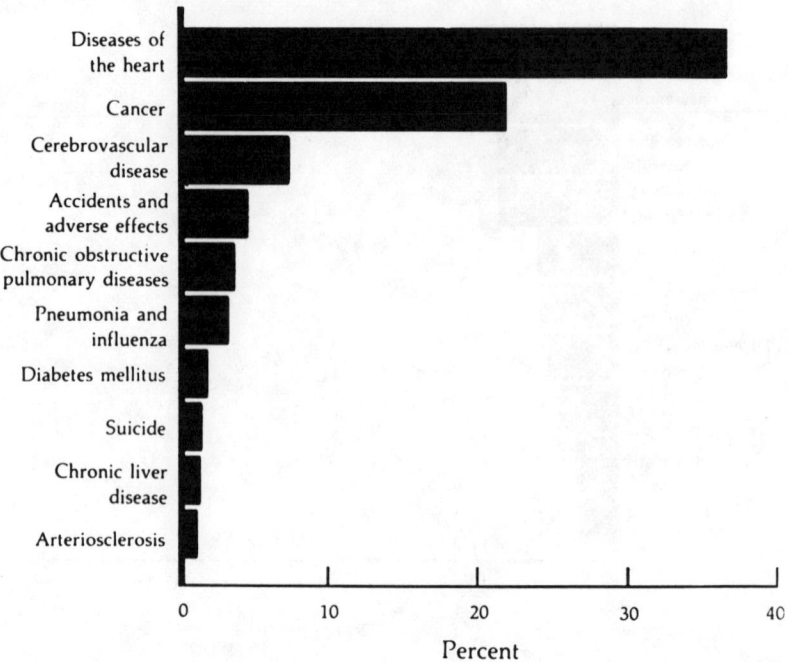

FIG. 5-2.
The ten leading causes of death as a percentage of all deaths: United States, 1985. From *Health, United States, 1987* (DHHS Publication No. PHS 88-1232) by the National Center for Health Statistics, 1988, p. 11, Washington, DC: U.S. Government Printing Office.

tional Center for Health Statistics, 1988). Risk factors for breast cancer include family history of the disease, age, and reproductive history.

Doing Better, Feeling Worse

Despite the major gains in the health status of the United States, the proportion of Americans satisfied with their own health and physical well-being has declined, from 61% in the 1970s to 55% in the mid-1980s (Barsky, 1988). Americans are reporting greater numbers of somatic problems, more general illness, and more disability. Barsky (1988) believes that four factors help account for this discrepancy between our actual and our perceived health. First, because medical science has made so many gains in the treatment of acute and infectious diseases, individuals now live long enough to acquire chronic, disabling illnesses. Because of these medical advances, some diseases increase rather than decrease in prevalence (Gruenberg, 1977). Second, health has become an increasingly important goal for many Americans, as reflected by the growing interest in diet, nutrition, and exercise. This interest has led to a heightened consciousness about personal health, amplifying awareness of symptoms and illness. Third, the increasing commercialization of health and the popularization of health issues in the mass media may contribute to dissatisfaction with one's own well-being. And fourth, the medicalization of daily life continues to increase, that is, individuals today consult physicians more frequently, seeing them for less serious reasons and for problems which, in the past, were typically considered unsuitable for medical intervention (e.g., baldness, fatigue, small breasts). This paradox of health contributes to disillusionment, disenchantment, and dissatisfaction with health care in this country.

TRENDS IN HEART DISEASE RESEARCH AND CONTROL

Cardiovascular disease (CVD) continues to be the leading cause of death in the United States, accounting for about 48% of annual mortality. Effective prevention of CVD depends on modification of behaviors associated with three primary risk factors: high blood cholesterol, high blood pressure, and cigarette smoking.

High Blood Cholesterol

The association between high blood cholesterol and increased risk of cardiovascular disease is well documented (Office of Medical Applications of Research, National Institutes of Health, 1985). A 1% decrease in serum cholesterol results in a 2% decrease in the risk of CVD (Lipid Research Clinics Program, 1984a, 1984b). During the past 20 years, there has been a 3-4% decrease in serum cholesterol in the United States, probably accounting in part for the overall reduction in mortality from CVD during this period (National Center for Health Statistics, 1987).

THE NATIONAL CHOLESTEROL EDUCATION PROGRAM

The National Cholesterol Education Program (NCEP), begun in November 1985, is one of three large risk education programs administered through the Office of Prevention, Education, and Control at the National Heart, Lung, and Blood Institute (NHLBI) of the NIH (U.S. Department of Health and Human Services, 1989c). The other two programs are the National High Blood Pressure Education Program, which served as the model for the development of the NCEP, and the NHLBI Smoking Education Program. A fourth program, the National Blood Resource Education Program, begun in 1987, is aimed at ensuring an adequate supply of safe blood in the United States.

The NCEP's goal is to help in the reduction of illness and death from coronary heart disease (CHD) by reducing the number of individuals with high blood cholesterol through the support of educational efforts aimed at health professionals and the general public. The Coordinating Committee of the NCEP consists of more than 20 member organizations from voluntary health societies, medical associations, and relevant community programs. In addition, a number of federal agencies have liaison representatives on the committee. The NCEP has been the driving force in this country in helping to raise awareness and understanding about high blood cholesterol as a CVD risk factor.

AWARENESS OF BLOOD CHOLESTEROL LEVELS

How many Americans know their blood cholesterol levels? Based on the 1987 Behavioral Risk Factor Surveillance system, a telephone survey using random-digit dialing conducted by state health departments, the answer is less than one in ten. Survey results indicated that only about 6% of respondents reported that they knew their cholesterol value (Centers for Disease Control, 1988a), similar to results of a 1986 survey which showed a 7% figure (Schucker et al., 1987). Approximately 47% of respondents have had their cholesterol tested, and 19% reported that they were told their value (Centers for Disease Control, 1988a). Although low, these values represent an increase from previous research. For example, an earlier survey in 1983 indicated that only 3% of respondents knew their cholesterol level (Schucker et al., 1987).

NEW GUIDELINES FOR TREATMENT

The *Report of the Expert Panel on Detection, Evaluation, and Treatment of High Blood Cholesterol in Adults* (U.S. Department of Health and Human Services, 1988a; Expert Panel on Detection, Evaluation, and Treatment of High Blood Cholesterol in Adults, 1988) provides new guidelines for identifying, evaluating, and treating high blood cholesterol in individuals 20 years of age and older. These guidelines detail who needs cholesterol-lowering treatment based on cholesterol levels and other risk factors for CHD. Blood cholesterol levels below 200 mg/dl are classified as "desirable blood cholesterol," those 200 to 239 mg/dl as "borderline-high blood cholesterol," and those 240 mg/dl and greater as "high blood cholesterol." About 30% of the adult population fall into the borderline-high-risk category (14% with CHD or two risk factors and 16% without CHD and two risk factors) and an additional 27% of adults are in the high-risk classification (Sempos et al., 1989). The proportion of individuals with cholesterol levels in these two classifications rises dramatically with increasing age. About 60 million adults in the United States are at sufficiently high risk of developing CHD and need to lower their blood cholesterol under medical supervision (Sempos et al., 1989).

Recommendations for individuals with cholesterol levels below 200 mg/dl include general dietary and other risk reduction educational information and instructions to be retested within the next 5 years. Individuals with cholesterols above 200 mg/dl are retested and the average of the two tests used. Those individuals with borderline values and CHD or with two other CHD risk factors, plus all individuals with high blood cholesterol, also receive lipoprotein analysis. Figure 5-3 illustrates this new initial classification based on total cholesterol. The final cholesterol value determines the treatment.

Intervention for individuals with borderline and high blood cholesterol begins with dietary therapy, usually by registered dietitians who ideally have had some behavioral training. The goal of dietary therapy is to reduce the cholesterol levels in two steps, the second more restrictive than the first in the intake of saturated fatty acids and cholesterol. For overweight patients, calories are also reduced. The "Step-One Diet" reduces total fat to less than 30% of calories, saturated fatty acids to less than 10% of calories, and cholesterol to less than 300 mg/day. Table 5-1 illustrates the kinds of changes in diet required by the Step-One Diet. The "Step-Two Diet" reduces saturated fatty acids even further, to less than 7% of calories and cholesterol to less than 200 mg/day (U.S. Department of Health and Human Services, 1988a). Table 5-2 illustrates the dietary therapy for high blood cholesterol.

Wood et al. (1988) examined the changes that occur in lipids and lipoproteins as a result of a low-fat, low-cholesterol diet versus an exercise regimen in overweight men. Compared with a control group ($n = 42$), both the low-fat diet group ($n = 42$) and the exercise group

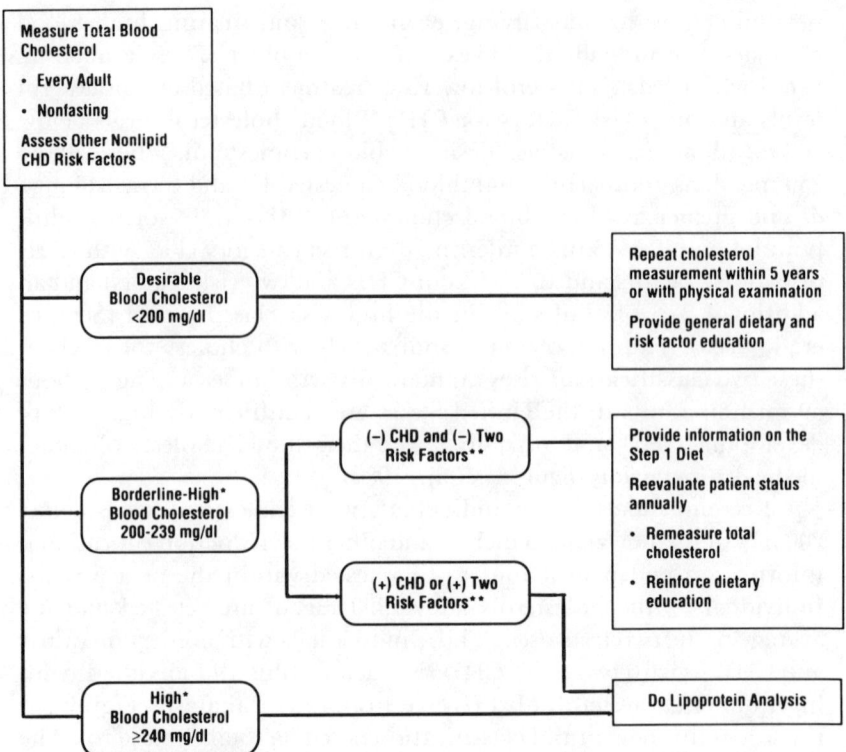

FIG. 5-3.
Initial classification based on total cholesterol. *Must be confirmed by repeat measurement; use average value. **One of which can be male sex. Adapted from *Report of the Expert Panel on Detection, Evaluation, and Treatment of High Blood Cholesterol in Adults* (NIH Publication No. 88-2925) by the U.S. Department of Health and Human Services, 1988a, p. 20, Washington, DC: U.S. Government Printing Office.

($n = 47$) had significant increases in plasma high-density lipoprotein cholesterol (HDL; the "good cholesterol"), the HDL subfractions (HDL$_2$ and HDL$_3$), and significant decreases in triglycerides. However, changes in total cholesterol and in plasma low-density cholesterol (LDL; the "bad cholesterol") were not different from the controls. None of the changes were different between the dieters and the exercisers, and the authors concluded that weight loss through either low-fat dieting or exercising produces comparable and beneficial changes in plasma HDL concentrations. This study also points out the value of weight loss in reducing the risk of CHD through changes in lipids and lipoproteins.

The key to success in the reduction of blood cholesterol is the individual's adherence to the dietary recommendations. Studies on long-term adherence to low-fat, low-cholesterol diets for lipid reduction suggest that individuals tend to make changes in the short-term while motivation is high, then gradually return to old habits (e.g., Foreyt, Scott, Mitchell, & Gotto, 1979; Reeves et al., 1983). With the trend in this field toward universal blood testing of all adult Americans for lipids at least once every 5 years and with a significant proportion of the adult population falling into an unhealthy range, behavioral scientists will be increasingly asked to devise effective maintenance approaches for large numbers of Americans. Results of research studies using dietary approaches as the sole intervention for cholesterol reduction have not been particularly encouraging.

Because of the great difficulty in lowering cholesterol into safe ranges with diet alone for individuals with dangerously high levels, the use of cholesterol-lowering drugs has become increasingly popular. For individuals with borderline and high cholesterol, at least 6 months of intensive dietary treatment and counseling are initially recommended before attempting drug treatment. After 6 months, the drugs of first choice include bile acid sequestrants, including cholestyramine and colestipol, and nicotinic acid. Newer drugs currently being evaluated include the HMG-CoA reductase inhibitors, for example, lovastatin, simvastatin, and pravastatin.

DIET-DRUG TRIALS

Gemfibrozil, a fibric acid derivative that elevates serum levels of HDL cholesterol and lowers levels of non-HDL cholesterol, was evaluated in the Helsinki Heart Study. The study was a randomized double-blind 5-year trial testing the drug's efficacy in 4,081 asymptomatic 40- to 55-year-old men with an average mean total cholesterol of 289 mg/dl. One group received the drug; the other group received a placebo. The study's authors reported that the cumulative rate of cardiac end points at 5 years was 27.3 per 1,000 in the gemfibrozil group and 41.4 per 1,000 in the placebo group, a significant reduction of 34% in the incidence of CHD (Frick et al., 1987). The drug was highly successful in increasing the HDL cholesterol and reducing the LDL cholesterol and triglycerides, resulting in significant reductions in the incidence of CHD without any major clinical adverse reactions. The results indicate that a combination intervention of lowering LDL and raising HDL cholesterol is more effective in reducing incidence of CHD than lowering LDL alone (Manninen et al., 1988). Similar to the earlier Lipid Re-

TABLE 5-1. Recommended Diet Modifications to Lower Blood Cholesterol: The Step-One Diet

	Choose	Decrease
Fish, chicken, turkey, and lean meats	Fish, poultry without skin, lean cuts of beef, lamb, pork, or veal, shellfish	Fatty cuts of beef, lamb, pork, spare ribs, organ meats, regular cold cuts, sausage, hot dogs, bacon, sardines, roe
Skim and low-fat milk, cheese, yogurt, and dairy	Skim or 1% fat milk (liquid, powered, evaporated), buttermilk	Whole milk (4% fat) (regular, evaporated, condensed), cream, half and half, 2% milk, imitation milk products, most nondairy creamers, whipped toppings
	Nonfat (0% fat) or low-fat yogurt	Whole-milk yogurt
	Low-fat cottage cheese (1% or 2% fat)	Whole-milk cottage cheese (4% fat)
	Low-fat cheeses, farmer or pot cheeses (all of these should be labeled no more than 2-6 g fat/ounce)	All natural cheeses (e.g., blue, roquefort, camembert, cheddar, swiss)
		Low-fat or "light" cream cheese, low-fat or "light" sour cream
		Cream cheeses, sour cream
	Sherbet, sorbet	Ice cream
Eggs	Egg whites (2 whites = 1 whole egg in recipes), cholesterol-free egg substitutes	Egg yolks

Fruits and vegetables	Fresh, frozen, canned, or dried fruits and vegetables	Vegetables prepared in butter, cream, or other sauces
Breads and cereals	Homemade baked goods using unsaturated oils sparingly, angel food cake, low-fat crackers, low-fat cookies	Commercially baked goods: pies, cakes, doughnuts, croissants, pastries, muffins, biscuits, high-fat crackers, high-fat cookies
	Rice, pasta	Egg noodles
	Whole-grain breads and cereals (oatmeal, whole wheat, rye, bran, multigrain, etc.)	Breads in which eggs are a major ingredient
Fats and oils	Baking cocoa	Chocolate
	Unsaturated vegetable oils: corn, olive, rapeseed (canola oil), safflower, sesame, soybean, sunflower	Butter, coconut oil, palm oil, palm kernel oil, lard, bacon fat
	Margarine or shortening made from one of the unsaturated oils listed above	
	Diet margarine	
	Mayonnaise, salad dressings made with unsaturated oils listed above	Dressings made with egg yolk
	Low-fat dressings	
	Seeds and nuts	Coconut

Note. From *Report of the Expert Panel on Detection, Evaluation, and Treatment of High Blood Cholesterol in Adults* (NIH Publication No. 88-2925) by the U.S. Department of Health and Human Services, 1988a, p. 39, Washington, DC: U.S. Government Printing Office.

TABLE 5-2. Dietary Therapy of High Blood Cholesterol

Nutrient	Recommended intake	
	Step-one diet	Step-two diet
Total fat	< 30% of total calories	
Saturated fatty acids	< 10% of total calories	< 7% of total calories
Polyunsaturated fatty acids	≤ 10% of total calories	
Monounsaturated fatty acids	10%–15% of total calories	
Carbohydrates	50%–60% of total calories	
Protein	10%–20% of total calories	
Cholesterol	< 300 mg/day	< 200 mg/day
Total calories	To achieve and maintain desirable weight	

Note. From *Report of the Expert Panel on Detection, Evaluation, and Treatment of High Blood Cholesterol in Adults* (NIH Publication No. 88-2925) by the U.S. Department of Health and Human Services, 1988a, p. 30, Washington, DC: U.S. Government Printing Office.

search Clinics' Coronary Primary Prevention Trial (Lipid Research Clinics Program, 1984a, 1984b), there was a lag of approximately 2 years between reduction of lipids and reduction of CHD.

In the Coronary Primary Prevention Trial, more than 3,800 middle-aged men with high cholesterol were placed on a low-fat diet and randomly assigned to either a cholestyramine bile acid sequestrant group or a placebo control group. At the end of the 7-year study, the experimental group reduced their total cholesterol and LDL cholesterol levels by 9% and 12%, respectively, compared with the controls. Definite CHD death and nonfatal myocardial infarction were 24% and 29% lower, respectively, in the drug group than the control group (Lipid Research Clinics Program, 1984a, 1984b).

In the Coronary Drug Project, a total of 3,908 men who had had heart attacks received either niacin or placebo. At the end of the 6-year study, the patients who had received the niacin had lowered their total blood cholesterol by 10% over the placebo control patients. No differences in total mortality were seen, although there was a slightly lower rate of reinfarction in the experimental group. At a 15-year measurement, 9 years after the end of the study, the mortality in the niacin group was 11% lower than in the placebo control group. This difference was attributed to the effect of the niacin on reducing the rate of reinfarction and the cholesterol-lowering effect of the medication (Canner et al., 1986).

In the Oslo Study Diet and Antismoking Trial (Hjermann, Holme, & Leren, 1986), 1,200 middle-aged men with high cholesterol were randomly assigned to intervention or control groups. At the conclusion of the 5-year study, total cholesterol values were lowered 13% in the intervention group and only 3% in the control group. The incidence of fatal and nonfatal myocardial infarction and sudden death was 47% lower in the intervention patients than the controls. The results were similar at a follow-up completed 3 to 4 years after completion of the study: the intervention patients had 45% fewer clinical coronary events than the control patients. Total mortality was also significantly different between the two conditions. There was a 33% lower incidence of mortality in the intervention patients at 5 years and a 40% lower incidence at 8 to 9 years.

In the Stockholm Ischaemic Heart Study, 560 patients who had had heart attacks were randomly assigned to either a treatment condition in which they received niacin and clofibrate or to a control group. At the end of the 5-year study, the intervention patients had lowered their total cholesterol by 13% and their triglycerides by 19%, had 26% fewer deaths, and had 36% fewer deaths due to ischemic heart disease compared with the control group (Carlson & Rosenhamer, 1988).

Finally, in the Cholesterol Lowering Atherosclerosis Study (Blankenhorn et al., 1987), 162 patients who had received coronary artery bypass surgery were given either nicotinic acid and colestipol or a placebo. Over 2 years, the intervention patients raised their HDL cholesterol by 37% and lowered their LDL cholesterol by 43%. Atherosclerotic regression was seen in 16% of the intervention patients compared with 3.6% of the placebo controls.

Despite recent attacks on the value of reducing cholesterol levels (Moore, 1989), these studies using lipid-lowering drugs and/or diets provide strong support that lowering total cholesterol and LDL cholesterol will reduce myocardial infarctions and mortality from CHD. In addition, the Helsinki Heart Study and the Cholesterol Lowering Atherosclerosis Study suggest that increasing HDL cholesterol also will reduce CHD events. Biobehavioral researchers are increasingly turning their attention away from diet-only approaches for high-risk patients to the more efficacious combined diet–drug interventions for effective control of lipids. This appears to be a strong growing trend in the entire behavioral medicine field.

Elevated Blood Pressure

High blood pressure affects 58 million Americans, about 30% of the adult population (Subcommittee on Definition and Prevalence of the

1984 Joint National Committee, 1985). There is a direct relationship between increasing diastolic blood pressure and cardiovascular mortality (Cupples & D'Agostino, 1987). Controlling high blood pressure reduces both cardiovascular morbidity and mortality.

THE NATIONAL HIGH BLOOD PRESSURE EDUCATION PROGRAM

The National High Blood Pressure Education Program (NHBPEP) was established in 1972 as a cooperative effort between the NHLBI, which coordinates its activities, and several professional and voluntary health agencies. Its goal is to reduce death and disability related to elevated blood pressure through professional, patient and public education. The NHBPEP is a coalition of approximately 15 federal agencies, 150 national agencies, almost all state health departments, and more than 2,000 community-based programs (Roccella & Horan, 1988).

Recent data suggest that the NHBPEP has been highly effective in accomplishing its aims. Public knowledge about high blood pressure has increased over the past several years. In 1973 only 24% of Americans knew that high blood pressure was a cause of heart disease and 29% knew it was a cause of stroke. By 1985 92% of Americans were aware that it increased their chances of developing heart disease and 77% knew that it could result in a stroke (U.S. Department of Health and Human Services, 1989c). Healthy behaviors have also improved. Physician visits for high blood pressure increased 74% between 1972 and 1986 compared with a 9% increase for all causes during the same time period. By 1984, 85% of individuals with high blood pressure were aware of their condition compared with 51% in 1972. The rate of control of high blood pressure more than tripled between 1972 and 1984, from 16% to 57%. Age-adjusted mortality rates for stroke declined 48% from 1972 through 1985 (Roccella & Horan, 1988).

NONPHARMACOLOGICAL TREATMENTS OF HYPERTENSION

Hypertension can be controlled by a number of pharmacological agents; however, concerns over the potential risks of using drugs has led to a large number of studies by behavioral scientists investigating the efficacy of various nonpharmacological interventions. The primary nonpharmacological approaches to lowering blood pressure are dietary: weight reduction for obese individuals, sodium restriction, and reduction of alcohol.

Weight Reduction. There is a strong relationship between increasing body weight and blood pressure. For example, the Framingham study documented clearly that relative weight, body weight change over time, and skinfold thickness are directly related to blood pressure and to the development of hypertension (Kannel, Brand, Skinner, Dawber, & McNamara, 1967; Dawber, 1980). About 44% of individuals with hypertension are obese compared with only 16% of normotensives (Horan & Roccella, 1988). The underlying mechanisms by which obesity may be associated with high blood pressure include expanded blood volume, elevated cardiac output associated with volume expansion, increased intake of dietary sodium and vascular responsiveness to sodium, and increased adrenergic output (Dustan, 1985).

Hovell's (1982) review of the literature documents the favorable short-term changes in blood pressure with weight reduction. Because of the evidence linking obesity with hypertension and the findings that reductions in weight tend to result in lowered blood pressure, along with positive changes in blood lipids, glucose, and uric acid, weight reduction and maintenance are major research priorities for control of this risk factor. Maintenance of desirable weight in reduced hypertensive formerly obese patients is among the most difficult behavioral research challenges.

Sodium Restriction. Although folklore tells us to cut down on salt to lower blood pressure, the actual role of sodium in the development and maintenance of hypertension is controversial, far more so than the relationship of obesity to blood pressure. Some individuals are sensitive to sodium and increasing the amount of dietary sodium raises their blood pressure. In others, sodium does not appear to affect blood pressure. Unfortunately, there is no available method for differentiating sodium-sensitive individuals from sodium-insensitive ones (Horan & Roccella, 1988). The lack of sensitivity to sodium in some individuals may help explain the mixed results reported in trials examining its relationship to hypertension (MacGregor et al., 1982; Richards et al., 1984).

The limited number of controlled studies on the effects of sodium restriction in hypertensive individuals to date have had small numbers of patients and have been of short duration (Horan & Roccella, 1988). However, because moderate restriction of sodium does not appear to be harmful to individuals, it is usually recommended for patients with high blood pressure. Data from the Dietary Intervention Study in Hypertension, for example, indicated that sodium restriction doubled the success of withdrawing drug therapy for hypertensive individuals controlled for 5 years (Langford et al., 1985). Research results to date, however, do not appear to be strong enough to recommend moderate sodium restriction to the general public.

Alcohol Restriction. From 5% to 11% of the hypertension in males is attributed to ingestion of alcohol (Friedman, Klatsky, & Siegelaub, 1982; MacMahon, Blacket, MacDonald, & Hall, 1984). This relationship appears to be independent of body weight, amount of exercise, smoking, and intake of sodium. Males who consume more than 80 mg of alcohol per day have a significantly higher prevalence of hypertension (Hennekens, 1983) than those who drink less. For hypertensive patients who drink, restriction of alcohol to less than 1 ounce of ethanol per day, the equivalent of approximately two 12-ounce cans of beer, or two 4-ounce glasses of wine, or two 1-ounce shots of distilled spirits, is recommended (Horan & Roccella, 1988).

Other Nonpharmacological Approaches. Other nonpharmacological approaches to the treatment of high blood pressure include increasing dietary potassium, calcium, or magnesium. Vegetarians tend to have lower blood pressures than meat eaters; thus, vegetarian-type eating plans have sometimes been recommended. Reducing dietary fat, protein, and simple carbohydrate and increasing dietary fiber have been attempted in several studies for reduction of blood pressure. Cutting down on caffeine and nicotine have also been tried. The role of exercise and blood pressure is a complex one, although, in general, individuals who exercise regularly tend to have lower blood pressures than sedentary ones (Blair, Goodyear, Gibbons, & Cooper, 1984; Paffenbarger, Thorne, & Wing, 1968). All of these strategies require additional research, especially studying the combination of diet and exercise with drug therapy. At present, not enough research evidence is available for any of these approaches to make clinical recommendations for their inclusion in programs for the treatment of high blood pressure (Horan & Roccella, 1988).

STRESS REDUCTION STRATEGIES

Stress reduction strategies for the control of blood pressure have received considerable interest from behavioral researchers in recent years. Relaxation therapy and biofeedback techniques are typically used as part of an overall treatment package. Studies suggest that modest reductions in blood pressure occur following their introduction (McCaffrey & Blanchard, 1985), although some studies show no changes (Blanchard, Miller, Abel, Haynes, & Wicker, 1979). For example, Blanchard, Khramelashvili, et al. (1988) reported the results of a cross-cultural comparison of thermal biofeedback and autogenic training to a self-relaxation control group in 59 unmedicated males with mild hypertension. Identical assessment and 10-week interventions were conducted in Albany, New York, and Moscow, USSR. Results showed comparable significant short-term decreases in diastolic blood pressure (DBP) for both interventions at both sites. The USSR patients had significantly higher baseline systolic blood pressures (SBP), and they also showed significant decreases at posttreatment; the American patients did not change their SBP. The Soviets showed better maintenance of gains than the Americans. At 1-year follow-up, 75% of the Soviets had DBP less than 90 mm Hg compared with only 24% of the Americans. The follow-up differences may have been due to the fact that the Soviets were younger, had been hypertensive longer, and had higher baseline SBP values. The Soviets also may have been more motivated to practice the stress reduction strategies or they may have perceived hypertension as a more serious illness than the Americans.

Aivazyan, Zaitsev, Salenko, Yurenev, and Patrusheva (1988) randomized 117 Soviet patients into groups receiving autogenic training, biofeedback, or breathing–relaxation training or to a placebo control group. Treatment lasted 6 weeks. The authors reported that the biofeedback and the breathing–relaxation training resulted in the greatest reductions in blood pressures. Overall, the effects of training were modest but lasted up through a 1-year follow-up.

The Hypertension Intervention Pooling Project began in 1983 by the NHLBI to assess the potential need for large-scale trials using behavioral stress reduction strategies for the treatment of high blood pressure. In 1984 the project began integrating data from 12 independent randomized studies on stress management-based interventions for high blood pressure. These studies totaled about 1,100 patients. Initial findings on a subset of 733 patients from nine studies covering baseline, posttreatment, and 1-year follow-up are now available (Kaufmann et al., 1988). Results from a number of the individual projects have also been published (Agras, Taylor, Kraemer, Southam, & Schneider, 1987; Blanchard et al., 1986; Chesney, Black, Swan, & Ward, 1987; Goldstein, Shapiro, & Thananopavaren, 1984; Goldstein, Shapiro, Thananopavaren, & Sambhi, 1982; Hatch et al., 1985; Jacob et al., 1986).

The overall meta analysis of the projects showed a modest benefit of the stress management strategies with respect to DBP but not to SBP on nonmedicated patients (Kaufmann et al., 1988). Patients with higher baseline blood pressures showed the greatest favorable changes.

The authors found no significant effect of the interventions on the medicated patients; however, they point out that potential differential effectiveness of the prescribed medications and the differences in compliance made it difficult to evaluate the effects of the behavioral interventions. At the 1-year follow-up, only one clinic had reported data on nonmedicated patients and controls. In that clinic, differences between treated patients and controls were not significant at either posttreatment or follow-up. The authors suggest that among the reasons for their modest results were the lack of selection criteria for admittance to the studies (i.e., the treatments may be more effective with some hypertensive subgroups than others) and the fact that most patients in the studies were only mildly hypertensive (i.e., patients with higher blood pressure at baseline do better regardless of treatment). The authors conclude by suggesting the need for studies concerning the predictors of treatment effectiveness to help identify patients more likely to benefit from stress reduction interventions.

Unfortunately, results of these analyses to date do not provide strong evidence of efficacy for large-scale clinical trials on these stress management approaches for control of hypertension. Their usefulness appears to be limited to subgroups of hypertensive patients who are most responsive to their effects and as components of comprehensive intervention programs for control of this risk factor.

Cigarette Smoking

NHLBI SMOKING EDUCATION PROGRAM

The NHLBI Smoking Education Program (SEP) was established in 1985 with a goal of reducing morbidity and mortality from tobacco-related cardiovascular and pulmonary diseases (U.S. Department of Health and Human Services, 1989c). SEP directs its efforts toward health professionals and interventions at the worksite. The program is aimed at motivating health professionals to intervene with their tobacco-dependent patients.

SURGEON GENERAL'S REPORT

The first Surgeon General's report on smoking and health was published in 1964 (U.S. Public Health Service, 1964), the 20th in 1989 (U.S. Department of Health and Human Services, 1989b). Over this quarter century, there have been dramatic shifts in attitudes toward tobacco

BEHAVIORAL MEDICINE

products and their use in the United States. These changes have been documented in the latest report of the Surgeon General, *Reducing the Health Consequences of Smoking: 25 Years of Progress*. The five major conclusions of the report are:

- The prevalence of smoking among adults decreased from 40% in 1965 to 29% in 1987. Nearly half of all living adults who ever smoked have quit.
- Between 1964 and 1985, approximately three-quarters of a million smoking-related deaths were avoided or postponed as a result of decisions to quit smoking or not to start. Each of these avoided or postponed deaths represented an average gain in life expectancy of two decades.
- The prevalence of smoking remains higher among blacks, blue-collar workers, and less educated persons than in the overall population. The decline in smoking has been substantially slower among women than among men.
- Smoking begins primarily during childhood and adolescence. The age of initiation has fallen over time, particularly among females. Smoking among high school seniors leveled off from 1980 through 1987 after previous years of decline.
- Smoking is responsible for more than one of every six deaths in the United States. Smoking remains the single most important preventable cause of death in our society. (U.S. Department of Health and Human Services, 1989b, p. 11)

Antismoking programs appear to have had a remarkable influence on the decline in smoking prevalence rates. In the absence of such programs, the report indicates that there would have been 91 million smokers age 15 and older in the United States in 1985 instead of 56 million. These figures suggest that an estimated 789,000 smoking-related deaths were avoided or postponed over the 25-year period. An estimated 2.1 million smoking-related deaths will be avoided or postponed between 1986 and the year 2000.

The report gives major research priority to several high-risk groups: children and adolescents, women, minorities, and blue-collar workers. Continuing declines in the prevalence of smoking are expected to slow unless organizations that represent these groups take active roles in education and intervention (U.S. Department of Health and Human Services, 1989b). Schools, parent organizations, women's groups, minority organizations, labor unions, and employers are needed to participate in programs for smoking prevention and cessation. The role of the behavioral researcher will increasingly turn to even more active involvement with these organizations, taking the lead in designing and evaluating efficacious programs for these high-risk subgroups. Other high-risk subgroups that need to be targeted for intervention include military personnel, high school dropouts, unemployed individuals, pregnant women, and heavy smokers (see Chapter 6, this volume, for research trends in the tobacco area).

RIP: TYPE A BEHAVIOR PATTERN

Like a shooting star that becomes brighter as it rises in the heavens and then falls to the earth extinguished, behavioral medicine's first cardiovascular risk factor, the Type A behavior pattern (TABP), seems to have finally burned itself out. Dating from the pioneering studies of Friedman and Rosenman in the 1950s, the TABP in only a short period of time became the most prominent and the most heavily researched behavioral factor associated with CHD.

The idea that an individual's state of mind affects one's heart certainly was not a new one. Scientists, poets, researchers, and clinicians have for years documented the relationship of feelings, personality traits, and behaviors on the heart and body. Psychological and behavioral factors do appear to play causal roles in the development of CHD. However, Friedman and Rosenman, two cardiologists, were the first to use the term "Type A behavior pattern" to refer specifically to a constellation of behaviors that described a large number of their own patients who came to them with CHD (Friedman & Rosenman, 1974). These patients were characterized by very high levels of competitiveness, impatience, a constant sense of time urgency, aggressive drive, and high levels of hostility (Friedman & Rosenman, 1974). The TABP was contrasted with the Type B behavior pattern, which tended to be just the opposite, much more easygoing, relaxed, less competitive, and less aggressive.

The TABP is typically assessed using the "structured interview" (SI; Rosenman et al, 1964) which was designed to examine patients' answers to questions about both everyday events and challenging situations. These interviews, which are conducted in a "mildly challenging" format (Rosenman, Swan, & Carmelli, 1988) by trained individuals, are tape recorded and rated by researchers who are taught to pay attention to various aspects of behavior. The patients then receive a global score, classifying them as Type A (either Type A1 or A2) or Type B (either B3 or B4). The SI has continued to be the favored method of assessment in this field, although there a number of self-report paper-and-pencil questionnaires that are also used, including the Jenkins Activity Survey (JAS; Jenkins, Rosenman, & Friedman,

1967), the Bortner Rating Scale (Bortner, 1969), and the Framingham Type A Scale (Haynes, Levine, Scotch, Feinleib, & Kannel, 1978).

Prospective Population Studies

The first major prospective trial that assessed the relationship of the TABP with CHD was the Western Collaborative Group Study (Rosenman et al., 1975). A total of 3,154 adult males free of CHD were followed for 8.5 years. Using the SI to assess behavior patterns, 50.4% were found to be Type A and 49.6% to be Type B at the beginning of the study. The trial was double-blind, with the investigators unaware of the subjects' behavior pattern or health status. At the end of 8.5 years, the subjects found to be Type A at baseline had a risk ratio of 2.2 for the development of CHD compared with the Type Bs. After statistically accounting for other CHD risk factors, the relationship persisted. Other analyses of the data using the JAS showed similar results (Jenkins, Rosenman, & Zyzanski, 1974; Brand, Jenkins, & Rosenman, 1978).

Data from the Framingham study have been used to assess the relationship of the TABP to CHD. A total of 949 women and 725 males, 45 to 77 years of age and free of CHD, were tested using the Framingham Type A Scale (Haynes et al., 1978). Multivariate analyses of 8-year incidence data showed that the TABP was an independent predictor of CHD and heart attacks in 45- to 64-year-old males and of CHD and angina in 45- to 64-year-old females (Haynes, Feinleib, & Kannel, 1980). Results were strongest in white-collar males. Similar results were found in the 10-year incidence data (Haynes & Feinleib, 1982).

In the French–Belgian Collaborative Study (French–Belgian Collaborative Group, 1982), 2,811 male civil servants and factory workers in Brussels and Ghent, Belgium, and in Paris and Marseilles, France, free from CHD, were assessed for the TABP by the Bortner Rating Scale (Bortner, 1969). Average follow-up time varied among groups, from 4.5 years to 8 years. Multivariate analyses of the combined data revealed that the TABP was a significant predictor of total CHD, myocardial infarction, and sudden death, although the data were not significant in each cohort analyzed separately (French–Belgian Collaborative Group, 1982).

A total of 1,958 males, 40 to 55 years of age, free of CHD, were followed for 5 years in the Belgian Heart Disease Prevention Trial (DeBacker, Dramaix, Kittel, & Kornitzer, 1983). The TABP was assessed using the JAS. Results indicated that the TABP predicted total CHD. A total of 2,187 males of Japanese descent, 51 to 70 years of age, were followed for 8 years in the Honolulu Heart Study (Cohen, Syme, Jenkins, Kagan, & Zyzanski, 1979). Subjects were tested with the JAS. After 8 years, no relationship between the TABP and CHD, myocardial infarction, or angina was found (Cohen & Reed, 1985).

Prospective Studies of High-Risk Individuals

The Multiple Risk Factor Intervention Trial (MRFIT) enrolled 12,772 males in 22 clinical centers. All subjects were free of CHD but had high cholesterol, high blood pressure, or smoked cigarettes. A total of 3,110 males from eight centers completed the JAS and a subset participated in the SI. Subjects were randomly assigned to special care or usual care conditions and followed for 7 years. Results showed no relationship between the TABP and mortality (Shekelle, Billings, et al., 1985).

In the Aspirin Myocardial Infarction Study, 2,070 males and 244 females, 29 to 69 years of age, who had had heart attacks, were randomly assigned to either an aspirin or a placebo group and followed for 3 years. The JAS was used to assess TABP. The TABP was not able to predict recurrence of myocardial infarction (Shekelle, Gale, & Norusis, 1985).

The aim of the Multicenter Post-Infarction Program was to identify factors predictive of long-term survival following a heart attack. A total of 548 patients of a total sample of 866 patients took the JAS within 2 weeks after their discharge from a coronary care unit. Results showed no relation between Type A and mortality, left ventricular ejection fraction, time to death for nonsurvivors, or duration of stay in a coronary care unit (Case, Heller, Case, & Moss, 1985).

A number of studies of patients referred for angiographic evaluation of coronary atherosclerosis did not find a relationship between the TABP and CHD severity (e.g., Bass & Wade, 1982; Dimsdale, Hackett, Block, & Hutter, 1978; Dimsdale et al., 1979; Kornitzer et al., 1982; Krantz et al., 1981; Scherwitz, McKelvain, & Laman, 1983).

Studies of high-risk groups have generally failed to support the notion that Type A is a cardiovascular risk factor for mortality or for recurrent cardiovascular events (e.g., Shekelle, Billings, et al., 1985; Shekelle, Gale, & Norusis, 1985; Case et al., 1985). The assessment tool used to measure the TABP has frequently been cited as a primary reason for failure to find significant results (e.g., Rosenman et al., 1988). The JAS, in particular, has been criticized as being ineffectual in assessing the TABP, and the SI is usually cited as the gold standard in this field. However, the SI was used in the MRFIT study on a subsample of patients and results were also negative (Shekelle, Billings, et al., 1985).

Proper training of interviewers in how to conduct the SI has also been addressed as a factor in affecting outcome. The SI is a subjective instrument and is affected by bias and interpretation of the interviewers. If training in the SI is really so difficult and restricted to relatively few individuals taught by only a few mentors, its clinical utility is seriously compromised. Blood pressure, cholesterol, and smoking are fairly easy to measure; if Type A is not, its clinical usefulness as a potential risk factor is limited.

Components of Type A

Given the number of recent studies that have failed to support the role of Type A as an independent risk factor for CHD, researchers have shifted their focus to an examination of the specific components of the profile in an attempt to assess whether or not some of them might be significant predictors of risk. Among the components currently being investigated include hostility, anger, competitiveness, numerous speech characteristics (e.g., speed, volume, explosive words, and short response latency), self-referencing, and self-aggrandizement (claims of superiority compared with others).

Hostility has the strongest research support to date implicating it as a factor associated with CHD. According to Williams and Barefoot (1988), hostility is a cynical, mistrusting attitude toward others, and a willingness to express openly the anger and contempt engendered by this attitude, and is the core component of coronary prone behavior. Competitiveness also appears to have some research support, as does a sense of time urgency (as measured by rate of speaking and immediateness).

Unfortunately, hostility, competitiveness, and time urgency do not appear to be any better defined than the TABP. They also seem to be rather vague constructs in need of operational definitions if they are going to replace the TABP and be of use in this area.

Trends in Type A Research

A number of large trials published in the 1980s that failed to replicate the earlier Western Collaboration Group Study have dampened the enthusiasm so prevalent in the 1970s for the usefulness of the Type A behavior pattern as a psychosocial risk factor for coronary heart disease. These recent trials, appearing one after another, each reported no associations between Type A and incidence of CHD.

Measurement of the TABP and its components continues to be a major hurdle for researchers. The easily administered self-report measures, like the JAS, do not appear to be particularly useful alternatives to the more difficult-to-give SI. The SI appears to be a useful diagnostic instrument only with white middle- and upper-class males.

The global Type A construct does not appear to be useful in predicting CHD. The weight of the prospective trials does not support its continued use in this area. Rather, behavioral researchers have begun an examination of what components of the behavior pattern should be assessed. Hostility as a construct seems to have the most research support at this time. Whether or not it will prove helpful will depend on the clarity of its definition and measurement and its long-term predictive ability in future prospective trials.

The TABP captured enormous attention and popular interest from the general public in the 1970s and from biobehavioral scientists. Although there is still a large amount of research being published in this field, at this time, it appears that Type A is not going to survive as a viable construct in the cardiovascular field. The future of components, such as hostility, will depend on further research.

TRENDS IN CANCER RESEARCH AND CONTROL

Cancer is the second leading cause of death in the United States, accounting for about 22% of annual mortality (National Center for Health Statistics, 1988). The prevalence of cancer increases with age and, unlike heart disease, the mortality rates over the past 35 years for all cancer sites have generally not declined. Even though our population is aging, the age-adjusted mortality has been increasing. Bailar and Smith (1986), in their review of progress against cancer, concluded that the intense efforts at improving treatment in recent years have been a "qualified failure" and that "we are losing the war against cancer" (p. 1231).

The National Cancer Institute (NCI) has set a number of optimistic objectives with respect to cancer prevention, screening, and treatment for the year 2000. These objectives are summarized in Table 5-3. Overall, the NCI hopes to see a reduction in cancer mortality of 25% to 50%.

Lung cancer is the major killer, accounting for about 25% of all cancer deaths and approximately 6% of all deaths in the United States. In general, overall cancer mortality has been decreasing among younger individuals and increasing among older ones. Examining

TABLE 5-3. Cancer Control Objectives for the Year 2000

Action	Target	Year 2000 objective	Estimated reduction in cancer mortality rate by year 2000[a]
Prevention	Smoking	Reduce the percentage of adults who smoke from 34% (in 1983) to ≤15%	8%–15%, depending on when objective is achieved
	Diet	Reduce average consumption of fat from 38% to ≤25% of total energy intake; increase average consumption of fiber from 8–12 to 20–30 g/day	8%
Screening	Breast	Increase percentage of women aged 50–70 yr who have an annual physical examination coupled with mammography to 80% from 45% for physical examination alone and 15% for mammography	
	Cervix	Increase percentage of women who have a Papanicolaou smear every 3 yr to 90% from 79% (ages 20–39 yr) and to 80% from 57% (ages 40–70 yr)	3%
Treatment	Transfer research results to practice	Increase adoption of state-of-the-art treatment	10%–26%

Note. Adapted from *Cancer Control Objectives for the Nation 1985–2000* (DHHS Publication No. 86-2880) by the U.S. Department of Health and Human Services, 1986, p. 11, Washington, DC: U.S. Government Printing Office.

[a]Total mortality reduction equals approximately 25%–50%.

age-specific death rates, taking age and changes over time into account, over the past 35 years deaths from cancer actually declined by approximately 25% to 65% in age groups up through 44 years, and recently have begun to decline in ages 45 to 54 years (Breslow & Cumberland, 1988). There is, however, an uninterrupted increase in cancer mortality above age 54 years that is responsible for the overall increase in mortality reported. For the groups older than 54 years, lung cancer has been increasing, and the cause attributed to 80% to 90% of lung cancer deaths is cigarette smoking (Breslow & Cumberland, 1988). As mentioned earlier, lung cancer has now caught up with breast cancer as the leading cause of cancer mortality in females (U.S. Department of Health and Human Services, 1989b). The relative risk of lung cancer in female smokers increased by a factor of more than four since the early 1960s and is now similar to that identified for males in that period. Cigarette smoking has also now been associated with cancer of the uterine cervix (U.S. Department of Health and Human Services, 1989b).

Smoking and Cancer

The control of cigarette smoking, both in prevention and cessation, is therefore a critical issue in reduction of cancer morbidity and mortality. The statistics suggest that the reduction of cancer mortality in younger age groups may in part be due to the successes experienced in reduced smoking rates in younger ages, particularly males, and the increased mortality in older groups may in part be due to the relative failure of intervention programs to control cigarette smoking in these individuals.

Overall, the reduced cancer mortality data illustrate the progress that has been made with younger groups in smoking prevention and cessation programs. Because of the considerable lag in the effects of both prevention and treatment interventions or cancer mortality, current reductions in cancer deaths of white males stem in part from efforts begun 25 years ago; benefits of current programs will show themselves over the next several decades (Breslow & Cumberland, 1988). Behavioral scientists continue to play critical roles in the development of both prevention and intervention programs (see Chapter 6, this volume, for a review of research trends in this area). Continued emphasis on prevention will undoubtedly solidify gains that have been made and continue to have a major impact in reduced death rates from lung cancer. Achieving the year 2000 objective of reducing the percent-

BEHAVIORAL MEDICINE

age of smokers to 15%, thereby reducing mortality rates by 8% to 15%, will require enormous behavioral support from NIH and other agencies and associations. Increasing research funds for prevention programs aimed at children would appear to have the greatest long-term benefits.

Diet and Cancer

It has been estimated that the proportion of cancer deaths attributed to diet is about 35% overall, with a 10% to 70% range (Doll & Peto, 1981). The underlying mechanisms accounting for the relationship of diet, digestive processes, and cancer include the following (U.S. Department of Health and Human Services, 1988b):

- Carcinogens in food (i.e., those that occur naturally, inadvertently, or through cooking or preserving).
- Diet-induced metabolic activation or deactivation of carcinogens.
- Biologic formation of carcinogens *in vivo*.
- Enhancement (such as by fats) of promotion.
- Impairment of immunity through nutrient imbalance.

Dietary factors that have been evaluated for possible relationships to cancer risk include fat, total calories, fiber, foods high in Vitamin A and carotenoids, and alcohol (U.S. Department of Health and Human Services, 1988b). Other dietary factors that also might be involved include salt-cured, salt-pickled, and smoked foods, protein, selenium, vitamin C, and vitamin E.

The Surgeon General's report has reviewed the literature on these dietary factors and their possible roles in increasing or decreasing risk of various cancers (U.S. Department of Health and Human Services, 1988b). Dietary fat, for example, is believed to increase the risk for the development of cancers of the breast, colon, rectum, endometrium, and prostate. Many researchers believe that lowering dietary fat has the potential for reducing the incidence of these cancers. Weight loss and maintenance of desirable weight may also decrease the risk for most of these cancers. Diets low in fiber may increase the risk for colon cancer. Those high in fiber may decrease risk for both colon and rectal cancers. Foods containing high levels of vitamin A and carotenoids may decrease the risk of developing epithelial cell cancers, including cancers of the lung, bladder, and oral cavity. Reduction of alcohol consumption may lower the risk of developing cancers of the mouth, esophagus, and pharynx. Selenium may decrease overall cancer risk and cancers of the colon and rectum. However, because too much selenium is toxic, raising current dietary levels has not been recommended.

High levels of protein have been linked to cancer development in some epidemiologic research; however, the evidence is insufficient at this time to recommend decreases in the consumption of protein. Some studies have linked consumption of salt-cured, salt-pickled, and smoked foods with development of stomach and esophageal cancers.

Based on the available and frequently contradictory research studies, the NCI has been conservative in recommending dietary guidelines for the general population. The NCI guidelines are similar to those issued by the American Cancer Society, the United States Department of Agriculture/Department of Health and Human Services, and the American Heart Association.

These NCI dietary guidelines are as follows (Butrum, Clifford, & Lanza, 1988):

- Reduce fat to 30% or less of total calories.
- Increase fiber intake to 20 to 30 g/day, with an upper limit of 35 g/day.
- Include a variety of vegetables and fruits in the daily diet.
- Avoid obesity.
- Consume alcohol in moderation, if at all.
- Minimize consumption of salt-cured, salt-pickled, and smoked foods.

Reviewing the evidence for the role of diet and cancer, it is clear that controlled human research on the possible benefits of following NCI's guidelines is lacking and needed. Although difficult and expensive, long-term prospective studies examining diet's relationship to various cancers should be vigorously pursued. The role of behavioral researchers is a critical one, aimed at ensuring long-term adherence to the dietary guidelines.

The Surgeon General's report (U.S. Department of Health and Human Services, 1988b, p. 227) lists several areas of special research priorities related to the role of diet and cancer. Table 5-4 lists these priorities.

AIDS

Behavioral scientists are being put to the ultimate test in dealing with the acquired immune deficiency syndrome (AIDS) epidemic. Do our

TABLE 5-4. Research and Surveillance

Research and surveillance issues of special priority related to the role of diet in cancer should include these investigations:

- Molecular mechanisms of carcinogenesis and the ways in which initiating or promoting events may be affected by specific components of dietary fat, fiber, protein, alcohol, vitamin A, carotenoids, and other vitamins or minerals
- Quantitative relationships between food and nutrient intake and cancer incidence through chemoprevention and dietary clinical trials
- The effect of specific components of dietary fat, fiber, vitamin A, and carotenoids on cancer etiology
- Interactions between dietary factors such as fat, fiber, calories, protein, and specific vitamins and minerals in cancer prevention and causation
- Development of biochemical markers of dietary intake to better monitor effects of dietary intervention on cancer risk
- Patterns of food intake best associated with cancer prevention
- Development of national population data on food and nutrient consumption patterns and specific cancer rates, including more accurate assessment of intake of specific dietary factors within relatively homogeneous population groups
- Levels of carcinogenic and mutagenic substances in the food supply
- Dietary guidance methods that are most effective in helping people improve patterns of food intake
- The causes of wasting and malnutrition in cancer patients and the effects of nutritional support on response to therapy and survival in these patients

Note. From *The Surgeon General's Report on Nutrition and Health* (DHHS Publication No. 88-50210) by the U.S. Department of Health and Human Services, 1988b, p. 227, Washington, DC: U.S. Government Printing Office.

current biopsychosocial theories of behavior change help us to understand why some infected individuals continue to spread the virus? Are the theories effective in helping design practical behavior modification programs to reduce the spread of the virus? Are our behavior change interventions powerful enough to help prevent further infection? What are the most appropriate roles for behavioral scientists in responding to the AIDS epidemic? What are the limitations of our theories and interventions?

As is now well known, AIDS is a disease that is predictive of cellular immune deficiency. It is caused by a virus, human immunodeficiency virus (HIV), that is responsible for the development of serum antibodies that infect and attack helper T-lymphocytes, the cells that activate immune system functioning. The virus is spread by infected blood and semen.

AIDS was first noticed in the United States in 1981. Since then, the total number of reported cases in this country has exceeded 100,000, with more than 59,000 AIDS-related deaths (Centers for Disease Control, 1989c). The first 50,000 cases of AIDS were diagnosed between 1981 and 1987, the second 50,000 between December 1987, and July 1989. By 1991, there will be approximately 270,000 cases of AIDS in the United States. In 1988 it ranked 15th among the leading causes of death (National Center for Health Statistics, 1989). Approximately 93% of all AIDS cases are male, and 70% are younger than 39 years. As many as 1.0 to 1.5 million people are infected with HIV (Office of the Assistant Secretary of Health, 1988). Individuals with HIV antibodies are considered to be carriers and capable of transmitting the virus to others (Centers for Disease Control, 1988b). About 54% of HIV-infected individuals will develop AIDS within 10 years of infection and up to 99% will eventually develop AIDS (Lui, Darrow, & Rutherford, 1988).

Because HIV reduces the helper T-lymphocytes, it reduces the immune system's ability to resist illnesses and infections. Among the diseases and infections commonly associated with AIDS include a number of malignancies (e.g., Kaposi's sarcoma, which affects about one-third of AIDS patients), viruses (e.g., cytomegalovirus, herpes, Epstein–Barr virus), protozoa (e.g., *Pneumocystis carinii* pneumonia, *Toxoplasma gondii*), fungi (e.g., candida, *Cryptococcus neoformans*), and bacteria (e.g., several mycobacterium species) (Kelly & St. Lawrence, 1988). Because AIDS is communicable and the only disease where mortality is substantially continuing to increase (Centers for Disease Control, 1988b), it is considered to be the number one health problem in this country (Pelosi, 1988).

The incidence of AIDS currently doubles every 8 to 10 months (Centers for Disease Control, 1988b). Approximately 70% of AIDS cases are homosexual males. Heterosexually transmitted AIDS accounts for only about 4% of total incidence (Centers for Disease Control, 1989b). Intravenous (IV) drug use accounts for about 21% of the incidence. The incidence of AIDS among blacks and hispanics is more than double the percentage of these minorities in this country. Ethnic minorities account for 40% of AIDS cases, with blacks accounting for about 24% and hispanics, 14%.

At a behavioral level, it is clear how to stop the AIDS epidemic. AIDS is a behaviorally transmitted disease. New HIV infection occurs through direct exposure to the semen or blood of an infected individual, primarily through sexual contact or sharing needles for IV drug use. Stop sexual contact and IV needle-sharing with infected individuals and AIDS will be stopped. Behaviorally, uninfected individuals should not engage in unprotected high-risk sexual behaviors (or, better yet, any sexual behaviors) with HIV-positive individuals. IV drug users should use clean needles and protect themselves from infected blood. If done, and the blood supply for transfusions, a public health issue, is tested and kept uninfected, the number of new HIV-infected individuals will decline to almost none. Because these are clearly behavioral issues, the role of behavioral medicine is a major one in this area. This is the chance for behavioral scientists to shine.

In actual practice, what we know about behavior change with respect to sexual and drug behavioral patterns is limited. Behavioral research has always been underfunded and undervalued as a means for developing effective prevention programs in the areas of drug abuse and high-risk sexual behaviors (Watkins, 1988).

What are the processes involved in the initiation, maintenance, and cessation of high-risk sexual and drug use behaviors? Why would anyone have unprotected sex with or continue to have sex with someone who was or might be infected with the virus? Why would anyone share a needle with someone else, given the possibility that it might be infected? Process data about how decisions are made in these areas are clearly needed.

To date, almost all efforts to prevent further infection have relied on the dissemination of health education messages about the behavioral risk factors associated with the spread of the virus (Stall, Coates, & Hoff, 1988). For example, Emmons, Joseph, Kessler, Montgomery, and Ostrow (1986) found that, of five psychosocial variables examined, knowledge about AIDS risk was the strongest measure correlated with reductions in risk-taking behaviors. McKusick, Horstman and Coates (1985) also reported preliminary data to suggest that making people aware of the high risks associated with unprotected sex leads to some reduction in risk-taking behavior.

Knowledge of AIDS antibody test results can lead to behavior change. In a group of gay and bisexual males who ultimately tested positive, the percent who practiced unprotected anal intercourse decreased from 48% to 12% (Coates, Morin, & McKusick, 1987). Van Griensven et al. (1988), Schechter et al. (1988), and McKusker et al. (1988) also have reported some beneficial effects of antibody testing. Similar data have been reported for IV drug users (Des Jarlais & Friedman, 1988).

Unfortunately, despite increased knowledge in this area, not all individuals change their behavior appropriately; a large number fail to adopt appropriate precautions and continue to expose themselves to potential infection (Becker & Joseph, 1988; Temoshok, Sweet & Zich, 1987). Siegel, Bauman, Christ, and Krown (1988) reported that despite adequate levels of knowledge concerning risk reduction guidelines, 48% of a sample of 162 asymptomatic gay and bisexual males studied continued to engage in risky sexual behavior. Similar to data in other health areas, knowledge of risk behaviors appears necessary but is not usually sufficient to ensure long-term behavior change. Increased knowledge is frequently correlated with initial changes in behavior but additional intervention is required for sustained change to occur. Additional research into the circumstances under which some people continue to engage in unsafe behaviors even with sufficient knowledge and understanding should be high priority in this area (Stall, Coates, & Hoff, 1988).

For example, individuals who combine alcohol or drugs with sexual activity are significantly more likely to engage in unsafe sexual practices than individuals who do not (Stall, Wiley, McKusick, Coates, & Ostrow, 1986; Stall & Ostrow, 1989). Health beliefs of individuals appear to play a major role in the practice of unsafe sexual behaviors. Males who agreed strongly with statements such as "sexual behaviors are difficult to change" tended to be more negative about the use of condoms and more positive about the exchange of semen during oral sex (Communications Technologies, Inc., 1984). Males with low self-efficacy, the belief that an individual is capable of making appropriate behavioral changes, tend to engage in high-risk sexual behaviors more than males with high self-efficacy (Joseph et al., 1987).

Current AIDS and Behavioral Research Needs

The Chairman of the Presidential Commission on the Human Immunodeficiency Virus Epidemic, Admiral James D. Watkins (retired) (1988), outlined a number of initiatives the Commission felt were necessary in order to enhance the behavioral research efforts in this area. These initiatives included the following:

- Expanded funding by the U.S. Department of Health and Human Services for research on adolescents and adults aimed at identifying the determinants of risk behavior, models of behavior change interventions, social factors and strategies to effect behavior change, and evaluation and other methodologies.
- Funding for sponsoring training programs through the National Institute of Mental Health and the Centers for Disease Control for graduate and postgraduate HIV behavioral researchers.
- Funding for long-term collaborative efforts in behavioral research.

- Studies of targeted groups to identify attitudes and behaviors that should be modified or reinforced prior to the development of education programs or other interventions.
- Studies on the cost-effectiveness and efficacy of various channels for reaching targeted groups.
- Research into effective prevention and treatment of drug and alcohol abuse.

Initially, AIDS was seen primarily as a medical problem. Today, it is clear that for the disease to be conquered, behavioral science research is crucial to the fight. With enough biobehavioral researchers as members of multidisciplinary teams and enough funding, the disease hopefully will eventually be controlled.

BEHAVIORAL MEDICINE AT THE WORKSITE

The workplace has seen an explosion of both research and clinical programs aimed at health promotion and disease prevention. Cooperative efforts among unions, employers, employees, and health care professionals have served to spur the growth of these programs. These programs typically are aimed at one or more of the cardiovascular risk factors, including weight management, dietary modification for control of lipids and blood pressure, exercise, and stress management. There are many excellent reviews of worksite programs available (e.g., Bibeau, Mullen, McLeroy, Green, & Foshee, 1988; Cataldo & Coates, 1986; Glanz & Seewald-Klein, 1986; Glasgow & Terborg, 1988; Klesges & Cigrang, 1988; Sallis, Hill, Fortmann, & Flora, 1986; Terborg, 1986).

Weight Control and Nutrition Education Programs

Jeffery, Forster, and Schmid (1989) described an intervention program for weight control and smoking cessation at a worksite of 485 employees. The company manufactures power equipment in Bloomington, Minnesota. Identical interventions were offered twice at 6-month intervals. Total participation over a 1-year program included 53% of the overweight employees and 23% of the smokers. The two series of classes resulted in similar enrollment. A total of 39% of employees in the first weight control class and 6% of the employees in the smoking cessation class reenrolled in the second series. Results indicated that weight losses and smoking cessation rates were similar for the two cycles, with a mean weight loss of about 7 pounds and a smoking cessation rate at 6 months of about 33%. Surveys of a random sample at baseline and at 12 months showed a 28% reduction in smoking but no changes in weight. Based on their encouraging preliminary results, the investigators are now conducting a controlled study in which 30 worksites are randomized to either treatment or control conditions.

Weight reduction programs like the one described by Jeffery et al. (1989) typically result in average weight losses of 7 to 17 pounds, depending on length of intervention and amount of obesity of the employees. A major problem in these programs has been attrition, with dropout rates of 50% to 75% not uncommon. Like all clinical programs for weight reduction, maintenance of lost weight is the other major concern, with regain inevitable in a majority of participants following the end of the intervention.

Nutrition programs to reduce cholesterol are fairly recent and little controlled evaluation has been done (e.g., see Foreyt, Scott, & Gotto, 1980, and Glanz & Seewald-Klein, 1986, for reviews). What research has been done is promising and, given the growing interest in cholesterol in our society, these programs can be expected to continue to increase.

Smoking Cessation Programs

Smoking cessation programs at the worksite that are multicomponent and behaviorally based tend to result in reported cessation rates of 30% to 40% at 1 year (Glasgow & Terborg, 1988). Among the major problems reported with these multicomponent programs, however, is the low participation rate. Incentive and competition-based interventions appear to increase participation and produce encouraging cessation rates, but better experimental designs, including control groups and objective assessment measures, are needed for external validity. There is wide variability in treatment outcome in smoking cessation programs at the worksite, which may be the result of an interaction of organizational characteristics (e.g., companywide smoking restrictions) with program characteristics (Glasgow & Terborg, 1988).

Hypertension Programs

Well-run screening programs at the worksite can result in the identification of almost 100% of hypertensive employees and, with interven-

BEHAVIORAL MEDICINE

tion, up to 85% of them can be successfully brought under control, usually through antihypertensive medications (Alderman, 1984). More recently, worksite programs aimed at controlling mildly elevated blood pressure using nonpharmacological approaches (e.g., diet, stress management) have been attempted, but more data are needed to assess their effectiveness. A primary need in this area continues to be research evaluating the combination of nonpharmacological strategies along with medication.

Exercise Programs

Low participation rates by individuals at risk for cardiovascular problems, such as obese employees, continue to limit the potential effectiveness of worksite interventions for increasing rates of employee fitness. Employees who take advantage of jogging tracks, basketball courts, swimming pools, and weights frequently are the ones who are healthy and who pose relatively little CVD risk. A research priority in this area is studies aimed at increasing participation in these programs by a more representative sample of employees. To date, participation rates at the worksite are similar to the population as a whole, about 25%.

Trends in Research at the Worksite

Worksite programs offer a wonderful opportunity for behavioral researchers to implement interventions developed in the laboratory, hospital, and clinic to a much wider audience. Unfortunately, studies to date indicate that when these programs are implemented, as developed in the laboratory, they tend to result in very high attrition and little sustained behavior change. Clearly, the idiosyncratic nature of each worksite must be taken into account if such programs are going to result in long-term healthy changes. Promising research trends in this area involve worksite competitions and incentives to increase participation rates and reduce dropouts. However, such approaches do not appear to help with long-term maintenance; for worksite programs to have an impact, process studies aimed at increasing our understanding the charactertistics of different types of worksites and employees need to be done. Presumably, changes at the worksite itself (e.g., healthful food available in the cafeterias, smoking bans at the office, time available for exercising, and health insurance contingencies) will play the greatest role in long-term behavioral change. Behavioral scientists have important contributions to make in this area if they pay attention to the participant, program, and company issues involved in the design, implementation, and evaluation of these interventions.

STATUS OF POTENTIALLY PROMISING RESEARCH TECHNIQUES

In 1984, the Army Research Institute asked the National Academy of Sciences to investigate a number of potentially promising techniques developed outside of mainstream science to enhance human performance (Druckman & Swets, 1988). These techniques tended to have rather unbelievable claims made about their effectiveness. The Committee on Techniques for the Enhancement of Human Performance was formed in 1985 and charged with the responsibility of examining these techniques and making recommendations to the Army for future study. The committee was composed of distinguished scientists, including a number of widely respected psychologists, including a past president of the Association for Advancement of Behavior Therapy, Gerald C. Davison.

A number of the techniques investigated are relevant to behavioral scientists, including biofeedback and other stress management strategies. The conclusions of the committee were thoughtful and reflect current state-of-the-art thinking in a number of areas.

Sleep Learning. One area examined was sleep learning. The committee concluded that there was no evidence that any learning occurs during verified sleep, as assessed by electrical recordings of brain activity. However, during lighter stages of sleep, presentations of certain material may enhance learning. These findings warrant more controlled research.

Mental Practice. Often, when I travel by plane, I receive an advertising catalog for a company called SyberVision. The company advertises audiotapes and videotapes for quitting smoking, losing weight, improving golf and tennis swings, increasing self-discipline, and even staying young. I was pleased to see that the committee evaluated SyberVision, even sending two of its members to visit the headquarters and interviewing the founder, Stephen DeFore, and the director of research, Karl Pribram. The committee members limited their review to an audiotape for improving achievement and to a number of videotapes for improving sport skills, including golf, skiing, tennis, bowling, racquetball, and baseball. After the interviews and a review of the literature, the committee members reported that they could not find any research that tested the efficacy of these SyberVision tapes and that the only basis for claims of improved performance was from anecdotal accounts and personal testimonials from a number of satisfied users.

Overall, the committee found that the SyberVision program was a broad-based package that included "elements of modeling and imagery, a training guide, tips from professional athletes, and common psychological characteristics of winners." However, "if performance gains were observed, they could not be attributed to mental practice" (Druckman & Swets, 1988, pp. 69–70). The research evidence for neuromuscular programming was scant and the committee found no direct scientific evidence that the brain acts like a holographic processor or performs Fourier transforms (Druckman & Swets, 1988). The committee concluded that packages like SyberVision should not be evaluated apart from the types of mental practice training that already have an established research core. Mental practice accounts for about half a standard deviation in performance gain over control groups. Performance gains for motor tasks with major cognitive components improve when the mental practice is combined with physical practice.

Visual Concentration. What about visual concentration used so frequently in cognitive-behavior therapy? According to the committee, the enhancement of cognitive and behavioral skills through improving visual concentration was not supported by data. Biofeedback came in for close critical scrutiny. The committee concluded that the effects of biofeedback on skilled performance still remain to be demonstrated.

Stress Management. With respect to stress management strategies, the committee found that biofeedback can reduce muscle tension; however, "it does not reduce stress effectively" (Druckman & Swets, 1988, p. 21). Providing knowledge and understanding about future events and helping to provide a sense of control were seen as the most effective strategies for reducing stress.

Social Processes. Another strategy, more popular several years ago among some clinicians, neurolinguistic programming (NLP), was critically evaluated. No evidence was found to support the use of NLP as a strategy for exerting influence.

Parapsychological Techniques. What I found especially interesting was the committee's lengthy report on their investigation of parapsychology. As expected, the committee members concluded that in their review of the literature they found no credible support for the existence of parapsychological phenomena.

Summary of Report. The committee is to be commended for a stimulating, well-researched report for the U.S. Army. The report

(Druckman & Swets, 1988) is highly recommended to researchers in behavioral medicine for its conclusions and its sensible recommendations for further study. A number of the strategies reviewed are highly relevant and widely used in behavioral medicine, and the committee's critical review of them will be helpful in shaping new research.

EDUCATION AND TRAINING TRENDS IN HEALTH PSYCHOLOGY

Education and training for health psychology service providers have received increasing attention as the field has continued to expand. What kinds of training should a psychologist who treats patients with headaches, eating disorders, or cancer have? Training in clinical psychology has traditionally followed the Boulder model with students completing Ph.D. programs taught how to conduct and evaluate research, perform psychological assessments, and do psychotherapy. Today, students graduating with Ph.D.'s in psychology are required to receive additional supervised experience before being licensed to practice independently.

The Arden House conference (Brownell, 1985; Stone, 1983) proposed that there be a range of training for students of health psychology, from predoctoral studies resulting in a Ph.D. (Boll et al., 1983), to a predoctoral internship of 1 year's duration (Strickland et al., 1983), plus a 2-year postdoctoral residency (Matarazzo et al., 1983).

At the predoctoral level, training should be consistent with American Psychological Association (APA) accreditation criteria and include a health psychology track consisting of instruction in human physiology, pathophysiology, neuropsychology, psychopharmacology, psychopathology, human development over the life cycle, and social systems theory. Specialized training specific to health psychology in epidemiological and prospective research skills, assessment, intervention, consultation, short-term psychotherapy, family interventions, group dynamics, and sensitization to group and ethnic norms was also recommended.

At the postdoctoral level, additional instruction in such areas as intervening with presurgical and postsurgical patients, chemically dependent and eating disordered patients, patients in pain and those with chronic illnesses, patients with cardiovascular diseases, and parents of high-risk infants was suggested. Training in how to supervise others and learning how to liaison with other disciplines was also considered important.

These skills were considered entry-level preparation for individuals entering this field, and the participants at the Arden House conference recommended that the 2-year postdoctoral training course be required for licensed health care service providers in health psychology (Stone, 1983). Sheridan et al. (1988) have recently published detailed guidelines for this 2-year specialty postdoctoral training program.

Students must have a Ph.D. or a Psy.D. from an APA-approved program of training in professional psychology. Prerequisites include having completed a track in health psychology and a 1-year predoctoral internship. The 2-year specialty training program is housed primarily in a general hospital or facility with a full range of medical and surgical services. Faculty supervisors include licensed interdisciplinary psychologists. Students complete at least two rotations during each of the 2 years and receive training in at least six of these nine areas: relaxation and biofeedback therapies; short-term individual, group, and family therapies; consultation and liaison skills; neuropsychological assessment and assessment of specific patient populations, such as pain patients and spinal cord injury patients; behavior modification principles; hypnosis; health promotion and public education skills; major treatment programs, such as eating disorders and chemical dependency; and compliance motivation (Sheridan et al., 1988).

Health psychology is a rapidly expanding specialty for health service providers in psychology. With its explosive growth, some formal criteria for certification are helpful. Sheridan et al., (1988) and the participants at the Arden House conference (Stone, 1983) have provided helpful guidelines for education in this field. The specialized training required for work in health psychology and behavioral medicine cannot be completely taught in traditional graduate programs. Practitioners in relevant disciplines must be comfortable in medical settings, working with interdisciplinary teams, and familiar with and competent in a broad range of interventions. I hope that other professionals in disciplines that are also increasingly becoming involved in aspects of health psychology and behavioral medicine, including nurses, registered dietitians, exercise physiologists, and others, will also develop similar appropriate training guidelines for their own professions.

CHAPTER

6

THE ADDICTIVE DISORDERS

JOHN P. FOREYT

INTRODUCTION

Research on the assessment and treatment of addictive disorders continues to increase. Journals such as *Addictive Behaviors, International Journal of Obesity,* and *Journal of Substance Abuse* are devoted solely to the publication of studies on these topics, and essentially all of the broader journals in medicine, psychology, nutrition, public health, and health promotion devote considerable space to the addictions. Reasons for this continued interest have to do in part with the great difficulty therapists have in helping patients suffering from any of these disorders achieve long-term success. For researchers and therapists, any information that provides a better understanding of the addictions is welcome news. Happily, there have been a number of recent advances in our understanding of these refractory disorders and they are reviewed in this chapter.

OBESITY

This chapter's section on obesity begins with new data on prevalence rates suggesting that despite all we read about the emphasis on health and fitness in the United States, obesity still afflicts more than one in five adults. As one indication of the intense interest in diet and nutrition, three major reports have been released since the last edition of this series. The Surgeon General has issued his first ever report on nutrition and health. The Committee on Diet and Health of the National Research Council has published its report, which suggests priorities for research in this area, and the Council of Scientific Affairs of the American Medical Association has released its report on the treatment of adult obesity. These three reports are reviewed and summarized.

Another development has been the increased attention to the treatment of moderate and severe obesity. Four treatment strategies are reviewed. First, the immense popularity of the very-low-calorie diets has caught many professionals by surprise. Do they work? Should behavior therapists get involved with them? Second, drug treatments are more prevalent than ever. What success have therapists had combining behavioral training with anorectic agents? Third, the gastric bubble craze has been here and burst. Did the bubble have any effect on weight loss? And fourth, the gastric bypass has now completely replaced the old jejunoileal bypass and appears to be the treatment of choice for severely obese patients by a large number of surgeons. Whom should behavior therapists refer for gastric bypass?

The treatment of choice for mild obesity continues to be a combination of low-fat diet, regular exercise, and behavior therapy. What advancements have been made in the treatment of adult mild obesity? A review of the literature (Bennett, 1987) suggests that no worthwhile progress has occurred in the dietary treatment of obesity since outcome studies in this area were first published over 50 years ago. Finally, new outcome data on longer treatments, the role of exercise in treatment, and the continued difficulty in achieving long-term maintenance are covered.

New Data on Prevalence

Prevalence estimates of obesity for 32 states and the District of Columbia were reported by the Centers for Disease Control (1989a) based on information from the 1987 Behavioral Risk Factor Surveillance System (BRFSS). State health departments collected data on a number of behavioral risk factors using random-digit telephone interviews of adults. The data are all self-reports and are adjusted for age, sex, and race. In the survey, overweight was defined as a body mass index—BMI = weight (kg)/height (m)^2—$\geq$ 27.8 for men and $\geq$ 27.3 for women. These BMI values are the 85th percentile for adults 20 to 29 years of age (National Center for Health Statistics, 1987b). The four states with the highest prevalence of overweight were Wisconsin (25.7%), Indiana (25.7%), West Virginia (25.1%), and Ohio (25.0%). The four states with the lowest prevalence were New Mexico (15.2%), Hawaii (15.5%), Utah (16.6%), and Montana (16.7%).

Table 6-1 lists the prevalence of overweight in selected states by sex. The median prevalence of overweight for all participating states was 21.1%. According to the survey, an estimated 21.8% of men and 21.1% of women are overweight. Overweight is highest in the Midwest (23.1%), followed by the South (22.0%) and the Northeast (19.8%), with the West (17.0%) having the lowest prevalence. The pattern did not change after adjustment for age, sex, and race. The authors (Centers for Disease Control, 1989a) suggest that their survey results may be underestimates because the data are all self-reported over the telephone. For example, the Second National Health and Nutrition Examination Survey (NHANES II; National Center for Health Statistics, 1987b), which relied on measured heights and weights, estimated that 24.2% of men and 27.1% of women are overweight (both NHANES II and BRFSS used the same BMI criteria for overweight). Nevertheless, overweight clearly differs by state and region. Reasons for these differences may involve the kinds and amounts of foods eaten and levels of activity. Having been born and raised in Wisconsin, I was not surprised by the way the results came out. The Midwest appears to me to be this country's "fat belt." I think that special efforts should be aimed at states with the highest levels of overweight. Hopefully, behavioral researchers in those states will use these data to mount campaigns aimed at encouraging healthful activity levels and reduction in high-fat food consumption. Come on, Wisconsin, shape up!

Surgeon General's Report on Nutrition and Health

The eagerly awaited, first-ever Surgeon General's Report on Nutrition and Health (U.S. Department of Health and Human Services, 1988b) proved disappointing to many readers, including behavior therapists involved in obesity research who had hoped that the book would have had a stronger behavioral emphasis. Unfortunately, the 723-page tome turned out to be primarily a compilation of existing knowledge about the by now well-known relationships between diet and chronic diseases. Although the report will be helpful to behavioral researchers looking to increase their understanding of the role of dietary factors with respect to morbidity and mortality, surprisingly little else will be of much interest. I was pleased to see basic chapters on child nutrition, aging, and drug–nutrient interactions, but was surprised that the Surgeon General was apparently not aware of the many advances that have occurred in the behavioral sciences in these areas.

The report appears to me to be overly cautious in its advice to the general public. Precise goals are absent. For example, although the report's major message is clearly the conclusion that Americans eat too much fat, nowhere does the Suregon General cite his recommended goal for fat consumption. Authoritative groups such as the American Heart Association and the American Cancer Society have long ago agreed upon a goal of no more than 30% of calories from fat. This lack of any precise recommendations in the Surgeon General's report based on current knowledge seriously limits its usefulness to behavior therapists and researchers who are interested in such goals for their work. Couching recommendations in broad generalities, although sure to offend no one, does a great disservice to the field. This surprisingly timid approach is especially disappointing given the strong, precise recommendations the Surgeon General has made in his numerous reports on the use of tobacco products. It appears evident that nutrition and health is not a priority, as is smoking, to the Surgeon General.

Table 6-2 presents the report's main conclusions. As you see, they are common-sense, well-known platitudes (e.g., eat less fat, eat more vegetables, etc.), and will cause little disagreement, but will do little behaviorally to advance changes in the American diet. The report would have been far more helpful to behavior therapists if it had included up-to-date reviews of the adherence and compliance literature with respect to dietary behaviors, discussions of prevention strategies especially related to children, and maintenance and relapse prevention research recommendations for both the general population and specific high-risk groups.

The chapter on obesity, for example, contains seven pages on the "Definition of Obesity" (pp. 279-285) and eight pages on the "Causes of Obesity" (pp. 290-297). Treatment of obesity is allocated a scant three pages (pp. 297-299), with only one paragraph (14 lines) devoted to the topic "Behavior Modification" (p. 298). Maintenance is not even mentioned.

Fifteen general recommendations for research related to the role of nutrition and exercise in obesity and weight management are mentioned. These recommendations are included in Table 6-3.

There is a chapter in the report entitled "Behavior"; however, it is a hodge-podge of various issues about the relationships between nutritional intake and behavioral patterns. Sections on the behavioral determinants of eating habits are promising and, although brief, are helpful. However, the chapter also attempts to review behavioral aspects of the eating disorders (obesity is apparently considered one), including

TABLE 6-1. Prevalence of Overweight in Selected States by Sex

State	Total[a]			Men			Women[a]		
	Sample size	Overweight[b] %	95% CI[c]	Sample size	Overweight[b] %	95% CI[c]	Sample size	Overweight[b] %	95% CI[c]
Alabama	1,135	22.3	±3	451	22.6	±4	684	22.1	±3
Arizona	1,128	17.3	±2	527	15.1	±3	601	19.5	±3
California	1,715	18.7	±2	750	20.6	±3	965	16.8	±3
District of Columbia[d]	1,051	23.1	±3	450	20.1	±4	601	25.8	±4
Florida	1,191	19.3	±3	515	20.7	±4	676	17.9	±3
Georgia	1,269	20.8	±3	529	23.3	±4	740	18.3	±3
Hawaii	1,804	15.5	±2	848	17.1	±3	956	13.7	±3
Idaho	1,718	20.0	±2	668	20.0	±3	1,050	20.0	±3
Illinois	1,690	21.9	±2	720	21.6	±3	970	22.2	±3
Indiana	2,034	25.7	±2	885	26.8	±3	1,149	24.6	±3
Kentucky	1,725	22.3	±2	712	23.1	±3	1,013	21.6	±3
Maine	1,167	23.1	±3	461	24.7	±4	706	21.6	±3
Maryland	993	19.8	±3	390	16.5	±4	603	23.0	±4
Massachusetts	1,370	19.8	±2	582	22.9	±4	788	17.0	±3
Minnesota	3,133	20.7	±2	1,467	21.8	±2	1,666	19.7	±2
Missouri	1,307	23.1	±3	536	23.8	±4	771	22.5	±3
Montana	1,141	16.7	±2	479	18.4	±4	662	15.0	±3

Nebraska	1,127	21.4	± 3	473	22.8	± 4	654	20.1	± 3
New Hampshire	1,144	17.7	± 3	522	17.8	± 4	622	17.6	± 3
New Mexico	1,125	15.2	± 2	535	16.7	± 4	590	13.8	± 3
New York	1,101	20.1	± 3	452	18.0	± 4	649	22.0	± 4
North Carolina	1,690	20.4	± 2	704	19.6	± 3	986	21.1	± 3
North Dakota	1,518	23.2	± 2	682	23.5	± 3	836	22.9	± 3
Ohio	1,430	25.0	± 2	647	26.8	± 4	783	23.3	± 3
Rhode Island	1,685	18.4	± 2	734	19.0	± 3	951	17.9	± 3
South Carolina	1,691	21.6	± 2	795	22.9	± 3	896	20.3	± 3
South Dakota	1,131	22.5	± 3	508	23.6	± 4	623	21.4	± 4
Tennessee	2,274	22.0	± 2	895	25.6	± 3	1,379	18.6	± 2
Texas	1,115	22.9	± 3	491	24.7	± 4	624	21.1	± 4
Utah	1,335	16.6	± 2	607	16.7	± 3	728	16.5	± 3
Washington	1,146	21.1	± 3	516	20.2	± 4	630	22.1	± 3
West Virginia	1,586	25.1	± 2	645	26.4	± 4	941	23.9	± 3
Wisconsin	1,306	25.7	± 3	630	26.9	± 4	676	24.6	± 4

Note. From "Prevalence of Overweight—Behavioral Risk Factor Surveillance System, 1987" by Centers for Disease Control, 1989a, *Morbidity and Mortality Weekly Report, 38,* 421–423.

[a]Pregnant women were excluded from the analysis.
[b]Overweight is defined as body mass index—weight (kg)/height (m)^2—≥ 27.8 for men and ≥ 27.3 for women.
[c]Confidence interval.
[d]For this study the District of Columbia is included among the states.

TABLE 6-2. Recommendations

Issues for most people

Fats and cholesterol
  Reduce consumption of fat (especially saturated fat) and cholesterol.
  Choose foods relatively low in these substances, such as vegetables, fruits, whole grain foods, fish, poultry, lean meats, and low-fat dairy products.
  Use food preparation methods that add little or no fat.

Energy and weight control
  Achieve and maintain a desirable body weight. To do so, choose a dietary pattern in which energy (caloric) intake is consistent with energy expenditure.
  To reduce energy intake, limit consumption of foods relatively high in calories, fats, and sugars, and minimize alcohol consumption.
  Increase energy expenditure through regular and sustained physical activity.

Complex carbohydrates and fiber
  Increase consumption of whole grain foods and cereal products, vegetables (including dried beans and peas), and fruits.

Sodium
  Reduce intake of sodium by choosing foods relatively low in sodium and limiting the amount of salt added in food preparation and at the table.

Alcohol
  To reduce the risk for chronic disease, take alcohol only in moderation (no more than two drinks a day), if at all.
  Avoid drinking any alcohol before or while driving, operating machinery, taking medications, or engaging in any other activity requiring judgment.
  Avoid drinking alcohol while pregnant.

Other issues for some people

Fluoride
  Community water systems should contain fluoride at optimal levels for prevention of tooth decay. If such water is not available, use other appropriate sources of fluoride.

Sugars
  Those who are particularly vulnerable to dental caries (cavities), especially children, should limit their consumption and frequency of use of foods high in sugars.

Calcium
  Adolescent girls and adult women should increase consumption of foods high in calcium, including low-fat dairy products.

Iron
  Children, adolescents, and women of childbearing age should be sure to consume foods that are good sources of iron, such as lean meats, fish, certain beans, and iron-enriched cereals and whole grain products. This issue is of special concern for low-income families.

Note. From *The Surgeon General's Report on Nutrition and Health* (DHHS Publication No. PHS 88-50210) by the U.S. Department of Health and Human Services, 1988b, p. 3, Washington, DC: U.S. Government Printing Office.

THE ADDICTIVE DISORDERS

TABLE 6-3. Research and Surveillance Issues of Special Priority Related to the Role of Nutrition and Exercise in Obesity and Weight Management

---

Determination of ideal or desirable body weights for individuals or for the population of various ages

Determination of the health risks associated with various degrees of overweight in children and adults

Identification of an effective means to measure total body fat and its regional distribution in individuals and in the population

Identification of the types of obesity most associated with increased chronic disease risk

Contribution of genetic and metabolic factors to obesity, including the molecular and genetic basis of energy metabolism and the nature of genetic aberrations in human obesity

Effects of diet, exercise, and weight loss on metabolism and thermogenesis

Effects of physical activity on maintenance of desirable body weight

Identification of dietary, behavioral, environmental, or genetic factors that predict development of obesity or the ability to lose weight successfully

Identification of the dietary, behavioral, environmental, social, or genetic factors that increase the risk of overweight in high-risk population groups

Health consequences of repeated cycles of weight gain and loss

Most effective individual, group, and community intervention strategies for weight management

Most effective intervention strategies for use with high-risk groups

Most effective means by which to educate individuals and the public about the factors predisposing to weight gain and loss

Most effective ways in which to promote increased physical activity in the population

Long-term effectiveness of existing weight control programs

Note. From *The Surgeon General's Report on Nutrition and Health* (DHHS Publication No. PHS 88-50210) by the U.S. Department of Health and Human Services, 1988b, pp. 301–302, Washington, DC: U.S. Government Printing Office.

problems like pica, which, according to the report (p. 523), "is common among people of either sex and all ages and races"! It also attempts to review the effects of various foods and nutrients on behavior, including short summaries of hyperactivity, hypoglycemia, and even antisocial behavior. Recommendations for research into the prevention of diet-related diseases and into the role of dietary factors in behavioral disorders are included in Table 6-4.

Hopefully, the next Surgeon General's report on nutrition and health will include an emphasis on the important issues affecting all of us: how the behavioral sciences can help people incorporate state-of-the-art nutritional recommendations into their lifestyles to maximize their chances of living long, healthy lives. The behavioral sciences have much to offer in this area. It is disappointing that the Surgeon General is apparently not aware of the advances that have occurred over the past several years.

TABLE 6-4. Research and Surveillance Issues of Special Priority Related to the Role of Behavior in the Prevention of Diet-Related Chronic Disease and to the Role of Diet in Behavioral Disorders

---

Behavioral factors that influence food selection patterns and dietary change
Most effective behavioral methods to encourage appropriate dietary changes
Behavioral factors that increase the risk for diet-related chronic disease
Behavioral factors that increase the risk for obesity, anorexia nervosa, bulimia, and pica
Prevalence of these eating disorders among different groups
Behavioral techniques effective in treatment of these disorders
Effects of foods and nutrients on etiology and treatment of behavioral disorders
Behavioral interventions that increase the long-term effectiveness of health promotion and chronic disease treatment programs

---

Note. From *The Surgeon General's Report on Nutrition and Health* (DHHS Publication No. PHS 88-50210) by the U.S. Department of Health and Human Services, 1988b, p. 530, Washington, DC: U.S. Government Printing Office.

National Research Council's Diet and Health Report

Another major report on the relationship of diet and health was released by the Committee on Diet and Health of the National Research Council (1989). It is aimed at reviewing the scientific issues related to nutrition policy for reducing risks of chronic diseases. The Committee did a thorough job summarizing much of the available literature in a number of nutritional areas and listed several research recommendations. The seven categories of research recommendations are as follows:

- Identifying foods and dietary components that alter risk of chronic diseases and explaining their underlying mechanisms of action.
- Improving the methodology for the collection and assessment of data on the exposure of humans to foods and dietary constituents that may alter risk of chronic diseases.
- Identifying markers of exposure and early indicators of risk of chronic diseases.
- Quantifying the adverse and beneficial effects of diet and determining the optimal ranges of intake of dietary macroconstituents and microconstituents that affect risk of chronic diseases.
- Assessing the potential for chronic disease risk reduction through intervention studies.
- Applying knowledge about diet and chronic diseases to public health programs.
- Expanding basic research in molecular and cellular nutrition.

The report has generated considerable interest from professionals in the area and will be a useful document for behavioral scientists for its extensive literature review and guidelines for future research trends.

Council on Scientific Affairs Report

The Council on Scientific Affairs of the American Medical Association presented an interesting report entitled "Treatment of Obesity in Adults" to their House of Delegates at their December 1987 Interim Meeting. It has now been published (Council on Scientific Affairs, 1988). The report reviews the current state-of-the-art on the role of diet, exercise, and behavior modification in the treatment of obesity. With respect to dietary treatments, the report concludes that fasting as a treatment strategy offers no benefits and results in rapid weight regain. The very-low-calorie diets are also seen as resulting in poor maintenance. According to the report, these diets should be limited to only severely obese individuals who receive appropriate cardiac evaluation in their initial screening and who remain under medical supervision.

Recommended for most obese patients are nutritionally balanced low-energy diets containing 50% carbohydrates, 20% protein, and no more than 30% fat, ranging from 1,000 to 1,200 kcal/day. Unbalanced low-energy diets, such as those containing low amounts of carbohydrate, are not recommended because the initial losses observed are likely to be the result of diuresis. Fatigue, nausea, orthostatic hypotension, dehydration, and electrolyte imbalance are also seen, along with weight regain following reintroduction of carbohydrate into the diet.

Physical activity is recommended as an important component of treatment for obesity. The report sidesteps the question of whether exercise alters the resting metabolic rate (RMR) by commenting that there is no general agreement on the issue. The Council suggests, however, that preliminary data indicate that the decrease in RMR that occurs during dieting may be prevented or reduced by adding exercise into a treatment program. No references are cited.

Studies on the relationship of exercise and food intake in obese women suggest that the addition of moderate exercise does not lead to an increase in food consumption. Studies on the thermogenic response to food and its interaction with exercise have shown contradictory results.

The report reviews briefly the data on the addition of behavioral strategies to the treatment of obesity. It mentions the need for relapse prevention training, social support strategies, and regular contacts with therapists during posttreatment periods. Guidelines for therapeutic weight control programs and for evaluating commercial weight loss clinics are presented.

The report concludes that the essential components of a weight control program are diet, exercise, and behavior modification and that all three are required for long-term weight control. The report emphasizes the need for long-term changes in eating behaviors and exercise levels and the necessity of addressing the psychological factors that limit adoption of these patterns. Prevention is seen as the "treatment" of choice. I found the report to be an excellent document summarizing current thinking in this field. Its recommendations are sensible, and they should be useful to physicians and other professionals in working with obese clients.

Very-Low-Calorie Diets

In the early 1980s, when I conducted workshops on the treatment of obesity, I always reviewed our work with very-low-calorie diets (VLCDs). Dietitians in the audience were almost always against the VLCD program, sometimes reacting violently (for dietitians). Nowadays, it seems to me that all the dietitians attending my workshops are employed by Sandoz Nutrition Corporation, which sells Optifast (a very-low-calorie product), or by one of the other VLCD companies. They are all interested in VLCD treatment programs. Times change.

VLCDs are now a huge fad in the obesity treatment field. It was reported that when Oprah Winfrey, a popular television talk show host, announced that she had lost 67 pounds on a VLCD, the company manufacturing and selling the product she used was swamped with 1 million telephone calls that day (about 150,000 actually got through)! A brief review and update of VLCDs are clearly in order.

VLCDs are usually defined as diets providing less than 800 kcal/day. Historically, they are predated by a number of studies of patients who ingested few or no calories. Fasting as a treatment strategy was especially popular in the 1950s and 1960s. Bloom (1959), for example, reported an 18-lb weight loss average for nine patients who fasted for 1 week. Drenick and Smith (1964) reported an average loss of 50 pounds in 32 patients who fasted for 51 days. Weight losses like these are difficult to attain by conventional dieting and they encouraged others to attempt the strategy. Unfortunately, losses like these are also difficult to maintain and rebound was inevitable (Innes et al., 1974; MacCuish, Munro, & Duncan, 1968). Also, fasting is dangerous. Several deaths related to fasting were reported in the literature (Spencer, 1968; Cubberley, Polster, & Schulman, 1965; Runcie & Thomson, 1970; Garnett, Bernard, Ford, Goodbody, & Woodhouse, 1969), and it was eventually abandoned as a treatment strategy.

In the 1960s and 1970s several researchers (Blackburn, Bistrian, & Flatt, 1975; Genuth, 1979; Howard & McLean Baird, 1977) began investigating ways to produce very rapid weight losses while preserving the lean body mass by providing dietary protein. Blackburn et al. (1975), for example, reported that 1.5 g protein/kg ideal body weight would generally maintain nitrogen balance (an indirect measure of lean body mass).

The source of protein comes either from animals (meat, fish, and fowl) and is eaten in this form or from a milk-based or an egg-based formula powder that is mixed with water and drunk as a liquid. Both approaches produce similar weight losses. These diets are frequently supplemented with multivitamins and with calcium, sodium chloride, potassium, and large amounts of water.

The diets are typically restricted to adults over age 18 who are at least 50 pounds overweight. Patients receive medical screening, including a complete physical examination, electrocardiogram, chest roentgenogram, SMA-20, blood count, and urinalysis. VLCDs are not used with patients who have had a recent heart attack, cerebrovascular disease, cancer, type I diabetes, hepatic disease, renal failure, lithium therapy, or any psychosis (Blackburn, Lynch, & Wong, 1986). Anyone becoming pregnant is immediately taken off the diet.

Patients are placed on the diet for about 12 to 16 weeks. They either consume their liquid three to four times each day, usually at the same time they would have eaten their meals, or eat the meat at their usual three mealtimes. Except for the supplements, nothing else is eaten. The daily caloric total is typically 400 to 800 kcal.

Weight losses are large at the beginning of the program, partly because of the diuresis effect, with 4 to 12 pounds typically reported at the end of the first week. Weekly losses then level off during the program and average about 2 pounds for women and 3 pounds for men. An average weight loss of about 45 pounds at the end of a 12-week program is typical, with males losing a little more, females somewhat less.

Following the VLCD, patients are usually refed a balanced normal diet over a 4-week period. Some type of maintenance program including nutrition education, exercise, and behavior modification strategies may then be utilized.

Wadden and Stunkard (1986) reported a controlled study comparing the effectiveness of a formula diet of 400 to 500 kcal/day with three groups: VLCD alone, behavior therapy alone, or VLCD plus behavior therapy. Mean weight losses at the end of treatment were 31, 31, and 42 pounds, respectively, with the losses for the third group significantly greater than the other two. At the 1-year follow-up, mean weight losses were 10, 21, and 28 pounds, respectively, with the losses for the third group significantly greater than the first group. A total of 29% of the third group and 44% of the second group maintained their weight losses within 4 pounds at follow-up. None of the first group did. The authors concluded that weight is regained very rapidly after treatment by VLCDs alone and that behavior therapy produces favorable long-term results when used in association with a standard 1,200 kcal/day diet or with a VLCD. Patients in the VLCD-alone condition regained two-thirds of their weight loss. Patients in the behavior-therapy-alone condition regained only half as much weight as the VLCD-alone condition, despite almost identical posttreatment losses. The combined treatment patients regained only one-third of their weight loss at the posttreatment measure. The authors suggested that their data supported the use of behavior therapy with VLCDs.

The authors (Wadden, Stunkard, & Liebschutz, 1988) have now published a 3-year follow-up of this well-done controlled study. Forty-five of the original 50 patients who completed the program were found. Mean weight losses were 8, 10, and 14 pounds, respectively. The differences between groups were not significant. At this 3-year follow-up, patients in all three conditions had regained between 74% and 85% of their end-of-treatment weight. Anecdotally, the authors reported that patients in both of the behavioral conditions told them that they rarely practiced the behavioral strategies they had been taught.

One interesting sidelight of this study was the number of patients who sought additional therapy after the 1-year follow-up assessment: 53% in the VLCD-alone, 36% in the behavior-therapy-alone group, and 38% in the combined group. The authors courageously calculated the effect of the additional treatment and corrected for it. With the correction, mean weight losses were 5, 8, and 11 pounds, respectively, with no significant differences between groups. The authors argue that failure to correct for the effects of additional therapy would result in a significant overestimation of the long-term effect of the original treatment.

Using the corrected weight data, the percent of patients regaining all of their weight losses were 47%, 43%, and 38%, respectively. The percent of patients maintaining their original weight losses within 4 pounds were 13%, 7%, and 19%, respectively.

No matter how the data were analyzed, long-term results were not good. Results of this study have clear implications for the field. Maintenance following treatment by VLCD, like other interventions, is poor. Putting most patients on VLCDs results in excellent initial weight losses with regain almost inevitable following treatment. Sikand, Kondo, Foreyt, Jones, and Gotto (1988), in a 2-year follow-up of patients on a VLCD, reported that even with exercise as an important component during treatment, patients regained 58% of the weight they lost while they were on the diet. Patients who had not received structured exercise training during intervention regained 96% of their end-of-treatment weight loss at the 2-year follow-up.

What do these findings mean for the vast majority of patients following such a program? Remember, 1 million people tried to call for information about a VLCD in one day when Oprah Winfrey told about her 67-pound treatment loss. The VLCD trend is definitely here. Additional long-term follow-up studies will be published in the next few years. Their impact on this fad will be of great interest.

Pharmacological Treatments for Obesity

Pharmacological treatments for obesity continue to be popular. Whether the pills are purchased in a drug store over the counter or by prescription, anorectic agents have long been seen as the most effortless way to lose weight. Only the sometimes dangerous side effects and rapid regain of lost weight following discontinuation of the drug have kept their potential usefulness in check.

Several pioneering studies by Craighead and colleagues (Craighead, 1984; Craighead, Stunkard, & O'Brien, 1981) investigated the combination of pharmacological therapy and behavior therapy. If drugs resulted in large weight losses, perhaps learning behavioral strategies would help with maintenance of the losses. Craighead et al. (1981) reported that patients who received fenfluramine hydrochloride alone, the drug plus behavior therapy, or behavior therapy alone achieved weight losses after 25 weeks of treatment of 32, 34, and 24 pounds, respectively. Unfortunately, at a 1-year follow-up, patients in the first two groups regained 18 and 24 pounds, respectively, and patients in the third group regained only 4 pounds.

Craighead (1984) also investigated whether different sequences of drug administration might enhance long-term effectiveness. Again, results were no different. It did not matter whether behavior therapy was taught before, after, or during the drug treatment. Regain occurred in all groups. It appeared that the drug treatments might have made it more difficult for patients to keep off weight, perhaps because they attributed the loss to the drug and did not learn or use behavioral strategies.

Other studies utilizing fenfluramine hydrochloride and behavior therapy (e.g., Bigelow, Griffiths, Liebson, & Kaliszak, 1980; Brownell & Stunkard, 1981; Ost & Gotestam, 1976) have generally found good losses during treatment but great difficulty with maintenance.

Rodin, Elias, Silberstein, and Wagner (1988) investigated a different anorectic agent, diethylpropion hydrochloride (Tenuate), with a 20-week cognitive-behavior therapy (CB) program. Comparison groups included a placebo plus CB, and CB alone. At the end of treatment, weight losses were 16, 17, and 20 pounds, for the CB alone, CB plus placebo, and drug plus CB groups, respectively, with the small group differences nonsignificant. At 1-year follow-up, weight losses were 10, 8, and 9 pounds, respectively, again with no main effect for group.

Results suggest that diethylpropion may be a weaker drug than fenfluramine hydrochloride and treatment-produced losses somewhat less. All groups regained significant weight following formal intervention. At a 6-month follow-up, the combination drug/CB group's regain was significant, whereas the regain in the other two groups was not.

Sullivan, Hogan, and Triscari (1987) reviewed new developments in pharmacological treatments for obesity, including appetite suppressants and drugs that inhibit lipid synthesis in rodents. One drug, Ro 22-0654, for example, suppresses the biosynthesis and enhances the oxidation of fatty acids. Its administration to lean and genetically obese Zucker rats reduces body weight gain and body fat levels selectively with body protein levels unchanged (Triscari & Sullivan, 1984a, 1984b). Also reviewed were drugs that stimulate thermogenesis in animals. One drug, Ro 16-8714, resulted in increased energy expenditure, as indicated by increased oxygen consumption, in both lean and obese rats. The drug was shown to stimulate thermogenesis for at least 6 hours following its administration. Studies on humans have not yet been attempted.

Unfortunately, at this writing, pharmacological therapy has so many disadvantages, including dangerous side effects, development of tolerance, potential for abuse, limited effectiveness with rapid regain of lost weight following withdrawal, and psychological attribution of loss to the drug, that its use should probably be restricted at this time to severely obese patients who need to lose weight rapidly in order to undergo surgery or other medical interventions (Brownell & Wadden, 1986). The combination of drug therapy plus behavior therapy to date has not worked. No potential breakthrough in this area is seen in the near future.

The Gastric Bubble

The Garren–Edwards gastric bubble is a free-floating intragastric device made of plastic. It was approved for use in the United States by the Food and Drug Administration in September 1985. Since that time, it has been used on more than 20,000 patients (Frank, Stern, & Fisher, 1987).

The idea for the bubble originated from an observation made by DeBakey and Ochsner (1938) that intragastric bezoars caused weight loss without any apparent adverse effects. The underlying reason for the weight loss is not well understood, although the smaller stomach volume results in reduced capacity, which presumably leads to earlier satiety. This early observation led to a number of case reports in which toy balloons and even silicone breast implants were placed in the stomach, all resulting in some weight loss (e.g., Muller, 1982; Nieben & Harboe, 1982; Taylor & Pullan, 1983; Percival, 1984).

Garren and Garren (1984) and Garren, Garren, Giordano, Webitt, and Plotzker (1986) reported their experiences placing a cylindrical polyurethane device in the stomach and then removing it endoscopically. Their encouraging preliminary results led to the bubble being approved for use in the United States.

Recent controlled investigations have cast doubt on the usefulness of the gastric bubble as an adjunct to an obesity treatment program. Benjamin et al. (1988) reported the results of a double-blind crossover study to evaluate the efficacy of the Garren–Edwards gastric bubble. Ninety patients at least 30% above ideal body weight were randomized into three groups: bubble–sham (BS), sham–bubble (SB), or bubble–bubble (BB) in two successive 12-week periods. Patients in the BS group received the bubble for 12 weeks followed by its removal (sham) for 12 weeks, etc., all done in a double-blind fashion. Patients participated in weekly dietary plus behavior therapy group classes during the 24-week treatment period. Sixty-one patients completed the entire treatment. At 12 weeks, mean weight loss was 19, 12, and 8 pounds, for the BS, SB, and BB groups, respectively. At 24 weeks, the losses were 23, 16, and 18 pounds, respectively. The authors reported that although weight loss occurred more consistently in patients with the bubble, there were no significant differences between any of the three groups at

12 or 24 weeks with respect to weight loss or BMI. They found that most of the weight loss occurred during the first 12 weeks, irrespective of whether or not the patients had the bubble. A number of side effects were reported. These included gastric erosions (26%), gastric ulcers (14%), small bowel obstruction (2%), Mallory–Weiss tears (11%), and esophageal laceration (1%).

Results of the Benjamin et al. (1988) study suggest that the Garren–Edwards gastric bubble is no more effective than diet and behavior therapy alone in the treatment of obesity. Weight loss occurred in all three groups and was unrelated to randomization to either bubble or sham. Looking at compliance, the authors found that compliant sham patients (those attending more than half of the 24 weekly classes) lost no less weight than noncompliant bubble patients. The presence of the bubble clearly was not a substitute for therapy. The bubble had no independent benefit beyond diet and behavior therapy. The authors concluded, "An ineffective device with this degree of morbidity is likely to have only a limited role in the treatment of obesity in its present form" (Benjamin et al., 1988, p. 587).

Meshkinpour, Hsu, and Farivar (1988) also reported the results of a randomized, double-blind, crossover study of the Garren–Edwards gastric bubble. Twenty-three patients more than 25% over ideal body weight were randomly assigned to receive either BS or SB over two 12-week periods. Patients received biweekly group classes of dietary and behavior therapy. Results showed that patients lost 12 pounds while on the bubble and 11 pounds during the sham period (nonsignificant). The order of administration of the bubble and sham did not significantly affect weight loss. The authors concluded, "The results of our randomized, double-blind, controlled study clearly indicate that the Garren–Edwards gastric bubble is no more effective than a sham as an adjuvant device for weight reduction" (Meshkinpour et al., 1988, p. 591). They go on to state, "In our opinion, the Garren–Edwards gastric bubble is of no value as an adjuvant device in weight reduction" (p. 592).

The Garren–Edwards gastric bubble was withdrawn for use in the United States in 1988. At present, seven different intragastric bubbles are available commercially in other countries for use in weight reduction ("Who Needs," 1988). These bubbles are generally used for about 3 to 4 months, but some of the newer ones may be used for longer periods of time.

At present, the use of a gastric bubble for 3 or 4 months does not result in greater weight losses than a sham procedure. The numerous reports of serious side effects (e.g., Holland, Bach, & Duff, 1985; Kirby, Mills, Kellum, Messmer, & Sugerman, 1987) suggest that as currently used the gastric bubble has no use in the treatment of obesity. Hopefully, controlled studies in the future will indicate whether the newer devices will have a contribution to make in this field. The studies to date clearly suggest that in the absence of diet and behavior therapy gastric bubbles are worthless.

Gastric Surgery

The first popular surgery for morbid obesity (i.e., patients who weigh more than 100 pounds over ideal body weight) was the jejunoileal bypass (Payne, DeWind, Schwab, & Kern, 1973; Scott et al., 1973). This short-circuiting of the small intestine resulted in rapid weight losses but was associated with a number of serious complications (Sugerman, 1987), which led to its eventual abandonment.

Mason and Ito (1967) divided the stomach surgically into a small upper pouch with a loop gastroenterostomy. The technique was later simplified by stapling the stomach, leaving only a small opening to allow food through the distal stomach and the duodenum (Pace, Martin, Tetirick, Fabri, & Carey, 1979). These gastroplasties are done by placing the staples either horizontally or vertically across the stomach. In the vertical-banded gastroplasty (Mason, 1982), a stapled opening is made and a strip of polypropylene mesh is wrapped around the stoma and sutured to itself.

Gastroplasties have been criticized for both their inability to produce significant weight losses and the high regain of lost weight (e.g., Laws & Piantadosi, 1981; Lechner & Callender, 1981; Linner, 1982; Pories, Flickinger, Meelheim, VanRij, & Thomas, 1982; Sugerman, 1987).

The gastric bypass is usually done with the staples placed in a vertical rather than horizontal direction because of less risk of injury (Sugerman, 1987). There have been a number of randomized, prospective studies comparing the efficacy of gastric bypass with unbanded gastroplasty procedures. Sugerman, Starkey, and Birkenhauer (1987) reported the results of a study comparing vertical-banded gastroplasty (VBGP) with Roux-en-Y gastric bypass (RYGBP) in a randomized, prospective trial. After the first 9 months of the study, the authors reported that they stopped the randomization procedure because after 20 patients had undergone each procedure the RYGBP was producing significantly greater weight losses. At 3-year follow-up, patients who had RYGBP had lost 64% of excess weight compared with 37% for patients who had undergone VBGP.

Patients had also been separated preoperatively as "sweets eaters" or "non-sweet eaters." Results showed that sweets eaters had a significantly worse weight loss after VBGP than RYGBP. There were no significant differences in weight losses between sweets eaters and non-sweets eaters in the RYGBP group. The most favorable weight loss in the sweets eaters after RYGBP versus the VBGP seemed to be the development of the dumping syndrome after RYGBP. Patients in the RYGBP group claimed that sweets produced a number of symptoms, including nausea, lightheadedness, flushing, and diarrhea, and most of them said that they had lost their desire for sweets. The authors concluded that the RYGBP appeared to be the most effective procedure for sweets eaters and the VBGP for non-sweets eaters.

In a follow-up study, Sugerman et al. (1989) selectivity assigned sweets eaters to RYGBP and non-sweets eaters to VBGP. Of 222 patients, 40 were defined as non-sweets eaters and underwent VBGP and 182 were defined as sweets eaters and underwent RYGBP. Compared with random assignment, the authors reported that the percentage excess weight loss at 2 years improved significantly from 53% to 68% with both groups combined. Comparing the randomized approach in their earlier study with the selective approach in this study at 2 years, in the VBGP group, the percentage of excess weight loss increased from 41% to 55%; in the RYGBP group, the percentage increased from 66% to 71%. With selective assignment to groups, the percentage excess weight lost with RYGBP was still better than that with VBGP. However, more complications were seen in the RYGBP group, and it was found to be ineffective with 19% of the patients. The authors concluded that VBGP should not be performed on morbidly obese patients who are addicted to sweets. However, it is the preferable procedure for non-sweets eaters because it results in good weight loss and tends to result in fewer complications than the RYGBP.

Surgical approaches should be considered for morbidly obese patients only after these patients have tried and failed numerous dietary and behavioral programs for more than 5 years. Exceptions should be made only when serious medical problems (e.g., renal insufficiency) exist. How a determination is made whether a patient is unable to lose weight on a rigorous behavior therapy program along with an aggressive dietary and exercise intervention is a considerable challenge. Behavioral assessment strategies in this field are still in their infancy. It is hoped that future research into this new field increases and will enable us all to have sensible guidelines for making these difficult decisions.

Behavior Therapy for Adult Obesity

Bennett (1987) published a rather scathing review of dietary treatments of obesity, including behavior therapy. He examined 26 studies published between 1977 and 1985 that were detailed enough to review adequately. All were dietary interventions, and many included behavior modification strategies. The studies totaled 1,861 subjects with a mean baseline weight of 207 pounds. He found that mean weight loss was 8.5% of baseline weight, similar to a finding in an earlier review of 57 studies totaling 3,864 subjects published between 1966 and 1977 (Wing & Jeffery, 1979). In that earlier review, Wing and Jeffery (1979) reported a mean loss of 8.9% of baseline weight. Bennett concluded that his finding suggests that "no material progress is being registered by interventions" (1987, p. 255) in this area.

Any improvement in follow-up results? Bennett (1987) also examined those studies that reported follow-up data. Final weight loss was 6% or less of baseline weight, which, according to Bennett, was "an essentially trivial result given that the median intake weight was 195 pounds (mean was 201)" (p. 256). The heaviest patients lost the most weight. Many studies reported statistical interpretation of results without giving the data, and Bennett (pp. 257-258) singled out "studies of behavior modification reported in the psychological literature" as being the greatest offenders.

He concluded his review by making an especially good point, namely, that it is very easy to recruit obese patients who are eager to lose weight, treat them with some behavioral/dietary intervention, and generate statistically significant results. However, these results are rarely clinically significant, and the longer the follow-up period, the more trivial the results become.

Bennett (1987) believes that no worthwhile progress has been made in the dietary treatment of obesity since outcome data were first reported in 1931 and that "the burden should now be on the investigator to establish a strong reason for undertaking yet another study of intake restriction, including studies employing behavior modification aimed primarily at altering eating behaviors" (p. 258). Focusing on eating behaviors, the heart of many behavioral programs, is, according to Bennett, an incomplete, probably wrong model, one that has not produced particularly enviable results. If the model itself is wrong,

Bennett asks, "Is there any justification for engaging clients in a behavior-modification program that provides them with deceptive information?" (p. 259). Ethically, according to Bennett, treatment of this nature should be labeled speculative.

Bennett makes several excellent points in his critique of interventions that treat obesity by focusing only on dietary intake, as many of the early behavioral studies tended to do. And I agree with him that focusing exclusively on dietary behaviors has not proved particularly helpful over the long-term for many obese patients. However, Bennett is incorrect in his appraisal of current behavioral programs. Learning from their shortcomings, behavior therapists today are much more comprehensive in their treatments than the stimulus-control-based interventions of the 1970s. Behavioral interventions today rely heavily on more complex models of behavior change and maintenance. Social support systems, relapse prevention, and emphasis on the development of exercise habits are critical elements in behaviorally based intervention programs. These multicomponent treatment programs are now producing clinically significant, substantial weight losses in patients. Maintenance of the losses, however, is still proving difficult, with substantial regain following formal treatment occurring in the majority of patients treated.

Bennett (1987) suggests that exploration of micronutrient effects might be a productive research track for the treatment of obese patients. If promising data did appear in this area, the use of behavioral approaches for adherence to the new dietary pattern would surely be indicated. Bennett's review is a welcome addition to the field. Hopefully, it will serve as a stimulus for better run and better written long-term intervention studies.

IMPROVING WEIGHT LOSSES

Behavioral treatment programs continue to get longer. Perri, Nezu, Patti, and McCann (1989) randomly assigned 48 obese patients to a standard behavioral treatment of 20 weekly sessions or to an extended treatment of 40 weekly sessions. Extending the treatment to 40 weeks significantly improved weight losses. Patients in the extended treatment condition increased their weight losses by 35% between week 20 and week 40. Average weight losses for the standard condition at weeks 20, 40, and 72 were 20, 14, and 10 pounds, compared with the results for the extended condition of 22, 30, and 22 pounds, respectively. Patients in the extended condition continued to lose weight between weeks 20 and 40, although at a slower rate. Adherence data were also better during this time period compared with the standard treatment. Once treatment was completed, however, the data showed deterioration in adherence in both groups. The authors suggest that initial formal treatment may need to be even longer than their 40-week program, perhaps a year or more for moderate and severe obesity. Therapeutic contacts during the maintenance period (perhaps forever?) may also be necessary.

This study is especially important because it illustrates the growing realization among behavior therapists of the need to conceptualize obesity as a chronic condition and the necessity of providing some form of long-term support for most patients following formal treatment. This trend is clearly here to stay. The long-held belief that obesity could be treated successfully in 8 or 12 sessions is hopefully gone. Note the regain of weight even in the 40-week condition at the 72-week follow-up visit.

ROLE OF EXERCISE

Exercise as both a weight loss strategy and a maintenance enhancer continues to receive increasing attention from behavior therapists and others in the field. For example, Pavlou, Krey, and Steffee (1989) reported that only patients who actively participated in a supervised exercise program were able to successfully maintain weight losses achieved during treatment utilizing a multidisciplinary approach. They found that subjects, all male police officers, who exercised at least three times a week to a caloric equivalence of 1,500 kcal/week were the ones who maintained their reduced weight. Supervision in exercise was important because only 5% of their group began exercise on their own.

CONTINUED DIFFICULTY ACHIEVING MAINTENANCE

As more behavioral studies report longer follow-up periods, the difficulty achieving maintenance in all but a few patients becomes painfully clear. A recent study by Kramer, Jeffery, Forster, and Snell (1989) is an excellent example. The authors reported 4-year follow-up data on 114 men and 38 women who completed a 15 week behavioral weight loss program. Long-term data were discouraging, with less than 3% of patients maintaining posttreatment weights throughout the 4 years of annual follow-up assessments. Nearly 40% of patients regained weight at least to baseline levels or above at some point during the follow-up assessments. More favorably, 18.5% of patients maintained at least half of their losses during follow-up visits and 34% of patients kept off at least one-fourth of their losses. Women lost less weight during treatment but maintained their losses better than men. Kramer et al. (1989) offered a particularly interesting speculation to explain their results: "Overall we are inclined to think that there is a powerful biological imperative involved in these weight regain phenomenon, but that under appropriate circumstances this imperative might be overridden. The means for doing so, however, clearly involve more clout than current behavioral methodologies" (p. 134).

TOBACCO USE

Several topics are reviewed in this section on tobacco use. Unlike obesity, the prevalence of smoking in the United States continues to decline. Despite this encouraging trend, new data clearly illustrate differences in this rate of decline among sociodemographic groups, suggesting research priorities for behavioral scientists. A recent Surgeon General's report on tobacco is among the strongest to date, labeling regular tobacco use an "addiction" and nicotine as the culprit. Nicotine chewing gum has become a fairly popular way of trying to quit smoking, and data on it and other pharmacological strategies are surveyed. Multicomponent intervention programs continue to be the most effective approach for the behavioral treatment of smoking. Finally, there has been an increase in the use of community intervention programs for smoking cessation. These programs appear to have a strong potential for decreasing the sales of tobacco products.

New Data on Prevalence

Despite encouraging declines in overall smoking prevalence, the rate of decline has differed among sociodemographic groups. According to data collected by the National Center for Health Statistics through the National Health Interview Surveys between 1974 and 1985, the estimated prevalence of smoking in the United States has declined steadily from 36.7% in 1974 to 30.4% in 1985, a decrease of 0.58% a year (Fiore et al., 1989). However, the decline has been steeper for men, 43.4% to 33.5%, than for women, 31.2% to 27.6%. The prevalence of smoking in blacks has remained higher than in whites. Blacks declined in prevalence of smoking from 44.0% to 35.4% compared with whites, who declined from 36.1% to 29.4% from 1974 to 1985. Both black and white men showed steeper declines in prevalence than black and white women, respectively.

Unfortunately, although smoking initiation decreased significantly in males from 44.8% to 33.4%, it increased slightly in women, from 33.4% to 34.6%, from 1974 to 1985 (Fiore et al., 1989). Looking at age, smoking initiation remained at about 34% among young women 20 to 24 years of age while declining about one percentage point per year between 1974 and 1985 to about 33% in young men. Overall, smoking prevalence decreased across all race-gender groups, although at a faster rate for men than women. Differences in initiation, more than cessation, appear responsible for the converging of prevalence rates among men and women in this country (Fiore et al., 1989).

Today, education level has replaced gender as the major sociodemographic predictor of smoking status (Pierce, Fiore, Novotny, Hatziandreu, & Davis, 1989a). Prevalence decreased 4.8 times faster among college graduates than among individuals with less than a high school education. In 1985 only 18% of college graduates smoked compared with 34% of individuals who did not graduate from high school. The more highly educated showed higher quit rates than the less educated and the gap appears to be widening. Regardless of gender, individuals are more than twice as likely to begin smoking if they do not attend college. Pierce et al. (1989a) suggest that antismoking interventions in the future need to be based much more on educational status than have been attempted to date.

Trends in Tobacco Use

Smoking prevalence has declined at a linear rate in the United States since 1974, and if this trend continues, only 22% of the adult population, 40 million individuals, will be smoking in the year 2000 (Pierce, Fiore, Novotny, Hatziandreu, & Davis, 1989b). Less than 10% of college graduates will be smoking compared with about 30% of individuals who do not receive an education beyond high school. About 20% of males and 23% of females will smoke in the year 2000. Looking at race, about 21% of whites and 25% of blacks will smoke.

Pierce et al. (1989b) conclude from their data that despite the overall decline in smoking prevalence, efforts by behavioral scientists and health researchers to prevent smoking initiation have been less effective than efforts to promote cessation. In the early 1980s, surveys suggested that each day about 3,000 young persons started smoking and became regular smokers (about 1 million per year). Research implications for behavioral scientists are clear. Efforts should be targeted at the prevention of smoking behavior in the young. Similarly, both prevention and cessation efforts should be aimed at the groups at greatest risk for smoking initiation, namely, the less educated members of our society, particularly adolescent female school dropouts.

Surgeon General's Report on Nicotine Addiction

A recent report of the Surgeon General on tobacco focuses on the pharmacological basis of tobacco addiction (U.S. Department of Health and Human Services, 1988c). Much of the report is spent reviewing evidence that tobacco use is addicting and that nicotine is the active pharmacological agent that causes the addiction. The report suggests that the terms "drug addiction" and "drug dependence" are scientifically equivalent because "both terms refer to the behavior of repetitively ingesting mood-altering substances by individuals" (U.S. Department of Health and Human Services, 1988c, p. 7). Both terms are used interchangeably in the report. The rationale for defining regular tobacco use as an addiction lies in the criteria used. The primary criteria used to define drug dependence are highly controlled or compulsive use, psychoactive effects, and drug-reinforced behavior. Additional criteria regarding addictive behavior are stereotypic patterns of use, use despite harmful effects, relapse following abstinence, and recurrent drug cravings. Finally, criteria regarding dependence-producing drugs are tolerance, physical dependence, and pleasant (euphoriant) effects (U.S. Department of Health and Human Services, 1988c, p. 7). According to the Surgeon General, regular use of tobacco meets those criteria, and it is therefore an "addiction."

Supporting the Surgeon General's report, Kozlowski et al. (1989) recently reported the results of a study in which they questioned about 1,000 individuals who were seeking treatment for alcohol or drug dependence about their difficulty, relative to cigarettes, of quitting alcohol or drugs, the strength of their strongest urges to use, and the pleasure they derived from use. Respondents tended to rate urges for cigarettes and difficulty in quitting cigarettes as high or higher than for their main alcohol or other drug problem. A total of 57% of respondents said that it would be easier to quit their alcohol or drug habit than to quit smoking. They also rated cigarettes as less pleasurable than alcohol or other drugs. Cigarette dependence was seen as being at least as "addictive" as other drug use but not as pleasurable.

THE ADDICTIVE DISORDERS

The major conclusions of the Surgeon General's report (U.S. Department of Health and Human Services, 1988c, p. 9) are as follows:

- Cigarettes and other forms of tobacco are addicting.
- Nicotine is the drug in tobacco that causes addiction.
- The pharmacologic and behavioral processes that determine tobacco addiction are similar to those that determine addiction to drugs such as heroin and cocaine.

Implications for Behavioral Scientists

The Surgeon General's report (U.S. Department of Health and Human Services, 1988c) goes into detail reviewing the literature on treatment approaches for habitual tobacco use. Behavioral interventions are singled out for their effectiveness in treatment. The fact that behavioral strategies received the most attention is not particularly surprising given the large number of prominent behavioral scientists who participated in the preparation of this excellent report. It is encouraging that so many behaviorally oriented researchers have made substantial contributions to this document. The Surgeon General's report on nutrition and health (U.S. Department of Health and Human Services, 1988b) reviewed earlier in this chapter reads for the most part as if it were written by well-meaning individuals with little behavioral knowledge; this one reads as if it were almost totally written by behavioral scientists. What a difference. In particular, the sections on intervention for cessation of tobacco use are clearly written and suggest practical implications for further study in this area. The conclusions regarding treatment of tobacco use are as follows (U.S. Department of Health and Human Services, 1988c, pp. 15–16):

- Tobacco dependence can be treated successfully.
- Effective interventions include behavioral approaches alone and behavioral approaches with adjunctive pharmacologic treatment.
- Behavioral interventions are most effective when they include multiple components (procedures such as aversive smoking, skills training, group support, and self-reward). Inclusion of too many treatment procedures can lead to less successful outcome.
- Nicotine replacement can reduce tobacco withdrawal symptoms and may enhance the efficacy of behavioral treatment.

This report published by the U.S. Public Health Service on the health consequences of tobacco use is the seventh during the tenure of C. Everett Koop, M.D., Sc.D., as Surgeon General. Dr. Koop did a remarkable job in this field as Surgeon General. He served as a spokesman, cheerleader, and driving force to advance the United States toward a smoke-free society. His leadership in the search for understanding the health consequences of tobacco usage is a superb achievement.

Pharmacological Treatments For Smoking: Nicotine Replacement

NICOTINE CHEWING GUM

Under the direction of Ferno, researchers at Leo Laboratories in Helsingborg, Sweden, developed Nicorette, a nicotine chewing gum, based on the assumption that because a smoking habit involves both a psychological and a nicotine dependence, providing an alternative source of nicotine would leave only the psychological aspects to be dealt with (Schwartz, 1987). Early work with the nicotine chewing gum (Westling, 1976) resulted in poor success rates, and the gum was reformulated, adding a carbonate buffer. By buffering above a pH of 8.0, the buccal absorption of nicotine was increased and the nicotine blood levels were similar to those produced by smoking cigarettes (Axelsson & Brantmark, 1977). A 2-mg dose of Nicorette apparently was similar to smoking one cigarette in terms of the time course of the response (Schwartz, 1987). In January 1984, the Food and Drug Administration of the United States approved the use of the 2-mg piece of Nicorette (nicotine polacrilex chewing gum).

In the United States, Nicorette is sold by prescription in the form of chewing gum. It is marketed through Merrell Dow Pharmaceuticals, a subsidiary of Dow Chemical Company. The company indicates that the gum should be used only as an aid in smoking cessation and not as a permanent replacement for tobacco. According to the company, the gum is a safe and helpful adjunct for patients trying to quit smoking.

There are several excellent reviews of the literature on the evaluation of nicotine chewing gum for the treatment of smoking (e.g., Schwartz, 1987; Fagerstrom, 1988; U.S. Department of Health and Human Services, 1988c). Schwartz (1987) evaluated 23 studies, which resulted in 28 trials of the gum by 20 different groups. Six of the 23 studies had at least a 6-month follow-up and 17 had a 12-month follow-up. The gum was the primary intervention in 14 trials, and it was a secondary intervention along with behavior therapy or other treatment in the other 14 trials.

The median quit rate for the trials using the gum as the primary intervention declined from 23% at 6 months to 11% at 12 months. When the gum was used as part of a more comprehensive intervention program, the quit rates were usually much higher than when used as the sole treatment. The median quit rate was 35% at 6 months and 29% at 12 months when the gum was combined with behavior therapy. For example, Hall, Tunstall, Rugg, Jones, and Benowitz (1985) assigned 120 subjects either to intensive behavioral treatment, to nicotine gum in a low-contact treatment, or to an intensive behavioral intervention plus the gum. The combined intensive treatment produced the highest abstinence rates, 59% at week 26 and 44% at week 52, than the other two conditions at all asessment periods. These differences were significant at 26 weeks from the start of the study, but not at 52 weeks. Hall et al. (1985, p. 257) concluded that "nicotine gum alone is not a panacea." In a later study, Hall, Tunstall, Ginsberg, Benowitz, and Jones (1987) assigned subjects in a 2 × 2 factorial design to an intensive behavioral intervention program or to a low-contact intervention and to nicotine gum or to placebo gum. Results at 52 weeks of follow-up showed significant effects only for the nicotine gum. No differences were found between the low-contact intervention and intensive behavioral intervention.

The dose–response effect has been examined by a number of researchers. For example, Tonnesen et al. (1988) randomly assigned 172 smokers to group counseling and 2-mg or 4-mg nicotine gum or to an "advice only" control group. After 4 weeks, the 4-mg gum was replaced by 2-mg gum. The success rate for the gum group was 45.6% versus 7.1% for the control group at 3 months, 33.3% versus 3.7% after 12 months, and 27.2% versus 5.7% after 22 months, respectively. No significant dose–response effect of the 2-mg and 4-mg gum was found.

OTHER PHARMACOLOGICAL TREATMENTS

In addition to the nicotine gum, a number of other nicotine replacement strategies have been attempted. Russell, Jarvis, Feyerabend, and Ferno (1983) and Jarvis (1986) have reported the use of a nasal nicotine solution that is squeezed into one's nose. This strategy is thought to result in more rapid absorption of nicotine than in the form of gum. Decreased craving and encouraging abstinence data have been reported (Jarvis, 1986). About two-thirds of 26 patients treated with the solution were abstinent at 6 months and one-third at 12 months. Although embarrassment was reported by some subjects, these preliminary data are encouraging and further study is indicated.

A nicotine transdermal patch has become somewhat popular recently as a treatment for smoking. Such a patch could help with steady-state delivery of nicotine, a potential improvement over the gum (Rose, Jarvik, & Rose, 1984; Rose, 1986). Rose, Herskovic, Trilling, and Jarvik (1985) reported reduced craving in a short-term (hours) study comparing a nicotine patch with a placebo patch. Nicotine vapor inhalers have also been tried, but to date their effectiveness as an intervention for smoking remains unknown (U.S. Department of Health and Human Services, 1988c).

How good are the pharmacological approaches, especially the nicotine gum? Studies to date suggest that the nicotine gum can be helpful for some motivated smokers if behavior therapy or some other supportive counseling is also provided. The gum appears to be most helpful for smokers more dependent on nicotine because the gum may reduce withdrawal symptoms, although studies are not consistent on this finding.

The critical determinant of success with nicotine gum seems to be its use as an adjunct along with comprehensive behavioral treatment. When used alone in a physician's practice, quit rates at 1 year range from 6% to 10% (Schwartz, 1987). Results improve when used by experienced practitioners combined with more intensive treatment.

Many of the research studies in this field have been criticized because of a number of shortcomings. With respect to posttreatment results, several studies have reported "follow-up" data while their patients were still using the gum. Because the gum is not considered a permanent replacement for tobacco, follow-up should be regarded as the time following withdrawal from the gum. When such a criterion is used, abstinence rates drop. A minimum 1-year follow-up after patients discontinue the use of the nicotine gum would help researchers interpret results. According to Schwartz (1987) who evaluated studies through 1986, only one trial measured follow-up results after gum use was discontinued; all others started their follow-up period when treatment was begun.

Another problem with the nicotine gum studies involves the amount of nicotine that subjects actually receive. Problems include poorly defined criteria for self-administration, low dosages, differing compliance rates, and variable absorption of nicotine from the gum (U.S. Department of Health and Human Services, 1988c). Additional research is needed in the areas of compliance and dosage effects, including use of the 4-mg gum with some highly dependent patients.

Pharmacological treatments have been used extensively with alcoholics, drug addicts, obese individuals, and other addictive disorders with rather limited success rates. Learning from the experiences of researchers in these other areas may be helpful in the tobacco area. For example, the study of individual differences (i.e., who is helped, who is not helped) may be a fruitful research path. Reducing physiological withdrawal may prove useful with only a subset of dependent smokers; lifestyle modification may ultimately be required for most habitual users of tobacco.

Behavior Therapy for Smoking Cessation

As reported in the previous volume in this series (Foreyt, 1987a), "Treatment programs for smoking that emphasize single strategies continue to give way to multicomponent interventions" (p. 223). Schwartz (1987) has published a thorough review of intervention studies by strategy used. Table 6-5 is his summary of follow-up quit rates of 416 smoking cessation trials, by method, reported between 1959 and 1985. Of the trials reviewed, 231 had at least a 12-month follow-up. A footnote reminds the reader that most of the quit rates were based only on self-report data. Definitions of follow-up varied between trials. As the table indicates, the highest median quit rates at 1-year follow-up were seen in physician intervention programs with cardiac patients (43%) and with multiple component programs (40%). Covered in the review were 17 multiple programs that had 1-year follow-ups, and, of those programs, two-thirds achieved at least a 33% success rate. There were 16 trials with cardiac patients, most with large numbers of subjects. Presumably, the impressive results were due at least in part to the high motivation levels many cardiac patients show.

Of the behavioral interventions reported, rapid smoking (30.5%) and satiation (34.5%) showed good results when combined with other procedures. However, when used as a singular intervention, the risky rapid smoking procedure showed only a 21% quit rate at 1-year follow-up.

Multicomponent interventions tend to differ in content, apparently the result of the therapists' or the investigators' beliefs in which components to include and which ones to emphasize. Because only a few multicomponent interventions assess process variables (e.g., Brandon, Tiffany, & Baker, 1986; Hall, Rugg, Tunstall, & Jones, 1984; Tiffany et al., 1986), the basis for the effectiveness of various components is unknown. For example, Kamarck and Lichtenstein (1988) treated 94 subjects in a behavioral program for smoking cessation, administering a weekly questionnaire that assessed their use of the popular behavioral strategies. They also administered an "affect-regu-

TABLE 6-5. Summary of Follow-Up Quit Rates of 416 Smoking Cessation Trials, by Method, Reported 1959-1985

Intervention method	At least 6-month follow-up				At least 1-year follow-up			
	Number	Range	Median	Percent 33%[c]	Number	Range	Median	Percent 33%[c]
Self-help	11	0-33	17	18	7	12-33	18	14
Educational	7	13-50	36	71	12	15-55	25	25
Five-day plan	4	11-23	15	0	14	16-40	26	21
Group[a]	15	0-54	24	20	31	5-71	28	39
Medication	7	0-47	18	14	12	6-50	18.5	17
Nicotine chewing gum	3	17-33	23	33	9	8-38	11	11
Nicotine chewing gum and behavioral treatment or therapy	3	23-50	35	67	11	12-49	29	36
Hypnosis: individual	11	0-60	25	36	8	13-68	19.5	38
Hypnosis: group	10	8-68	34	50	2	14-88	—	50
Acupuncture	7	5-61	18	29	6	8-32	27	0
Physician advice or counseling	3	5-12	5	0	12	3-13	6	0
Physician intervention more than counseling	3	23-40	29	33	10	13-38	22.5	20

Method							
Physician intervention							
Pulmonary patients	10	10-51	24	20	6	25-76	31.5	50
Cardiac patients	5	21-69	44	80	16	11-73	43	63
Risk factor	—	—	—	—	7	12-46	31	43
Rapid smoking	12	7-62	25.5	33	6	6-40	21	17
Rapid smoking and other procedures	21	8-67	38	57	10	7-52	30.5	50
Satiation smoking[b]	11	14-76	38	64	12	18-63	34.5	58
Regular-paced aversive smoking[b]	13	0-56	29	31	3	20-39	26	33
Nicotine fading[b]	7	26-46	27	29	16	7-46	25	44
Contingency contracting[b]	9	25-76	46	89	4	14-38	27	25
Multiple programs[b]	13	18-52	32	38	17	6-76	40	65

Note. From *Review and Evaluation of Smoking Cessation Methods: The United States and Canada, 1978-1985* (DHHS Publication No. 87-2940) by J. L. Schwartz, 1987, p. 130, Washington, DC: U.S. Government Printing Office.

[a]Three group trials had 5-month follow-ups.

[b]Other procedures may have been used, and some trials may be included in more than one method.

[c]Percent 33% is the percentage of trials with quit rates of at least 33%. Median not calculated for less than three trials. Caution: Quit rates provided suggest overall trends. Most quit rates were based on self-reports. Some quit rates were recalculated to include all subjects, but most quit rates were based on reports by investigators. Some quit rates omitted subjects who did not complete treatment or persons who did not reply to follow-ups. Definitions of follow-up may vary between trials.

lation" coping inventory before and after treatment. They found that short-term maintenance was associated with an extensive affect-regulation repertoire (e.g., use of relaxation skills, talking about feelings, joking about things that were upsetting) and the use of stimulus-control strategies. Long-term maintenance was associated with consistent self-monitoring of smoking during treatment.

When elements like self-monitoring are used as single-treatment strategies, results tend to be short-lived (e.g., Pechacek, 1979). Why the combination of elements appear effective is unknown. Apparently, the interaction of strategies may be more powerful than the individual components. Obesity researchers tried unsuccessfully to isolate effective elements during the 1970s. However, theory-driven interventions should result in more progress than the crazy-quilt approaches now frequently seen. It is critical that investigators closely link their approaches to some theoretical model if progress into our understanding of the processes involved is going to continue to move forward.

Early studies relied on self-report of smoking behavior as the primary dependent variable. Similar problems plagued the early alcohol and obesity literature. Fortunately, biochemical verification of self-report data has become the norm in most controlled trials of tobacco dependency. Such verification, at least on random samples of participants, should be mandatory for peer review publication. Cotinine, a major metabolite of nicotine, although expensive, is the preferred measure.

Adoption of standards for the evaluation of smoking cessation programs would improve reporting of data. The American Heart Association, the American Lung Association, the American Cancer Society, and other organizations have endorsed the standards developed by the National Interagency Council on Smoking and Health (U.S. Department of Health and Human Srvices, 1988c). The primary definition of success in these standards is complete cessation from all forms of tobacco for 1 year. Tightening these standards to include biochemical validation of abstinence would make them stronger.

Lando (1981) has reminded us that simply adding more strategies in multicomponent programs, the "kitchen-sink" approach, does not necessarily improve effectiveness. Too many procedures tend to overwhelm some individuals, not only in the treatment of smoking, but also in the treatment of drug usage, obesity, and alcohol. One promising trend in this field is the combination of a multicomponent behaviorally based treatment program with nicotine gum for highly dependent smokers who have tried to quit many times (U.S. Department of Health and Human Services, 1988c).

Effectiveness of Community Programs

The three large community programs funded by the National Heart, Lung, and Blood Institute aimed at reduction of cardiovascular disease—namely, the Stanford Five City Project, the Minnesota Heart Health Program, and the Pawtucket Heart Health Project—were reviewed in the previous volume of this series (Foreyt, 1987b). With respect to tobacco use, the Stanford study hopes to show a 9% net change in the proportion of smokers in their communities. The Minnesota study expects to show a difference of 20% in quit smokers or the amount smoked in their experimental communities, relative to their comparison communities. The Pawtucket study also plans to show significant reductions in smoking in their experimental community. All three of these studies are nearing completion, and final reports should provide definitive data on the effectiveness of community programs for reduction of smoking behavior.

One recent study reported by Altman, Foster, Rasenick-Dous, and Tye (1989) illustrates the impact that community organization can have on reduction of cigarette purchasing. Although it is illegal in most states to sell tobacco products to minors, the laws are rarely enforced (DiFranza, Norwood, Garner, & Tye, 1987; Kirn, 1987). Altman et al. (1989) reported an aggressive community program aimed at reducing the sales of cigarettes to minors. The authors hired 18 minors 14 to 16 years of age to visit and attempt to purchase cigarettes from 412 stores in Santa Clara County, California, and from 30 outlets that had cigarette vending machines. Three interventions were then implemented. First, all communities in the county received an educational program about the problem of tobacco availability. Mass media, small media, and presentations to community groups were utilized. Second, all stores were randomly assigned to one of three conditions: (1) no personal contact, (2) mailed information, or (3) personal visit from project staff. Third, certified letters were sent to the chief executive officers of 24 company-owned chain and franchise operations in the county, requesting them to issue a companywide directive telling store managers that they would not tolerate illegal sales of tobacco to minors, require managers to post notices about this policy, implement employee training programs about the policy, and develop a mechanism to monitor the policy. The 18 minors then revisited each store or outlet 6 months later, following the intervention program, and again attempted to purchase cigarettes.

Results showed that over-the-counter sales to these minors decreased from 74% at baseline to 39% at the second visit. However, vending machine sales were not reduced at posttreatment, remaining at 100% at both visits. The stores that received the mailed education kits or the personal visits increased the number of warning signs in the stores, but there was no differential effect on sales as a function of type of contact among the three conditions.

The authors suggest that a law similar to the one enacted in King County, Washington, serve as a model for other counties. This law requires that vending machines must be electronically disabled until a store clerk is certain of the purchaser's age; all tobacco merchants must be licensed and each one is tested yearly by minors attempting to purchase cigarettes; sales of individual cigarettes are banned; penalties for sales to minors are $100 for the first offense and up to $1,000 and suspension of license for 9 to 18 months for the third offense; minors caught purchasing cigarettes can be subjected to community service programs and required to attend smoking cessation programs.

In addition to the law, Altman et al., (1989) suggest that federal laws be passed requiring a minimum age of 21 for the purchase of tobacco and uniform enforcement of both alcohol and tobacco laws; all businesses selling tobacco be licensed; fines for illegal sales be increased substantially; stronger enforcement of current laws; required posting of warning signs about sales to minors; elimination of all cigarette vending machines; and a national campaign to inform the general public, health professionals, community groups, and businesses about the problem and provide help to them for dealing with it. This study is an excellent example of the kind of community intervention programs that can make a difference. Their practical recommendations are particularly helpful for public health researchers and for those in health promotion.

ALCOHOLISM

Several topics are surveyed in this section on alcoholism. New data on the prevalence of drinking in the United States suggest that about 18 million adults experience significant problems associated with their use of alcohol. Among adolescents, two-thirds of high school students reported on a survey that they used alcohol within the past month. Adolescents tend to perceive drinking as a relatively low-risk activity compared with other drug use, a finding that has clear implications for behavioral scientists when attempting to design effective awareness and treatment programs for this young population. Several recent articles about the Sobell and Sobell (1973a, 1973b) controlled drinking controversy prompted one more comment on this long-running story. Behavioral self-management training programs for problem drinkers continue to show impressive posttreatment results, and the trend toward multifaceted, eclectic interventions appears here to stay. As behavior therapy's role in assessment and treatment expands in this area, further successes seem likely.

New Data on Prevalence

The United States is a nation of drinkers. Per capita consumption in 1984 was the equivalent of 2.65 gallons of pure alcohol per person 14 years and older (Williams, Doernber, Stinson, & Noble, 1986). That amount of alcohol equates to about 50 gallons of beer, or 20 gallons of wine, or more than 4 gallons of distilled spirits. Excluding abstainers, consumption increased to about 4 gallons of pure alcohol per person. Figure 6-1 illustrates the long-term consumption of alcoholic beverages in gallons of pure alcohol from the repeal of Prohibition through 1984. Note the continued decline in total consumption during the 1980s. This 3-year decrease was the first seen since Prohibition. Both beer and spirits showed a decrease, and wine registered a slight increase. Consumption of spirits has declined steadily since 1970, a decrease of about 17%. Half of the alcohol consumed in the United States is drunk by 10% of the drinking population (Secretary of Health and Human Services, 1987).

An estimated 18 million adults 18 years of age and older experience problems because of their use of alcohol (Williams, Stinson, Parker, Harford, & Noble, 1987). Among their problems are withdrawal symptoms, binge drinking, inability to cut down on their drinking, inability to stop drinking until they are intoxicated, and loss of memory. The National Institute on Alcohol Abuse and Alcoholism (NIAAA) defines individuals with dependence symptoms as alcoholics (Secretary of Health and Human Services, 1987). The NIAAA defines alcohol abusers as those, who, although not showing dependence symptoms, do experience negative personal or social consequences of using alcohol, including health problems, impairment of job performance, difficulties with interpersonal relationships, or arrests. Adolescent alcohol abusers include those who are involved with law enforcement personnel, have difficulties with their parents, or have trouble in school.

Excluding abstainers, the survey data suggest that 7% of all adults experience moderate levels of dependence symptoms and 10% experi-

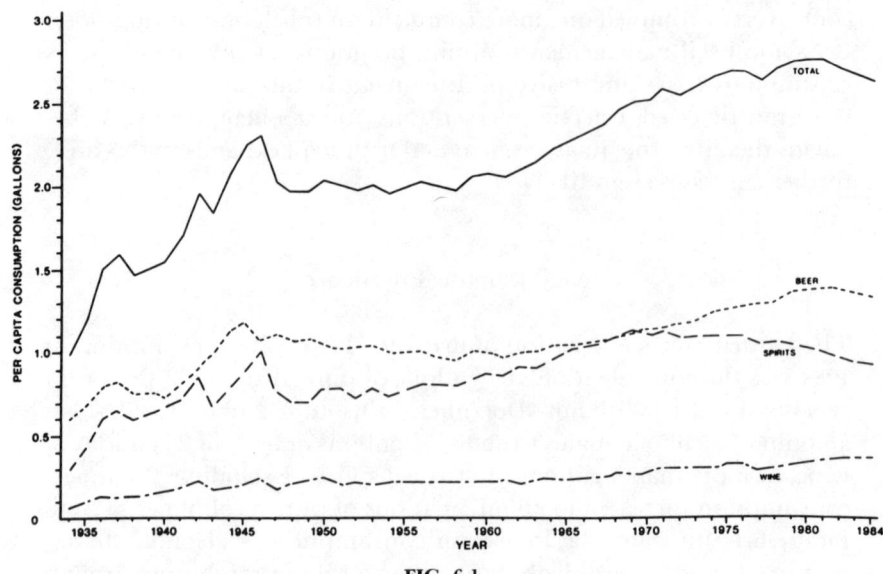

FIG. 6-1.
Apparent U.S. per capita consumption of alcoholic beverages in gallons of pure alcohol, from the end of Prohibition to 1984. Sources of data: *U.S. Apparent Consumption of Alcoholic Beverages Based on State Sales, Taxation, or Receipt Data. U.S. Alcohol Epidemiologic Data Reference Manual* (Vol. 1) by the National Institute on Alcohol Abuse and Alcoholism, Alcohol Epidemiologic Data System, 1985, Rockville, MD: National Institute on Alcohol Abuse and Alcoholism; and "National, State, and Regional Trends in Apparent Per Capita Consumption of Alcohol" by G. D. Williams, D. Dorenberg, F. Stinson, and J. Nobel, 1986, *Alcohol, Health and Research World, 10,* 60–63. From *Sixth Special Report to the U.S. Congress on Alcohol and Health* (DHHS Publication No. ADM 87-1519) by the Secretary of Health and Human Services, 1987, p. 2, Washington, DC: U.S. Government Printing Office.

ence moderate levels of tangible social or personal consequences associated with alcohol abuse (Hilton, 1987). More men than women are affected, with 14% of men and 6% of women reporting a moderate level of tangible consequences due to alcohol.

According to an annual nationwide survey of about 17,000 high school seniors conducted by the National Institute of Drug Abuse, alcohol consumption among adolescents has shown a slow, gradual decline through 1985 (Johnston, O'Malley, & Bachman, 1986). Use of cocaine has increased. Almost 5% of high school seniors drank every day in 1985. Heavy drinking, five or more drinks at a time during the preceding 2 weeks, was reported by 37% of seniors. Even though consumption of alcohol among adolescents is apparently on the decline,

92% of high school seniors reported having used alcohol at least once and about 66% reported having used it during the preceding month.

High school seniors were also surveyed about their perceptions of the degree of risk associated with various levels of alcohol. A total of 24% reported that they perceived a great risk in the consumption of one or two drinks nearly every day; 43% perceived that there was a great risk in five or more drinks at one time once or twice each weekend, and 70% perceived a great risk in consuming four or five drinks nearly every day (Johnston et al. 1986).

Figure 6-2 illustrates the perceived harmfulness of drugs by high school seniors through 1985. The regular use of cocaine continues to be seen as the most risky, followed by regular use of marijuana and one or two packs of cigarettes per day. Consuming five or more drinks once or twice each weekend or one or two drinks nearly every day is perceived as considerably less risky. These data have treatment implications for behavior therapists. If adolescents perceive drinking as relatively low risk compared with other drugs, intervention efforts may first have to be directed at raising the knowledge levels of the potential dangers of prolonged misuse of alcohol before any prevention or treatment campaigns in schools or communities will have much of an effect.

The Controlled Drinking Controversy: Epilogue

I know that I promised in the previous volume of this series that final comments on the Sobell and Sobell (1973a, 1973b, 1976) controlled drinking controversy had been written and that the story had been laid to rest. Unfortunately, another article, along with several rejoinders, has been published; thus, some comment needs to be made for those readers still following the saga. Readers unfamiliar with the history are referred to the original articles (Sobell & Sobell, 1973a, 1973b, 1976; Caddy, Addington, & Perkins, 1978; Pendery, Maltzman, & West, 1982) and reviews of the controversy in Volumes 9, 10, and 11 of this series (Brownell, 1984, 1985; Foreyt, 1987b)

The latest article is one by Maltzman (1989), in which he states the same allegations he has made over the past several years. Reading his article, I could not find anything new in it that I had not read previously. The article appears to me to simply repeat what he has already written (e.g., Pendery et al., 1982).

In the same issue of the *Journal of Studies on Alcohol* is a strong editorial statement by Nathan (1989). He comments that the Maltzman

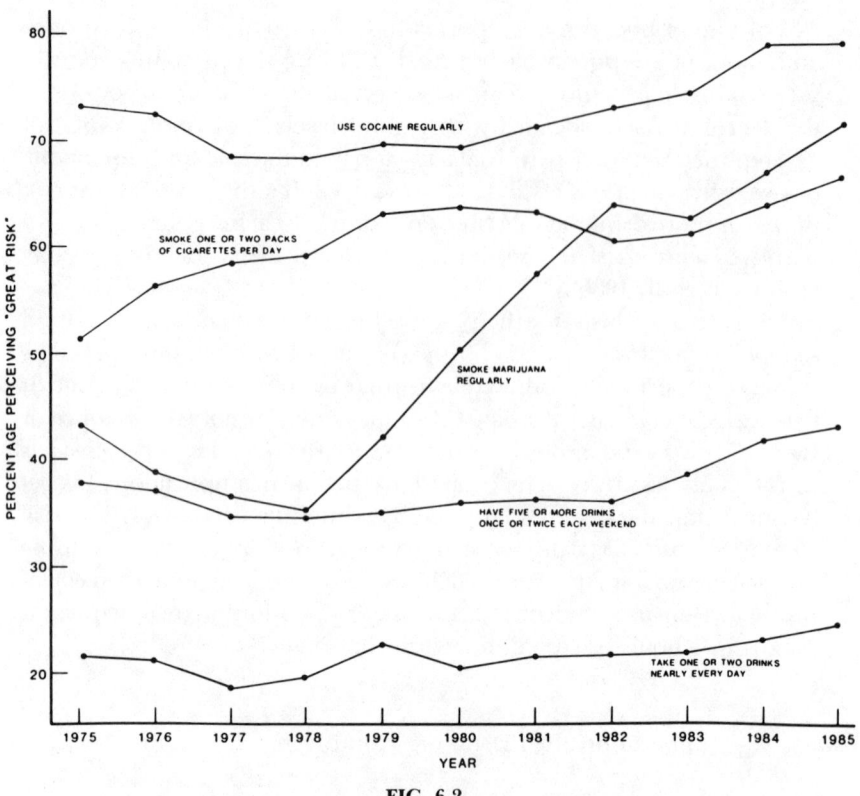

FIG. 6-2.
Perceived harmfulness of drugs as reported by high school seniors, United States, 1985. Source of data: *Drug Use Among American High School Students, College Students, and Other Young Adults: National Trends through 1985* (DHHS Publication No. ADM 86-1450) by L. D. Johnston, P. M. O'Malley, and J. G. Bachman, 1986, p. 112, Washington, DC: U.S. Government Printing Office. From *Sixth Special Report to the U.S. Congress on Alcohol and Health* (DHHS Publication No. ADM 87-1519) by the Secretary of Health and Human Services, 1987, p. 16, Washington, DC: U.S. Government Printing Office.

article was accepted by a field editor and that the journal later requested that it be withdrawn because parts were thought to be inappropriate. The request was refused and the article was published to honor the journal's commitment. Nathan also writes that, in his reading, Maltzman raises no new issues, and that there have been a number of separate and competent inquiries that have investigated and essentially vindicated the Sobells with respect to the original allegations (see Foreyt, 1987b, for a review of the inquiries).

There also is a response to the Maltzman article by Cook (1989), which includes a strong rejoinder, and a comment by Baker (1989). Baker was an undergraduate research assistant working with the Sobells on their study and he presents an interesting perspective about what went on during the time he was there. His conclusions are supportive of the Sobells and the various inquiries.

Finally, in the same issue, there is an article written by the Sobells (Sobell & Sobell, 1989) entitled "Moratorium on Maltzman: An Appeal to Reason," in which they carefully review once again the allegations raised by Maltzman and colleagues, and they summarize the findings of each of the inquiries into the conduct of their study. Reading the article by the Sobells again reminded me of the agony and suffering they must have gone through during the past several years. Reviewing the entire controversy one more time, I was again impressed with how thoughtfully and impressively the Sobells handled each of the attacks on them and their work. Although minor errors in the reporting of their data were found, none of these errors appeared to have affected the study's outcome. Only because the Sobells kept such detailed records of their study, including original tapes and notes, were the inquiries able to arrive at their conclusions. The outcomes of the inquiries indicate that the results of their study are correct. This latest article by Maltzman does not add any new information as far as I can determine.

The Sobells state that enough is enough, that they are going to get on with their lives, and that they are calling a halt to their side of the controversy. Their study has been essentially vindicated by five separate inquiries. It has been drawn out long enough, and it has diverted attention away from the growing number of reports investigating the role of controlled drinking with individuals who have difficulty handling alcohol. The Sobells write that they anticipate that their calling a halt will be welcomed by most who have followed the controversy. I for one agree with them. Let's call it quits and turn our priorities to other issues in this field.

Behavioral Treatment of Alcohol Abuse

Hester and Miller (1989) have published an excellent handbook of treatment approaches for alcoholism. I recommend it highly to all behavior therapists working with problem drinkers. They begin their book by stating three myths about alcoholism treatment: "Nothing works; there is one particular approach which is superior to all others; all treatment approaches work about equally well" (p. 3). Then they proceed to discredit each of them. The authors provide a helpful developmental history of the ways in which alcohol has been conceptualized, and they review 11 models of addictive behaviors and each model's implications for treatment. Table 6-6 summarizes these models.

A number of excellent reviews have surveyed the current state of the art in the treatment of alcohol abuse and the reader is referred to them for in-depth coverage (e.g., Hester & Miller, 1989; Miller & Hester, 1986; Riley, Sobell, Leo, Sobell, & Klajner, 1987; Sobell, Toneatto, & Sobell, 1990; Sobell, Wilkinson, & Sobell, in press).

Over the past few years behavioral treatment programs for alcohol abuse have continued to become more comprehensive and eclectic. I think that this is the result of a growing realization among behavior therapists of the limitations of narrowband, traditional behavioral approaches. The application of aversion therapy or covert sensitization or social skills training to an addicted individual within the context of a one-on-one therapeutic situation rarely leads to long-term favorable changes, especially in an area as complex as alcohol abuse. Our conceptualizations of alcoholism have become much more integrative and sophisticated. The continuation of the overall trend in the behavioral field to incorporate cognitive constructs (Donovan & Marlatt, 1988; Marlatt & Gordon, 1985) into our conceptualizations has also contributed to the refreshing advances in the study of alcohol abuse.

Does Controlled Drinking Work for Problem Drinkers?

Behavioral self-management training programs continue to receive increasing attention in this field. The overall goal of these programs is the attaining of either abstinence or, more usually, moderate, nonproblematic drinking. The programs typically incorporate a number of behavioral techniques, including self-monitoring, goal setting, specific rewards for the attainment of goals, a functional analysis of drinking situations, and training in the acquisition of alternative coping skills. The training can be either self-directed using a self-help manual or therapist-directed using a group setting with weekly meetings for a specified number of weeks. According to Hester and Miller (1989), these programs have been extensively studied and have been subjected to more controlled evaluations than any other intervention in the alcohol abuse field. Hester and Miller (1989) conclude that the research studies on these behavioral procedures indicate that they do work with some problem drinkers and that some drinkers can sustain moderate and nonproblemmatic drinking over extended time periods. They find that a number of patients decide to become totally abstinent and, when patients are randomly assigned to intervention programs with abstinence or moderation as goals, the long-term results tend to be comparable.

For example, Sanchez-Craig, Annis, Bornet, and MacDonald (1984) randomly assigned 70 problem drinkers to a behavioral treatment program with either an abstinence or controlled drinking goal. Patients received five or six sessions of cognitive-behavior therapy. The authors reported that significant improvements in drinking were achieved in both groups at posttreatment with no significant differences between them. Over a 2-year follow-up, the authors found no changes in the proportion of patients in the outcome categories; regardless of the patient's initial assignment, 70% moderated their drinking over the follow-up compared with 5% who abstained.

Foy, Nunn, and Rychtarik (1984) reported the successful reduction of drinking in two groups of patients who received cognitive-behavior therapy and training in drinking management. The group that received training in controlled drinking reported fewer abstinent days and more abusive drinking at 6 months, but there were no differences between the groups at 12 months. The authors have now published a 5- to 6-year follow-up of their data, and they reported no significant differences in drinking, with 20% of all subjects abstinent and 18% drinking moderately (Rychtarik, Foy, Scott, Lokey, & Prue, 1987).

Skutle and Berg (1987) randomly assigned 48 problem drinkers to one of four conditions: self-control-oriented bibliotherapy, therapist-assisted self-control therapy, coping skills treatment, or coping skills treatment plus self-control therapy. No significant group differences were found at posttreatment with all groups showing decreases in alcohol consumption. At the 12-month follow-up, 7% of the patients were abstinent and 24% were drinking moderately with no reported episodes of heavy drinking.

Alden (1988) assigned 127 problem drinkers to one of three conditions: behavioral self-control, drug counseling, or a waiting list control group. The two treatment groups did not differ on any measure: both decreased their drinking, had lower peak blood alcohol levels, and had more abstinent and controlled drinking days than the controls. Graber and Miller (1988) randomly assigned 24 problem drinkers to a behavioral self-control treatment with either an abstinence or a reduced drinking goal. Again, no differences were found, with both groups significantly reducing their alcohol consumption. Gains were

TABLE 6-6. A Developmental History of Models of Addictive Behaviors and Their Implications for Intervention

Model	Examples	Emphasized casual factors	Implied interventions	Appropriate intervention agent
Moral	Abuse as sin	Spirituality	Spiritual direction	Clergy
	Abuse as crime	Personal responsibility	Moral suasion	Law enforcement agents
			Social sanctions	
Temperance	Prohibition	Alcohol	Exhortation	Abstainers
	WCTU		Abstinence/prohibition	Legislators
American disease	AA	Irreversible constitutional	Identification/confrontation	Recovering alcoholics
	NA	Abnormality of individual	Lifelong abstinence	Peer support
Educational	Lectures	Lack of knowledge	Education	Educators
	Affective education	Lack of motivation		
Characterological	Psychoanalysis	Personality	Psychotherapy	Psychotherapists
		Traits/dispositions	Risk identification	
		Defense mechanisms	Self-image modification	
Conditioning	Classical conditioning	Conditioned response	Counterconditioning	Behavior therapists
	Operant conditioning	Reinforcement	Altered contingencies	
			Relearning, "disenabling"	

Model	Examples	Etiology	Intervention	Providers
Biomedical	Heredity Brain (THIQ)	Genetic Physiological	Risk identification Medical treatment	Diagnosticians Physicians
Social learning	Cognitive therapy Relapse prevention	Modeling Expectancies Skill deficits	Appropriate models/goals Cognitive restructuring Skill training Self-control training	Cognitive-behavior therapists Appropriate models
General systems	Transactional analysis Adult children of alcoholics	Family dysfunction	Family therapy Recognition, peer support	Family therapist Support groups
Sociocultural	Control of consumption	Environmental Cultural norms	Supply-side intervention Social policy Server intervention	Lobbyists/legislators Social policy makers Retailers/servers
Public health	World Health Organization National Academy of Sciences	Interactions of host, agent, and environment	Comprehensive, multifaceted	Interdisciplinary

Note. From "Treating Alcohol Problems: Toward an Informed Eclecticism" by W. R. Miller and R. K. Hester, 1989, in R. K. Hester and W. R. Miller (Eds.), *Handbook of Alcoholism Treatment Approaches: Effective Alternatives*, p. 10, New York: Pergamon Press. Copyright 1989 by Pergamon Press. Reprinted by permission.

maintained at a 3.5-year follow-up. A total of 16.5% of patients in both groups attained abstinence. Only 8.5% of patients with moderation as their goal were able to successfully reduce their drinking.

Overall the data suggest that behavioral self-management programs, when they have moderate drinking as their goal, are more effective with less severe problem drinkers and are not recommended for severely dependent patients. These programs can, however, also be implemented with abstinence as their goal. For severely dependent alcoholics, abstinence is still the primary treatment goal (Nathan, 1986; Nathan & Skinstad, 1987).

Current Status of Behavior Therapy for Problem Drinkers

Most of the behavioral research over the past several years has used a package of self-management intervention strategies. These programs do result in reduced drinking at posttreatment. We do not know, however, whether these strategies are superior to other behavioral or nonbehavioral interventions (Sobell et al., 1990). Like the obesity and smoking literature, a number of techniques have been grouped under the rubric "self-management training." Like the literature in these other areas, the effectiveness of the strategies may not lie in the components themselves but rather in the nonspecifics of therapeutic change processes that are common to any intervention (Foreyt, Goodrick, & Gotto, 1981; Sobell et al., 1990).

Treatment for alcoholism today appears to be increasingly guided by a more informed eclecticism (Hester & Miller, 1989). This informed eclecticism has blossomed because researchers and clinicians understand that there is no one single best approach to treatment for all patients, that different types of individuals appear to respond to different treatments, and that it is becoming increasingly more possible to match individuals to their best treatment, increasing both efficiency and effectiveness (Hester & Miller, 1989).

Is Inpatient Detoxification for Alcoholics Needed?

Today's treatment programs for alcoholics typically involve 6 to 8 weeks of inpatient hospitalization following detoxification, including both individual and group psychotherapy, enlisting support from family members, and referring to Alcoholics Anonymous (Klerman, 1989). A recent study questioned the value of inpatient detoxification for patients with mild to moderate symptoms of alcohol withdrawal. The report reflects the growing trend toward outpatient interventions for addictive disorders. Hayashida et al. (1989) randomly assigned 164 male veterans who had applied to a Veterans Administration Alcoholism Treatment Unit for alcohol detoxification over a 2-year period to either outpatient ($n = 87$) or inpatient ($n = 77$) detoxification. To be accepted into the study, patients showed evidence of the alcohol withdrawal syndrome to require detoxification, including coarse tremors of the hands and at least one other symptom of withdrawal. The patients assigned to the outpatient group were evaluated medically and psychiatrically and prescribed decreasing doses of oxazepam at daily clinic visits. The inpatient group received similar treatment in the hospital.

Results showed that the mean duration of treatment was only 6.5 days for the outpatients compared with 9.2 days for the inpatients. Fewer outpatients (72%) than inpatients (95%) completed detoxification; there were no serious medical complications seen in either of the groups. Substantial improvement was observed in both groups at 1- and 6-month follow-ups. There were no group differences found at the 6-month follow-up. Also, the authors found no differences in the subsequent use of other alcoholism treatment services. Major savings in cost per patient were seen: outpatient costs per patient were $175 to $388; inpatient costs were $3,319 to $3,666. The authors concluded that outpatient medical detoxification is "an effective, safe, and low-cost treatment for patients with mild-to-moderate symptoms of alcohol withdrawal" (Hayashida et al., 1989, p. 358).

Unanswered Questions in the Treatment of Alcohol Abuse

A number of unanswered questions with respect to the current treatment of alcoholics remain. For example, is an inpatient treatment program always needed to begin an intervention program? If inpatient treatment is necessary, how long should it be? Should the alcoholism unit be part of a general hospital, or are other arrangements effective? How critical is abstinence? How feasible is controlled drinking for some alcohol abusers?

There is little prospect of any new technological breakthroughs in the treatment of alcoholism in the near future (Klerman, 1989). No pharmacological agents are going to be available soon to help reverse dependency. Research efforts therefore need to be directed toward evaluating the efficacy, costs, and safety of current therapeutic approaches. A comprehensive report on the treatment of alcoholism currently being prepared by the Institute of Medicine of the National Academy of Sciences should be extremely helpful in focusing priorities in this area of growing research interest by behavior therapists. Behavioral scientists have an enormous amount of expertise to contribute in this area that has for so long been dominated by one predominant faction in this country.

CHAPTER

7

BEHAVIOR THERAPY WITH CHILDREN AND ADOLESCENTS

CYRIL M. FRANKS

INTRODUCTION

Preparation for this chapter involved a screening of many child-relevant articles. In general, case studies and investigations dealing with narrowly focused issues or problems of assessment were excluded. My main concerns were twofold: (1) to evaluate the extent to which the limited mainstream return to conceptualization and the development of a systems/ecologically oriented perspective noted in Chapter 1 is also evident in the present context, and (2) to place recent child-relevant behavioral events in perspective.

Developments in child behavior therapy parallel the mainstream. The shift from a linear model to a more systems-oriented interactionism is beginning to filter through to child behavior therapists and those administrators and professionals who work either directly or indirectly with young people (e.g., Powers, 1987). Kuhn (1970) defines a paradigm shift as "a series of tradition-bound periods punctuated by non-cumulative . . . revolutionary breaks." In drawing attention to this definition, Whittaker, Schinke, and Gilchrist (1986) suggest that we are near such a shift in both policy and practice with respect to young people and their well-being. It is social support systems, networks, life skills evaluation, and the individual as a group member within a total environment that are now the focus, and Holahan, Wilcox, Spearly, and Campbell (1979) offer a twofold strategy for identification and utilization of this emerging paradigm: an environmental emphasis establishing or strengthening social support, and a transactional focus upon individual competencies for dealing with environmental blocks.

The literature offers some modest evidence for the efficacy of child welfare social support systems (e.g., Whittaker, Garbarino, & Associates, 1983). Polansky and Gaudin (1983) address the question of how a family's neighborhood environment can help or hinder the quality of childrearing. Social isolation was found to be a frequent correlate of families involved in neglect and abuse. For Polansky and Gaudin, one avenue leading to reduction of social isolation and the availability of neighborhood social support is the improvement of parenting behaviors to conform with the community norm. The research of Dumas and Wahler (1983) bears directly on this point. Ecological variables have a powerful, if at times indirect, impact upon mother–child behavior change. Parental training programs that overlook contextual factors, especially in high-risk families, may inadvertently turn the treatment experience into one of failure and helplessness.

Increasingly, the evidence points to the need to combine social support systems with the teaching of specific life skills. According to Whittaker et al., the presence or absence of such community support systems, especially within the context noted above, appears to be a better predictor of youth progress than status at discharge, case work predictions, severity of presenting problems, or type of treatment.

Kiesler's (1985) perceptive review of the policy implications of such research raises critical questions that are likely to inform and guide both policy debate and research within the 1990s. Until then, Kiesler advocates a wait-and-see policy, whereas Whittaker et al. conclude that sufficient evidence already exists to warrant revision of current strategies.

In 1961 Bijou and Baer proposed extending behavioral analysis to the area of child development, a proposal that lost impetus with the ascendance of Bandura's social learning theory and Piagetian cognitive development. The notion remains alive in the form of an updated integration of applied behavior analysis, interbehaviorism, systems theory, and developmental psychology (see Chapter 1, this volume; also Franks, 1989; Morris & Hursh, 1979).

Similarly, Simon and Johnston (1987) make a spirited pitch for a nonlinear, systems-oriented approach within school and family settings. Both traditional psychodynamicists and behavior therapists, it is argued, emphasize individuals rather than human interactions. Family stress and symptoms of behavioral disorders cannot be adequately described in terms of simple cause and effect. The nonlinear approach they advocate stresses the notion of circular or reciprocal interaction.

School personnel, for example, fall readily into the fallacious position of seeing the single parent as responsible for the behavioral disorders of their children. The single parent who has difficulty in scheduling school conferences is labeled as difficult, uncaring, or irresponsible, laying fertile ground for a deteriorating relationship between school and parent, with the hapless child caught in the middle (Power & Bartholomew, 1985). Unfortunately, as Simon and Johnston note, shifting from a linear to an interactive model is likely to go against the grain of traditional school planning and thereby arouse much resistance. Evans and Scheuer (1987) make a similar point in their discussion of response repertoires in childhood aggression, but for them the solution lies in Staats's (1975) social behaviorism. According to Staats, the individual child's personality can be thought of as a system of interrelated behaviors learned through prior experience but functioning in an interactive, causative manner so as to influence subsequent experience and learning. Behaviors are inseparable from the interactions between individuals and their social milieu.

Plas's (1986) school psychology text likewise makes a plea for systemic thinking. However, while recognizing the value of mechanistic Western formulations, she also wants the reader to take into account the holistic metaphysics of Eastern philosophy. According to Plas, systems psychology, with its focus on rules of communication rather than individuals and patterns rather than discrete causes, offers a meaningful synthesis between these two perspectives. The major problem with this ambitious book is that it attempts to accomplish too much in too little space (see also Franks, 1987b; Harris, 1987).

This broader perspective influences all aspects of behavior therapy, from initial assessment through intervention to outcome evaluation (Cone & Hoier, 1986; Voeltz & Evans, 1982). Acceptability, with its enlarged sphere of influence, offers a good example of this new look struggling to emerge. Factors now reported to influence acceptability include problem severity, treatment approach, time needed for treatment, implementation, treatment integrity, effectiveness of treatment, and mutual consideration of the opinions of all concerned (Witt & Elliott, 1985; Reimers, Wacker, & Koeppl, 1987). And yet, these encouraging trends notwithstanding, many studies still focus on acceptability from the perspective of the therapist and the adult community exclusively rather than that of the child (e.g., Tarnowski, Kelly, & Mendlowitz, 1987). Fortunately, this blinkered view of the world can be modified by appropriate adult education (Singh & Katz, 1985) and the active involvement of parents, school personnel, and child (Dadds, Adlington, & Christensen, 1987).

Two of the new texts warrant discussion. Hersen and Van Hasselt's (1987) *Behavior Therapy with Children and Adolescents* offers an excellent across the board overview of new developments, but school and family contexts are underrepresented, developmental psychology is given short shrift, and systems/ecological perspectives are hardly mentioned. Nevertheless, for those seeking an up-to-date survey of traditional child behavior therapy, this volume has much to offer.

Finally, there is Kazdin's (1987) *Conduct Disorders in Childhood and Adolescence*. Kazdin, a seasoned campaigner, more than accomplishes his assignments: to present relevant new theory and research; to bridge and integrate theory, research, and clinical practice; to assess current status; and to point to new directions. Attention is drawn to the need for increased specificity in the identification of symptom patterns pertaining to peer relations and the many settings within which the child functions. Profiles of antisocial youth and their functioning environments could lead to more effective intervention strategies. Most current treatment programs for antisocial behavior, notes Kazdin, are directed toward the more moderate levels of disturbance. Such strategies might be better deployed in the development of programs geared toward secondary prevention. In terms of secondary, and perhaps primary, prevention, Kazdin's proposal to consider conduct disorders as chronic conditions requiring intervention and monitoring at many levels throughout the life span is particularly intriguing. It is too bad that Kazdin does little more than raise rather than explore these issues.

HOME AND FAMILY IN BEHAVIOR THERAPY

Contemporary family behavior therapy is systems-oriented. Turnbull, Summers, and Brotherson (1984) used a case study methodology to identify the many interlocking systems within which families with handicapped children operate. For example, the economic function of the family may be affected due to increased medical and educational costs, not to mention the increased time required to provide care at the expense of more economically productive pursuits. Greater demands are often placed on the family's physical care function with respect to their handicapped child, and opportunities for family rest, recuperation, and socializing thereby become restricted. Virtually all spouse, sibling, and extrafamily relationships can be affected. Knowledge of coping strategies and the manner in which these impinge upon various family systems is now an established component of most behavioral family therapy research (Schilling & Schinke, 1988).

Social interaction research and family systems research are closely related. However, the bulk of social interaction research to date has focused on peer relationships in educational settings. Direct analyses of parent–sibling interactions in terms of other relationships are rare (Fox & Savelle, 1987). (Patterson's well-known studies of coercive family process involving conduct-disordered children is a notable exception to this generalization; e.g., Patterson, 1982.) According to Fox and Savelle, the few observational studies of the in-home, family interaction patterns of children that are available, especially those who are behaviorally disordered, suffer from serious methodological limitations. Global categories and lack of procedural standardization predominate. Understandably then, the findings are equivocal, to say the least.

Dadds and his associates have long been concerned with ecological relationships between family variables and child behavior. Their particular interest is in what they term "oppositional children" and the institution of multimodality-based family interventions (Dadds, 1987). The leading behavioral models of family interaction come from Patterson, Wahler, and their associates (e.g., Patterson & Reid, 1984; Wahler & Dumas, 1984). Each family member's behavior is conceptualized in terms of functional, mutually dependent interactions with other family members. In social learning terms, oppositional behavior is both a response and a stimulus for the behavior of others in the system. Engaging in aggressive behavior is thought to maximize short-term gains for child and/or parent without necessarily invoking more complex and lasting social behaviors. Until recently, as Dadds notes, these models have been based largely on data limited to observations of dyadic interactions between mother and child. Nowadays, the trend is turning toward the individual's role in relation to more general social systems (e.g., Griest & Wells, 1983).

Patterson and Reid's (1984) social interactional perspective and Wahler and Dumas's (1984) systems interaction model are highly compatible. Both assume that a child's behavior is determined by a network of subsystems that form the components of other more complex systems. At each level, component elements are interdependent in the ways they function, and each level is affected by the dynamics of levels above and below it. Throughout, pertinent family characteristics need to be taken into consideration.

Dadds and his associates arrive at their conclusions through carefully controlled studies supplemented by clinical observation. For example, to study the patterns of marital discord and their effects upon family interactions during behavioral parent training for parents with oppositional children, four families were subjected to systematic intensive observation. A multiple-baseline design was used to assess the effects of different treatment conditions on parent–parent and parent–child interactions. All families underwent baseline observation, child management training, partner support training, and 6-months follow-up. Measures of parent and child behavior were obtained by independent observers who recorded family interactions in the home during evening meals and in other settings. Both at baseline and during child management training, parents engaged in aversive interchanges with their spouses. For the most part, these interchanges coincided with misbehaviors by their children. During partner support training, aversive behavior decreased and problem-solving behavior increased. These results are consistent with theories of social learning, which emphasize the functional relationship of aggressive child behavior to marital and other family interactional systems.

The authors of this article, Dadds, Sanders, Behrens, and James (1987), are careful to point out that only limited generalizations can be made from a study involving four families. Nevertheless, the finding that partner support training, in particular the phase that focused on escalating day-to-day crises, was associated with decreases in parent–parent aversiveness for all families still engaging in these behaviors following child management training is important. This unique study demonstrates that parents can implement treatment suggestions focusing on marital interactions within the context of behavioral parent training. Another finding worthy of follow-up is that the father's presence did not consistently influence any of the mother–child interactions. In a related study with a larger sample, Dadds, Schwartz, and Sanders (1987) found that significant improvement was in evidence as long as 6 months after discontinuation of the program.

Ramsey and Walker (1988) were interested in parents of antisocial versus nonantisocial middle-school boys. Specifically, the family management practices of an antisocial and a nonantisocial control group were contrasted. The 80 fourth-grade boys and their families included in this study were part of an extensive, longitudinal investigation of families identified as being at greater than normal risk for development of antisocial behavior. The antisocial family interactions that emerged were characterized by negativism, stern disciplinary practices, inconsistency, lack of structure, and relatively low levels of competence in parenting skills. As Ramsey and Walker note, the correlational and descriptive nature of this study precludes the ascribing of any causal or functional role to family practice differences between their two groups. However, the findings do approximate closely those reported by Patterson and his group in which causal relationships have been systematically explored (e.g., Patterson, 1986).

It is Wahler and Dumas's (1986) contention that antisocial behavior patterns can continue across generations. Children exposed to harsh, negative, and generally incompetent parenting styles are predisposed to developing similar parenting styles with their own children when they grow up. Thus, Ramsey and Walker reasonably speculate that the antisocial subjects in their study are substantially at risk for long-term negative developmental outcomes as well as the creation of family societies that place their own children at risk at higher than normal risk for the development of such behavior patterns.

Most research pertaining to contact disorders in children has focused primarily upon boys. There is little evidence that such an association exists between marital problems and the childhood problems of girls. When Johnson and O'Leary (1987) compared conduct-disordered and non-conduct-disordered girls, using parental reports about themselves and their children and child reports on themselves and both parents, as predicted parents of conduct-disordered girls were more hostile in non-child-directed contexts than were parents of girls who were non-conduct-disordered. Although these negative features were evident for both mothers and fathers, the mothers' behavior patterns tended to be more closely associated with the children's behavior patterns than were those of the fathers. Additionally, the more hostile the mother was toward her spouse, the more likely she was to perceive her child's behavior as unsatisfactory. In this event, the infusion of brief marital interaction strategy into the overall parent training program may be helpful (Dadds, Schwartz, & Sanders, 1987).

Attention has already been drawn to the need for acceptability ratings by the children directly concerned. Furthermore, although parent training studies of child management interventions from the parents' perspectives are much more commonplace, virtually all samples consist primarily of middle class participants (Heffer & Kelley, 1987). Regardless of acceptability, there would seem to be a negative relationship between program success, on the one hand, and socioeconomic status and deficit social interactions, on the other. In particular, there would seem to be a negative relationship between low income and successful parent training outcome. It may be that low-income parents have poorer reading ability, greater marital conflict, and a dearth of pretreatment child management skills. It has also been suggested that coercive interchanges between disadvantaged mothers and adults outside the home may lead to negative parent–child interactions. Dumas and Wahler's (1983) disadvantaged, insular mothers, for example, seemed to lack the necessary social or problem-solving skills either to benefit directly from parent training or to generalize to new situations.

Heffer and Kelley draw attention to a hitherto unexplored hypothesis to account for the high failure rate of parent training with low-income parents, namely, that different income groups vary in their perceptions of the social validity of treatment procedures. If, for example, lower-income parents view an intervention as unacceptable, they may be more likely to drop out of parent training or to use the techniques inappropriately. Thus, commonly utilized behavioral interventions may be less socially valid when taught to low-income mothers. Most investigators confine themselves to parental perceptions following participation in the training programs, with parents generally reporting satisfaction with treatment received. However, satisfaction ratings have usually been obtained only from those individuals who complete treatment. Thus, given that low-income parents are more likely to terminate treatment prematurely, little can be said about consumer satisfaction ratings with low-income families. No study seems to have systematically examined the social validity of behavioral interventions from the relative perspectives of white and nonwhite, middle class, and lower-income parents.

To shed light on this problem, Heffer and Kelley assessed the effects of race and income on mothers' ratings of the acceptability of five management interventions. The participants were 83 mothers of children between the ages of 2 and 12 years recruited from pediatric outpatient waiting rooms. Data were collected from 45 black or white low-income mothers, and 38 middle- to upper-income mothers, 18 black and 20 white. Participants were presented with a hypothetical case description and five methods that might be used to correct the behavior problems described. These consisted of positive reinforcement, response cost, time-out, spanking, and medication. The order of treatment descriptions was randomized across participants and each subject was asked to complete a 15-item questionnaire designed to measure adult acceptance of the treatment used.

Parents consistently rated response cost and positive reinforcements significantly more acceptable than the other treatments. Even more interesting, low- and middle-to-upper-income parents differed in their acceptance of specific treatments. For example, low-income families evaluated time-out as significantly less acceptable than either positive reinforcement or response cost, and spanking and medication as equally unacceptable. In contrast, middle-to-upper-income mothers viewed time-out, response cost, and reinforcement as equally acceptable and significantly more acceptable than the remaining treatments. Unfortunately, because Heffer and Kelley's study utilizes a hypothetical case and data based solely on self-report, it is of limited value in understanding the reasoning involved.

Clinic-referred children display rates of deviancy similar to those of nonclinic children, suggesting that a child may be referred to a clinic for reasons other than deviant behavior, for example, maternal depression. If this is so, argue Rickard, Graziano, and Forehand (1986), part of the child's "problem" may lie in the mother's perception. Perhaps it is the mother who should be the principle focus of the intervention in addition to the child. The second, not necessarily unrelated, determinant of clinic referral is the parents' knowledge and expectations. Parents with limited knowledge of child development norms and unrealistically high expectations may perceive deviancy where little is actually present.

To explore these possibilities, Rickard et al. developed a 67-item questionnaire for the assessment of parental knowledge, beliefs, and expectations about children and child-rearing practices. Their clinic group consisted of 16 mothers and their children who had contacted the University of Georgia Psychology Clinic for treatment of child behavior problems. The nonclinic group consisted of 88 mothers and their children who responded to written announcements in community kindergarten and day-care centers. Mother–child interactions were also assessed during home observations.

Three significant points emerged. First, there do seem to be relatively stable and measurable individual differences in parental knowledge and expectations about children and child-rearing practices. Second, individual differences within a clinic-referred group can be used to predict mother–child interactions in the home. Third, individual differences in parental knowledge and expectations about children and child-rearing practices do discriminate between child-referred and nonclinic mother–child pairs. In arriving at these conclusions, Rickard et al. are careful to draw attention to the correlational nature of their study and the limitations of causal inference. Additionally, the hypothetical construct of parental knowledge and expectancies was operationalized exclusively in terms of the mothers' responses. What about the fathers' knowledge and expectations and their relationships to mother and child responses? Even with these limitations, their study has significant practical implications. For example, when a child is referred to a psychological clinic, the extent to which the "problem" lies in the interpretation of the child's behavior by others, particularly the mother, needs to be carefully explored. Furthermore, to increase intervention effectiveness, it may be necessary to offer parents basic normative information about their children in addition to child management techniques.

Public Law 94-142 codified the role of families, primarily the parents, in the education of their handicapped children. The Individualized Educational Plan (IEP) provides the vehicle through which parents mandated active roles in the education of their exceptional children. Unfortunately, few parents take advantage of this opportunity, and because most research in this area has focused on the opinions of professionals rather than the parents themselves, we have little idea why this might be so (Weber & Stoneman, 1986). It would seem that professionals are only minimally supportive of a strong role for parents, and most team members perceive the influence and contributions of parents at planning meetings to be low. Those relatively few parents who do attend IEP meetings tend to be generally satisfied even though they report a desire for more input into the decision-making process. Little, however, is known about parents who do not attend program meetings. It seems probable that families with lower incomes, older children, and children with more severe developmental difficulties are less likely to participate in parent educational programs, advisory boards, political advocacy organizations, etc. (Suelzle & Keenan, 1984).

Weber and Stoneman studied 72 low-income families with parental education ranging from grade school or less to advanced graduate degrees. Forty-six of the families were white, the rest black. The children were all mentally retarded, about half lived at home, and the rest at a residential facility. All families were invited to attend all IEP meetings.

As expected, nonattending families tended to have lower incomes, less parental education, and to include more single-parent and nonwhite families. Mothers from nonattending families were inclined to place more responsibility for their children's educational programs on professionals and had significantly less information about the program than mothers from other families. These mothers also knew less about their children's educational goals and the support services that were available to them. Interestingly enough, mothers who attended the program planning meetings believed that they benefitted from attending, but many expressed the opinion that their presence made little or no difference to the outcome of the meeting.

It would seem important that ways be found to communicate to families inclined not to participate that they have important contributions to make. Most training workshops and parental meetings are not effective. Printed materials describing Public Law 94-142, Rights and Procedures, tend to be less than comprehensible to a large number of the parents for whom they are intended.

Finally, there is Eyberg's (1988) intriguing parent–child interaction therapy. In essence, this is a modification and updating of a successful combination of operant conditioning and traditional play therapy as spelled out more than two decades earlier by Hanf and her associates (see Eyberg, 1988) and described in some detail in previous volumes in this series. In the first of Hanf's two stages, the mother is instructed to let the child lead the play and taught how to give differential attention. In the second stage, the mother leads the play, gives clear instructions, praises her child for obeying, and punishes the child with time-out for not obeying.

Half's model is essentially an operant one even though it does make use of natural play situations. Eyberg decided to expand this approach and teach parents skills used by play therapists as well as those of behavior therapists. Although her focus is primarily descriptive, as yet the limited evidence that is available points to a high degree of parental compliance and treatment satisfaction as well as improved parental attitudes toward the child and generally enhanced psychological well-being within the family. It will be of interest to see what future research uncovers.

BEHAVIORAL PARENT TRAINING

Being a parent is an ubiquitous phenomenon, and it probably comes as no great surprise that behavioral parent training is one of the more thoroughly investigated areas within child behavior therapy. When the needs are special, as with the physically impaired or developmentally disabled child, behavioral parent training is likely to assume even greater prominence. It used to be thought that only children with mild forms of mental retardation and no serious behavioral problems were appropriate subjects either for behavioral parent training programs or placement in community-based schools (Matson, 1987). Stimulated in large part by the passage of Public Law 94-142, a dramatic shift has occurred, and it is now believed that training for most mentally retarded children is best conducted in the natural environment. Additionally, the prevailing emphasis is upon positive reinforcements and structured activities rather than aversive procedures (Romanczyk, 1986). However, unanticipated adverse side effects can occur. According to Kozloff, Helm, and Cutler (1987), even the best of these programs often produces changes that are limited both in scope and durability, promoting quantitative modification of isolated behaviors rather than substantial qualitative enrichment of functional repertoires.

As reviewed by Kozloff et al., behavioral parent training research is methodologically deficient. Given the thrust toward the development of such programs, this conclusion is discouraging. Little seems to be known about such basic variables as the characteristics of the parents and the family system as they impinge upon the parenting process, or even about the durability of change itself. Even when the need is great and the intervention seemingly effective over the short term (e.g., Scott & Stradling's [1987] six-session program for low-income, single-parent or state-benefit families with problem-behavior children), the long-term benefits remain unknown.

Kozloff et al. do not spare themselves in this indictment. Throughout the years, Kozloff and his associates were accustomed to evaluating their own programs on a regular basis, identifying weaknesses and suggesting revisions for incorporation into the next project. Their most recent thrust seems to be toward the strengthening of previously unnoticed competencies. It would seem that handicapped children possess a much greater repertoire of competencies in both social interactions and the performance of self-help tasks than had hitherto been suspected. Systematic observation and program modification over the years led Kozloff et al. to conclude that what most parents need is training at an early stage in tailoring programs to the specific requirements of their children. This is a formidable task, and Kozloff and his associates admit to major insufficiencies beyond their power to correct. Families need more than Kozloff can give them and more than they can give themselves.

The school system is apparently a particularly weak link in the chain. For a variety of reasons, administrators and teachers resist active parental participation, and gains painfully won during the school year tend to be lost during the summer. Thus, for many families, behaviorally oriented training programs geared toward summers and extended day ventures in addition to in-home assistance need to be implemented. (See Wood, 1986, for additional discussion of training programs for mentally handicapped children.)

Increasingly, mentally retarded couples express a wish to have children of their own, there are many reasons for this. First, more and more mildly and moderately retarded persons are being returned to the community from institutional settings. Second, this is the era of equal rights in the areas of marriage and parenting, and court decisions tend to favor this trend. Third, both involuntary and parent-requested sterilization is banned in many jurisdictions. Contrary to popular belief, low IQ (above 50) is not necessarily predictive of inadequate parenting. The problem would seem to be that although most of these parents could develop sufficient competency to raise their children, such families require considerable and specialized support from social service agencies, and this is not always forthcoming (Feldman, 1986).

Young children of retarded parents are at particular risk for developmental delay, particularly in language. Furthermore, mental development is related to the quality of maternal interactions, and retarded mothers are deficient in providing stimulating interactions during play, particularly with respect to giving appropriate praise and reinforcing child vocalizations.

Feldman uses these observations as a starting point for the development of individualized programs for mentally handicapped parents. Although still a long way from any claim that parent training and early intervention for these families can reduce the risk of developmental delay, cultural–familial retardation, maltreatment, and neglect, the findings to date are encouraging. Longitudinal studies are now needed to identify the significant predictors of developmental delay and subsequent school and home problems (Feldman et al., 1986).

Virtually all parents of handicapped children, mentally retarded or otherwise, are subject to mental and physical strain. When even short-term respite care is available, requests for residential placement are considerably reduced. Unfortunately, as Neef, Parrish, Egel, and Sloan (1986) note, quality respite care services are often not available. In part, this is because training programs for respite caregivers are not available. The few programs that are available rarely include either a comprehensive treatment package or requisite skills or sufficiently precise behavioral specification to permit reliable observation and evaluation.

Neef et al. systematically analyzed the effectiveness of what seemed to be a particularly promising instructional package for respite care workers. Taken together, their four controlled studies suggest that, when combined with modeling and behavior rehearsal, a well-designed self-instructional manual can be a cost-effective, consumer-acceptable alternative to the workshop format that is customarily employed in the training of respite personnel. Most important, the method can be readily used by agency personnel for evaluating trainee performance. It would seem that the customary written examination is not necessarily predictive of actual performance. Trainees who perform well in role-playing situations tend to perform well in carefully monitored respite care situations.

By now, the acceptability of a good number of treatment programs has been well researched. Children, parents, undergraduate students, hospital staff, teachers, and others have repeatedly been shown to be able to distinguish among alternative treatments on the basis of acceptability (Calvert & McMahon, 1987). Interventions designed to increase deficit behavior (e.g., positive reinforcement) are generally rated as more acceptable than interventions designed to decrease inappropriate or excessive behavior (e.g., time-out, medication).

Forehand and McMahon's (1981) much cited behavioral parent training program utilizes a controlled learning environment to teach parents how to change maladaptive interactions with their children. Sessions are conducted with individual families in a clinic setting. Social validity is demonstrated by way of consumer satisfaction methods. However, consumer satisfaction is not necessarily synonymous with treatment acceptability. In contrast to treatment acceptability, consumer satisfaction measures completed after treatment termination give no indication of how the same program may have been evaluated prior to treatment. Conceivably, such ratings could be affected by the perceived efficacy of the different procedures. Furthermore, consumer satisfaction measures usually apply only to subjects who finish the full program. Those who drop out or choose not to enter this type of treatment are not included (Calvert & McMahon, 1987).

In many behavioral parent training programs, despite substantial evidence that instructions facilitate both understanding and performance, parents are told to implement their newly acquired parenting techniques without prior explanation or demonstration. For such reasons, Calvert and McMahon reevaluated their 1981 project in terms of treatment acceptability for both individual components and the overall program. Additionally, they were interested in evaluating the relative acceptabilities of having parents provide their children with a verbal rationale plus modeling prior to use of the various parenting techniques or no rationale at all. Because it has already been demonstrated that a verbal rationale and/or modeling can enhance child behavior and parental satisfaction with the procedure, it was also deemed important to determine whether the inclusion of these methods of introduction would likewise enhance parental evaluations of treatment acceptability.

Ninety nonreferred mothers of 3- to 8-year-old children were evaluated for treatment acceptability of their behavioral parent training program in terms of five individual parenting skills (attends, rewards, ignoring, commands, time-out), three methods of introducing each new skill to the child (rationale plus modeling, no rationale, no modeling), and in terms of the program as an entity. All aspects of the program were rated very positively on overall ratings of acceptability. Strategies designed to increase deficit behavior (rewards, commands, attends) were rated as more acceptable than those used to reduce behavioral excesses (time-out, ignoring). Presenting a rationale was rated as the most acceptable method of introducing new parental strategies to the children. Comparisons with previous research by McMahon and associates also suggest that techniques embedded within an overall program tend to be perceived as more acceptable than techniques presented independently.

Limited parental or child acceptability is but one reason why behavioral parent training may not "take." Stress factors, family variables, setting events, child variables, marital disharmony, socioeconomic variables, and others have all been implicated at one time or another. Unfortunately, the correlational nature of most of these investigations precludes meaningful causal inference (Dumas, 1986). Recognizing these limitations, Dumas extended his earlier methodology to make causal inferences possible. His basic premise was that child variables are related to parental perception but not to outcome and that socioeconomic variables are related to outcome but not to parental perception. By contrast, parental variables were hypothesized to be related both to outcome and parental perception.

In general, his findings, which included a 12-month follow-up, provide partial support for the theoretical model. Parental perception may be determined by child characteristics and parental personal and interpersonal functioning, whereas treatment involvement in outcome may be primarily a function of socioeconomic variables. In other words, different causal processes may be at work in the two situations. Not only may these two aspects of behavior be unrelated, they may also be under the control of different sets of contingencies. These are important findings that merit serious consideration and further investigation. From a theoretical perspective, Dumas's model helps differentiate and unravel the complex elements involved in parental perception, treatment involvement, and outcome.

Most investigators conclude that potential consumers prefer positive techniques. However, many of their studies are based upon analogue rather than real-life situations and, therefore, of limited value. Additionally, the perceptions of the children themselves are rarely investigated. In this respect, it is noteworthy that nonclinic children have repeatedly been shown to be able to voice consistent preferences between disciplinary measures. The evidence with respect to clinic-referred children is more conflicting. Parents of clinic-referred children tend to use more punitive, coercive disciplinary measures than parents of nonreferred children. Thus, if children tend to rate procedures highly in relation to those used by their parents, it would seem reasonable to expect clinic-referred children to give ratings of parental disability techniques that are different from those of nonclinic children. It might also be speculated that these children's ratings should change in response to any changes in parental behavior following behavioral management training.

To explore these possibilities, Dadds, Adlington, and Christensen (1987) examined the acceptability ratings of five maternal behaviors or disciplinary techniques (permissiveness, physical punishment, directed discussion, quiet time, time-out) across four different situations (noncompliance with an initiating instruction, aggression toward others, noncompliance with a terminating instruction, and noncompliance with known rules) by samples of clinic and control children. Both groups were found to be alike in rating permissiveness as less acceptable than any of the other behaviors across most situations and rating it as unacceptable in absolute terms. In agreement with previous findings, young children were found to prefer actively interventionist to permissive parents.

Many parents express concern about the use of seclusion. The Dadds study suggests that time-out is acceptable to most behavior problem children as long as the procedure is explained beforehand. How these perceptions relate to sex, age, and other developmental variables must await further research.

There is a widespread belief that for parent training to have any chance of success, parents must attend meetings regularly and carry out instructions faithfully with their children. Dumas and Albin (1986) studied 82 families with noncompliant, aggressive children participating in a behavioral parent training program geared toward the modification of dysfunctional family relationships. At follow-ups ranging from 1 to 3 years, each family was assigned to one of two groups according to treatment outcome status (success, no success). The groups were then compared on eight measures of social and material standing found to be predictive of outcome in previous research and two measures of parental involvement in treatment.

Contrary to prediction, measures of parental attendance at scheduled meetings and compliance with program instructions failed to account for any significant outcome variance. Dumas and Albin offer two ways of accounting for these results. First, if attendance at treatment sessions and compliance with instructions are necessary conditions for standardized parent training programs to succeed with every family, then it could be that the two measures used in their study to quantify these variables were simply inadequate. Alternatively, although parental involvement in treatment is necessary for training to succeed, such involvement may not be sufficient in many high-risk families. If this is so, then many families characterized by numerous adverse setting events may be unable to benefit from parent training no matter how regular their treatment sessions and how well they comply with instructions. If this is correct, then the dyadic, parent–child perspective within which these dysfunctional family interactions have commonly been conceptualized and treated needs to be expanded. The inability of a fragile single mother on welfare to learn to control her child's aversive behavior may reflect more than a lack of parenting skills or the presence of an inadequate training program. It could also reflect the broad ecological content within which parents and children function. Behavioral training programs may also need to address these issues.

Positive reinforcement alone is not sufficient to achieve or maintain behavior change in deviant children. In the treatment studies reviewed by Forehand (1986), time-out emerged repeatedly as a necessary procedure for meaningful change to occur—this despite the fact that positive reinforcement is generally viewed very favorably by parents. While not recommending that positive reinforcement be eliminated from parent training programs, Forehand does suggest that a thorough prior assessment is necessary. Even if time-out or some similar strategy is indicated as an auxiliary procedure, there are several reasons why positive reinforcement should also be included in the training program. First, positive reinforcement is viewed very favorably by parents and children alike. Second, positive reinforcement and time-out can be effectively combined to function interactively. Thus, it is not positive reinforcement per se that needs to be evaluated so much as its role within the total parent behavioral repertoire.

It is important that parents and professionals communicate effectively. In an excellent chapter on parent and family training which could well be expanded into a book, Budd and Fabry (1986) focus upon the role of the practitioner in fostering healthy functioning in families with seriously disturbed children. To date, most efforts to improve parent–professional interactions have been directed toward enhancing the communication skills of the professional (Kohr, Parrish, Neef, Driessen, & Hallinan, 1988). What of the parents? Kohr et al. began by identifying target skills on the basis of social validation ratings by external judges of sample interactions between parents and professionals. Eight parents were then trained in these skills by way of an instructional package embedded in a multiple baseline design. Not altogether to their surprise, targeted skills acquired in simulated conference situations tended to generalize well to real-life settings.

This pioneering study paves the way for a behavioral definition of parent–professional communication, one more step in the development of a comprehensive, ecologically based parent training. Further research is now required to examine the complex relationships among family variables, training procedures, and treatment outlook. Dadds, Sanders and James (1987), for example, assessed a broad range of parent and child behaviors in diverse home and community child care settings during baseline, child management training, and a 3-month follow-up. Although treatment gains occurred in the home training setting with the therapist present, little generalization to other findings was found. By follow-up, the gains made in the training setting had largely reverted to baseline levels. In a subsequent study, these investigators added generalization training (planned activities and a social–marital support intervention). It was found to be associated with further improvements in nontraining settings with respect to both parent and child behavior. These results were maintained or further improved at follow-up.

Behavioral approaches to delinquency prevention have been reviewed in Chapter 1. Nearly two decades of clinical research at the Oregon Social Learning Center are at long last beginning to shape a meaningful theory of antisocial behavior in boys. Although selected parents trained in the principles of behavioral family management can learn to cope more effectively with their antisocial children, little is known about generalization of this methodology to the large urban populations where it is most needed (Bank, Patterson, & Reid, 1987).

As noted, approximately 20 years earlier Hanf developed a program for teaching parents more effective ways of dealing with their noncompliant children. In the decades that followed, Barkley extended this program to hyperactive, attention deficit, conduct-disordered, and more seriously disturbed children. Detailed instructions for use by trained professionals are provided in his latest manual, but as Barkley (1987) points out, overall success is critically related to the nature and severity of the child's problems, the extent and severity of the family psychopathology, and the levels of parental intelligence, education, and motivation. Little can be taken for granted.

The two most widely used behavioral treatments for attention deficit disorders are behavioral parent training and the teaching of self-control techniques coupled with problem solving. Although both strategies are of demonstrable value during intervention, taken separately, neither has been found to produce significant generalization and maintenance of treatment effects. It could be, argue Horn, Lalongo, Popovich, and Peradotto (1987), that a combined approach might prove maximally beneficial by altering those contingencies in the home that maintain the maladaptive behaviors while also helping the child develop more adaptive behavioral skills through instruction in self-control. When the child begins to apply those newly acquired strategies, the home becomes "primed" to reinforce use of these new skills. The child may then be more likely to extend these new skills to situations outside the home.

To augment speculation with the data, Horn et al. employed a multiple-outcome group design to compare home-based behavioral parent training, self-control instruction, and a combination of the two in 24 hyperactive school children. Although all groups showed significant improvement over time maintained at 1-month follow-up, there was no evidence for generalization to the classroom. Children who were better able to reflect on problems, who admitted to greater self-control problems, and who had a more internal locus of control showed the greatest improvements.

Mothers experiencing greater isolation from support figures outside the home reported less improvement in their children than mothers who perceived themselves as receiving greater extrafamilial social support. There is now a growing body of evidence to suggest that a lack of adequate social support networks is a good predictor of resistance to psychological interventions.

Given the limitation of their sample size, there is little reason to assume that a combination of behavioral parent training and cognitive-behavioral self-control therapy is necessarily superior to either treatment alone. What future research has to determine is whether the addition of a school behavioral consultation component and/or psycho-stimulant medication to behavioral parent training, self-control therapy, or the combination of the two is going to enhance generalization.

If parents of problem children can be trained to become successful cotherapists, what of their efficacy as coteachers for children with academic learning difficulties? Once again, there is mounting evidence to suggest that home-based remedial teaching programs can produce gains in children's academic behavior that generalize to the school. As Glynn (1987) observes, the power of parents is grossly underused. According to Glynn, existing behavioral research is already capable of providing a tentative specification for a better technology of home and school interface. For example, the frequency of parent–teacher contact suggest that a significant proportion of these children can eventually be integrated into the educational mainstream (Egel & Gradel, 1988).

The nature of most handicapping conditions requires that parents or parent surrogates be major participants in the intervention process, and this is particularly true as far as autistic children are concerned. Unfortunately, parents seldom have the necessary knowledge, skills, and competence to participate effectively in parent training and, even more regrettably, the opportunity to acquire the needed "know-how" is rarely made available. The fact that parents often have to cope with overwhelming daily problems of grief and isolation in addition to other excessive demands upon their limited resources presents further difficulties (Kozloff et al., 1988). Understandably, therefore, positive changes are not easy to maintain.

Since 1967 Kozloff and his associates have conducted 12 training programs for persons living and working with handicapped children: seven for parents exclusively, two for parents and professionals together, and three for professionals alone. Their design generally followed a standard pretest, posttest, delayed-training control group format, with continual outcome evaluation and families allocated randomly to either an experimental or a control group. Their major findings are as follows. First, in the absence of training, the delayed-training control group showed no improvement. This suggests that, to the extent that they are effective, parenting training programs are a necessity rather than a luxury. Second, prior to training, parents' teaching skills may be associated less with their children's performance during sessions than they are with their children's enthusiasm, effort, attentiveness, and cooperation. Third, participation scores tended to be strongly related to task performance. If parental signaling, prompting, and reinforcement can get the children to pay attention, cooperate, and expend effort, then the children may be more likely to perform tasks within their potential behavioral repertoires. By the end of training, not only had parent's teaching skills and participation significantly improved but so had the relationship between the two. It is as if the greater enthusiasm and attention displayed by the parents makes the children more enthusiastic and attentive, and this, coupled with greater technical proficiency on the part of the parents, begins to result in positive changes in task performance.

To understand the change process better, further analyses are needed. How do parents perceive themselves and their children before and after training? Do other beneficial changes take place that home visit data fail to capture? If home visit data indicate that children's performances change little (either because they were already rather high or because the children have profound handicaps), do parents still perceive significant improvements? When home visit data do indicate substantial improvements, do parental perceptions match those of the investigators? What factors might account for parents' perceptions in addition to the performance of their children? The decision to encourage community resource leaders to offer parent training as a regular service rests in part upon the resolution of such issues.

A particularly frustrating problem is that newly acquired behaviors typically fail to generalize to settings and people beyond the original training environment (Schreibman, 1988). In addition, response generalization is rarely achieved, children tend to learn rote responses with minimal variability and minimal changes in other behaviors. Schreibman's literature review suggests that, although generalization of behavior change is superior for those children whose parents have been trained, serious limitations are evident. For example, gains evidenced in the presence of the parents are much less likely to occur when the parents are not present.

Schreibman's program is geared toward the development of maximum generalization. Identification of procedures to enhance generalization led to an improved parent training package. The next step (to be implemented by Schreibman shortly) is the field testing of these procedures and a components analysis to assist in the identification of the most effective and efficient training package (see also Schreibman, Koegel, Mills, & Burke, 1984).

Finally, attention is drawn to the possibility of training siblings to work with their autistic brothers and sisters. To date, all work in this area has focused on teaching siblings one aspect of behavior management skills or on having them teach the handicapped child one task or new behavior. Recognizing this limitation, Schreibman, O'Neill, and Koegel (1983) developed a program to teach siblings a set of generalizable behavior modification skills that could then be used in a variety of settings with a variety of target behaviors. Three main questions were addressed in their preliminary investigations: (1) Could siblings of autistic children be taught to conduct correct behavior modification procedures in a proficient manner? (2) If so, would this implementation generalize to nontraining environments during unstructured play activities? (3) Would the implementation of these behavior modification procedures by the siblings produce measurable improvement in the behavior of their autistic brothers and sisters?

Three sibling pairs participated in a multiple-baseline analysis of the effects of training the normal sibling to use behavior modification procedures to teach their autistic brother or sister simple learning tasks. All experimental sessions were conducted in the children's homes, except for the generalization probe sessions, which were carried out in a separate building. Data were collected during each baseline and training session, and the probes conducted in a setting designed to resemble a living room, with a variety of toys readily available. The sibling was instructed to interact and play with his or her autistic brother or sister while alone in the room. Social validation consisted of inquiries to the parents designed to evoke sibling comments about their brothers and sisters before and after training. Following training, there was a decrease in negative statements and an increase in positive observations. Siblings learned to use these behavioral procedures at high levels of efficiency that generalized to a different setting, and there were observed improvements in the behavior of the autistic children.

CHILD ABUSE AND NEGLECT

According to the American Humane Association (1984) nearly 1 million cases of child abuse and neglect are reported to child protection agencies in the United States each year and this number is escalating. Although several excellent resource books and guides to intervention are available, nothing that even remotely resembles a "breakthrough" is in sight. This is not surprising in view of the complexity of the problem. Abusive parents are not a homogeneous subset of adults. They are not easily identified by their symptoms and they rarely seek treatment on their own.

Among numerous recent texts, the following seem worthy of special mention: Finkelhor and Associates' (1986) source book on child sexual abuse, a comprehensive overview of the past decade; Haugaard and Reppucci's (1988) insightful guide to current knowledge and intervention strategies for sexually abused children and their families; a behaviorally oriented model of child abuse and its implications for child development and psychopathology by Wolfe (1987); and an edited text by Wyatt and Powell (1988), which takes a hard look at possibly lasting effects of child sexual abuse, posing and offering tentative answers to such questions as, What kinds of psychological problems are children who are sexually abused subject to in later life? Can early detection of child sexual abuse reduce the likelihood of long-term psychological trauma? What forms of treatment are currently available for adults who were sexually abused as children?

Then there are the numerous review articles of the past year or so. Some are inconsequential, such as Hoier's (1987) sketchy survey in which the only conclusion of significance is that little attention has been paid to long-term intervention. Others are more substantive. For example, Finkelhor and Williams (1988) use review data derived from approximately 270 cases of sexual abuse in day-care facilities for young children to generate recommendations for detection and prevention. In 1981 Dixen and Jenkins reviewed strategies for the treatment and prevention of incestuous sexual abuse of children. It is now time for an update. In their searching analysis of primary and secondary approaches to child sexual abuse, Miller-Perrin and Wurtele (1988) review both the initial effects of childhood sexual victimization and the more long-term impact on adult functioning. Only recently, with the realization of the epidemic proportions and the negative consequences of child sex abuse, has primary prevention achieved recognition as a potentially viable option. Unfortunately, prevention tends to be implemented primarily by well-meaning but inadequately trained professionals, local service agencies, police departments, parents and educators.

Miller-Perrin and Wurtele (1988) classify prevention in terms of three subsets. In primary prevention, the intent is to prevent sexual abuse from ever occurring. To bring this about, it is necessary to eliminate possible causes of dysfunction and promote mental health through the development of positive competencies. Once identified, the concern of secondary prevention is with the interruption of the pathological sequence as early as possible. Tertiary prevention, prevention in name only, seeks to reduce the resulting impairment by minimizing the consequences of abuse and facilitating rehabilitation.

For children thought to be at high risk for sexual victimization, identification is the paramount task. Finkelhor's (1984) Sexual Abuse Risk Factor Checklist contains eight risk signals: (1) the child has a stepfather; (2) the child has lived without his or her mother at some time; (3) the mother–child relationship is distant; (4) the child's mother did not complete high school; (5) the child's mother is often punitive; (6) physical or emotional affection from the father is lacking; (7) family income is less than $10,000 per year; and (8) the child has fewer than three friends.

An alternative approach, rather than working directly with the children themselves, is to target parents of at-risk children. Miller-Perrin and Wurtele (1988) offer as examples of this strategy the provision of sexual abuse awareness information to custodial parents who are remarrying, parents of disabled children, or parents seeking help for problems related to marital dysfunction, depression, alcoholism, and battering. Another group of parents who could be specially targeted are those who were themselves victimized as children.

Only a small percentage of victimized children report the abuse, and even smaller numbers are detected by parents, teachers, or physicians. Parents and professionals are sometimes not aware of the "masked" signs and symptoms associated with abuse. Sexually abused children often come to the attention of others for problems other than the abuse (e.g., school problems or depression).

In their review of the literature, Browne and Finkelhor (1986) remind us once again of the many serious methodological limitations that frequently invalidate the findings. In interpreting the effects of sexual abuse, long-term impact is overemphasized as the ultimate criterion. Effects are considered less "serious" if their impact becomes less apparent over time. Browne and Finkelhor refer to this tendency to assess everything in terms of long-term effects as "adulto-centric" bias. As they remind their readers, rape is a painful and alarming event whether its impact lasts 1 year or 10 years. Similarly, childhood trauma should not be prematurely dismissed because no so-called long-term effect can be demonstrated.

According to Brunk, Henggeler, and Whelan (1987) two models of maltreatment have emerged: the social-situational model and the ecological model. Rooted in social learning theory, the social-situational model stresses the development of parental capacity to increase positive child interactions and thereby reduce aversive child behaviors. Within the ecological model, child maltreatment is viewed from a systems paradigm. Maltreatment is thought to result from the interaction of multiple factors nestled within four ecological levels: the background of the parent, family relations, family transactions with extrafamilial systems, and cultural variables that support maltreatment. The multisystemic therapy of Henggler and colleagues (1986) is consistent with this model. Individuals are viewed as imbedded in multiple systems exerting both direct and indirect influences on behavior. Both cognitive variables and extrafamilial variables maintaining behavior problems are taken into consideration.

Brunk et al. distinguish between child abuse and child neglect. Abusive parents are described as rigid and intrusive in their relationships, whereas neglecting parents, in sharp contrast, exhibit lower rates of interaction with their children and seem to be less responsive in both short-term and long-term parent–child interactions. This suggests that the treatment of abusive families should be geared toward the promotion of increased parental flexibility in responding to child behavior, whereas the treatment of neglecting families should aim at the development of increased cohesion and greater parental responsibility.

To compare the two models, Brunk et al. randomly assigned 18 abusive families and 15 neglecting families to one of two treatment conditions. Eight abusive families and eight neglecting families received multisystemic therapy and ten abusive families and seven neglecting families completed social–situational behavioral training. Self-report measures were used to assess perceptions of change at individual, family, and social system levels. Observational measures were used to assess changes in parental control strategies, parental responsivity, and child compliance. The behavioral training program emphasized a linear conceptual model, whereas the multisystemic approach leaned heavily upon circular causality. Multisystemic therapy was found to be more effective than parent training in restructuring parent–child relationships, whereas parent training was more effective than multisystemic therapy at reducing identified social problems.

Behavioral intervention strategies have been shown on many occasions to be effective and economical alternatives to out-of-home placement in bringing about desired changes among abusive families. It is somewhat surprising, therefore, that behavioral methods are not usually considered as early intervention strategies of choice for preventing the deterioration of parent–child relationships and the concomitant abuse and neglect that can occur. Social agency services for at-risk parents typically follow a family support model that attempts to eliminate family stress in whatever ways it can, chiefly by assistance with basic needs and alleviating immediate situational crises on a short-term basis.

Agency-based family support services, speculate Wolfe, Edwards, Manion, and Koverola (1988), would have a greater impact on high-risk families if supported by parent training. To provide the necessary data for this contention, Wolfe et al. randomly assigned 30 mother–child dyads to one of two conditions: (1) an information-only group offered by the child protection agency, or (2) a special program of behavioral parent training in addition to agency information. Most of these dyads consisted of single-parent, female-headed households on welfare. In both groups the children tended to be mildly delayed in physical, motor, perceptual, and cognitive development. Traditional types of control groups had to be ruled out because of the needs of this population. The therapists for parent training consisted of supervised graduate students, and both self-report and observational measures were used to evaluate outcome. Parents and children were reassessed approximately 3 months after posttesting, and mothers in the parent training group completed a Consumer Satisfaction Questionnaire. The control group received an open-ended opinion survey.

Although both groups showed improvements, case worker ratings significantly favored families who had received parent training in addition to information. Given the present state of knowledge, it would seem that the diverse needs of families at risk of maltreatment are probably better addressed through a coupling of family support and individually tailored instruction in behavioral child management. A policy of waiting until the parent–child relationship deteriorates to the point of social or legal recognition is extremely undesirable.

Project 12-Ways has been the subject of much favorable discussion in this series (e.g., Volume 11, 1987, p. 254ff). In 1987 Lutzker and Rice compared Project 12-Ways families with families receiving other child protection services in terms of child abuse incidence and impact. Project 12-Ways families were found to be significantly less likely to injure or neglect their children.

According to Lutzker and his associates, parental characteristics (such as emotional disturbance), child characteristics (such as physical or mental handicap), and what has been termed "ecological instability" within the family's ecosystem can all contribute to child abuse and neglect. The family ecosystem is particularly sensitive to such variables as joblessness, unsafe neighborhoods, hazardous homes, and medical problems.

Early prevention has to cut across physical, sociological, interpersonal, and psychological determinants. Tangible hazards need to be taken into account as well as those of a more subtle nature. Project 12-Ways, for example, focuses on teaching families to eliminate common household risks. When earlier endeavors turned out to be impractical for anyone other than the most highly trained counselling personnel (Tertinger, Greene, & Lutzker, 1984), Lutzker and his associates came up with a streamlined program, equally effective and readily usable by virtually any counselor or state agency (Barone, Greene, & Lutzker, 1986).

Belsky and Vondra (1987) conceptualize child abuse as an extreme point on a continuum of parental function–dysfunction, with insight into etiology and treatment best gained indirectly. To achieve reciprocal interactivity, they draw upon a notion of life span maturation that incorporates causal elements originating at all levels of the developmental ecosystem. This ambitious undertaking is in sharp contrast to the prevailing single-focus emphasis on the parent rather than the total context. In so doing, they fault both traditional behavioral and psychotherapeutic interventions. Behavioral approaches, they argue, are concerned primarily with changing the behavior and cognitions of the maltreating individual. However, bringing new insight and emotional assistance to abusive parents by various forms of psychotherapy without demonstrating alternative patterns of behavior or developing specific skills is likely to be equally fruitless.

Parents Anonymous, the primary group for abusive parents, is cited as an example of one of the better multidimensional programs. Taking its cue from Alcoholics Anonymous, emotional support is combined with concrete assistance. Parents are connected to available community services and drawn into new social networks, but these programs are subject to numerous limitations. Lack of motivation and fear of social stigma are hard to overcome. Furthermore, by the time remediation is offered, the damage has already been done in terms of child costs, strained family relations, parental self-concept, and social labeling. It is therefore understandable that even the best of these programs have poor success rates (Burgess & Richardson, 1984).

Belsky and Vondra's prevention-based parent support model is predicated upon three basic principles. First, parental functioning is viewed as being multiply determined by forces of influence derived from the parent, the child, and the social context in which the parent–child relationship is embedded. Intervention efforts are aimed at multiple rather than single causes. Second, the forces that shape parenting operate directly and indirectly. Therefore, one should address parental behavior directly through behavior modification and parental well-being through a traditional psychotherapy that also takes into account the social ecology of parent–child relationships. Their third principle, somewhat more complex, rests upon the notion that there is a continuum of influence ranging from stress to support. Furthermore, when operating in a supportive versus a stressful mode, the processes that sometimes undermine parental functioning and generate child maltreatment can also be used to generate parental competence. The basic principle derived from this notion is that is it not necessary to focus exclusively on remedying already dysfunctional parenting or the child-rearing practices of parents at risk for maltreating their offspring because efforts geared toward enhancing the functioning of all parents may prove equally beneficial. Belsky and Vondra further suggest that such endeavors could even reduce the incidence to a greater extent than efforts targeted more directly toward this goal.

BEHAVIOR MODIFICATION AND EDUCATION

Few fields in psychology are better suited to the study of education than behavioral psychology and fewer therapies are more appropriate. If the proliferation of recent texts is a valid measure, writing about these matters is an even more visible spinoff from this liaison. But as Durand (1988) notes, behavioral scientists able to tell us *how* to teach are not yet in a position to offer informed counsel about *what* to teach. The majority of these new texts are primarily "how-to" in nature (e.g., Sulzer-Azaroff & Mayer, 1986). Others combine practical and theoretical considerations in a more equitable mix (e.g., Maher & Forman, 1987). Of them all, Witt, Elliott, and Gresham's (1988) *Handbook of Behavior Therapy in Education* is probably the most comprehensive. To single out but a few contributions to this massive "handbook": Elliott (1988) takes a hard look at acceptability research and the variables that influence teacher selections, Anderson and Kratochwill (1988) examine training issues, and Correo and Melton (1988) view behavior therapy in the school system from a legal perspective. Although the caveats noted by Correo and Melton are certainly in order, they do not seem unique to behavior therapy, as the title of their chapter implies.

Wheldall's (1987) literally less weighty paperback is geared toward the British school system. In this edited text, Glynn (1987) reminds us that the often overlooked power of parents to remedy their academic learning difficulties of children is great. Home-based remedial teaching programs can produce gains that generalize significantly to the school setting, and vice versa. It seems surprising that schools are still loathe to harness the support of their most powerful allies, the parents.

In the same volume, Berger, Yule, and Wigley (1987) report on their long-term social-learning-theory-based Teacher–Child Interactional Project (TCIP), and Wheldall and Merrett (1987) outline recent developments with their Behavioral Approaches to Teaching Package (BATPACK) (reviewed in detail in Volume 11). BATPACK's major deficit, more than balanced by its strengths, would seem to be the limited attention given to maintenance and generalization of behavior change. Once teachers are trained, how can the school environment be made to support gains made (Murphy, 1985)?

Finally, Merrett and Wheldall (1987) devote attention to a theme much beloved by behavior therapists in the United States but largely overlooked in the United Kingdom: the acceptance of behavioral procedures by school personnel, the utilization of these strategies, and the differences they make, if any. British teachers seem to hold negative or neutral views largely as the results of ignorance, incomplete knowledge, or factually incorrect knowledge. They tend to express much more positive attitudes once these deficiencies have been corrected, but there is no firm evidence to suggest that teaching teachers about behavioral methods necessarily improves classroom performance. What behavioral training does seem to accomplish is making teachers more amenable to future use. What is refreshing about this chapter and those cited above is the admission of failure when it occurs.

Anderson, Kratochwill, and Bergan's (1986) concern in the big handbook is with behavioral training for teachers from an American perspective in which the focus is upon the behavior therapist as consultant. As school psychologists increase their consultative roles, other school personnel, especially teachers, must also assume new roles, namely, those of consultee and behavior change agents. The success of behavioral consultation and the implementation of behavioral interventions in the classroom may well depend in large part upon teacher attitudes, a conclusion strikingly similar to that of Merrett and Wheldall (1987) in the United Kingdom.

Anderson et al. evaluated the relative effectiveness of two teacher training packages and two analogue consultation conditions in a 2×2 factorial design. Their subjects were 56 elementary urban school teachers subjected either to training in classroom behavior modification plus consultation or to the procedural aspects of consultative services delivery within a multidisciplinary team setting (the nonspecific control group). The consultation conditions included one variant in which specific questions were posed and another in which much more general, rather vague, consultant questionnaires were presented by way of problem identification and analysis of behavioral consultation analogue interviews. Effectiveness was measured in terms of pencil and paper knowledge of behavior modificational principles and observed behavior in analogue consultation interviews. Relationships between pretraining teacher attitudes about behavior modification and training outcome were also investigated.

The experimental training package increased both knowledge of behavioral procedures and the frequency of pertinent verbalizations. Problem clarification skills were also improved following contact with skilled behavioral personnel. By and large, the overall conclusion was that, while consultant skills are essential to successful consultative problem solving within the school, teacher training in basic behavioral principles is equally necessary.

At this point, one might not unreasonably ask why it is that behavioral approaches are not in general classroom use in either this country or the United Kingdom. How does it come about that, despite the ready availability, easy applicability, and demonstrable effectiveness of a broad array of techniques appropriate to educational settings, endorsement of these procedures by the educational community is still limited? (The noteworthy exception to this disheartening conclusion lies in the application of behavior modification to the education of severely retarded children.)

Powers and Franks (1988) offer three possible clues: the perceived arrogance of applied behavior analysts, the absence of sufficient "system pain" to motivate change, and the absence of an ecological/ systems perspective. Many behavior analysts are perceived as brash individuals who attempt to impose their strategies upon the educational community. Educators respond negatively and, in turn, behavior analysts and behavior therapists become polarized away from the mainstream educational community.

As to the second clue, schools are social organizations, a complex series of systems within an even more complex systemic superstructure (Plas, 1986). As such, collaborative, interdependent relationships between administrators, faculty, related service professions, support staff, parents, students, and members of various educational and local government boards are essential components of the school setting as a social organization. Yet, schools are different from many other organizational strategies in that they are less vulnerable to the effects of competition and more vulnerable to community pressures on a day-to-day basis. It is these daily problems and pressures that are more likely to lead to "system pain." Educators tend to respond much more quickly to the disequilibrium created by short-term crises. In so doing, their goals are to quell the disturbance, satisfy the concerned parties, return to the status quo, and get back to the business of teaching. Neither administrators nor teachers are likely under such circumstances to feel sufficient system pain to countenance the major changes recommended by the behavior analyst. Third, despite increasing evidence of the need for a nonlinear ecological/systems-oriented perspective rather than the more traditional direct cause-and-effect approach advocated by early behavior therapists, many behavioral clinicians still think in these outdated terms.

For Baer and Bushell (1981; Baer, 1988a), the answers to these questions lie not so much in the school system as in those areas of society in which decisions are being made about schools. The contrast between behavior-analytic and educational assumptions is only part of the problem. A behavioral analysis of the decision-making process within the larger social system has to be the first step toward answers and resolution.

As far as the contrast between educators and behavior analysts is concerned, Baer and Bushell detail four arenas of possible paradigm clash. The first is at the level of the organism. Behavior analysts work with specific children's behaviors; educators believe that children must be treated as entities. The second clash is at the level of behavior. Behavior analysts assume that behaviors change as responses to environmental controls programmable by teachers and parents. Educators assume that behaviors change because of maturational processes within the organism. Children who are ready will profit by assigned practice, and those who are not can be conveniently categorized as difficult-to-teach and segregated as such within special classes. The third clash follows from the second; it is at the level of strategy. For the teacher, student failure is rarely the teacher's fault. The teacher has made the correct assignment according to grade level and the rest is the student's responsibility. For the behavior analyst, teaching is the arrangement of various procedures leading to behavior change. The fourth clash is at the level of technique. Educators teach assigned texts and grade test results. By contrast, behavior analysts arrange contingencies that support curricula of behavior change chosen to fit the individual child's set of current abilities and deficits. When behavior changes do not occur readily, behavior analysts assign failing grades to themselves and make monitored changes in contingencies and tasks to bring about success.

By way of remedy, Baer and Bushell suggest that behavioral analysis be explicitly taught to education and school psychology students and that demonstration projects be maintained in the hope that they will eventually be seen as needed by the educational community. Their final recommendation is more action-oriented, no less than a switch from the school exclusively to the political arena, as noted above.

Baer and his associates are not the only ones to sound the note of alarm and respond accordingly. In 1983 the National Commission on Excellence in Education issued a report provocatively entitled "A Nation At Risk: The Imperative for Educational Reform." To remedy this "alarming status of American education," sweeping changes in content, standards, expectations, teaching strategies, leadership, and general support were proposed. In so doing, perhaps for the reasons outlined above, the commission and the public it represents overlooked completely the role that behavioral technology could play in the improvement of education.

In a well-organized, unsolicited, response, Sulzer-Azaroff (1985) examined each recommendation from the perspective of the behavior analyst, noting what can be said at this time, what might be currently addressed and remediated, and what profitably might be explored further. Part of the need is to communicate honestly and effectively with both educators and the general public (Sulzer-Azaroff, 1986; Sulzer-Azaroff & Mayer, 1986).

With their developmental colleagues, behavior therapists are particularly qualified to make significant contributions to education in terms of the acquisition of normative data. There is, for example, a need for further information about the social interactions of normal children. When Ballard and Crooks (1986) made repeated observations of kindergarten children, there was much evidence of session-by-session variability. If, then, social behavior is setting-dependent, it would seem important to obtain normative data in each setting of interest.

Slate and Saudargas's (1986) concern was with a different problem, the differences in classroom behavior between behaviorally disordered and regular class children. Children who exhibit severe behavioral or emotional difficulties may be classified under Public Law 94-142 guidelines into the seriously emotionally disturbed or behaviorally disordered category. According to Epstein, Kauffman, and Cullinan (1985), the following school behaviors, obtained primarily from teacher and parent ratings, are characteristic of more serious emotional disturbance: (1) disrupts other children, (2) compulsive, (3) does not complete required work, (4) destructive to own and others' belongings, (5) does not follow commands from authority figures, (6) undependable, (7) exhibits inappropriate behavior, (8) unhappy or depressed and (9) exhibits poor interpersonal relationships.

Ratings require teachers, parents, or peers to rank behavioral characteristics through a series of interactions. When Cosper and Erickson (1984) examined the relationships between teachers' ratings of their male students' behavior and direct observational data, significant differences were obtained. Direct observational data appeared to measure a different facet of behavior to that assessed by teacher ratings. Teacher ratings may not predict actual behavior with sufficient validity or accuracy.

Drawing attention to the methodological limitations of most studies to date, Slate and Saudargas investigated the classroom behavior of behaviorally disordered and regular class third, fourth, and fifth grade boys. An average of 80 minutes of direct classroom observational data was recorded for each child to determine which behaviors best differentiated the behaviorally disordered from the regular classroom children. Ten behaviors accounted for about 81% of the variance in group membership. Child- and teacher-based data alone failed to differentiate between the two groups. From these data, its seems reasonable to conclude that the behaviorally disordered child is best examined within a regular classroom setting that takes into account the behavior of both child and teacher.

Related, if partially contradictory, findings are reported by Schachar, Sandberg, and Rutter (1986) in their study of the agreement between teacher ratings and hyperactivity, inattentiveness, and defiance scores as measured by the widely used Conners Teacher Rating Scale (CTRS). Conclusions about the validity of this scale have generally been based on its high reliability, its sensitivity to drug-induced behavior changes, and its ability to differentiate normal children from those diagnosed as hyperkinetic. However, as noted by Schachar et al., these features fail to establish the validity of the CTRS as either a diagnostic instrument or a measure of activity. To be valid, the ratings should correlate with independent measures of the same behavior, they should not be excessively influenced by other behaviors, and they should be able to distinguish hyperactive from nonhyperactive disturbed children. According to Schachar et al., low correlations between individual CTRS factors and observations of similar behavior could be due either to halo effects or to the global nature of the CTRS.

In any event, when Schachar et al. examined the utility of the CTRS with 6- to 7-year-old boys, there was a high degree of association between observed behavior and scale ratings. This association varied with the nature of the behavior being rated. Defiancy was more reliably rated than hyperactivity or inattentiveness. Halo effects were particularly evident with respect to ratings of hyperactivity, inattentiveness, and behavioral problems. Clearly, manifest defiance toward the teacher seemed to increase the likelihood that a child would be rated as hyperactive or inattentive regardless of his observed level of activity or attentiveness. These findings were construed by Schachar et al. as supporting evidence for the continuing use of rating scales such as the CTRS as screening measures. Even more to the point, this study is of value in drawing attention to the fact that a child's defiance and disobedience can be significant and possibly primary causes of misclassification.

When Simpson and Halpin (1986) used a revised version of the Behavior Problem Checklist to collect parent and teacher ratings of middle school children, there was a general lack of agreement between parent and teacher ratings with respect to the identification of children rates as mildly or highly deviant. It may be, as these authors suggest, that such judgments are rater-dependent. It is also possible that the child's behavior may be situation-specific. Finally, teachers and parents observing the same behaviors may perceive these behaviors differently. Teachers, for example, may tend to evaluate a child's behavior relative to the hundreds of children with whom they have come into contact in the school setting, whereas parents may compare a child's behavior only to that of siblings or the children of social acquaintances.

How teachers rate their charges may well determine the manner in which they offer approval and disapproval of various activities. Contingent verbal approval is probably the most effective means of influencing children within the classroom setting (O'Leary & O'Leary, 1977, p. 55). Another form of teacher attention is disapproval, a frequently used but rarely studied teacher consequence of questionable value according to Wyatt and Hawkins (1987).

White's (1975) study is still widely cited; approval and disapproval rates were assessed for 104 suburban teachers of first through twelfth grade pupils. Teachers gave more disapproval than approval, with teachers in higher grades giving less of either. Approvals tended to be related to formal learning and disapprovals to more general classroom management. Although subsequent studies cited by Wyatt and Hawkins (1987) generate inconsistent and sometimes directly contradictory conclusions, their own investigation offers qualified endorsement of White's findings. The mean rates of both approval and disapproval were highest in first grade and lower in the upper grades, with the partial exception of the ninth grade, but other findings led them to question White's conclusion that disapproval predominates after the second grade and that this may account for the disillusionment of children in grades thereafter. Transition time between activities was the only occasion during which disapproval exceeded approval. Interestingly, neither approval nor disapproval rates were related to teachers' ages, years of experience, or recency of training. Overall, their main recommendation was that teacher training focus on verbal approval, particularly in classroom management and that such training be conducted by trained behavior analysts within the classroom setting.

Among the many leverage strategies proposed for maximizing teacher resources, behavioral self-management and peer-mediated intervention seem the most promising in terms of teacher and child benefits and demonstrable success. Unfortunately, school personnel tend not to view these techniques with favor. Why is this so? According to Fantuzzo, Rohrbeck, and Azar's (1987) review of about 34 self-management studies, at least four major obstacles need to be surmounted. First, the label "self-management" covers a variety of different combinations of specific self-management skills and there is no viable procedure for the comparison of these various strategies. Second, there is still active debate with respect to the extent to which self-management interventions are truly *self*-managed or managed primarily by the teachers. The concept of the self is probably a matter for philosophic and personal rather than experimental resolution, and it is unlikely that consensus will be obtained in the near future. Be this as it may, it is not surprising that this diversity of positions filters through to the more day-to-day levels of teachers and school administrators. Third, inadequate procedural details make replication difficult and application even more difficult. Fourth, guidelines with respect to age levels and other subject or situational variables are rarely provided. Witt (1986) and Sulzer-Azaroff (1985) come to similar conclusions. No wonder, then, that teachers are reluctant to use this technology.

Peer tutoring can be viewed from three perspectives: psychological, educational, and social. In her penetrating review, Cohen (1986) fragments peer tutoring into separate learning and teaching experiences that together form a social process, thereby providing a framework for both research and practice. As learning and teaching experiences, the components include reinforcement, modeling, the closeness of pupil and teacher, and the process of individualization, manifested in individualized pacing predicated upon systematic attention, explanation, demonstration, and immediate, direct feedback. Alternatively, the process can be conceptualized as a cooperative educational system in which the cooperation is mainly unidirectional because only the tutor is fully cooperative. From a behavioral perspective, this process may be best described as a group reinforcement structure contingent on the performance of the individual.

For Schunk (1987), the effectiveness of classroom peers rests in large part on the perceived similarities between model and observer. From this perspective, peer modeling and, by implication, peer training are forms of social comparison. When objective standards of behavior are unclear or unavailable, observers evaluate themselves through comparisons with others, and the most accurate self-evaluations are derived from comparisons with those who are similar with respect to the ability or characteristic being evaluated (Festinger, 1954). It is argued that, given these considerations, peer models should be especially influential in situations in which perceived similarities convey relevant information about one's abilities or the appropriateness of one's behaviors. Similarity serves as an important source of information for gauging behavioral appropriateness, formulating expectations, and assessing self-efficacy for learning or task performance.

According to Schunk's reading of the literature, model–observer age similarity is less important in the learning of skills, rules, and novel responses than the functional value of behaviors whether they lead to successes or failures. Children tend to pattern their actions after models veiwed as competent. Positive peer modeling behavior is likely to emerge to the extent that these peers are viewed as competent as adults. When children question the competence of peers, the tendency is to revert to available adults as role models. It also seems that peers may be more effective models when children hold self-doubts about their learning or performance capabilities. Viewing a peer successfully complete a task can raise a child's performance self-efficacy more than observation of an adult.

The influence of developmental factors upon the processes of attention, retention, production, and motivation involved in observational learning has been insufficiently investigated. This is especially true with respect to childhood developmental disabilities and the role of peer modeling. With the present emphasis on mainstreaming, teachers routinely work with students possessing various developmental and learning problems. Do regular students make acceptable models for such children or are these students more likely to benefit by observing other students with similar problems?

Peer modeling is much more complex than one might at first think. Inadvertently or otherwise, children may support undesirable behavior by mechanisms readily discernible to the behavior therapist. What are the potential hazards associated with monitoring procedures? How can they be minimized? In raising these issues, Fowler (1988) draws particular attention to the risk that peers will use coercion in monitoring or that peers will retaliate against monitors. It is important to think in terms of appropriate training, adult supervision, and the development of a reward system that promotes cooperative behavior as potential avenues for risk reduction if teacher misgivings are to be allayed.

Two relatively recent studies illustrate the manner in which good research in this area can be conducted. In the first, Fowler (1986) developed peer-monitoring and self-monitoring procedures to decrease disruption and nonparticipation during classroom and nearby transitional activities of a special kindergarten class. During peer monitoring, 10 children were assigned to one of three teams, each taking turns to serve as team captain. Team captains monitored each member of their team and awarded points at the end of each of four transition activities to team members and to themselves for following instructions. Following a substantial reduction in inappropriate behavior, the self-monitoring procedure was introduced. The children continued to be assigned to teams, with each child responsible for awarding his or her own points at the end of the transition activities.

Improvements achieved during peer-monitoring were maintained throughout self-monitoring. It is also significant to note that the inclusion of teacher feedback in addition to team feedback during the initial peer-monitoring conditioning seems to be a necessary tool for teaching these children to implement the monitoring procedure accurately within the classroom. It may also serve to differentiate acceptable behaviors from those that are unacceptable. This is an important prerequisite for accurate self-evaluation.

The National Commission on Excellence in Education (1983) calls for increasing the length of the school year as a basic strategy of educational reform. The mounting evidence that peer tutoring can sometimes be more cost-effective than other methods of improving student achievement, including computer-assisted instruction, reducing class size, or increasing learning time (e.g., Levin, Glass, & Meister, 1984) seems to have been completely overlooked by the members of this commission. A recently reported, long-term field replication study of classwide peer tutoring applied to spelling instruction stands in sharp contrast to the conclusions of this learned body: 211 inner city first and second grade students in four schools participated in this key project. Classwide peer tutoring and direct teacher instruction were systematically compared in a standard group replication design. Both teacher instructional procedures and classwide peer tutoring were effective in increasing spelling performance above preschool levels. However, peer tutoring produced consistently greater gains relative to teacher procedures for both low and high performance students (Greenwood et al., 1987).

To conclude this section of the review, I turn now to another important issue: To what extent can behavior modification procedures be utilized as preventive measures and thereby minimize both future social disruption and the more immediate needs for specialized education and rehabilitation?

The evidence that school-related factors are potentially important contributors to delinquency and other social problems is unequivocal. What is far less understood is the nature of these factors and their interactions with extraschool variables (Lane & Murakami, 1987). Traditionally, the school's responses to delinquency have been exclusion, the reduction of school time, and/or a vocationally oriented component grafted onto the routine educational program. It is only within the last decade or so that behavioral interventions within the school system have assumed significant impact. According to Lane and Murakami, the current trend is to think in terms of traditional behavioral programs linked to broad-based ecologically oriented organizational change. The trend seems to be away from the control or elimination of unwanted, antisocial behaviors toward the teaching of prosocial activities. Expanding the behavioral repertoires of young people to include adaptive skills could thereby increase their chances of surviving successfully within the community and, at the same time, provide them with behaviors that may be incompatible with delinquency. Much less research has been carried out with interventions directed at the environmental level.

Bry and her associates have developed a program of early intervention for junior high school students with school adjustment problems that incorporates similar principles (Bien & Bry, 1980; Bry, 1982; Bry & George, 1979, 1980). Typical outcome measures include grades, attendance and promptness, discipline referrals, disruptive classroom behavior, and teacher ratings of severity of school problems. One-year follow-up led to the following findings. First, intervention students encountered significantly fewer serious school problems than those reported for members of a matched control group. Second, significantly more intervention than control group students obtained at least one job by the time of the follow-up interview. Third, at least according to student self-report, no between-group difference was demonstrated for either drug or alcohol abuse. Fourth, whereas 11 intervention students reported a total of 19 instances of criminal behavior, 18 of the control students reported 45 such instances. At 5-year follow-up, significantly fewer intervention students had county court files than did members of the control group.

As noted, comparatively little research has been directed toward the environmental level. In this respect, Mayer, Butterworth, Nafpaktitis, and Sulzer-Azaroff's (1983) behavioral intervention program is a noteworthy exception. Over a 3-year period, teams of school personnel from 18 elementary and junior high schools attended training strategy classes for reducing student vandalism and disruption. In addition, these teams met on a regular basis at their respective schools to plan and implement these strategies on a schoolwide basis. A multiple-baseline design was used to evaluate the program and its outcome. Rates of praise delivered by teachers in the project schools increased significantly whether or not the teachers were directly involved in the project. Rates of acceptable off-task behavior increased significantly following treatment. Finally, vandalism costs decreased more in the treatment than in the control schools.

Lane and Murakami's evaluation of four school-based behavioral programs led to the following conclusions. First, these programs are able to bring about positive short-term changes in academic performance. Students, however, had to participate in the program for at least 1 year for these results to be realized. Second, the evidence is unclear with respect to the impact of these programs on negative in-school behavior. Only one of the four programs reviewed by Lane and Murakami reported short-erm effects. This finding is particularly troublesome in view of the by now extensive body of literature, which seems to support the efficacy of behavioral procedures in the reduction of disruptive school behavior. Third, there is no evidence that any change is maintained for more than 1 year posttreatment. Fourth, although these programs do seem to enhance student entry into high school, without special programming participants still perform poorly and fail to graduate in greater numbers than nonparticipants. Fifth, there is little indication that these programs are effective in reducing the likelihood of subsequent delinquent behavior. Only Bry (1982) reported positive findings in this respect. Finally, attention is drawn once again to the encouraging Mayer et al. study with its strong suggestion that school-focused environmental interventions can contribute significantly to delinquency prevention and reduction. Behavioral preventive intervention, suggest Lane and Murakami, should begin prior to entrance into elementary school rather than waiting until junior high or high school. The data further indicate that additional intervention is necessary to maintain achieved gains during high school and prevent dropout. If provided in the high school setting, to the extent that this is possible, it is important that students be expected to remain in the mainstream. Self-contained classroom intervention should be avoided.

BEHAVIOR MODIFICATION AND THE EDUCATION OF THE ATYPICAL CHILD

Although learning-disabled children share many common characteristics, they are a more diverse group than some educators and psychologists would have us believe. This may account for the fact that many traditional research designs fail to produce significant differences and thereby fail to pinpoint the potential efficacy of specific interventions for specific learning-disabled students. Differences can be obscured by variability within the learning-disabled sample. The question of appropriate programming, suggest Kneedler and Meese (1988) in the Witt handbook, is not one of either teacher- or student-directed intervention. Both of these may be appropriate. Direct instruction, for example, may be appropriate for younger learning-disabled children or for those children first acquiring particular academic skills. However, self-monitoring procedures may be more appropriate for those learning-disabled youngsters whose primary deficits are in the attentional domain or for those children who need encouragement to maintain or generalize newly acquired skills.

Much of the early behavioral research with mentally retarded adults focused on the more severely disturbed, usually institutionalized, individual. As Matson and Schaughency (1988) noted, it is only recently that mild and moderately retarded individuals have received research attention. However, even in this short period of time behavioral psychologists have acquired both the knowledge and the techniques for direct application with these populations.

Carlson and Lahey (1988) use the Witt handbook to review the many strategies currently available for the treatment of conduct and attention deficit disorders. In addition to behavioral programs that rely on teachers, peers, parents, or the children themselves as agents of change, it now seems possible to manipulate environmental and task variables to bring about improvements in classroom performance. The handbook also contains Wacker and Berg's (1988) thoughtful formulation of issues to be confronted in the habilitation of students with severe handicaps. Generalization and independence are their major treatment goals, and guidelines for defining, implementing, and evaluating individualized treatment programs are presented with these in mind.

Ever since the passing of the Education for All Handicapped Children Act of 1985 (Public Law 94-142), mainstreaming has remained a matter of controversy. In the 1960s, this controversy was confined primarily to the field of special education and the debate centered on the ethics and efficacy of the then prevailing special class model. In the 1970s, largely as a function of the new act, the locus shifted to general education and the issue became one of the capacity of the regular school system to comply (Skrtic, 1987). Today, a new mainstreaming debate is beginning to emerge. There is growing recognition that for many students mainstreaming is failing (e.g., see Will, 1985). Consequently, the current debate within the special education community is about the possibility of a new, restructured mainstream. A new text by Meisel (1986) focuses exclusively upon these issues, drawing attention to the need for recognition of social as well as academic outcomes; Meisel's cautiously positive summing up rests largely on an optimistic reading of the relevant research and its ready application to the integration of effective new procedures with everyday practices in special education.

Attempts to repeal, deregulate, or otherwise modify Public Law 94-142 tends to overlook an important compliance monitoring mechanism built into the act to ensure free, appropriate education for all handicapped children. Federal agencies monitor states, and states are required by law to monitor local agencies. Although federal regulations formally encourage active parent participation in this process, in practice this recommendation is rarely implemented. What is needed, argue Smith and Tawney (1983), is the active, direct involvement of parents in the monitoring process and, in particular, the asking of questions about individual plans and programs. Such activities could increase the opportunities for appropriate handicapped student education regardless of the act's ultimate fate.

Even under ideal circumstances, mainstreamed handicapped children experience acceptance difficulties. Teachers are not as receptive to the social integration of these children as the founding mothers and fathers of Public Law 94-142 had hoped. Regular classroom and resource room teachers seem to differ systematically in their perceptions of their handicapped pupils. The regular classroom teachers tend to rate their handicapped pupils as significantly more maladjusted (Fabre & Walker, 1987). (For a brief but informative discussion of issues involved in the training of teachers and other school personnel for working with severely impaired students, see Kerr, 1986).

Teacher perceptions of pupil behavior can affect teacher–pupil interactions and, if for this reason alone, further investigation is mandatory. When Center and Wascom (1986) compared teacher perceptions of 534 youngsters classified as either learning disabled or socially normal, striking differences emerged. Socially normal pupils were perceived as evidencing significantly more prosocial behavior and significantly less antisocial behavior. Females were perceived as exhibiting significantly more prosocial behavior than males.

If perceptions differ, what of the rewards used to bring about behavior change? Should rewards used in remedial classrooms be made available in the regular classroom and should items and activities that occur routinely in the regular classroom be used in remedial settings?

Martens, Muir, and Meller (1988) were interested in both the identification of rewarding activities, consequences, and materials commonly found in regular and special educational classrooms, and in comparing the ratings of these rewards by handicapped and nonexceptional students, respectively. When 72 students completed a 12-item questionnaire designed to investigate the desirability of various rewards, ratings by nonexceptional students in regular classroom settings did not differ significantly from those of their handicapped peers in self-contained room placements. Rewards rated as most desirable by both groups included good grades and free time privileges for work completed. Neither the opportunity to engage in further academic work of their choice, either with peers or teachers, nor additional socializing with friends fared as well.

As the investigators note, their study suffers from several limitations. The subjects were primarily black, middle and high school level, lower socioeconomic pupils, and the study was confined to perceptions of the desirability of the various classroom reinforcers. The correspondence between these ratings and reward effectiveness in the classroom remains unknown. Nevertheless, the failure to obtain significantly different ratings between students in regular and self-contained room placements does raise the possibility that a common set of rules may be validly employed in both settings.

Attention has been drawn in the preceding section of this chapter to peer tutoring as an activity of potential benefit to both tutor and tutee. At first, Mastropieri, Jenkins, and Scruggs (1985) believed that behaviorally disturbed students could have a special, beneficial role as tutors because they themselves exhibit the type of deficits in social functioning and attitudes toward school upon which tutoring interventions are said to impact positively. Later, based both on their own observations and their searching review of the evidence, Scruggs, Mastropieri, Tolfa Veit, and Osguthorpe (1986) came to the conclusion that the beneficial effect of such procedures is minimal and that, until more compelling positive evidence becomes available, it would seem prudent for teachers to employ other means of enhancing social functioning. Once again, it would seem that the teacher reservations noted in the preceding section of this chapter are not unfounded.

According to Hollinger (1987), a combination of social skills training and attention to the negative social perception biases of their peers might facilitate acceptance of behaviorally disordered children in mainstream settings. McEvoy and Odom (1987) come to a similar conclusion with respect to social interaction training for preschool children with behavioral disorders. Eventually, such strategies could lead to a valid basis for the utilization of behaviorally disturbed children as tutors. As yet, this is far from the case.

Follow-up studies of students who have participation in special education programs raise an interesting question: How well have special education programs prepared the youth they were designed to serve? When Neel, Meadows, Levine, and Edgar (1988) first reviewed the postgraduation adjustment of 160 students formally classified as behaviorally disordered, the data seemed to be encouraging. According to the students' parents, nearly two-thirds of these behaviorally disordered former students had found jobs and adjusted satisfactorily. They seemed to have accomplished this with minimal assistance from agencies, institutions, or schools. On closer inspection, however, Neel et al. conclude that the overall picture is not as bright. Less than one in five of these young people originally classified as severely behaviorally disordered was involved in any form of secondary postgraduate program. This may be contrasted with an approximately 50% involvement on the part of a comparable nonhandicapped population. Furthermore, when compared with national figures, the rate of unemployment of these disturbed youths was nearly three times as high (40% vs. 15%). Perhaps the most alarming finding was that nearly one-third of this population were not receiving the necessary training and support for participation in the adult world. Perhaps understandably, despite reports of satisfactory adjustment, approximately one-third of the parents also felt dissatisfied with the manner in which the schools had helped their children, and one-third were flatly dissatisfied with the jobs their children eventually found. Once again, this is in marked contrast to similar reports by parents of nonhandicapped youths. Their study and its disconcerting conclusions merit concerned attention from administrators, educators, and researchers.

To conclude on a less pessimistic note, let me draw attention to an innovative blueprint by Evans and his associates for the evaluation of programs for children with disabilities. As Evans, Brown, Weed, Spry, and Owen (1987) noted, merely documenting effective intervention strategies does not lead automatically to a more effective technology of application. Even the best documented procedure requires sophisticated monitoring, program adjustments based on individual needs, and countless feedback-based daily decisions. This, in turn, required meaningful student assessment and systematic program evaluation. To find out how this might come about, the reader is referred directly to the timely monograph of Evans et al.

CONCLUSIONS

As noted in the introduction, preparation for this series rests largely upon a continual monitoring of the relevant literature with an eye to both continuity and developments of significance. In so doing, I have been increasingly led over the years to the conclusion that, despite the seemingly disparate natures of specific areas, there is an underlying unity of approach that characterizes all behavior therapy. Areas of focus may differ, we may be concerned primarily with children, technique innovation, or social change, but throughout, a commonality of purpose and strategy remains: a combination of learning theory, behavioral science, and a willingness to "think out of the box" and seek new conceptual horizons as either the data or changing times dictate. It is this combination that gives behavior therapy the right to call itself unique among therapeutic modalities, not its treatment successes (or failures, for that matter).

Thus, target audiences and subject matter apart, from a conceptual vantage there is little that is unique to child behavior therapy per se. Given this premise, it is understandable and desirable that developments within child behavior therapy parallel what is happening within the parent body. On this account, child behavior therapy, like its parent model, seems to be technologically and professionally alive and flourishing. Although conceptual or even methodological breakthroughs are conspicuously lacking—few new principles or fundamentally innovative techniques have emerged within the past three decades—the 1980s have seen two important trends: an ecological systems-oriented sensitivity to the multifaceted needs of our times and a still evolving nonlinear but rigorous methodology.

Behavior therapy is more fortunate than physics. According to the Heisenberg uncertainty principle, it is possible to measure precisely either the location of an atomic particle or its velocity but not both at the same time. In behavior therapy, there are the few whose primary concerns are with concept and theory, and there are the many who focus upon clinical and professional issues. Unlike physics, however, in behavior therapy it is not axiomatically impossible for the same individual or investigative team to think in terms of both perspectives; it is merely unusual. Such individuals are rare. In the belief that, in the long run, all of behavior therapy is open to benefit from this liaison and not just child behavior therapy, I have tried to draw attention to these developments wherever it seems to me that they occur.

CHAPTER

8

CLINICAL ISSUES AND STRATEGIES IN THE PRACTICE OF BEHAVIOR THERAPY

G. TERENCE WILSON

The range of therapeutic strategies encompassed by behavior therapy continues to widen, and their clinical applications continue to expand. These heterogeneous strategies and diverse activities also continue to be accompanied by familiar points of contention among different groups within behavior therapy and between behavior therapists and other forms of psychotherapy.

Dominant themes from previous years continue to provoke lively discussion and debate. In this chapter we return to the question of commonalities between behavior therapy and other forms of psychotherapy. Everyone agrees on the desirability of replacing what has often been internecine warfare among competing schools of psychological therapy with greater cooperation and consensus. But how best to go about this difficult task? Is some superordinate form of psychological therapy that integrates existing approaches feasible or desirable at this stage of development? Are there alternative strategies to integrationism? The question of treatment outcome remains a crucial issue. The advocacy of integrationism is buttressed by assertions rejecting differential effects among diverse treatments. There are now legal as well as ethical and clinical implications of the attempt to avoid grappling with the difficult and divisive matter of treatment outcome.

Another overriding issue is the relationship between research and clinical practice. The behavior therapy literature has been criticized as clinically naive, as failing the practicing clinician. Other critics la-ment what they perceive as the estrangement of clinical practice from its conceptual and research bases. These concerns blend ineluctably into existing controversies about models of clinical training for psychologists. The role of the therapist–patient relationship has attracted increased attention within behavior therapy. And novel suggestions for clinical practice have come from an unexpected source, radical behaviorism.

COMMONALITIES AMONG PSYCHOLOGICAL THERAPIES

The interest in integrating different forms of psychotherapy continues to be one of the "hottest" topics in the field (Norcross, 1986; Wachtel, 1987). As we have noted in our commentaries in previous volumes in this series, a critical issue in attempts to integrate the psychological therapies has been the extent of the commonalities and differences between psychodynamic therapy and behavior therapy (Arkowitz & Messer, 1984). There are several reasons for this focus on the potential rapprochement between psychodynamic and behavioral therapies.

Cognitive-behavior and psychodynamic therapies are, as the Smith (1982) survey indicates, probably the two most influential approaches among clinical and counseling psychologists. When self-described eclectic therapists are asked to define which approaches they most favor, they refer to psychodynamic and behavioral therapies (Garfield & Kurtz, 1976). Goldfried and Safran (1986) cite a study by Friedling, Goldfried, and Stricker (1984) that similarly shows evidence of convergence among therapists from different theoretical orientations. Graduates from a behavioral (Stony Brook) and a psychodynamic (Adelphi) clinical training program completed a questionnaire designed to assess their therapeutic activities. An attempt was made to couch the questions in neutral language that that did not clearly favor either theoretical approach. Of the aspects of clinical practice sampled in this questionnaire, 56% were reportedly used by both groups of respondents; only 29% were used exclusively by one of the groups. Graduates from Stony Brook were more likely to be eclectic if they were full-time practitioners as opposed to academics. (Graduates from Adelphi were solely practitioners, so the comparable comparison could not be made.) Not surprisingly, the psychodynamic therapists reported more eclectic activities the more they treated patients from lower socioeconomic strata. Eclectic therapists stated that they drew upon both approaches, but there is a history of marked conflict and rivalry between psychodynamic and behavioral therapists themselves. Psychodynamic therapists, for example, have often criticized behavior therapy as being superficial and failing to address the real causes of clinical disorders. Behavior therapists have always attacked psychoanalysis as unscientific, untestable, and lacking any evidence of therapeutic effectiveness. In some ways, these two approaches represent polar opposites in their basic philosophies, theories, and treatment methods. Success in finding ways to bridge these apparent differences would greatly advance the development of a more integrated approach to psychotherapy.

The ideal of an integrated, unified approach to psychological treatment that would that would embrace demonstrably effective therapeutic strategies from diverse theoretical orientations has obvious appeal. Few therapists would dissent from the view that proponents of different psychological approaches might make greater efforts to understand and perhaps incorporate each other's principles or techniques. The question is how to go about it. Different solutions have been proposed, and the more prominent alternatives are examined here.

Technical Eclecticism

Eclecticism has always loomed large as an alternative to any particular theoretical approach to psychological therapy. Smith's (1982) survey of members of the clinical and counseling divisions of the American Psychological Association confirmed what has been evident for some time, that the majority of practitioners advocate some form of eclectism in psychological treatment. A recent text by Norcross (1986) points out that eclecticism is not a unitary construct or approach. Different kinds of eclecticism within psychotherapy are possible.

Unsystematic Eclecticism

One kind of eclecticism is what Lazarus (1988) has labeled unsystematic eclecticism. This approach permits openness and flexibility but also encourages the indiscriminate use of different concepts and methods from what may be fundamentally conflicting systems. This approach is subject to therapeutic fads that have neither an adequate theoretical rationale nor an empirical support. It is this type of eclecticism that has frequently been criticized as incompatible with scientific progress. For example, Eysenck (1986, p. 378) writes that "an eclectic point of view by definition means an anti-scientific point of view: Eclecticism has always been the enemy of scientific understanding."

Systematic or Technical Eclecticism

Lazarus (1988, 1989d) rejects what he calls fusionism, the attempt to integrate the different concepts and techniques of varying systems of psychological therapy into a unified, harmonious whole. He suggests that the field of psychotherapy is too fragmented and insufficiently developed to permit conceptual integration of this sort. According to Lazarus, the preferred alternative is technical eclecticism. In this approach the therapist is free to draw upon techniques from any type of psychotherapy without necessarily subscribing to the theoretical tenets that gave rise to the techniques in question.

Lazarus's espousal of technical eclecticism has been the source of considerable controversy within behavior therapy over the years. A critical analysis of this matter has often featured prominently in previous volumes of this series (e.g., Volume 8). As we have previously indicated, the majority of techniques used by Lazarus are standard methods within behavior therapy (Wilson, 1982a). In addition, however, technical eclectism makes use of several nonbehavioral methods. It has never been clear the extent to which these nonbehavioral methods characterize technical eclecticism. Nevertheless, advocating the use of nonbehavioral techniques drawn from widely differing approaches helped to set aside Lazarus's position from orthodox behavior therapy.

In his most recent analysis of technical eclecticism, Lazarus (1988) addresses many of the criticisms that have dogged his approach. Most notably perhaps, he rejects the criticism that his approach is atheoretical despite its openness to techniques from other therapeutic systems. He looks mainly to social and cognitive learning theory for explanatory constructs because

> all of its tenets are grounded in research and are open to verification and disproof. By operating from a consistent, testable, theoretical base and then drawing on useful techniques from any discipline without necessarily subscribing to the theoretical tenets that gave rise to the techniques in question, one avoids the jumble, the melange, and the subjective bias of theoretical eclecticism and integrationism. (p. 64)

This statement, grounding his approach firmly within social learning theory and rejecting "integrationism," makes it more difficult to distinguish between Lazarus's approach and contemporary cognitive-behavior therapy.

The question we have raised before is this: By what criteria are nonbehavioral methods chosen for use within technical eclecticism? Lazarus (1988) illustrates his approach with reference to the empty chair technique. This method involves pretending that a significant other is sitting in an empty chair, whereupon a dialogue is enacted. The client expresses thoughts and feelings to the imagined person in the empty chair and then changes places, now occupying the formerly empty chair and acting as that other person. This technique is drawn from Gestalt therapy (Yontef & Simkin, 1989), in which it is aimed at helping the patient to work through painful emotions attached to prior relationships and what is called "unfinished business." It might be used, for instance, to help a patient resolve emotional conflicts with a parent who has died.

One would not select this method based on empirical evaluation. There is no good research evidence demonstrating that this method is effective, let alone that it has incremental effectiveness when combined with other methods. Nor can we say that this technique derives from social learning theory. With some creative post hoc analysis, we might be able to make a case for it not being inconsistent with social learning theory. Lazarus (1988) states that the technique is used as a variant of behavior rehearsal, that it is employed primarily to modify current maladaptive patterns of behavior. This pragmatic approach seems sensible and has clinical appeal, but it leaves unanswered questions. For instance, why do we need a variant of behavior rehearsal? Why this particular variant? What can be said at this point is that the empty chair technique is frequently chosen by behavior therapists as a nonbehavioral method they would use. In addition to Lazarus (1988), this arguably most favored of nonbehavioral methods has been endorsed in one way or another by Arnkoff (1983), Goldfried and Safran (1986), Haaga (1986), and Hayes (1987).

Psychotherapy Integration

One of the most thoughtful and systematic attempts to move toward a uniform, integrated psychotherapeutic approach has been proposed by Goldfried and his colleagues. The essence of Goldfried's proposals for integration in psychotherapy, and how they differ from other related proposals, was described in a previous volume in this series (Wilson,

1982a). Goldfried and Safran (1986) have provided an update on this approach. Briefly, they suggest that the first step toward any integration must identify the specific commonalities and differences among the various psychological therapies. To this end they recommend that we focus on the appropriate level of conceptual analysis and develop a neutral language with which to describe commonalities.

A clinical strategy falls at some intermediate point of abstraction between a concrete therapeutic technique (e.g., interpretation) on the one hand, and an overall theoretical framework (e.g., behaviorism) on the other. Examples of clinical strategies include corrective experiences, providing patients with feedback on their behavior, and the therapist–patient relationship. (Whether these strategies are really common across different forms of psychological therapies, or only represent relatively trivial, surface similarities, has been debated elsewhere; Wilson, 1982a.) The recommended language is that of cognitive psychology. Goldfried and Safran argue that not only is it "neutral with respect to past histories of conflict among rival psychotherapeutic systems, but also that it reflects what has become a dominant force in experimental psychology" (p. 467).

As numerous commentators have observed, cognitive constructs from experimental psychology find ready acceptance among clinicians and their patients alike. They appear more congenial than the often harsh language of environmental control that characterizes some behavioral approaches. The similarity of cognitive constructs to everyday language and the manner in which people construe and interpret their experience is one of the dangers radical behaviorists have warned against. The allure and acceptance of common sense sounding but nonobservable and internal mediating variables confirm the behaviorist's worst nightmare. Increasingly, traditional psychotherapeutic processes are being recast in the more modern language of cognitive psychology. A good illustration of this trend is provided by Westen's (1988) examination of the psychodynamic concept of transference from an information processing perspective.

Westen (1988) restates the classic psychodynamic view that during development, and childhood in particular, individuals experience primitive wishes, conflicts, and other negative affective responses. These dysphoric affective responses are avoided (unconsciously repressed) to reduce their untoward emotional effects.

> As a result, they may remain encapsulated in "pockets" of unworked-through cognitive–affective networks and may continue to direct thought and behavior. By bringing these cognitive–affective structures to consciousness, the patient can begin to reassess as an adult whether these

structures are realistic and whether the way they were regulated in childhood should continue to operate. (p. 175)[1]

Westen reinterprets this process by likening it to the recall of mood-dependent memory (e.g., Bower, 1987) and schema-related affect (Derry & Kuiper, 1981), both important constructs within current cognitive psychology.

Westen (1988) also endorses the classic psychodynamic view that transference is the only way to access these cognitive–affective structures. He gives the following example:

> A borderline patient whom I had been seeing for over a year started to withdraw without clear cause, refusing to talk and sitting glumly in her chair. We had previously discussed a similar pattern in her life of suddenly severing relations with people important to her, but the pattern was now emerging—with corresponding affect—in the transference. She was aware of her actions but angrily told me that she would not and could not explain them. I suggested to her that someone does not pull away from another person like that unless she is afraid of something, at which point she volunteered that she did not know what she feared, but that she was sure something terribly bad would happen if she did not run. The combination of her experiencing this feeling with me and eliciting thoughts and memories congruent with the affect allowed us to explore the fear behind her behavior, and repeated experiences of this sort allowed her both to reanalyze (cognitively) conditions under which fear has been inappropriately evoked, and to see that, in fact, her fears are not confirmed in interaction with me. This latter aspect of use of the transference is similar to in vivo exposure techniques in behavioral treatment. (p. 175)

The foregoing clinical anecdote may well indicate that the therapist had accessed a cognitive–affective structure that was intimately associated with the patient's interpersonal behavior. Cognitive-behavior therapists would explore the significance of this sample of behavior and possibly use it as an important opportunity for therapeutic change, but to say as much is not to accept the seminal role accorded transference in psychodynamic therapy. There is still no acceptable evidence that transference is either necessary or sufficient for therapeutic change. Even if a goal of cognitive–behavioral treatment were to elicit and then modify some feature of interpersonal functioning (i.e., to "work through" some conflicted pattern of behavior), it can be argued that the therapist–patient relationship is unlikely to be the optimal crucible for change.

---

[1] The term "cognitive–affective structure" is receiving increasing play within the behavior therapy literature. For example, Barlow (1988), in his book on anxiety and its disorders, makes cognitive–affective structure the cornerstone of his theory of anxiety.

Behavior therapists do make direct use of the therapeutic relationship to alter some patterns of behavior. (For more detail on this subject see Volume 10 of this series, pp. 313–314.) The utility of the therapeutic relationship in this regard is limited. Mischel's still devastating critique of cross-situational consistency of personality traits (Mischel & Peake, 1982) underscores the necessity of promoting corrective emotional experiences within the appropriate situational context. That context, for most patients, is not their relationship with a therapist in an artificial treatment setting; it is more likely to be specific interpersonal relationships under particular conditions in their everyday environment. (Note, however, that Kohlenberg & Tsai, 1987, have proposed a behavioristic analysis of treatment, which strongly disputes this assertion, as discussed below.)

CRITIQUE

Goldfried and Safran (1986) are quick to acknowledge that certain risks attach to their proposals for psychotherapy integration. They worry openly about the possibility that "the growing interest in eclecticism and psychotherapy integration may result in a renewed competition, the arena being to determine who can formulate the best eclectic or integrated system" (p. 480). My own view, given psychotherapy's tradition of competing and conflicting schools that flourish in impressionistic quicksand devoid of any empirical foundation, is that such competition for the "best" integrated system is inevitable. There are signs of it already. For example, Lazarus (1988, 1989d) blasts away at approaches such as "fusionism" while advocating technical eclecticism. The rejoinders are not far off. Goldfried and Safran (1986) explicitly embrace what they call a "rational empirical approach" as a general framework for developing an integrated psychotherapy. It is not hard to think of influential psychotherapists who share little, if any, enthusiasm for an empirical approach to understanding human behavior.

I am reminded of the recent history of meta analysis. Smith, Glass, and Miller (1980) stated that this quantitative technique would rid the field of biased, "literary" reviews, and show once and for all that all forms of psychotherapy produced equal and significantly greater benefit to patients than no treatment. We now know that the result was different. In Volume 11 of this series I pointed out that the proliferation of meta analyses of treatment outcome had rehashed many of the old controversies (Wilson, 1987a). What happened was that the controversies were simply raised to another level (Garfield, 1983).

CLINICAL ISSUES AND STRATEGIES IN PRACTICE

In trying to identify commonalities among different treatments, it makes sense, as Goldfried and Safran (1986) recommend, to focus comparative studies on specific clinical disorders. Addressing a particular disorder ensures a more problem-focused, pragmatic attitude. More abstract, ideological differences are less likely to come into play. I discuss one example of this strategy, using bulimia nervosa as the clinical disorder, later in this chapter.

What is most troubling about Goldfried and Safran's (1986) position (and all other integrationist proposals) is their apparent acceptance that the widely different forms of psychological treatment they wish to integrate are equally effective. Consider, for example, their statement that "if we are truly interested in understanding similarities and differences between psychotherapy approaches, we must develop a better understanding of the subtle psychological change processes through which different interventions achieve their impact" (p. 471). What, however, is the established "impact" of some of the therapies they seek to integrate? If they mean effectiveness, then we cannot escape the contentious but all-important question of treatment outcome effects.

Curiously, Goldfried and Safran (1986), in warning against the dangers of premature integration, include the following quote from Kazdin (1984):

> Integrationism as a general movement represents a highly significant development in psychotherapy. However, it may be the general movement that is worth promoting rather than the specific attempt to integrate psychodynamic and behavioral views. At this point, individual positions suffer from loose concepts and weak empirical bases, problems that are not resolved and perhaps may even be exacerbated by their combination. The overall goal is establishing an empirically based and theoretically viable account of therapy. Premature integration of specific positions that are not well supported on their own may greatly impede progress. (pp. 141–142)

Here Kazdin is voicing precisely the same concerns I underscore above, namely, do not try to integrate therapies that are not well supported (i.e., shown to be effective). The authors do not reconcile this advice with their exclusive reliance on process research at the expense of any serious consideration of outcome research. Goldfried and Safran (1986) make a number of useful and sophisticated suggestions about carrying out good process research, but there is no point in conducting fine-grained analyses of process variables in therapies that are simply ineffective.

A primary commitment to process research may be an increasing trend within psychotherapy research. For example, Vandenbos (1986), in his introduction to a special issue of the *American Psychologist* on psychotherapy research, states that by 1980, "a consensus of sorts was reached that psychotherapy, as a generic treatment process, was demonstrably more effective than no treatment" (p. 111). To document his sweeping conclusion, Vandenbos cited many reviewers but selectively excluded those who have disagreed with his optimism. And although Vadenbos acknowledges that some effort be made to assess outcome in the move toward process research, those who do not necessarily share his blanket enthusiasm for the effectiveness of psychotherapy will be left with the impression that he believes that the outcome issue has been largely decided.

That the outcome issue goes to the heart of the integration movement is revealed in a recent paper by Beitman, Goldfried, and Norcross (1989), which seems designed to represent a consensus statement on the nature of integration of different psychotherapies. These authors assert that a major reason for the integration movement "is the general inability to show that one therapeutic approach is clearly superior to any other in manifest outcome" (p. 140). Beitman et al. (1989) reaffirm the "Dodo bird" verdict of Luborsky, Singer, and Luborsky (1979) that all therapies are equally effective.

There are clearly two camps when it comes to this issue of alleged equality of outcome among different therapies. Those who pronounce such a verdict rely heavily on the Smith et al.'s meta analysis in support of their argument. In so doing, they ignore the well-documented inadequacies in this particular meta analysis, ranging from fundamental conceptual shortcomings to simple failure to include a large number of highly relevant studies (Paul, 1985; Wilson & Rachman, 1983). In addition, they pointedly exclude other meta analyses that consistently show differences among treatments (see Wilson, 1985b). This refusal even to address let alone accept evidence that is uncongenial to their position undermines the credibility of Beitman et al.'s (1989) position.

Those who reject the view that all therapies are equally effective argue that there are preferred treatments for specific disorders (Kazdin & Wilson, 1978; Lazarus, 1989c). This is not to say that for some relatively minor or intractable problems no differences among treatments are likely to emerge, but differential treatment effects across a range of common and disabling disorders cannot be overlooked in the rush toward integration. The implications of uncritically accepting the view that all therapies are equally effective are taken up more fully below.

Beitman et al. (1989) not only assert that different treatment methods are equally effective but also that they have a modest role in producing change. Relying once more on the Smith et al. (1980) meta analysis, these authors attribute only 10% to 12% of outcome variance to technique variables. Preexisting patient factors are said to account for most of the variance, followed by therapist personal factors. If all therapeutic methods are created equal, and are largely ineffective, there seems to be little point in comparing different approaches or in trying to integrate them. Beitman et al. (1989) are essentially led to a conclusion similar to that of Smith et al.'s (1980). It does not seem to matter what method is used, in what form (individual or group), for how long, or by whom (therapist experience was unrelated to treatment outcome in that meta analysis). Psychotherapy can ill-afford such advocacy. Beitman et al. (1989) themselves leave the reader with the following recommendation:

> Our efforts might be more profitably expended in tailoring the therapeutic relationship and clinical method to the patient. To the extent that there are some specific technique effects (and refined research may discern still more), treatment success can be maximized by altering the therapist's stance and operations to the patient's presenting problem, interpersonal style, personality configuration, readiness to change, and related variables. To the degree that clinicians are able to modify and enlarge their practices to fit the patient's needs, the benefits are potentiated. (p. 141)

This vaguely stated injunction offers a poor blueprint for future advances.

In what is purported to be an updated analysis of what the research literature can contribute to the practitioner, Strupp (1989) also endorses the view that all therapies are equally effective, namely, "research has made relatively little headway in demonstrating that specific techniques are uniquely effective in treating particular disorders" (p. 717). He tends to dismiss all specific therapeutic methods as "disembodied techniques." The dubious conclusion that specific techniques are not differentially effective has been taken up elsewhere. Here the notion that techniques are "disembodied," at least in behavior therapy, must be questioned. Presumably for Strupp, techniques are disembodied because they are not part of his personal view of psychotherapy and mechanisms of change, namely, the therapist-patient relationship that he construes in traditional transference terms. In behavior therapy, which is based on a broad cognitive-social learning model of behavior change, specific techniques are one component (and often a critically important one) of diverse psychosocial factors (including the therapist-patient relationship) that may influence the patient's behavior. At the level of behavior change processes, specific techniques are conceptually related to the therapeutic relationship (e.g., Lazarus & Fay, 1984; Jacobson, 1989b; Wilson & Evans, 1977).

Many proponents of the equivalency verdict apparently fail to grasp its ramifications for psychotherapy, as we have already noted. Strupp's (1989) paper offers a clear illustration of this irony. He asserts that no single psychological method is superior to another. He also, however, defines conditions for effective and ineffective (or harmful) psychotherapy. With regard to the former, "Nothing is of greater importance than the transactions between patient and therapist in the here and now of each therapy hour."[2] In terms of the latter, therapists "except in rare instances should desist from giving advice, guidance, and the like" (p. 719). This reasoning is unsound.

Providing advice, making suggestions, and offering encouragement to patients have been part and parcel of behavior therapy since its inception. Challenging patients' dysfunctional cognitions and actively prompting them to engage in behavioral experiments to test personal beliefs and assumptions largely defines all forms of cognitive therapy (e.g., Beck et al., 1979). Strupp announces that therapists who adopt such strategies will be ineffective at best, harmful at worst. Yet in embracing the verdict that all therapies are equally effective he himself accepts that there are no differences in outcome effectiveness among psychological therapies, including cognitive-behavioral methods. The reasoning is inherently contradictory.

Strupp's (1989) prescription that therapists should "rarely confront or challenge patients" and refrain from "giving . . . guidance" is all the more puzzling because it flies in the face of so much empirical evidence not to mention common sense. As Lazarus (1989c) comments, "Sound advice, intelligent support, and responsible encouragement are apt to enhance the patient–therapist relationship, facilitate treatment adherence, and foster the attainment of viable treatment goals." Cognitive-behavior therapy has unquestionably been shown to be effective in several well-controlled clinical studies for several disorders (e.g., O'Leary & Wilson, 1987). Whether it is the optimal or preferred form of psychological treatment for some anxiety disorders, depression, sexual dysfunction, and bulimia nervosa, to take some examples, may be arguable. What is undeniable, however, is that the approach has been shown to work; no evidence suggests that it might be less effective than alternative methods.

In trying to identify commonalities among different treatments it makes sense, as Goldfried and Safran (1986) recommend, to focus comparative studies on specific clinical disorders. Addressing a particular

---

[2]It should be noted that this sweeping reaffirmation of psychoanalytic faith is still hotly debated and, in my view, without credible empirical support.

disorder ensures a more problem-focused, pragmatic attitude. More abstract, ideological differences are less likely to come into play. I discuss one example of this strategy, using bulimia nervosa as the clinical disorder, later in this chapter.

Toward an Empirical Approach

It is easier to be critical than to be constructive. Thus, although it is well and good to point out problems in the integrationist position adopted by Goldfried and his associates, it behooves us to recommend an alternative approach to the shared goal of developing a more encompassing therapeutic framework than our individual orientations have allowed.

Some years ago, in response to the then-building enthusiasm for integrationism, I suggested that "we resist the temptation to begin what is likely to prove a futile search [for an integrated approach] and devote our energies to developing replicable, testable, and effective methods of therapeutic change within the social learning framework of behavior therapy and invite other theoretical orientations to do the same" (Wilson, 1982a, p. 327). Agras (1987) has more recently reemphasized this approach. His view is that ony after outcome studies have established the effectiveness of psychodynamic psychotherapies will there be any basis for finding common practice between behavioral and psychodynamic treatments.

At the start of this decade these proposals were just a promissory note. It is now possible, however, to point to outcome studies that provide the opportunity to examine commonalties between methods that are effective. Take the case of interpersonal psychotherapy (IPT), a form of time-limited psychotherapy developed primarily for the treatment of depression (Klerman, Weissman, Rounsaville, & Chevron, 1984). IPT shares some features of psychodynamic therapy but differs in many important respects. In IPT the therapist recognizes the intrapsychic conflicts that are the focus of psychodynamic therapy but does not interpret the patient's current problems as an expression of these underlying conflicts. Rather, the patient's behavior is explored in terms of his or her interpersonal relationships. Unlike psychodynamic therapy with its seminal focus on the transference relationship, in IPT the therapeutic relationship is not the primary focus of treatment. Drawing parallels between this relationship and others in the patient's life is done selectively. IPT also overlaps with cognitive-behavior therapy.

Like behavioral and other forms of brief therapy, IPT is directive (at least in the early beginning and intermediate stages), focused on well-defined problems, and time-limited. Some of the specific techniques used, such as modeling, role playing, problem identification, and decision analysis, closely resemble common cognitive–behavioral methods, as discussed below. In common with Beck's (1976) cognitive therapy, IPT identifies dysfunctional thinking and directs patients' attention to its impact on interpersonal relations. The difference between IPT and cognitive therapy lies in the fact that

> IPT . . . makes no attempt to uncover such distorted thoughts systematically, by giving "homework" or other assignments, nor is there an attempt to help the patient develop alternative thought patterns through prescribed practice. Rather, when evidence arises during the course of therapy the therapist calls the patient's attention to distorted thinking in relation to significant others. From there, the therapist insists that the patient explore the effect of this maladaptive thinking on interpersonal relationships. (Klerman et al., 1984, p. 16)

What is of particular interest about IPT is that it has been shown to be effective in well-controlled outcome studies. It has, for example, been shown to be an effective treatment for depression (Klerman et al., 1984). It can be described precisely, is replicable by different therapists, and can be differentiated, procedurally, from cognitive-behavior therapy (DeRubeis, Hollon, Evans, & Bemis, 1982).

More recently, Fairburn (1988) has reported a major comparative outcome study in which IPT was as effective as cognitive-behavior therapy (CBT) in the treatment of bulimia nervosa. Both IPT and CBT achieved superior results to a strictly behavioral treatment. Fairburn was careful to ensure that his IPT and CBT treatments were procedurally distinctive. In some ways the comparison is more interesting than in the depression treatment research because a treatment manual was developed for treating bulimia nervosa, which explicitly omitted some aspects of IPT that obviously overlap with CBT (Fairburn, 1988). The theoretical implications of these findings are significant not only for understanding the nature of the clinical disorders in question but also in advancing our knowledge about commonalities between procedurally distinct therapies.

One explanation of the apparent parity in outcome is simply the common impact of the "nonspecifics" of any formal psychological treatment. Although this parsimonious view cannot be dismissed given the relatively scant data that are available, it is most improbable. Other studies clearly show that some treatments are superior to others. For example, Garner (1988) has found that CBT is significantly more effective than psychodynamic therapy. Although Fairburn's study needs to be replicated, it would appear that IPT has specific therapeutic effects.

An alternative explanation of the roughly comparable success of CBT and IPT in Fairburn's (1988) study is that different treatments achieve success through different mechanisms. Fairburn suggests that whereas CBT works by directly modifying core psychopathological beliefs about body shape and weight, IPT is effective because it alters patients' negative self-evaluation: "The patients who respond seem to develop an increased sense of self-worth and competence and, as a result, their tendency to evaluate themselves largely in terms of their shape and weight lessens in intensity. This erosion of a central aspect of the psychopathology of the disorder appears in turn to lead to a change in their eating habits" (p. 641).

A third explanation is that, independent of any effect on eating behavior and attitudes toward shape and weight, CBT may also change self-evaluation and affect, either directly or indirectly, which then mediates improvement. Resolution of this matter is complicated because CBT programs vary widely in terms of how seriously they address issues beyond those related directly to weight and eating behavior. Fairburn's (1988) CBT treatment is carefully limited to these targets, but it is apparent that other CBT treatments, although modeled on Fairburn's, have had a broader purview. For example, Wilson, Rossiter, Kleifield, and Lindholm (1986) attributed the success of their CBT treatment to alterations in patients' self-efficacy for coping with food-related high-risk situations. Developing coping skills may be even more important than radically altering concern about ideal body image. Patients might continue to be concerned with body shape and weight but cease to be bulimic. Even if it is confirmed that bulimics have a distinctive preoccupation with body image, it could be argued that changes in dysfunctional self-evaluation and related emotional well-being might secondarily reduce the pathological concern with body weight and shape that is unique to bulimics.

What is needed now is continued comparative outcome research in which the hypothesized behavior change mechanisms are carefully assessed and linked to treatment outcome. It is at this juncture that Goldfried and Safran's (1986) analysis of process variables common to different treatment approaches might yield valuable data. Process research of this sort might then indicate whether the two different procedures work for different reasons or whether both depend on the same mechanisms of change.

CRITIQUE

Haaga (1986) sees problems ahead for the empirical approach advocated by Agras (1987) and Wilson (1982a). He questions "the likelihood that various orientations will produce evidence of accomplishment that would convince therapists of other orientations." Haaga's point is well taken. Behavior therapists and other empirically minded mental health researchers require well-controlled, experimental outcome studies. Such research has not been done and will not likely be completed by therapists from orientations that have long been indifferent to rigorous methodological standards. Nonetheless, the prospects are not entirely grim. The development and evaluation of IPT is a refreshing exception to this trend. Some psychodynamic therapists are also committed to empirical evaluation of their methods. Luborsky (1987) and his colleagues, for example, have completed several empirical studies of his form of psychodynamic psychotherapy (see Volume 11 of this series, pp. 296–297).

Rather than waiting for proponents of nonbehavioral therapies to complete controlled research, Haaga recommends that behavior therapists themselves study the utility of incorporating techniques from other approaches. He cites Arnkoff's (1983) description of supplementing cognitive therapy with strategies such as the Gestalt empty chair technique. In so doing, Haaga observes, Arnkoff remained faithful to a cognitive–behavioral conceptual framework as opposed to adopting a purely eclectic approach. What Haaga is prescribing here seems indistinguishable from Lazarus's (1988) technical eclecticism, as we have discussed.

A Contextual Approach

A novel approach to the question of integration has recently been proposed by Hayes (1987). He has described a complex therapeutic approach based squarely on radical behaviorism. Within this approach Hayes prescribes the use of traditional Gestalt and psychodynamic techniques. Hayes justifies this technical eclecticism as follows:

> In my opinion, behavior therapy is not a body of techniques. Rather, it is an approach to therapy that is organized, rationalized, and evaluated in terms of behavioral philosophy, concepts, and methodology. Thus, "psychodynamic," "Gestalt," or any other set of techniques can be part of behavior therapy when (but only when) this occurs. In fact, many so-called behavior therapy techniques are really not behavioristic in a radical behavioral sense of the term. (pp. 367–368)

CLINICAL ISSUES AND STRATEGIES IN PRACTICE

The similarity between the technical eclecticism espoused by Hayes (1987) and Lazarus (1988) is obvious. The critical difference lies in their respective theoretical positions. Lazarus favors a broad, empirically based cognitive–social learning framework. Hayes insists on nothing less than radical behaviorism.

Hayes's approach is unusual in more than one sense. It is an understatement to say that there seem to be few clinical practitioners working with outpatients who adhere faithfully to the tenets of radical behaviorism. One has only to examine the contents of *Journal of Applied Behavior Analysis* to confirm this impression. Clinical practitioners, for better or worse, have been unwilling to forgo the use of mediational (typically cognitive) concepts and an eclectic range of procedures. As Jacobson (1987a) notes, "The incorporation of cognitive theory and therapy into behavior therapy has been so total that it is difficult to find pure behavior therapists working with outpatients" (pp. 4–5).

Hayes (1987) offers a somewhat novel view and greater technical breadth than one would automatically associate with operant conditioning. As a radical behaviorist, he reduces "cognitive control" to verbal control, but unlike Skinner (1953), Hayes contends that verbal control is qualitatively different from the discriminative control that is studied in animal conditioning experiments. In another major departure from the conventional Skinnerian view, Hayes argues that verbal control, or what he also calls "rules," may influence behavior in ways that are inconsistent with environmental contingencies.[3] For Hayes, analyzing how rules exert generalized effects on behavior is the key to understanding adult clinical phenomena.

How Hayes derives his therapeutic strategies from his analysis of verbal control or rule-governed behavior is complex and beyond the scope of the present chapter. Briefly, a critical strategy is to change the contingencies that determine the rules (verbal control) rather than first trying to alter the rules themselves. What this leads to is a proscription

---

[3]Cognitive theorists assume that different cognitive structures and processes filter the impact of environmental contingencies on behavior. Is Hayes (1987) simply presenting a post hoc behavioristic interpretation of this well-established phenomenon? His claim is that he differs from cognitive theorists in addressing the question, "What are the contingencies that might produce verbal rules and might cause them to influence other forms of human action?" (p. 336). Yet, cognitive–social learning theory emphasizes this question. Self-efficacy theory provides one of numerous examples. Perceptions of efficacy influence thoughts, physiology, and behavior, but efficacy expectations themselves are derived from particular types of commerce with the environment. This is precisely what reciprocal determinism is all about. Hayes would seem to be presenting a truncated and unrepresentative view of "cognitive control" in his analysis.

of attempts to change thoughts or feelings directly. Moreover, patients are encouraged to alter their own view that their thoughts and feelings are causing their problems, and to change their perception of themselves as being able to directly control their thoughts and feelings. To accomplish this end, Hayes advocates a number of strategies in which the use of paradox features prominently.

CRITIQUE

The theoretical thrust of the contextual approach is unlikely to have much influence other than among the true adherents of radical behaviorism. The thesis that radical behaviorism does not ignore private events, and the attempt to conceptualize cognition as just another form of behavior, is well worn. So too are the many criticisms of this nonmediational approach (see, e.g., Bandura, 1986). Hayes does take the position that learning in humans is different from that in animals, and he centers this distinction on the role played by verbal rules. Nevertheless, this view will do little to alter the nature or outcome of the debate between radical behaviorists and cognitive-social learning theorists.

Of greater interest and potential impact are the strategies Hayes outlines for doing therapy. There is much in common between this approach and that of strategic therapy, as Jacobson (1987b) points out. The raison d'être of contextual therapy notwithstanding, it could be argued that much of what Hayes actually prescribes is consistent with conceptual models of behavior change other than radical behaviorism.

The acid test for this contextual approach will be its success in generating therapeutic strategies that can be shown to work. Hayes is mindful of this challenge and tentatively presents preliminary evidence of success. He reports impressive success in an uncontrolled series of patients with anxiety disorders as well as a comparative outcome study of depressed patients in which his method was superior to that of Beck's (1976) cognitive therapy. New therapies are, of course, almost always heralded by their originators as superior to existing methods. Whether this approach can deliver on its ambitious claims remains to be seen.

One of the problems in testing Hayes's approach will be the difficulty in specifying the method so that it can be evaluated within comparative studies. The approach is complex and heavily reliant on general philosophical assumptions rather than specific procedures. Hayes (1987) himself comments that "this is an approach that is very difficult to teach to others because its assumptions and techniques differ so much from the mainstream culture" (p. 384).

Functional Analytic Psychotherapy

Kohlenberg and Tsai (1987) also attempt to apply radical behaviorism to outpatient clinical settings. Whereas Hayes (1987) attempts to go beyond the original Skinnerian framework in applying radical behaviorism to human behavior, Kohlenberg and Tsai (1987) return to the traditional operant view in their therapeutic applications. Their approach, which they call functional analytic psychotherapy, underscores the critical importance of what occurs between the therapist and patient during the treatment session. The goal is to structure the session so as to elicit "clinically relevant behaviors" (CRBs). These include both the problem and target behaviors. When a CRB is evoked, the therapist can modify it using the principle of reinforcement. The reinforcers the therapist uses are his or her emotional and interpersonal reactions to the patient's behavior. Kohlenberg and Tsai emphasize the importance of using what Ferster (1979) once called "natural" (i.e., the therapist's reactions) as opposed to "arbitrary" reinforcers (i.e., external or tangible rewards). Jacobson (1989b) uses Kohlenberg and Tsai's emphasis on natural reinforcers to remind practitioners about the importance of genuineness in the therapeutic relationship. Specifically in regard to treating depression, Jacobson (1989b) suggests that depressed patients "are likely to harbor suspicions about the therapist's behavior being attributable to the role of being therapeutic, rather than genuine regard for the client. The best defense against the negating impact of these attributions is for the therapist to only provide regard when it is, in fact, genuine, and for the focus to periodically shift from the therapeutic relationship to important interpersonal processes in the natural environment" (p. 93). Beck et al. (1979), among others, have cautioned that therapists take note of patients' attributional propensities in tailoring their therapeutic style to particular cases. Jacobson (1989b), however, carries his suggestion further in speculating that "this may mean that therapists can only work to maximum effectiveness with depressives that they like, or it could be that good cognitive behavior therapists are able to separate the qualities of people that make them unlovable from their inherent likability as human beings" (p. 93). Although I suspect many practitioners would concur with Jacobson, it is unclear that therapists are more effective with patients they like. And even if they are, there are reasons other than perceived genuineness of the therapist, which might account for it.

Kohlenberg and Tsai (1987) observe that their approach is most suitable for patients who need "an intensive, emotional, in-depth therapy experience. It is also well suited for clients who have not improved adequately with behavior therapy, who have difficulties in establishing intimate relationships, or who have diffuse, pervasive, interpersonal problems typified by Axis II diagnoses in DSM-III" (p. 389). The authors argue that these interpersonal problem behaviors occur far more frequently during the therapeutic session than most behavior therapists believe. To the extent that the problem behavior does occur in the session, then behavior therapists can and do use their relationship with the patient to effect change (Arnkoff, 1983). Cognitive-behavior therapists would go beyond the principle of reinforcement in altering maladaptive behavior, but they would be addressing the same sample of in-session behavior.

Is functional analytic psychotherapy a restatement of psychoanalysis in operant terms? Is it an example of an important commonality between behaviorism and psychoanalysis applied to the clinical setting? Despite their insistence on the primary importance of the interaction between therapist and patient as the vehicle of therapeutic change, Kohlenberg and Tsai (1987) reject this equation. They observe that the overt problem behavior expressed in the session is the target behavior; it is not an indirect reflection of some early childhood conflict. Moreover, as an operant, the problem behavior will occur only if the conditions that control any behavior are present. Transference, they state, is assumed to occur almost automatically in psychodynamic sessions. Finally, they argue that "the psychodynamic view is that the therapist should 'disengage from the emotional climate presented by the client' in order to avoid responding to the client with reactions that might occur naturally in the social environment. The radical behavioral view is that natural therapist reactions are the primary change agent" (p. 437). What this behavioral analysis of in-session change using the therapist's reinforcement does not satisfactorily explain is how this narrow situational control over behavior is extended to the world outside of the therapist's office. Generalization of treatment-induced change is a recurring problem for all treatment approaches.

TREATMENT OUTCOME: THE PATIENT'S RIGHT TO EFFECTIVE THERAPY

Psychological/psychiatric training and literature make frequent reference to patients' right to treatment and their right to refuse treatment. But what about patients' rights to safe and *effective* treatment? In my

CLINICAL ISSUES AND STRATEGIES IN PRACTICE

Presidential Address to the Association for Advancement of Behavior Therapy (Wilson, 1982c), I noted that "procedures that are grounded in empirical research are used sparingly, if at all, in general clinical practice, whereas unsupported and even discredited methods continue to flourish." I went on to quote Liberman's (1980) perceptive observation that "after almost 20 years of behavioral analysis and therapy, workers in the field must realize that political, personal, and social factors determine upwards of 90% of the success and survival of technical procedures. . . . Implementation, survival, and dissemination of empirically validated interventions require much more than data and journal publications" (Wilson, 1982c, p. 309). Recent events have provided some of the first signs that effective treatments might be legislated even though some psychoanalysts continue to ignore evidence of effectiveness.

Klerman (1990) has provided a revealing analysis of the *Osheroff v. Chestnut Lodge* case, a likely landmark case in which a patient sued the psychiatric institution where he was hospitalized for persisting in ineffective treatment while withholding effective treatment. Dr. Osheroff, a nephrologist, was hospitalized in 1979 for anxiety and depressive symptoms at Chestnut Lodge in Rockville, Maryland. This institution has played a significant role in the history of modern psychiatry as a center for the clinical practice of psychoanalytic and interpersonal forms of psychotherapy. Dr. Osheroff's condition worsened during 7 months of hospitalization during which he received therapy four times a week. The patient's family had a senior psychiatrist try to intercede on his behalf, but the institution's staff refused to alter their treatment. At the end of 7 months he was admitted to another institution where he was immediately placed on antidepressant medication. Dr. Osheroff showed improvement after 2 to 3 weeks and was discharged after 3 months. He resumed his medical practice and has suffered no interference with his professional or social functioning while receiving outpatient psychotherapy and medication.

In 1982 Dr. Osheroff sued Chestnut Lodge claiming that the withholding of effective drug treatment deprived him of income he would otherwise have had from his medical practice, and resulted in him losing custody of his two children. Dr. Osheroff's suit was heard by the Maryland Health Care Arbitration Panel (HCAP). Several expert psychiatric witnesses participated in this review process. The HCAP awarded him $500,000 in damages. Both sides appealed, and Dr. Osheroff requested a jury trial. A settlement was reached before court action, however.

Here is a case in which the issue of right to effective treatment seems clear. As Klerman (1990) points out, there was no evidence whatsoever to support the use of the intensive, long-term psychoanalytic therapy for depression used by Chestnut Lodge. Also, there was convincing evidence for the effectiveness of alternative treatments (e.g., medication), which the staff rejected. Klerman cautioned,

> It should not be concluded there is no evidence for the value of any psychotherapies in the treatment of depressive states. Depressive states are heterogeneous, and there are multiple forms of psychotherapy. There is very good evidence from controlled clinical trials for the value of a number of brief psychotherapies for nonpsychotic and nonbipolar forms of depression in ambulatory patients [Weissman, Jarrett, & Rush, 1989]. The psychotherapies for which there is evidence include cognitive–behavioral therapy [Beck et al., 1979], interpersonal psychotherapy [Klerman et al., 1984], and behavioral therapy [Lewinsohn, 1974]. However, no clinical trials have been reported to support the claims for efficacy of psychoanalysis or intensive individual psychotherapy based on psychoanalytic theory for any form of depression. (p. 413)

Klerman provides an informative analysis of the legal and public health implications of *Osheroff v. Chestnut Lodge* and suggests that practitioners who persist in using ineffective methods where more effective alternatives exist may be placing themselves in jeopardy for legal action. Among Klerman's recommendations to the practicing clinician is the suggestion that "the patient has the right to be informed as to the alternative treatments available, their relative efficacy and safety, and the likely outcomes of these treatments" (pp. 416–417). This emphasis on discriminating among different treatment methods for different disorders on the basis of evidence from controlled clinical trials will be welcomed by behavior therapists who share similar views (Agras, 1987; Kazdin & Wilson, 1978; Lazarus, 1989b). It offers a very different prospect from those (e.g., Beitman et al., 1989; Smith et al., 1980; Strupp, 1989; Vandenbos, 1986) who would deny significant differences in effectiveness among the bewildering array of typically untested and unproven psychological therapies.

BIOBEHAVIORAL APPROACHES: COMBINING BEHAVIOR THERAPY WITH PHARMACOTHERAPY

In contrast to most of the psychological therapies that are the focus of the "integrationist" approach, pharmacotherapy has a history of experimental evaluation. That specific drug treatments are demon-

CLINICAL ISSUES AND STRATEGIES IN PRACTICE   293

strably effective for particular clinical disorders is beyond question. As such, they invite comparison, and possible combination, with cognitive–behavioral methods. Indeed, the increasing interaction between behavioral and pharmacological approaches to treatment is one of the more exciting and desirable therapeutic developments. As Agras (1987) has observed, combinations of behavioral and drug treatments have been applied to a variety of disorders, including obesity, bulimia, anorexia nervosa, anxiety disorders, depression, smoking cessation, childhood hyperactivity, and chronic schizophrenia.

The evidence on the effectiveness of a combination of behavioral and drug treatments for anxiety disorders is summarized in Chapter 3. In the case of agoraphobia, data exist indicating that a combined treatment approach is more effective than behavioral treatment alone (Telch, Agras, Taylor, Roth, & Gallen, 1985). Agras (1987) similarly argues that a combination of cognitive-behavior therapy and tricyclic medication is the preferred treatment for depression. He bases this conclusion on evidence showing that patients receiving drug treatment alone experience greater rates of relapse than those receiving combined treatment (Simons, Garfield, Murphy, 1984). Drug treatment, however, produces more rapid improvement than cognitive–behavioral treatment.

The treatment of bulimia nervosa provides another example of active research on cognitive–behavioral and pharmacological therapies. Antidepressant drugs are more effective than placebo controls in producing short-term reductions in binge eating and purging (Agras & McCann, 1987). Nevertheless, the results obtained using these drugs are generally less impressive than those of cognitive–behavioral treatment (Fairburn, 1988; Wilson & Smith, 1987). Only one controlled study to date has evaluated the combined effects of an antidepressant drug (imipramine) and cognitive–behavioral treatment (Mitchell, 1988). The results showed that the combined treatment was no more effective than cognitive-behavior therapy plus a drug placebo. Although these findings require replication, they argue against the value of combined drug/cognitive–behavioral treatments at this point. This recommendation is reinforced by the absence of systematic long-term follow-ups of pharmacotherapy for this eating disorder (Fairburn, 1988).

The point to be underscored here is that there is a growing literature of methodologically sound (double-blind, placebo-controlled) studies of the effects of antidepressant treatment of bulimia nervosa and related eating disorders. The findings from these studies not only allow comparison with the effects of cognitive–behavioral treatment but also have begun to bear on the nature of the eating disorder itself. There is an established basis for exploring commonalities in treatment mechanisms, an exploration that might help explain the disorder and lead to more effective treatment strategies.

Compare the foregoing healthy state of affairs with the status of psychological therapies. Family therapy is widely regarded as a preferred form of treatment for eating disorders in general and bulimia nervosa in particular (Schwartz, Barrett, & Saba, 1985). Nevertheless, Fairburn (1988) in his review of the treatment literature could find only a single controlled outcome study of family therapy. This study revealed scant benefit of family therapy for patients hospitalized for bulimia nervosa (Russell, Szmukler, Dare, & Eisler, 1987). It would be a mistake, however, to take this finding as representative of the value of family therapy. The patients in this study constituted an unusually refractory group (Fairburn, 1988). Some variant of family therapy may well be effective, as its proponents claim. We simply do not know how effective family therapy is in the absence of appropriate studies.

Psychodynamic therapies are routinely used in the treatment of eating disorders. Only one study has evaluated the effects of psychodynamic therapy. This study was conducted by Garner (1988), a cognitive–behavioral researcher. He found that cognitive–behavioral treatment was significantly more effective than the psychodynamic treatment carried out by committed psychodynamic therapists. A recent book edited by Schwartz (1988) sets forth the psychoanalytic approach to bulimia nervosa. As Stunkard (1989) notes in a review of the book, "In the 549 pages the only mention of effectiveness is an occasional offhand reference to a therapeutic triumph. No evidence is presented that psychoanalysis of psychoanalytic treatment is any more effective than no treatment at all. Nor is it mentioned that such evidence exists for other therapies." And taking a position in line with that of Klerman's (1988), Stunkard emphasizes that this book raises an important ethical question:

> How does one justify psychoanalysis for the treatment of bulimia. . . . Until it can be answered with assurance it would appear essential that anyone considering psychoanalysis for bulimia be informed that there is no evidence that such treatment is effective and that there is such evidence for other treatments. Informed consent for psychoanalytic treatment for bulimia is not now required.

Contrary to the integrationist approach, it would seem premature to attempt to integrate either family therapy or psychodynamic therapy with cognitive–behavioral treatment for bulimia nervosa on the assumption that there are important commonalties among them.

INTEGRATING RESEARCH AND PRACTICE

In previous volumes in this series we have discussed the often voiced view that the behavior therapy literature does not speak to the clinical practitioner (e.g., Volume 10, pp. 296–298). Jacobson (1987a) has bluntly restated this objection in the following terms: "There is no literature on how to treat many of the clients confronting clinicians on a day-to-day basis. The long and the short of it is that, in our quest for internal validity, we have evaluated the efficacy of our treatments on such restrictive client populations that behavior therapy technology has not been extended to cover many of those who sit in our outpatient waiting rooms hoping for our help" (p. 3). To remedy this situation, Jacobson (1987b) has edited a volume entitled, *Psychotherapists in Clinical Practice: Cognitive and Behaivoral Perspectives*. The respective authors in this anthology were selected in part because of their active involvement in clinical practice. Each contribution includes sections on topics such as the therapeutic relationship, coping with resistance, the influence of the therapist's values, and the nature of therapist errors.

Levis (1988) adds another voice to the chorus of protests about the perceived gap between research and clinical practice in behavior therapy. In his view, a "key factor in the continued influence of psychoanalytic theory is the ability of the theory to address a number of clinical [phenomena] commonly and regularly observed in clinical practice which the behavioral movement arbitrarily has denied or considered unimportant (p. 95). He bewails "how conceptually shallow, oversimplistic, and unrelated to clinical experience are the vast majority of behavior techniques. Not only do these techniques appear to be developed in an academic vacuum but their incorporation of learning principles and theory are all too often naive, simplistic, and lacking integration, let alone creative thoughts" (p. 95).

The point that behavior therapy can benefit from increased attention to clinical practice in all of its complexity is well taken. Yet, Levis's judgment seems unduly harsh and unhelpful. He fails to acknowledge such practical and clinical sophisticated analyses as Foa and Emmelkamp's (1983) book on failures in behavior therapy, Barlow's (1985) clinical handbook, and Jacobson's (1987b) anthology, to mention only a few sources. Nor does he credit the increasing emergence of highly detailed and "clinician-friendly" treatment manuals (e.g., Barlow & Cerny, 1988; Beck et al., 1979; Fairburn, 1985; Mathews et al., 1981; not to mention the availability of numerous unpublished manuals). Luborsky (1987) has hailed this development as a "small revolution." Behavior therapists, more than anyone else, have helped blaze this particular trail.

The clinical observations that Levis (1988) charges are being ignored by behavior therapists have a distinctly Freudian ring. Psychopathology is primarily a product of traumatic fear/avoidance learning. The stimuli/memories associated with such early traumatic learning are encoded in a way that prevents their being reactivated and deconditioned; the "defense mechanism of dissociation" protects against deconditioning; and reactivation and deconditioning require deconditioning strategies elaborated by Levis and Stampfl in their rationale for implosion therapy (e.g., Levis & Malloy, 1982).

Discussions of the role of encoded memories and cognitive-affective structures in behavior change have been increasingly common in the cognitive-behavior therapy literature during the past decade (Meichenbaum & Cameron, 1982). Particularly important in this respect is the accessibility of these largely unconscious, affective processes or structures to cognitive and behavioral interventions (Rachman, 1983). These analyses have been part of a wider interest in the interaction between cognition and affect (Barlow, 1988; Wilson, 1982b). Bower (1986, 1987), for example, described an influential model in which emotion is viewed within the context of modern cognitive psychology. Relying upon learned, associative mechanisms, Bower explains how affect (mood) and cognition (memory) come to have reciprocal influences on each other. His is a testable and heuristic theory that encompasses, among other phenomena of clinical interest, the activation of the emotionally charged memories to which Levis (1988) alludes.

Levis (1988) seems to overlook the foregoing advances in research and theory because of his insistence on explaining phenomena such as encoded memories within the Mowrer (1960) two-factor conditioning framework. He criticizes "so-called behavior therapists" for deemphasizing a conditioning interpretation of psychopathological phenomena. There is no need to rehash the details of this particular criticism here. Denunciations of "second and third generation" behavior therapists for leading the field astray by going beyond early classical and operant conditioning theories have been addressed more than once in this series. And in Chapter 3 of the present volume, we note that such sentiments may fail to appreciate theoretical advances in classical conditioning itself. The irony is that it may well be the contemporary cognitive perspective in behavior therapy, to which Levis objects, which will provide useful analyses (devoid of excess psychoanalytic baggage) of the clinical phenomena he has in mind (Marzillier, 1989).

Commentators on the state of behavior therapy have for many years now expressed concern about the increasing focus on technical applications at the expense of basic research and theoretical refinement (e.g., Franks & Wilson, 1982; Hayes, Rincover, & Solnick, 1980; Meichenbaum & Cameron, 1982; Ross, 1985). In his provocative Presidential Address to the Association for Advancement of Behavior Therapy, Ross (1985) laments that "behavior therapists cite each other when they are not citing themselves. When they do make reference to work outside their immediate field, it is usually to the sources of scales or measures they used in their study. One often has the impression that other citations serve the prime purpose of lending an aura of scholarship to yet another technical report" (p. 197).[4]

There can be no doubt that the clinical applications of behavior therapy have outstripped its conceptual and empirical foundations (Franks & Wilson, 1982). There is a sense in which criticism of the kind advanced by Ross (1985) is unfounded. Research in behavior therapy has become increasingly specialized. More and more, it is the treatment of particular clinical disorders that determines the research agenda. In concentrating their attention on the treatment of specific clinical disorders, behavior therapists have focused on understanding their etiology and nature. In so doing, behavior therapists have necessarily been consumers of the basic research literature within each of these specific domains of psychopathology.

In several domains proponents of a cognitive–behavioral approach have often been at the forefront of research that has advanced our understanding of the etiology and maintenance of specific disorders. Among the many examples that could be cited to illustrate this interaction between basic research and clinical practice are research on the nature of anxiety disorders (e.g., Barlow, 1988; Clark, 1988b; Rachman & Maser, 1988; see also Chapter 3, this volume), on obesity (e.g., Brownell & Foreyt, 1986), on anorexia and bulimia nervosa (e.g.,

---

[4]Ross (1985) based his observations on the contents of the journal *Behavior Therapy*. Different journals take on fairly specific identities, and it is difficult to judge a field by what is one of numerous index journals. The journal *Behaviour Research and Therapy*, for example, covers a broader range of topics. Many of the papers in this journal address basic theoretical and research interests. *Behaviour Research and Therapy* was the first journal devoted exclusively to behavior therapy and continues to help shape the field. The journal and its publishers celebrated its 25th anniversary in 1987. The question of maintaining a balance between clinical and research papers in *Behaviour Research and Therapy*, albeit with slightly different considerations in mind, apparently confronted the journal's founders with a dilemma at its inception. Wolpe (1988) offers some interesting historical insights into this matter.

Fairburn, 1988; Garner & Garfinkel, 1985; Rossiter, Agras, Losch, & Telch, 1988), on sexual disorders (Barlow, 1986; Rosen & Beck, 1988), and on the wide range of problems embraced by the field of behavioral medicine (e.g., Agras, 1982; Blanchard, 1982). This research has already helped alter the way these major disorders are conceptualized and treated. There is little "standing still" in these areas; the picture is more one of intellectual excitement, innovative research at basic and applied levels, and evolving implications for treatment. To answer the question Agras (1987) posed, this is where behavior therapy, at least an important part of the field, is going.

MODELS OF TRAINING

The training of clinical psychologists in the United States continues to stir up controversy, especially in the wake of recent developments within the American Psychological Association (APA).[5] The implications for training behavior therapists are significant in that behavior therapy is predicted on the analysis and application of basic and applied research.

One aspect of the debate centers on the respective mertis of the scientist-practitioner versus the professional school model of clinical training for psychologists, a controversy we addressed in Volume 10 (pp. 291–294) of this series. A recent series of papers have delineated the points of contention. Davison (1987), in a persuasive statement about the value of the scientist-practitioner model, cites the following excerpt from an early publication by Davison, Goldfried, and Krasner (1970):

> The philosophical foundations of behavior therapy as a segment of applied general psychology are the same as those characterizing the area of general experimental psychology. There is an emphasis on operationally defined terms, careful and dispassionate experimentation, a tendency to look for principles in the experimental [and empirical] area rather than in the more speculative portions of contemporary psychology, as well as a recognition that the psychological principles that we are currently attempting to apply are in a continual state of reevaluation and revision. . . . The behavior therapist is a clinically oriented psychologist who realizes the tentativeness of current knowledge—vis-a-vis both prin-

---

[5]In 1988, many of the most distinguished scientists within APA formed a new organization, the American Psychological Society, the better to represent scientific interests and needs in psychology. The long-term consequences of this breakaway from APA are unknown, but the move underscores the deep divisions between scientists (academics) and practitioners. A separate Assembly of Scientist-Practitioner Psychologists, representing a third, overlapping constituency, had been formed in August 1987.

ciples and techniques—and who sees his [or her] most powerful tool as being the research activities and critical thinking in which he and his colleagues engaged. . . . We [therefore] find it particularly appropriate for . . . training to be carried on within an academic psychology department, for it is here that one is most likely to find psychologists whose Weltanschauung best corresponds to the above, and people whose professional lives are devoted to asking certain kinds of questions about behavior, its nature, and control. (p. 767)

Davison (1987) argues that professional schools that divorce clinical training from mainstream academic psychology departments cutoff clinical practice from its theoretical and empirical base. Peterson (1987), a founding father of the professional school movement and formerly director of the Ph.D. program at the University of Illinois, which produced several leading behavior therapists, rejects this view. He reaffirms that

the basis of professional education is disciplined knowledge. Although any profession must involve educationally communicable techniques, nobody here or elsewhere has ever proposed that professional education be restricted to training in techniques. Any techniques we employ should be linked with the large, complex body of theoretical, methodological and substantive knowledge we call psychology. (p. 8)

He adds that there is an inherent incompatibility between being an academic and a practitioner and that scientific and professional training are fundamentally different in ways that dictate separate professional schools within the university.

Can graduates from professional schools be the equal of their scientist–practitioner peers in critical thinking and an understanding of the underlying discipline of psychology as Peterson claims? Are they better or worse practitioners/behavior therapists? We do not know. Perry (1987) does make the point that the development of professional schools has "reinforced the misperception held by some that applied psychology has moved away from research . . . and that people trained in clinical psychology cannot or do not do research regardless of the type of program they graduated from" (p. 10). He goes on to provide evidence that contradicts these perceptions.

The views of Davison (1987) and Perry (1987) exemplify the position within clinical psychology that research training and expertise distinguishes clinical psychologists from other mental health professions, such as social work. If research training is critical to behavior therapists, what then do we make of the training of behaviorally oriented social workers? Training in social work only rarely emphasizes research.

Thyer (1987) provides an informative review of the role of behavior therapy in social work. There are several reasons for being concerned about this role. Thyer points out that social workers represent a large segment of human service providers: "In mental health organizations the ratio of social workers to either psychologists or psychiatrists is approximately two to one" (p. 131). An even more important reason, as Thyer notes, is that social workers traditionally work with "the poor and disenfranchised, the oppressed, those treated by society in an unjust manner, racial and ethnic minorities, and the most severely disabled" (p. 132).

According to Thyer (1987), one-third of surveyed clinical social workers report that behavior therapy is their preferred approach. It is difficult to reconcile this rosy estimate with his conclusion that "the perspective remains a minority view and is misunderstood by the majority of the profession" (p. 134). Worse still, we learn that "empiricism is ridiculed and phenomenologically-oriented academics contend that there is no such thing as 'objective reality'—and the faculty member with a behavioral orientation may be viewed with suspicion or humor" (p. 133)!

Thyer (1987) defines behavioral social work as "the informed use by professional social workers of interventive techniques based upon empirically-derived learning theories, including but not limited to, operant conditioning, respondent conditioning, and observational learning. Behavioral social workers may or may not subscribe to the philosophy of behaviorism" (p. 134). This definition limits behavioral social work to traditional learning principles and seems to exclude cognitive principles and procedures. Thyer argues that given the populations they serve and the problems they face, behavioral social workers are likely to find the techniques of applied behavior analysis most helpful. Here he refers to the commitment to single-case analyses and the emphasis on observable change in socially important behaviors. Nevertheless, a case could be made that social workers might add to their effectiveness by drawing upon the broader compass of cognitive-behavior therapy.

CONCLUSIONS

Despite the various divisions and controversies within behavior therapy, and despite the occasional now to-be-expected prediction that the field will die unless fealty to a favored theoretical position prevails, behavior therapy is alive and well. The clinical literature continues to grow, and the number of controlled clinical outcome studies (with "real" patients) is increasing (Agras, 1987). The conceptual and clinical bases of behavior therapy continue to expand. Behavior therapists have not remained a narrowly focused, parochial in-group. They have reached out and are interacting with other professionals of different theoretical persuasions and from different disciplines. This welcome trend is particularly evident in, but hardly restricted to, behavioral medicine. Given their commitment to controlled, experimental research at both the basic and applied level, behavior therapists have inevitably been involved in studies of the etiology and nature of different forms of psychopathology. Behavior therapists are even members of several key committees of the American Psychiatric Association, which are charged with developing the criteria for DSM-IV.

Professional interest in behavior therapy is still most evident among psychologists. The Association for Advancement of Behavior Therapy, an interdisciplinary body, is flourishing. The continued success of AABT, with its blend of basic and applied interests, is all the more important now that the American Psychological Association seems to be self-destructing over the interaction between scientists and practitioners. This is not to say that similar tensions have not been felt within AABT, but thus far good sense and tolerance for our differences have prevailed. Finally, only 30 years after the publication of Wolpe's landmark text, *Psychotherapy by Reciprocal Inhibition*, September 1988 marked the Third World Congress of Behavior Therapy in Edinburgh, Scotland. The meeting was a major success, for which the organizing committee and the British Association for Behavioural Psychotherapy deserve special plaudits. Particularly significant was the strong European participation in the congress. Behavior therapy is broadening its international appeal.

REFERENCES

Achenbach, T. M., & Edelbrock, C. S. (1983). *Manual for the Child Behavior Checklist and revised Child Behavior Profile.* Burlington, VT: University Associates in Psychiatry.

Adams, H. (1989). Has behavior therapy progressed? *Contemporary Psychology, 34,* 557–558.

Adler, C. M., Craske, M., Kirshenbaum, S., & Barlow, D. H. (1989). "Fear of panic": An investigation of its role in panic occurrence, phobic avoidance, and treatment outcome. *Behaviour Research and Therapy, 27,* 391–396.

Affleck, G., Tennen, H., Croog, S., & Levine, S. (1987). Causal attribution, perceived benefits, and morbidity after a heart attack: An 8-year study. *Journal of Consulting and Clinical Psychology, 55,* 29–35.

Agras, W. S. (1982). Behavioral medicine in the 1980s: Nonrandom connections. *Journal of Consulting and Clinical Psychology, 50,* 797–803.

Agras, W. S. (1987). So where do we go from here? *Behavior Therapy, 18,* 203–217.

Agras, W. S., & McCann, U. (1987). The efficacy and role of antidepressants in the treatment of bulimia nervosa. *Annals of Behavioral Medicine, 9,* 18–22.

Agras, W. S. Taylor, S. B., Kraemer, H. C., Southam, M. A., & Schneider, J. A. (1987). Relaxation training for essential hypertension at the worksite: II. The poorly controlled hypertensive. *Psychosomatic Medicine, 49,* 264–273.

Aivazyan, T. A., Zaitsev, V. P., Salenko, B. B., Yurenev, A. P., & Patrusheva, I. F. (1988). Efficacy of relaxation techniques in hypertensive patients. *Health Psychology, 7,* 193–200.

Alden, L. (1988). Behavioral self-management controlled drinking strategies in a context of secondary prevention. *Journal of Consulting and Clinical Psychology, 56,* 280–286.

Alderman, M. H. (1984). Worksite treatment of hypertension. In J. D. Matarazzo, S. M. Weiss, J. A. Herd, N. E. Miller, & S. M. Weiss, S. M. (Eds.), *Behavioral health: A handbook of health enhancement and disease prevention* (pp. 862–869). New York: Wiley.

Alloy, L. B. (1988). (Ed.). *Cognitive processes in depression.* New York: Guilford Press.

Altman, D. G., Foster, V., Rasenick-Douss, L., & Tye, J. B. (1989). Reducing the illegal sale of cigarettes to minors. *Journal of the American Medical Association, 261,* 80–83.

Amaral, P. L. (1987). The special case of compliance in the elderly. In K. E. Gerber &

A. M. Nehemkis (Eds.), *Compliance: The dilemma of the chronically ill* (pp. 128-157). New York: Springer Publishing Co.

American Humane Association. (1984). *Trends in child abuse and neglect: A national perspective.* Denver, CO: American Humane Association.

American Psychiatric Association. (1980). *Diagnostic and statistical manual of mental disorders* (2nd ed.). Washington, DC: American Psychiatric Association.

American Psychiatric Association. (1987). *Diagnostic and statistical manual of mental disorders* (3rd ed.). Washington, DC: American Psychiatric Association.

American Psychological Association. (1989). NIH hails behavioral research. *Science Agenda, 1,* 1-2.

Anderson, T. K., & Kratochwill, T. R. (1988). Dissemination of behavioral procedures in the schools: Issues in training. In J. C. Witt, S. N. Elliott, & F. M. Gresham (Eds.), *Handbook of behavior therapy in education* (pp. 217-244). New York: Plenum Press.

Anderson, T. K., Kratochwill, T. R., & Bergan, J. R. (1986). Training teachers in behavioral consultation and therapy: An analysis of verbal behaviors. *Journal of School Psychology, 24,* 229-241.

Arkowitz, H., & Messer, S. B. (Eds.). (1984). *Psychoanalytic therapy and behavior therapy: Is integration possible?* New York: Plenum Press.

Arnkoff, D. B. (1983). Common and specific factors in cognitive therapy. In M. J. Lambert (Ed.), *Psychotherapy and patient relationships* (pp. 85-125). Homewood, IL: Dorsey.

Arnkoff, D. B., & Smith, R. J. (1988). Cognitive processes in test anxiety: An analysis of two assessment procedures in an actual test. *Cognitive Therapy and Research, 12,* 425-439.

Auerbach, S. M., & Kilmann, P. R. (1977). Crisis intervention: A review of outcome research. *Psychological Bulletin, 84,* 1189-1217.

Axelsson, S., & Brantmark, B. (1977). The antismoking effect of chewing gum with nicotine of high and low bioavailability. In J. Steinfeld, W. Griffiths, K. Ball, & R. M. Taylor (Eds.), *Health consequences, education, cessation activities, and social action. Vol. II: Proceedings of the 3rd World Conference on Smoking and Health, 1975* (DHEW Publication No. (NIH) 77-1413). Washington, DC: U.S. Department of Health, Education and Welfare.

Azar, S. T., & Rohrbeck, C. A. (1986). Child abuse and unrealistic expectations: Further validation of the parent opinion questionnaire. *Journal of Consulting and Clinical Psychology, 54,* 867-868.

Baer, D. M. (1988a). The future of behavioral analysis in educational settings. In J. C. Witt, S. N. Elliott, & F. M. Gresham (Eds.), *Handbook of behavior therapy in education* (pp. 823-828). New York: Plenum Press.

Baer, D. M. (1988b). If you know why you're changing a behavior, you'll know when you've changed it enough. *Behavioral Assessment, 10,* 219-223.

Baer, D. M., & Bushell, D. (1981). The future of behavior analysis in the schools? Consider its recent past, and then ask a different question. *School Psychology Review, 10,* 259-270.

Baeyens, F., Crombez, G., Van den Bergh, O., & Eelen, P. (1989). Once in contact always in contact: Evaluative conditioning is resistant to extinction. *Advances in Behaviour Research and Therapy, 10,* 179-200.

Bailar, J. C. III, & Smith, E. M. (1986). Progress against cancer? *New England Journal of Medicine, 314,* 1226-1232.

Bailey, J. S. (1988). The marketing of behavior analysis. *Journal of Applied Behavior Analysis, 21,* 3-4.

REFERENCES

Baker, T. (1989). An open letter to *Journal* readers. *Journal of Studies on Alcohol, 50,* 481-483.
Baltes, M. M., Kindermann, T., Reisenzein, R., & Schmid, U. (1987). Further observational data on the behavioral and social worlds of institutions for the aged. *Psychology and Aging, 2*(4), 390-403.
Ballard, K. D., & Crooks, T. J. (1988). Some normative data on preschool children's social behaviors. *Behaviour Change, 3,* 41-47.
Bandura, A. (1969). *Principles of behavior modification.* New York: Holt, Rinehart & Winston.
Bandura, A. (1975). The ethics and social purposes of behavior modification. In C. M. Franks & G. T. Wilson (Eds.), *Annual review of behavior therapy: Theory and practice* (Vol. 3, pp. 13-20). New York: Brunner/Mazel.
Bandura, A. (1977). Self-efficacy: Toward a unifying theory of behavioral change. *Psychological Review, 84,* 191-215.
Bandura, A. (1986). *Social foundation of thought and action: A social cognitive theory.* Englewood Cliffs, NJ: Prentice-Hall.
Bandura, A. (1988a, August). *Human agency in social cognitive theory.* Invited address to the International Congress of Psychology, Sydney, Australia.
Bandura, A. (1988b). Self-efficacy conception of anxiety. *Anxiety Research, 1,* 77-98.
Bandura, A., Cioffi, D., Taylor, C. B., & Brouillard, M. E. (1988). Perceived self-efficacy in coping with cognitive stressors and opioid activation. *Journal of Personality and Social Psychology, 55,* 479-598.
Bandura, A., Taylor, C. B., Williams, S. L., Mefford, I. N., Barchas, J. D. (1985). Catecholamine secretion as a function of perceived coping self-efficacy. *Journal of Consulting and Clinical Psychology, 53,* 406-414.
Bank, L., Patterson, G. R., & Reid, J. R. (1987). Delinquency prevention through parent training in family management. *The Behavior Analyst, 10,* 75-82.
Barber, K., Barber, M., & Clark, H. B. (1983). Establishing a community-oriented group home and ensuring its survival: A case study of failure. *Analysis and Intervention in Developmental Disabilities, 3,* 227-238.
Barkley, R. A. (1987). *Defiant children: A clinician's manual for parent training.* New York: Guilford Press.
Barlow, D. H. (Ed.). (1985). *Clinical handbook of psychological disorders.* New York: Guilford Press.
Barlow, D. H. (1986). Causes of sexual dysfunction. *Journal of Consulting and Clinical Psychology, 54,* 140-157.
Barlow, D. H. (1988). *Anxiety and its disorders.* New York: Guilford Press.
Barlow, D. H., & Cerny, J. A. (1988). *Psychological treatment of panic.* New York: Guilford Press.
Barofsky, I. (1978). Compliance, adherence and the therapeutic alliance: Steps in the development of self-care. *Social Science and Medicine, 12,* 369-376.
Barone, V. J., Greene, B. F., & Lutzker, J. R. (1986). Home safety with families being treated for child abuse and neglect. *Behavior Modification, 10,* 93-114.
Barrett, E. T., & Gleser, G. C. (1987). Development and validation of the Cognitive Status Examination. *Journal of Consulting and Clinical Psychology, 55,* 877-882.
Barrett, R. P. (Ed.). (1986). *Severe behavior disorders in the mentally retarded: Non-drug approaches to treatment.* New York: Plenum Press.
Barsky, A. J. (1988). The paradox of health. *New England Journal of Medicine, 318,* 414-418.
Bass, C., & Wade, C. (1982). Type A behavior: Not specifically pathogenic? *Lancet, 2,* 1147-1150.

Bays, K., & King, N. (1988). Staff attitudes towards data collection in behavioural programming for the intellectually disabled. *Behaviour Change, 5,* 19-27.

Beck, A. T. (1967). *Depression: Clinical, experimental, and theoretical aspects.* New York: Harper & Row.

Beck, A. T. (1976). *Cognitive therapy and the emotional disorders.* New York: International Universities Press.

Beck, A. T. (1988). Cognitive approaches to panic disorder: Theory and therapy. In J. Rachman & J. D. Maser (Eds.), *Panic: Psychological perspectives* (pp. 91-111). Hillsdale, NJ: Erlbaum.

Beck, A. T. (1989, June). *Cognitive therapy and research: A 25-year retrospective.* Keynote address to World Congress on Cognitive Therapy, Oxford University, Oxford, England.

Beck, A. T., & Emery, G. (1985). *Anxiety disorders and phobias: A cognitive perspective.* New York: Basic Books.

Beck, A. T., Epstein, N., Brown, G., & Steer, R. A. (1988). An inventory for measuring clinical anxiety: Psychometric properties. *Journal of Consulting and Clinical Psychology, 56,* 893-897.

Beck, A. T., Laude, R., & Bohnert, M. (1974). Ideational components of anxiety neurosis. *Archives of General Psychiatry, 31,* 319-325.

Beck, A. T., Riskind, J. H., Brown, G., & Steer, R. A. (1988). Levels of hopelessness in DSM-III disorders: A partial test of content specificity in depression. *Cognitive Therapy and Research, 12,* 459-469.

Beck, A. T., Rush, A. J., Shaw, B. F., & Emery, G. (1979). *Cognitive therapy of depression.* New York: Guilford Press.

Becker, M. H., & Joseph, J. G. (1988). AIDS and behavioral change to reduce risk: A review. *American Journal of Public Health, 78,* 394-410.

Beidel, D. C., & Turner, S. M. (1986). A critique of the theoretical bases of cognitive-behavioral themes and therapy. *Clinical Psychology Review, 6,* 177-197.

Beitman, B. D., Goldfried, M. R., & Norcross, J. C. (1989). The movement toward integrating the psychotherapies: An overview. *American Journal of Psychiatry, 146,* 138-147.

Belsky, J., & Vondra, J. (1987). Child maltreatment: Prevalence, consequences, causes, and interventions. In D. H. Crowell, I. M. Evans, & C. R. O'Donnell (Eds.), *Childhood aggression and violence: Sources of influence, prevention and control* (pp. 159-206). New York: Plenum Press.

Benjamin, S. B., Maher, K. A., Cattau, E. L., Jr., Collen, M. J., Fleischer, D. E., Lewis, J. H., Ciarleglio, C. A., Earll, J. M., Schaffer, S., Mirkin, K., Cooper, J., & Altschul, A. M. (1988). Double-blind controlled trial of the Garren-Edwards gastric bubble: An adjunctive treatment for exogenous obesity. *Gastroenterology, 95,* 581-588.

Bennett, W. (1987). Dietary treatments of obesity. In R. J. Wurtman & J. J. Wurtman (Eds.), *Human obesity* (pp. 250-263). New York: New York Academy of Sciences.

Bennun, I., Hahlweg, K., Schindler, L., & Langlotz, M. (1986). Therapist's and client's perceptions in behaviour therapy: The development and cross-cultural analysis of an assessment instrument. *British Journal of Clinical Psychology, 25,* 275-283.

Berger, M., Yule, W., & Wigley, V. (1987). The Teacher-Child Interaction Project (TCIP): Implementing behavioural programming with troublesome individual children in the primary school. In K. Wheldall (Ed.), *The behaviourist in the classroom* (pp. 90-111). London: Allen & Unwin.

Berkman, L., & Syme, S. L. (1979). Social networks host resistance and mortality: A nine year follow-up of Alameda County residents. *American Journal of Epidemiology, 109*, 186-204.

Bernard, M. E., & DiGiuseppe, R. (1989). Rational–emotive therapy today. In M. E. Bernard & R. DiGiuseppe (Eds.), *Inside rational–emotive therapy: A critical appraisal of the theory and therapy of Albert Ellis* (pp. 1-8). San Diego: Academic Press.

Bernstein, D., & Borkovec, T. D. (1973). *Progressive relaxation training: A manual for the helping professions.* Champaign, IL: Research Press.

Beutler, L. E., Scogin, F., Kirkish, P., Schretlen, D., Corbishley, A., Hamblin, D., Meredith, K., Potter, P., Bamford, C. R., & Levenson, A. I. (1987). Group cognitive therapy and alprazolam in the treatment of depression in older adults. *Journal of Consulting and Clinical Psychology, 55*, 550-556.

Bibeau, D. L., Mullen, K. D., McLeroy, K. R., Green, L. W., & Foshee, V. (1988). Evaluations of worksite smoking cessation programs: A critique. *American Journal of Preventive Medicine, 4*, 87-95.

Bien, N. Z., & Bry, B. H. (1980). An experimentally designed comparison of four intensities of school-based prevention programs for adolescents with adjustment problems. *Journal of Community Psychology, 8*, 110-116.

Bigelow, G. E., Griffiths, R. R., Liebson, I., & Kaliszak, J. E. (1980). Double-blind evaluation of reinforcing and anorectic actions of weight control medications. *Archives of General Psychiatry, 37*, 1118-1123.

Bijou, S. W., & Baer, D. M. (1961). *Child development: Vol. 1. A systematic and empirical theory.* Englewood Cliffs, NJ: Prentice-Hall.

Black, D. R., Aller, D. D., Madonna, M. R., & Skinner-Smith, J. D. (1983). Changing behavior in the pharmacy by ignoring it. *Patient Counseling in Community Pharmacy, 2*, 9-12.

Black, D. R., Madonna, M. R., Skinner-Smith, J. D., & Blinde, L. (1983). Positive words in the pharmacy: Good words for good behavior. *Patient Counseling in Community Pharmacy, 2*, 2-8.

Black, D. R., Madonna, M. R., Skinner-Smith, J. D., & Thompson-Skinner, M. F. (1984). Model behavior in the pharmacy: How to set an effective example. *Patient Counseling in the Community Pharmacy, 3*, 11-14.

Blackburn, G. L., Bistrian, B. R., & Flatt, J. P. (1975). Role of a protein-sparing modified fast in a comprehensive weight reduction program. In A. N. Howard (Ed.), *Recent advances in obesity research* (pp. 279-281). London: Newman.

Blackburn, G. L., Lynch, M. E., & Wong, S. L. (1986). The very low-calorie diet: A weight-reduction technique. In K. D. Brownell & J. P. Foreyt (Eds.), *Handbook of eating disorders: Physiology, psychology, and treatment of obesity, anorexia, and bulimia* (pp. 198-212). New York: Basic Books.

Blair, S. N., Goodyear, N. N., Gibbons, L. W., & Cooper, K. H. (1984). Physical fitness and incidence of hypertension in healthy normotensive men and women. *Journal of the American Medical Association, 252*, 487-490.

Blanchard, E. B. (1982). Behavioral medicine: Past, present, and future. *Journal of Consulting and Clinical Psychology, 50*, 795-796.

Blanchard, E. B., Andrasik, F., Guarnieri, P., Neff, D., & Rodichok, L. D. (1988). Two-, three-, and four-year follow-up on the self-regulatory treatment of chronic headache. *Journal of Consulting and Clinical Psychology, 55*, 427.

Blanchard, E. B., Khramelashvili, V. V., McCoy, G. C., Aivazyan, T. A., McCaffrey, R. J., Salenko, B. B., Musso, A., Wittrock, D. A., Berger, M., Gerardi, M. A., & Pangburn, L. (1988). The USA–USSR collaborative cross-cultural comparison of autogenic training and thermal biofeedback in the treatment of mild hypertension. *Health Psychology, 7*, 175-192.

Blanchard, E. B., McCoy, G. C., Musso, A., Gerardi, M. A., Pallmeyer, T. P., Gerardi, R. J., Cotch, P. A., Siracusa, K., & Andrasik, F. (1986). A controlled comparison of thermal biofeedback and relaxation training in the treatment of essential hypertension: I. Short-term and long-term outcome. *Behavior Therapy, 17*, 563-579.

Blanchard, E. B., Miller, S. T., Abel, G. G., Haynes, M. R., & Wicker, R. (1979). Evaluation of biofeedback in the treatment of borderline essential hypertension. *Journal of Applied Behavior Analysis, 12*, 99-109.

Blanchard, E. B., & Schwarz, S. P. (1988). Clinically significant changes in behavioral medicine. *Behavioral Assessment, 10*, 147-158.

Blankenhorn, D. H., Nessim, S. A., Johnson, R. L., Sanmarco, M. E., Azen, S. P., & Cashin-Hemphilly, L. (1987). Beneficial effects of combined colestipol-niacin therapy on coronary atherosclerosis and coronary venous bypass grafts. *Journal of the American Medical Association, 257*, 3233-3240.

Bloom, W. L. (1959). Fasting as an introduction to the treatment of obesity. *Metabolism, 8*, 214-220.

Blowers, C., Cobb, J., & Mathews, A. (1987). Generalized anxiety: A controlled treatment study. *Behaviour Research and Therapy, 25*, 493-502.

Boivin, M. J., Sweell, R. G., & Scott, K. (1986). Attitudes toward behavior modification: A companion of prison, criminal justice, and other undergraduate populations. *Behavior Modification, 10*, 435-456.

Boll, T., Thoresen, C., Adler, N., Hall, J., Millon, T., Moore, D., Olbrisch, M. E., Perry, N., Weiss, L., Woodring, J., & Wortman, C. (1983). Working Group of Predoctoral Education/Doctoral Training. *Health Psychology, 2*(Suppl.), 123-130.

Bommer, M., Gratto, C., Gravander, J., & Tuttle, M. (1987). A behavioral model of ethical and unethical decision making. *Journal of Business Ethics, 6*, 265-280.

Bonneson, C. I., & Hartsough, D. M. (1987). Development of the Crisis Call Outcome Rating Scale. *Journal of Consulting and Clinical Psychology, 55*, 612.

Borkovec, T. (1982). Facilitation and inhibition of functional CS exposure in the treatment of phobias. In J. Boulougouris (Ed.), *Learning approaches to psychiatry* (pp. 95-102). New York: Wiley.

Borkovec, T. D., & Mathews, A. (1988). Treatment of nonphobic anxiety disorders: A comparison of nondirective, cognitive and coping desensitization therapy. *Journal of Consulting and Clinical Psychology, 56*, 877-884.

Borkovec, T. D., Mathews, A. M., Chambers, A., Ebrahimi, S., Lytle, R., & Nelson, R. (1987). The effects of relaxation training with cognitive therapy or nondirective therapy and the role of relaxation-induced anxiety in the treatment of generalized anxiety. *Journal of Consulting and Clinical Psychology, 55*, 883-888.

Bortner, R. W. (1969). A short rating scale as a potential measure of pattern A behavior. *Journal of Chronic Diseases, 20*, 525-533.

Boudewyns, P. A., & Fry, T. J. (1986). Token economy programs in VA medical centers: Where are they today? *the Behavior Therapist, 9*, 126-127.

Bower, G. H. (1986). Prime time in cognitive psychology. In P. Eelen & O. Fontaine (Eds.), *Behavior therapy: Beyond the conditioning framework* (pp. 22-47). Hillsdale, NJ: Erlbaum.

Bower, G. H. (1987). Commentary on mood and memory. *Behaviour Research and Therapy, 25*, 443-456.

Branch, M. N. (1987). Behavior analysis: A conceptual and empirical base for behavior therapy. *the Behavior Therapist, 10*, 79-84.

REFERENCES

Brand, R. J., Jenkins, C. D., & Rosenman, R. H. (1978). Comparison of coronary heart disease prediction in the Western Collaborative Group Study using the Structured Interview and the Jenkins Activity Survey assessments of the coronary-prone Type A behavior pattern. *American Heart Association Cardiovascular Disease Epidemiology Newsletter, 24,* 1. (Abstract)

Brandon, T. H., Tiffany, S. T., & Baker, T. B. (1986). The process of smoking relapse. In F. M. Tims & C. G. Leukefeld (Eds.), *Relapse and recovery in drug abuse* (pp. 104-117) (DHHS Publication No. ADM 86-1473). Washington, DC: U.S. Department of Health and Human Services.

Brandon, T. H., Zelman, D. C., & Baker, T. B. (1987). Effects of maintenance sessions on smoking relapse: Delaying the inevitable? *Journal of Consulting and Clinical Psychology, 55,* 780-782.

Braswell, L., Kendall, P. C., Braith, J., Carey, M. P., & Vye, C. S. (1985). "Involvement" in cognitive-behavioral therapy with children: Process and its relationship to outcome. *Cognitive Therapy and Research, 9,* 611-630.

Braukmann, C. J., & Wolf, M. M. (1987). Behaviorally based group homes for juvenile offenders. In E. K. Morris & C. J. Braukmann (Eds.), *Behavioral approaches to crime and delinquency: A handbook of application, research, and concepts* (pp. 135-159). New York: Plenum Press.

Breslow, L., & Cumberland, W. G. (1988). Progress and objectives in cancer control. *Journal of the American Medical Association, 259,* 1690-1694.

Brewin, C. (1988). *Cognitive foundations of clinical psychology.* Hillsdale, NJ: Erlbaum.

Brooks, P. H., & Baumeister, A. A. (1977). A plea for consideration of ecological validity in the experimental psychology of mental retardation: A guest editorial. *American Journal of Mental Deficiency, 81,* 407-416.

Browne, A., & Finkelhor, D. (1986). Impact of child sexual abuse: A review of the research. *Psychological Bulletin, 99,* 66-77.

Browne, M. A., & Mahoney, M. J. (1984). Sports psychology. *Annual Review of Psychology, 35,* 605-625.

Brownell, K. D. (1984). Behavioral medicine. In G. T. Wilson, C. M. Franks, K. D. Brownell, & P. C. Kendall, *Annual review of behavior therapy: Theory and practice* (Vol. 9, pp. 180-210). New York: Guilford Press.

Brownell, K. D. (1985). Behavioral medicine. In C. M. Franks, G. T. Wilson, P. C. Kendall, & K. D. Brownell, *Annual review of behavior therapy: Theory and practice* (Vol. 10, pp. 164-187). New York: Guilford Press.

Brownell, K. D., & Foreyt, J. P. (Eds.). (1986). *Handbook of eating disorders: Physiology, psychology, and treatment of obesity, anorexia, and bulimia.* New York: Basic Books.

Brownell, K. D., & Stunkard, A. J. (1981). Couples training, pharmacotherapy, and behavior therapy in the treatment of obesity. *Archives of General Psychiatry, 38,* 1224-1229.

Brownell, K. D., & Wadden, T. A. (1986). Behavior therapy for obesity: Modern approaches and better results. In K. D. Brownell & J. P. Foreyt (Eds.), *Handbook of eating disorders: Physiology, psychology, and treatment of obesity, anorexia, and bulimia* (pp. 180-197). New York: Basic Books.

Brunk, M., Henggeler, S. W., & Whelan, J. P. (1987). Comparison of multisystemic therapy and parent training in the brief treatment of child abuse and neglect. *Journal of Consulting and Clinical Psychology, 55,* 171-178.

Bry, B. H. (1982). Reducing the incidence of adolescent problems through preventive intervention: One- and five-year follow-up. *American Journal of Community Psychology, 10,* 265-276.

Bry, B. H., & George, F. E. (1979). Evaluating and improving prevention programs: A strategy from drug abuse. *Evaluation and Program Planning, 2*, 127-136.

Bry, B. H., & George, F. E. (1980). The preventive effects of early intervention on the attendance and grades of urban adolescents. *Professional Psychology, 11*, 252-260.

Budd, K. S., & Fabry, P. L. (1986). Parents and family training. In R. P. Barrett (Ed.), *Severe behavior disorders in the mentally retarded: Nondrug approaches to treatment* (pp. 235-271). New York: Plenum Press.

Burchard, J. D. (1987a). Social and political challenges to behavioral programs with delinquents and criminals. In E. K. Morris & C. K. Braukmann (Eds.), *Behavioral approaches to crime and delinquency: A handbook of application, research and concepts* (pp. 577-596). New York: Plenum Press.

Burchard, J. D. (1987b). Social policy and the role of the behavior analyst in the prevention of delinquent behavior. *The Behavior Analyst, 10*, 83-88.

Burchard, J. D., & Burchard, S. N. (Eds.). (1987). *Prevention of delinquent behavior.* Newbury Park, CA: Sage.

Burgess, R. L., & Richardson, R. A. (1984). Coercive interpersonal contingencies as a determinant of child maltreatment: Implications for treatment and prevention. In R. F. Dangel & R. A. Polster (Eds.), *Parent training: Foundations of research and practice* (pp. 239-259). New York: Guilford Press.

Burgio, L. D., & Burgio, K. L. (1986). Behavioral gerontology: Application of behavioral methods to the problems of older adults. *Journal of Applied Behavior Analysis, 19*, 321-328.

Burns, D. (1980). *Feeling good.* New York: Morrow.

Butcher, J. N., Dahlstrom, G., Graham, J., & Tellegen, A. (1989). *MMPI-2.* Minneapolis: University of Minnesota Press.

Butler, G. (1989). Issues in the application of cognitive and behavioral strategies to the treatment of social phobia. *Clinical Psychology Review, 9*, 91-106.

Butler, G., & Anastasiades, P. (1988). Predicting response to anxiety management in patients with generalized anxiety disorders. *Behaviour Research and Therapy, 26*, 531-534.

Butler, G., Cullington, A., Hibbert, G., Klimes, I., & Gelder, M. (1987). Anxiety management for persistent generalized anxiety. *British Journal of Psychiatry, 151*, 535-542.

Butler, G., Cullington, A., Munby, M., Amies, P., & Gelder, M. (1984). Exposure and anxiety management in the treatment of social phobia. *Journal of Consulting and Clinical Psychology, 52*, 642-650.

Butler, G., Gelder, M., Hibbert, G., Cullington, A., & Klimes, I. (1987). Anxiety management: Developing effective strategies. *Behaviour Research and Therapy, 25*, 517-522.

Butrum, R. R., Clifford, C. K., & Lanza, E. (1988). NCI dietary guidelines: Rationale. *American Journal of Clinical Nutrition, 48*(Suppl.), 888-895.

Caddy, G. R., Addington, H. J., & Perkins, D. (1978). Individualized behavior therapy for alcoholics: A third year independent double-blind follow-up. *Behaviour Research and Therapy, 16*, 345-362.

Calvert, S. C., & McMahon, R. J. (1987). The treatment acceptability of a behavioral parent training program and its components. *Behavior Therapy, 18*, 165-179.

Cameron, R., & Best, J. A. (1987). Promoting adherence to health behavior change interventions: Recent findings from behavioral research. *Patient Education and Counseling, 10*, 139-154.

Camper, P. M., Jacobson, N. S., Holtzworth-Munroe, A., & Schmaling, K. B. (1988). Causal attributions for interactional behaviors in married couples. *Cognitive Therapy and Research, 12*, 195-209.

Canner, P. L., Berge, K. G., Wenger, N. K., Stamler, J., Friedman, L., Prineas, R. J., & Friedwald, W. (1986). Fifteen year mortality in coronary drug project patients: Long-term benefit with niacin. *Journal of the American College of Cardiology, 8*, 1245-1255.

Carey, M. P., Faulstich, M. E., Gresham, F. M., Ruggiero, L., & Enyart, P. (1987). Children's Depression Inventory: Construct and discriminant validity across clinical and nonreferred (control) populations. *Journal of Consulting and Clinical Psychology, 55*, 755-761.

Carlson, C. L., & Lahey, B. B. (1988). Conduct and attention deficit disorders. In J. C. Witt, S. N. Elliott, & F. M. Gresham (Eds.), *Handbook of behavior therapy in education* (pp. 653-677). New York: Plenum Press.

Carlson, L. A., & Rosenhamer, G. (1988). Reduction of mortality in the Stockholm ischaemic heart disease secondary prevention study by combined treatment with clofibrate and nicotinic acid. *Acta Medica Scandinavica, 223*, 405-418.

Carsrud, A. L., Carsrud, K. B., Dodd, B. G., LeUnes, A., Rhine, J., & Trout, S. (1984). Effects of institutional tours on attitudes toward the mentally retarded and their institutional settings. *Applied Research in Mental Retardation, 5*, 99-105.

Carstensen, L. L. (1986). Social support among the elderly: Limitations of behavioral interventions. *the Behavior Therapist, 9*, 111-113.

Carstensen, L. L., & Erickson, R. J. (1986). Enhancing the social environments of elderly nursing home residents: Are high rates of interaction enough? *Journal of Applied Behavior Analysis, 19*, 349-355.

Case, R. B., Heller, S. S., Case, N. B., & Moss, A. J. (1985). Type A behavior and survival after acute myocardial infarction. *New England Journal of Medicine, 312*, 737-741.

Casey, R. J., & Berman, J. S. (1985). The outcome of psychotherapy with children. *Psychological Bulletin, 98*, 388-400.

Cataldo, M. F., & Coates, T. J. (Eds.). (1986). *Health and industry: A behavioral medicine perspective*. New York: Wiley.

Center, D. B., & Wascom, A. M. (1986). Teacher perceptions of social behavior in learning disabled and socially normal children and youth. *Journal of Learning Disabilities, 19*, 420-425.

Centers for Disease Control. (1988a). Cholesterol awareness in selected states—behavioral risk factor surveillance, 1987. *Morbidity and Mortality Weekly Report, 37*, 245-248.

Centers for Disease Control. (1988b). *AIDS weekly surveillance report for June 6, 1988 (Center for Infectious Diseases)*. Atlanta, GA: Centers for Disease Control.

Centers for Disease Control. (1989a). Prevalence of overweight—behavioral risk factor surveillance system, 1987. *Morbidity and Mortality Weekly Report, 38*, 421-423.

Centers for Disease Control. (1989b). Update: Heterosexual transmission of acquired immunodeficiency syndrome and human immunodeficiency virus infection—United States. *Morbidity and Mortality Weekly Report, 38*, 423-434.

Centers for Disease Control. (1989c). First 100,000 cases of acquired immunodeficiency syndrome—United States. *Morbidity and Mortality Weekly Report, 38*, 561-563.

Chadsey-Rusch, J., & Rusch, F. R. (1986). Habilitation programs. In R. P. Barrett (Ed.), *Severe behavior disorders in the mentally retarded: Non-drug approaches to treatment* (pp. 99-122). New York: Plenum Press.

Chesney, M. A., Black, G. W., Swan, G. E., & Ward, M. M. (1987). Relaxation training for essential hypertension at the worksite: I. The untreated mild hypertensive. *Psychosomatic Medicine, 49,* 250–263.

Chhokar, J. S. (1987). Safety at the workplace: A behavioural approach. *International Labour Review, 126,* 169–178.

Christensen, H., Hadzi-Pavlovic, D., Andrews, G., & Mattick, R. (1987). Behavior therapy and tricyclic medication in the treatment of obsessive–compulsive disorder: A quantitative review. *Journal of Consulting and Clinical Psychology, 55,* 701–711.

Christensen, L., & Mendoza, J. L. (1986). A method of assessing change in a single-subject: An alteration of the RC index. *Behavior Therapy, 17,* 305–308.

Clark, D. A. (1986). A cognitive approach to panic. *Behaviour Research and Therapy, 24,* 461–470.

Clark, D. A. (1988a). The validity of measures of cognition: A review of the literature. *Cognitive Therapy and Research, 12,* 1–20.

Clark, D. A. (1988b). A cognitive approach to panic. In J. Rachman & J. Maser (Eds.), *Panic: Psychological perspectives.* Hillsdale, NJ: Erlbaum.

Clark, D. A. (1989). Special review of C. Brewin, *Cognitive foundations of clinical psychology. Behaviour Research and Therapy, 27,* 691–693.

Clark, L. (1989). The anxiety and depressive disorders: Descriptive psychopathology and differential diagnosis. In P. C. Kendall & D. Watson (Eds.), *Anxiety and depression: Distinctive and overlapping features.* (pp. 83–127). New York: Academic Press.

Coates, T. J., Morin, S. F., & McKusick, L. (1987). Consequences of AIDS antibody testing among gay men. *Journal of the American Medical Association, 258,* 1989.

Cohen, J. (1986). Theoretical considerations of peer tutoring. *Psychology in the Schools, 23,* 175–186.

Cohen, J. B., & Reed, D. (1985). Type A behavior and coronary heart disease among Japanese men in Hawaii. *Journal of Behavioral Medicine, 8,* 343–352.

Cohen, J. B., Syme, S. L., Jenkins, C. D., Kagan, A., & Zyzanski, S. J. (1979). Cultural context of Type A behavior and risk for CHD: A study of Japanese American males. *Journal of Behavioral Medicine, 2,* 375–384.

Cohn, A. W. (1987). Behavioral objectives in probation and parole: A new approach to staff accountability. *Federal Probation, 51,* 40–49.

Collins, F. L., & Thompson, J. K. (1988). On the use of symbolic labels in psychotherapy outcome research: Comment on Wills, Faitler, and Snyder. *Journal of Consulting and Clinical Psychology, 56,* 932–933.

Committee on the Review of Medicine. (1980). Systematic review of the benzodiazepines. *British Medical Journal, 280,* 910–912.

Communications Technologies, Inc. (1984). *Designing an effective AIDS prevention campaign strategy for San Francisco: Results from the first probability sample of an urban gay male community.* San Francisco: Communication Technologies, Inc.

Compas, B. E., Davis, G. E., Forsythe, C. J., & Wagner, B. M. (1987). Assessment of major and daily stressful events during adolescence: The adolescent Perceived Events Scale. *Journal of Consulting and Clinical Psychology, 55,* 534–541.

Compas, B. E., Forsythe, C. J., & Wagner, B. M. (1988). Consistency and availability in causal attributions and coping with stress. *Cognitive Therapy and Research, 12,* 305–320.

Condiotti, M. M., & Lichtenstein, E. (1981). Self-efficacy and relapse in smoking cessation programs. *Journal of Consulting and Clinical Psychology, 49,* 648–658.

Cone, J. D., & Hoier, T. S. (1986). Assessing children: The radical behavioral perspective.

REFERENCES

In R. J. Prinz (Ed.), *Advances in behavioral assessment of children and families* (Vol. 2, pp. 1-27). Greenwich, CT: JAI Press.
Cook, D. R. (1989). A reply to Maltzman. *Journal of Studies on Alcohol, 50,* 484-486.
Cook, E. W., Melamed, B. G., Cuthbert, B. N., McNeil, D. W., & Lang, P. J. (1988). Emotional imagery and the differential diagnosis of anxiety. *Journal of Consulting and Clinical Psychology, 56,* 734-740.
Correo, J., & Melton, G. B. (1988). Legal issues in school-based behavior therapy. In J. C. Witt, S. N. Elliott, & F. M. Gresham (Eds.), *Handbook of behavior therapy in education* (pp. 377-402). New York: Plenum Press.
Cosper, M., & Erickson, M. (1984). Relationships among observed classroom behavior and three types of teacher ratings. *Behavioral Disorders, 9,* 189-195.
Costello, E. J., Costello, A. J., Edelbrock, C., Burns, B., Dulcan, M. K., Brent, D., & Janiszewski, S. (1988). Psychiatric disorders in pediatric primary care. *Archives of General Psychiatry, 45,* 1107-1116.
Council on Scientific Affairs. (1988). Treatment of obesity in adults. *Journal of the American Medical Association, 260,* 2547-2551.
Craighead, L. W. (1984). Sequencing of behavior therapy and pharmacotherapy for obesity. *Journal of Consulting and Clinical Psychology, 52,* 190-199.
Craighead, L. W., Stunkard, A. J., & O'Brien, R. M. (1981). Behavior therapy and pharmacotherapy for obesity. *Archives of General Psychiatry, 38,* 763-768.
Craske, M. G., & Rachman, S. J. (1987). Return of fear: Perceived skill and heart rate responsivity. *British Journal of Clinical Psychology, 26,* 187-200.
Cubberley, P. T., Polster, S. A., & Schulman, C. L. (1965). Lactic acidosis and death after treatment of obesity by fasting. *New England Journal of Medicine, 272,* 628-630.
Cummings, C., & Nehemkis, A. M. (1986). How society contributes to non-compliance. In K. E. Gerber & A. M. Nehemkis (Eds.), *Compliance: The dilemma of the chronically ill* (pp. 213-239). New York: Springer Publishing Co.
Cupples, L. A., & D'Agostino, R. B. (1987). *Some risk factors related to the annual incidence of cardiovascular disease and death using pooled repeated biennial measurements: Framingham heart study. 30 year follow-up* (DHHS Publication No. NIH 87-2703). Washington, DC: U.S. Government Printing Office, National Heart, Lung, and Blood Institute.
Dadds, M. R. (1987). Families and the origins of child behavior problems. *Family Process, 26,* 341-357.
Dadds, M. R., Adlington, F. M., & Christensen, A. P. (1987). Children's perceptions of time out and other maternal disciplinary strategies: The effects of clinic status and exposure to behavioural treatment. *Behaviour Change, 4,* 3-13.
Dadds, M. R., Sanders, M. R., Behrens, B. C., & James, J. E. (1987). Marital discord and child behavior problem: A description of family interactions during treatment. *Journal of Clinical Child Psychology, 16,* 192-203.
Dadds, M. R., Sanders, M. R., & James, J. E. (1987). The generalization of treatment effects on parent training with multidistressed parents. *Behavioural Psychotherapy, 15,* 289-313.
Dadds, M. R., Schwartz, S., & Sanders, M. R. (1987). Marital discord and treatment outcome in behavioral treatment of child conduct disorders. *Journal of Consulting and Clinical Psychology, 55,* 396-403.
Davison, G. C. (1987). On keeping the Boulder model alive and well. *Clinical Psychologist, 40,* 62-64.
Davison, G. C., Goldfried, M. R., & Krasner, L. (1970). A postdoctoral program in behavior modification: Theory and practice. *American Psychologist, 25,* 767-772.

Davison, G. C., & Stuart, R. B. (1975). Behavior therapy and civil liberties. *American Psychologist, 30,* 755-763.

Dawber, T. R. (1980). *The Framingham Study: The epidemiology of atherosclerotic disease.* Cambridge, MA: Harvard University Press.

DeBacker, G., Dramaix, M., Kittel, F., & Kornitzer, M. (1983). Behavior, stress, and psychosocial traits as risk factors. *Preventive Medicine, 12,* 32-36.

DeBakey, M. E., & Ochsner, A. (1938). Bezoars and concretions: A comprehensive review of the literature with an analysis of 303 collected cases and a presentation of 8 additional cases. *Surgery, 4,* 934-963.

Deitz, S. M. (1987). On the relation between the experimental analysis of human behavior and applied behavior analysis. *Psychological Record, 37,* 29-33.

Delprato, D. J. (1989). Developmental interactionism: An emerging integrative framework for behavior therapy. *Advances in Behaviour Research and Therapy, 9,* 173-205.

Derry, P., & Kuiper, N. (1981). Schematic processing and self-referents in clinical depression. *Journal of Abnormal Psychology, 90,* 286-297.

DeRubeis, R., Hollon, S., Evans, M., & Bemis, K. (1982). Can psychotherapies for depression be discriminated? A systematic investigation of cognitive therapy and interpersonal therapy. *Journal of Consulting and Clinical Psychology, 50,* 744-756.

De Silva, P., & Rachman, S. (1981). Is exposure a necessary condition for fear-reduction? *Behaviour Research and Therapy, 19,* 227-232.

Des Jarlais, D. C., & Friedman, S. R. (1988). The psychology of preventing AIDS among intravenous drug users: A social learning conceptualization. *American Psychologist, 43,* 865-870.

DiFranza, J. R., Norwood, B. D., Garner, D. W., & Tye, J. B. (1987). Legislative efforts to protect children from tobacco. *Journal of the American Medical Association, 257,* 3387-3389.

Dimsdale, J. E., Hackett, T. P., Block, P. C., & Hutter, A. M. (1978). Type A personality and extent of coronary atherosclerosis. *American Journal of Cardiology, 42,* 583-586.

Dimsdale, J. E., Hackett, T. P., Hutter, A. M., Block, P. C., Catanzano, D. M., & White, P. J. (1979). Type A behavior and angiographic findings. *Journal of Psychosomatic Research, 23,* 273-276.

Dixen, J., & Jenkins, J. O. (1981). Incestuous child sexual abuse prevention: A review of treatment strategies. *Clinical Psychology Review, 1,* 211-222.

Dobson, K. S. (1989). A meta-analysis of the efficiency of cognitive therapy for depression. *Journal of Consulting and Clinical Psychology, 56,* 414-419.

Dobson, K. S., & Shaw, B. F. (1988). The use of treatment manuals in cognitive therapy: Experience and issues. *Journal of Consulting and Clinical Psychology, 56,* 673-680.

Dodge, C. S., Hope, D. A., Heimberg, R. G., & Becker, R. E. (1988). Evaluation of the Social Interaction Self-Statement Test with a social phobic population. *Cognitive Therapy and Research, 12,* 211-222.

Doll, R., & Peto, R. (1981). The causes of cancer: Quantitative estimates of avoidable risks of cancer in the United States today. *Journal of the National Cancer Institute, 66,* 1191-1308.

Donovan, D. M., & Marlatt, G. A. (Eds.). (1988). *Assessment of addictive behaviors.* New York: Guilford Press.

Drenick, E. J., & Smith, R. (1964). Weight reduction by prolonged starvation. *Postgraduate Medicine, 36,* 95-100.

REFERENCES

Druckman, D., & Swets, J. A. (Eds.). (1988). *Enhancing human performance: Issues, theories, and techniques.* Washington, DC: National Academy Press.

Dumas, J. E. (1986). Parental perception and treatment outcome in families of aggressive children: A causal model. *Behavior Therapy, 17,* 420-432.

Dumas, J. E., & Albin, J. (1986). Parent training outcome: Does active parental involvement matter? *Behaviour Research and Therapy, 24,* 227-230.

Dumas, J. E., & Wahler, R. G. (1983). Predictors of treatment outcome in parent training: Mother insularity and socioeconomic disadvantage. *Behavioral Assessment, 5,* 301-313.

Durand, V. M. (1988). Are we talking to ourselves? Review of Maher and Forman's "A behavioral approach to education of children and youth." *Contemporary Psychology, 33,* 807-808.

Durham, R. C., & Turvey, A. A. (1987). Cognitive therapy vs. behaviour therapy in the treatment of chronic general anxiety. *Behaviour Research and Therapy, 25,* 229-232.

Dush, D. M., Hirt, M. L., & Schroeder, H. E. (1989). Self-statement modification in the treatment of child behavior disorders: A meta-analysis. *Psychological Bulletin, 106,* 97-106.

Dustan, H. (1985). Obesity and hypertension. *Annals of Internal Medicine, 106,* 1047-1049.

D'Zurilla, T. (1986). *Problem-solving therapy: A social competence approach to clinical intervention.* New York: Springer Publishing Co.

Edelstein, B. A. (1985). Empirical evaluation of clinical training. *the Behavior Therapist, 8,* 67-70.

Edelstein, B. A. (1989). Generalization: Terminological, methodological and conceptual issues. *Behavior Therapy, 20,* 311-324.

Eelen, P., & Fontaine, O. (Eds.). (1986). *Behavior therapy: Beyond the conditioning framework.* Leuven, Belgium: Leuven University Press.

Egel, A. L., & Gradel, K. (1988). Social integration of autistic children: Evaluation and recommendations. *the Behavior Therapist, 11,* 7-11.

Ehlers, A., Margraf, J., Roth, W., Taylor, C. B., & Birbaumer, N. (1988). Anxiety induced by false heart rate feedback in patients with panic disorder. *Behaviour Research and Therapy, 26,* 1-12.

Elias, M., & Clabby, J. F. (1989). *Social decision making skills: A curriculum for the elementary grades.* Rockville, MD: Aspen Publishers.

Elliott, S. N. (1988). Acceptability of behavioral treatments in educational settings. In J. C. Witt, S. N. Elliott, & F. M. Gresham (Eds.), *Handbook of behavior therapy in education* (pp. 121-150). New York: Plenum Press.

Ellis, A. (1980). Rational-emotive therapy and cognitive behavior therapy: Similarities and differences. *Cognitive Therapy and Research, 4,* 325-340.

Ellis, A. (1989a, June). *Is rational-emotive therapy (RET) "rationalist" or "constructivist"?* Address to World Congress on Cognitive Therapy, Oxford University, Oxford, England.

Ellis, A. (1989b). Comments on my critics. In M. E. Bernard & R. DiGiuseppe (Eds.), *Inside rational-emotive therapy: A critical appraisal of the theory and therapy of Albert Ellis* (pp. 199-260). San Diego: Academic Press.

Emerson, E., & Emerson, C. (1987). Barriers to the effective implementation of habilitative behavioral programs in an institutional setting. *Mental Retardation, 25,* 101-106.

Emmelkamp, P. M. G., Visser, S., & Hoekstra, R. J. (1988). Cognitive therapy vs. exposure *in vivo* in the treatment of obsessive-compulsives. *Cognitive Therapy and Research, 12,* 103-114.

Emmons, C. A., Joseph, J. G., Kessler, R. C., Montgomery, S., & Ostrow, D. (1986). Psychosocial predictors of reported behavior change in homosexual men at risk for AIDS. *Health Education Quarterly, 13,* 331-345.

Epstein, M., Kauffman, J., & Cullinan, D. (1985). Patterns of maladjustment among the behaviorally disordered: II. Boys aged 6-11, boys aged 12-18; girls aged 6-11, and girls aged 12-18. *Behavioral Disorders, 10,* 125-134.

Erwin, E. (1978). *Behavior therapy: Scientific, philosophical and moral foundations.* Cambridge, MA: Cambridge University Press.

Erwin, E. (1988). Cognitive and behaviorist paradigms in clinical psychology. In D. B. Fishman, F. Rotgers, & C. M. Franks (Eds.), *Paradigms in behavior therapy: Present and promise* (pp. 109-140). New York: Springer Publishing Co.

Evans, I. M., Brown, F. A., Weed, K. A., Spry, K. M., & Owen, V. E. (1987). The assessment of functional competencies: A behavioral approach to the evaluation of programs for children with disabilities. In R. J. Prinz (Ed.), *Advances in behavioral assessment of children and families* (Vol. 3, pp. 93-121). Greenwich, CT: JAI Press.

Evans, I. M., & Scheuer, A. D. (1987). Analyzing response relationships in childhood aggression: The clinical perspective. In D. H. Crowell, I. M. Evans, & C. R. O'Donnell (Eds.), *Childhood aggression and violence: Sources of influence, prevention, and control* (pp. 75-94). New York: Plenum Press.

Expert Panel on Detection, Evaluation, and Treatment of High Blood Cholesterol in Adults. (1988). Report of the National Cholesterol Education Program Expert Panel on Detection, Evaluation, and Treatment of High Blood Cholesterol in Adults. *Archives of Internal Medicine, 148,* 36-39.

Eyberg, S. (1988). Parent-child interaction therapy: Integration of traditional and behavioral concerns. *Child and Family Behavior Therapy, 10,* 33-46.

Eysenck, H. J. (1982). Neo-behavioristic (S-R) theory. In G. T. Wilson & C. M. Franks (Eds.), *Contemporary behavior therapy: Conceptual and empirical foundations* (pp. 205-276). New York: Guilford Press.

Eysenck, H. J. (1986). Consensus and controversy: Two types of science. In S. Modgil & C. Modgil (Eds.), *Hans Eysenck: Consensus and controversy* (pp. 275-398). London: Falmer Press.

Eysenck, H. J. (1988). Psychotherapy to behavior therapy: A paradigm shift. In D. B. Fishman, F. Rotgers, & C. M. Franks (Eds.), *Paradigms in behavior therapy: Present and promise* (pp. 45-76). New York: Springer Publishing Co.

Eysenck, H. J., & Martin, I. (Eds.). (1987). *Theoretical foundations of behavior therapy.* New York: Plenum Press.

Fabre, T. R., & Walker, H. M. (1987). Teacher perceptions of the behavioral adjustment of primary grade level handicapped pupils within regular and special education settings. *Remedial and Special Education, 8,* 34-39.

Fagerstrom, K. O. (1988). Efficacy of nicotine chewing gum: A review. In O. F. Pomerleau & C. S. Pomerleau (Eds.), *Nicotine replacement: A critical review* (pp. 109-128). New York: Alan R. Liss.

Fairburn, C. G. (1985). Cognitive-behavioral treatment for bulimia. In D. M. Garner & P. E. Garfinkel (Eds.), *Handbook of psychotherapy for anorexia nervosa and bulimia* (pp. 160-192). New York: Guilford Press.

Fairburn, C. G. (1988). The current status of the psychological treatments for bulimia nervosa. *Journal of Psychosomatic Research, 32,* 635-645.

Fantuzzo, J. W., Rohrbeck, C. A., & Azar, S. T. (1987). A component analysis of behavioral self-management intervention with elementary school students. *Child and Family Behavior Therapy, 9,* 33-43.

Faraone, S. V., & Dorfman, D. D. (1989). Testing the significance of interobserver agreement measures in the presence of autocorrelation: The jacknife procedure. *Journal of Psychopathology and Behavioral Assessment, 10*, 39-48.

Fawcett, S. B., Seekins, T., & Braukmann, C. J. (1981). Developing and transferring behavioral technologies for children and youth. *Children and Youth Services Review, 3*, 319-342.

Felce, D., deKock, V., & Repp, A. C. (1986). An eco-behavior analysis of small community-based houses and traditional large hospitals for severely and profoundly mentally handicapped adults. *Applied Research in Mental Retardation, 7*, 393-408.

Feldman, M. A. (1986). Research on parenting by mentally retarded persons. *Psychiatric Perspectives on Mental Retardation, 9*, 777-796.

Feldman, M. A., Towns, F., Betel, J., Case, L., Rincover, A., & Rubino, C. A. (1986). Parent education project: II. Increasing stimulating interactions of developmentally handicapped mothers. *Journal of Applied Behavior Analysis, 19*, 23-37.

Fellner, D. J., & Sulzer-Azaroff, B. (1984). A behavioral analysis of goal setting. *Journal of Organizational Behavior Management, 6*, 33-51.

Ferguson, D. G., & Cullari, S. (1983). Behavior modification in facilities for the mentally retarded: Problems with the development and implementation of training programs. In S. E. Browning, J. L. Matson, & R. P. Barrett (Eds.), *Advances in mental retardation and developmental disabilities* (Vol. 1, pp. 177-197). London: JAI Press.

Ferster, C. B. (1979). A laboratory model of psychotherapy. In P. Sjoden (Ed.), *Trends in behavior therapy*. New York: Academic Press.

Festinger, L. (1954). A theory of social comparison processes. *Human Relations, 7*, 117-140.

Finch, A. J., Lipovsky, J. A., & Casat, C. D. (1989). Anxiety and depression in children and adolescence: Negative affectivity or separate constructs? In P. C. Kendall & D. Watson (Eds.), *Anxiety and depression: Distinctive and overlapping features* (pp. 191-204). New York: Academic Press.

Fincham, F. D., & Beach, S. R. H. (1988). Attribution processes in distressed and nondistressed couples: 5. Real versus hypothetical events. *Cognitive Therapy and Research, 12*, 505-514.

Finkelhor, D. (1984). *Child sexual abuse: New theory and research*. New York: Free Press.

Finkelhor, D., & Associates. (1986). *A sourcebook on child sexual abuse*. Newbury Park, CA: Sage.

Finkelhor, D., & Williams, L. M. (1988). *Sexual abuse in day care: Red Riding-Hood revisited*. Newbury Park, CA: Sage.

Fiore, M. C., Novotny, T. E., Pierce, J. P., Hatziandreu, E. J., Patel, K. M., & Davis, R. M. (1989). Trends in cigarette smoking in the United States: The changing influence of gender and race. *Journal of the American Medical Association, 261*, 49-55.

Fischler, G. L., & Kendall, P. C. (1988). Social cognitive problem solving and childhood adjustment: Qualitative and topological analysis. *Cognitive Therapy and Research, 12*, 133-154.

Fishman, D. B. (1988). Pragmatic behaviorism: Saving and nurturing the baby. In D. B. Fishman, F. Rotgers, & C. M. Franks (Eds.), *Paradigms in behavior therapy: Present and promise* (pp. 254-293). New York: Springer Publishing Co.

Fishman, D. B., Rotgers, F., & Franks, C. M. (Eds.). (1988). *Paradigms in behavior therapy: Present and promise*. New York: Springer Publishing Co.

Floyd, F. J., & Markman, H. (1984). An economical observational measure of couples communications skill. *Journal of Consulting and Clinical Psychology, 52,* 97–103.

Floyd, F. J., O'Farrell, T., & Goldberg, M. (1987). Comparison of marital observation measures: The Marital Interaction Coding System and the Communication Skills Test. *Journal of Consulting and Clinical Psychology, 55,* 423–429.

Foa, E. B., & Emmelkamp, P. M. G. (Eds.). (1983). *Failures in behavior therapy.* New York: Wiley.

Foa, E. B., & Kozak, M. J. (1985). Treatment of anxiety disorders: Implications for psychopathology. In A. H. Tuma & J. Maser (Eds.), *Anxiety and the anxiety disorders.* Hillsdale, NJ: Erlbaum.

Foa, E. B., Rothbaum, B. O., & Kozak, M. J. (1989). Behavioral treatments for anxiety and depression. In P. C. Kendall & D. Watson (Eds.), *Anxiety and depression: Distinctive and overlapping features.* New York: Academic Press.

Foley, F. W., Bedell, J. R., LaRocca, N. G., Scheinberg, L. C., & Reznikoff, M. (1987). Efficacy of stress inoculation training in coping with multiple sclerosis. *Journal of Consulting and Clinical Psychology, 55,* 919–922.

Forehand, R. (1986). Parental positive reinforcement with deviant children: Does it make a difference? *Child and Family Behavior Therapy, 8,* 15–21.

Forehand, R., Breiner, J., McMahon, R. J., & Davies, G. (1981). Predictors of cross-setting behavior change in the treatment of child problems. *Journal of Behavior Therapy and Experimental Psychiatry, 12,* 311–313.

Forehand, R., & McMahon, R. J. (1981). *Helping the noncompliant child: A clinician's guide to parent training.* New York: Guilford Press.

Foreyt, J. P. (1987a). The addictive disorders. In G. T. Wilson, C. M. Franks, P. C. Kendall, & J. P. Foreyt, *Review of behavior therapy: Theory and practice* (Vol. 11, pp. 187–233). New York: Guilford Press.

Foreyt, J. P. (1987b). Behavioral medicine. In G. T. Wilson, C. M. Franks, P. C. Kendall, & J. P. Foreyt, *Review of behavior therapy: Theory and practice* (Vol. 11, pp. 154–186). New York: Guilford Press.

Foreyt, J. P., Goodrick, G. K., & Gotto, A. M. (1981). Limitations of behavioral treatment of obesity: Review and analysis. *Journal of Behavioral Medicine, 4,* 159–174.

Foreyt, J. P., Scott, L. W., & Gotto, A. M., Jr. (1980). Weight control and nutrition education programs in occupational settings. *Public Health Reports, 95,* 127–136.

Foreyt, J. P., Scott, L. W., Mitchell, R. E., & Gotto, A. M., Jr. (1979). Plasma lipid changes in the normal population following behavioral treatment. *Journal of Consulting and Clinical Psychology, 47,* 440–452.

Fowler, S. (1986). Peer-monitoring and self-monitoring: Alternatives to traditional teacher management. *Exceptional Children, 52,* 573–581.

Fowler, S. A. (1988). The effects of peer-motivated interventions on establishing maintenance, and generalizing children's behavior changes. In R. H. Horner, G. Dunlap, & R. L. Koegel (Eds.), *Generalization and maintenance: Life-style changes in applied settings* (pp. 143–170). Baltimore: Paul H. Brookes.

Fox, D. K., Hopkins, B. L., & Anger, W. K. (1987). The long-term effects of a token economy on safety performance in open-pit mining. *Journal of Applied Behavior Analysis, 20,* 215–224.

Fox, J., & Savelle, S. (1987). Social interaction research and families of behaviorally disordered children: A critical review and forward look. *Behavioral Disorders, 12,* 276–291.

Foxall, D. J. (1984). Evidence for attitudinal-behavioural consistency: Implications for consumer research paradigms. *Journal of Economic Psychology, 5,* 71–92.

REFERENCES

Foxall, D. J. (1985). Consumer spending on designer jeans: An operant conditioning interpretation. *Journal of Consumer Studies and Home Economics, 9,* 147-150.

Foxall, G. R. (1986a). Theoretical progress in consumer psychology: The contribution of a behavioural analysis of choice. *Journal of Economic Psychology, 7,* 393-414.

Foxall, G. R. (1986b). Consumer theory: Some contributions of a behavioural analysis of choice. *Management Bibliographies and Reviews, 12,* 27-51.

Foxall, G. R. (1986c). Consumer choice in behavioural perspective. *European Journal of Marketing, 20,* 7-18.

Foy, D. W., Nunn, L. B., & Rychtarik, R. G. (1984). Broad-spectrum behavioral treatment for chronic alcoholics: Effects of training in controlled drinking skills. *Journal of Consulting and Clinical Psychology, 52,* 218-230.

Frank, B. B., Stern, W. R., & Fisher, A. H. (1987). Survey of gastric bubble use: Preliminary results (Abstract). *Gastrointestinal Endoscopy, 33,* 171.

Franks, C. M. (Ed.). (1969). *Behavior therapy: Appraisal and status.* New York: McGraw-Hill.

Franks, C. M. (1985). Behavior therapy: An overview. In C. M. Franks, G. T. Wilson, P. C. Kendall, & K. D. Brownell, *Annual review of behavior therapy: Theory and practice* (Vol. 10, pp. 1-46). New York: Guilford Press.

Franks, C. M. (1987a). Behavior therapy: An overview. In G. T. Wilson, C. M. Franks, P. C. Kendall, & J. P. Foreyt, *Review of behavior therapy: Theory and practice* (Vol. 11, pp. 1-39). New York: Guilford Press.

Franks, C. M. Foreword. In M. D. Powers (Ed.). (1987b). *Expanding systems of service delivery for persons with developmental disabilities* (pp. xi-xiv). Baltimore: Paul H. Brookes.

Franks, C. M. (1987c). Behavior therapy and the AABT: Personal recollections, conceptions and misconceptions. *the Behavior Therapist, 10,* 171-174.

Franks, C. M. (1989). Review of D. H. Ruben & D. J. Delprato (Eds.), "New ideas in therapy: Introduction to an interdisciplinary approach." *Child and Family Behavior Therapy, 11,* 79-81.

Franks, C. M., & Wilson, G. T. (Eds.). (1982). *Contemporary behavior therapy: Conceptual and empirical foundations.* New York: Guilford Press.

French-Belgian Collaborative Group. (1982). Ischemic heart disease and psychological patterns: Prevalence and incidence studies in Belgium and France. *Advances in Cardiology, 29,* 25-31.

Frick, M. H., Elo, O., Haapa, K., Heinonen, O. P., Heinsalmi, P., Helo, P., Huttunen, J. K., Kaitaniemi, P., Koskinen, P., Manninen, V., Maenpaa, H., Malkonen, M., Manttari, M., Norola, S., Pasternack, A., Pikkarainen, J., Romo, M., Sjoblom, T., & Nikkila, E. A. (1987). Helsinki heart study: Primary-prevention trial with gemfibrozil in middle-aged men with dyslipidemia: Safety of treatment, changes in risk factors, and incidence of coronary heart disease. *New England Journal of Medicine, 317,* 1237-1245.

Friedman, G. D., Klatsky, A. L., & Siegelaub, A. B. (1982). Alcohol, tobacco, and hypertension. *Hypertension, 4,* III143-III150.

Friedman, M., & Rosenman, R. H. (1974). *Type A behavior and your heart.* New York: Knopf.

Fuoco, F. J., & Christian, W. P. (1986). *Behavior analysis and therapy in residential programs.* New York: Van Nostrand Reinhold.

Furtkamp, E., Gifford, D., & Schiers, W. (1982). In Class evaluation of behavior modification knowledge: Parallel tests for use in applied settings. *Journal of Behavior Therapy and Experimental Psychiatry, 13,* 131-134.

Garfield, S. L. (1983). Does psychotherapy work? Yes, no, maybe. *Behavioral and Brain Sciences, 6,* 292-293.

Garfield, S. L. (1989). The client-therapist relationship in rational-emotive therapy. In M. E. Bernard & R. DiGiuseppe (Eds.), *Inside rational-emotive therapy: A critical appraisal of the theory and therapy of Albert Ellis* (pp. 113-134). San Diego: Academic Press.

Garfield, S. L., & Kurtz, R. (1976). Clinical psychologists in the 1970's. *American Psychologist, 31,* 1-9.

Garner, D. M. (1988, September). *The current status of cognitive treatments for anorexia nervosa and bulimia nervosa.* Paper presented at the World Congress of Behavior Therapy, Edinburgh, Scotland.

Garner, D. M., & Garfinkel, P. E. (Eds.). (1985). *Handbook of psychotherapy for anorexia nervosa and bulimia.* New York: Guilford Press.

Garnett, E. S., Bernard, D. L., Ford, J., Goodbody, R. A., & Woodhouse, M. A. (1969). Gross fragmentation of starvation for obesity. *Lancet, 1,* 914-916.

Garren, L. R., & Garren, M. (1984). The Garren gastric bubble: An endoscopic aid to treatment of morbid obesity. *Gastrointestinal Endoscopy, 30,* A153. (Abstract)

Garren, L. R., Garren, M., Giordano, F., Werbitt, W., & Plotzker, R. (1986). Further experience with the Garren-Edwards gastric bubble as an adjunctive therapy in obesity. *Gastrointestinal Endoscopy, 32,* A170-A171. (Abstract)

Geller, E. S. (1986). Prevention of environmental problems. In B. A. Edelstein & L. Michelson (Eds.), *Handbook of prevention* (pp. 361-383). New York: Plenum Press.

Gendreau, P., & Ross, R. R. (1979). Effective correctional treatment: Bibliotherapy for cynics. *Crime and Delinquencies, 25,* 463-489.

Genuth, S. (1979). Supplemented fasting in the treatment of obesity and diabetes. *American Journal of Clinical Nutrition, 32,* 2579-2586.

Gerber, K. E. (1986). Compliance on the chronically ill: An introduction to the problem. In K. E. Gerber & A. M. Nehemkis (Eds.), *Compliance: The dilemma of the chronically ill* (pp. 12-23). New York: Springer Publishing Co.

Gerber, K. E., & Nehemkis, A. M. (Eds.). (1986). *Compliance: The dilemma of the chronically ill.* New York: Springer Publishing Co.

Gesten, E. L., & Jason, L. A. (1987). Social and community intervention. *Annual Review of Psychology, 38,* 427-460.

Glanz, K., & Seewald-Klein, T. S. (1986). Nutrition at the worksite: An overview. *Journal of Nutrition Education, 18*(Suppl.), S1-S12.

Glasgow, R. E., & Terborg, J. R. (1988). Occupational health promotion programs to reduce cardiovascular risk. *Journal of Consulting and Clinical Psychology, 56,* 365-373.

Glass, C. R., Merluzzi, T. V., Biever, J. L., & Larsen, K. H. (1982). Cognitive assessment of social anxiety: Development and validation of a self-statement questionnaire. *Cognitive Therapy and Research, 6,* 37-55.

Glynn, T. (1987). More power to the parents: Behavioural approaches to remedial tutoring at home. In K. Wheldall (Ed.), *The behaviourist in the classroom* (pp. 69-89). London: Allen & Unwin.

Goldfried, M. R., & Safran, J. (1986). Future directions in psychotherapy integration. In J. C. Norcross (Ed.), *Handbook of eclectic psychotherapy.* New York: Brunner/Mazel.

REFERENCES

Goldiamond, I. (1984). Training parent trainers and ethicists in nonlinear analysis of behavior. In R. F. Dangel & R. A. Polster (Eds.), *Parent training: Foundations of research and practice* (pp. 504-546). New York: Guilford Press.

Goldman, L., & Cook, E. F. (1984). Decline in ischemic heart disease mortality rates: An analysis of the comparative effects of medical intervention and changes in lifestyle. *Annals of Internal Medicine, 101*, 825-836.

Goldstein, I. B., Shapiro, D. S., & Thananopavaren, C. (1984). Home relaxation techniques for essential hypertension. *Psychosomatic Medicine, 46*, 398-414.

Goldstein, I. B., Shapiro, D. S., Thananopavaren, C., & Sambhi, M. P. (1982). Comparison of drug and behavioral treatments of essential hypertension. *Health Psychology, 1*, 7-26.

Gotlib, I. H., & Cane, D. B. (1989). Self-report assessment of depression and anxiety. In P. C. Kendall & D. Watson (Eds.), *Anxiety and depression: Distinctive and overlapping features* (pp. 131-170). New York: Academic Press.

Gottlieb, J. (1975). Public, peer, and professional attitudes toward mentally retarded persons. In M. J. Begab & S. A. Richardson (Eds.), *The mentally retarded and society: A social science perspective* (pp. 99-125). Baltimore: University Park Press.

Graber, R. A., & Miller, W. R. (1988). Abstinence or controlled drinking goals for problem drinkers: A randomized clinical trial. *Psychology of Addictive Behaviors, 2*, 20-23.

Gray, M. (1983). Communicating with elderly people. In D. Pendleton & J. Hasler (Eds.), *Doctor-patient communication* (pp. 46-72). London: Academic Press.

Green, L., & Kagel, J. H. (Eds.). (1987). *Advances in behavioral economics* (Vol. 1). Norwood, NJ: Ablex.

Greenwood, C. R., Dinwiddie, G., Bailey, V., Carta, J. J., Dorsey, D., Kohler, F. W., Nelson, C., Rotholz, D., & Schulte, D. (1987). Field replication of classwide peer tutoring. *Journal of Applied Behavior Analysis, 20*, 151-160.

Gross, J., Rosen, J. C., Leitenberg, H., & Willmuth, M. E. (1986). Validity of the Eating Attitudes test and the Eating Disorders Inventory in Bulimia Nervosa. *Journal of Consulting and Clinical Psychology, 54*, 875-876.

Gruenberg, E. M. (1977). The failures of success. *Milbank Memorial Fund Quarterly, 55*, 3-24.

Griest, D. L., & Wells, K. C. (1983). Behavioral family therapy with conduct disorders in children. *Behavior Therapy, 14*, 37-53.

Haaga, D. (1986). A review of the common principles of approach to integration of psychotherapies. *Cognitive Therapy and Research, 10*, 527-538.

Haaga, D. A. F., & Davison, G. C. (1989). Outcome studies of rational-emotive therapy. In M. E. Bernard & R. DiGiuseppe (Eds.), *Inside rational-emotive therapy: A critical appraisal of the theory and therapy of Albert Ellis* (pp. 155-198). San Diego: Academic Press.

Haas, J. R., Rosenfarb, I. S., & Hayes, S. C. (1987). Back to basics: The formation of a special interest group concerned with the contribution of philosophy, theory, and basic research to behavior therapy. *the Behavior Therapist, 4*, 88.

Halford, W. K., & Sanders, M. R. (1988). Assessment of cognitive self-statements during marital problem-solving: A comparison of two methods. *Cognitive Therapy and Research, 12*, 515-530.

Hall, G. C., Proctor, W. C., & Nelson, G. M. (1988). Validity of physiological measures of pedophilic sexual arousal in a sexual offender population. *Journal of Consulting and Clinical Psychology, 56*, 718.

Hall, S. M., Rugg, D., Tunstall, C., & Jones, R. T. (1984). Preventing relapse to cigarette smoking by behavioral skill training. *Journal of Consulting and Clinical Psychology, 52,* 373-382.

Hall, S. M., Tunstall, C., Ginsberg, D., Benowitz, N. L., & Jones, R. T. (1987). Nicotine gum and behavioral treatment: A placebo controlled trial. *Journal of Consulting and Clinical Psychology, 55,* 603-605.

Hall, S. M., Tunstall, C., Rugg, D., Jones, R. T., & Benowitz, N. (1985). Nicotine gum and behavioral treatment in smoking cessation. *Journal of Consulting and Clinical Psychology, 53,* 256-258.

Hammen, C. (1981). Assessment: A clinical and cognitive emphasis. In L. P. Rehm (Ed.), *Behavior therapy for depression* (pp. 255-277). New York: Academic Press.

Hammen, C. (1985). Predicting depression: A cognitive-behavioral perspective. In P. C. Kendall (Ed.), *Advances in cognitive-behavioral research and therapy* (Vol. 4, pp. 4-29). New York: Academic Press.

Handleman, J. S. (1986). A glimpse of current trends in the education of autistic children. *the Behavior Therapist, 9,* 137-139.

Harackiewicz, J. M., Sausone, C., Blair, L. W., Epstein, J. A., & Mauderluik, G. (1987). Attributional processes in behavior change and maintenance: Smoking cessation and continued abstinence. *Journal of Consulting and Clinical Psychology, 55,* 372-378.

Harris, S. L. (1986). Families of children with autism: Issues for the behavior therapist. *the Behavior Therapist, 9,* 175-177.

Harris, S. L. (1987). Parent training: An ecological/system perspective. In M. D. Powers (Ed.), *Expanding systems of service delivery for persons with developmental disabilities* (pp. 53-65). Baltimore: Paul H. Brookes.

Hartlage, L. C. (1986). The future of behavioral neuropsychology. *the Behavior Therapist, 6,* 115-116.

Hartlage, L. C. (1987). Behavioral neuropsychology/behavior therapy: The role of the behavioral neuropsychology special interest group of the AABT. *the Behavior Therapist, 10,* 216.

Hatch, J. P., Klatt, K. D., Supik, J. D., Rios, N., Fisher, J. G., Bauer, R. L., & Shimotsu, G. W. (1985). Combined behavioral and pharmacological treatment of essential hypertension. *Biofeedback and Self Regulation, 10,* 119-138.

Haugaard, J. J., & Reppucci, N. D. (1988). *The sexual abuse of children.* San Francisco: Jossey-Bass.

Hayashida, M., Alterman, A. I., McLellan, A. T., O'Brien, C. P., Purtill, J. J., Volpicelli, J. R., Raphaelson, A. H., & Hall, C. P. (1989). Comparative effectiveness and costs of inpatient and outpatient detoxification of patients with mild-to-moderate alcohol withdrawal syndrome. *New England Journal of Medicine, 320,* 358-365.

Hayes, B., & Hesketh, B. (1989). Attribution theory, judgmental biases, and cognitive behavior modification: Prospects and problems. *Cognitive Therapy and Research, 13,* 211-230.

Hayes, S. C. (1987). A contextual approach to therapeutic change. In N. S. Jacobson (Ed.), *Psychotherapists in clinical practice: Cognitive and behavioral perspectives* (pp. 327-387). New York: Guilford Press.

Hayes, S. C., & Haas, J. R. (1988). A reevaluation of the concept of clinical significance: Goals, methods, and methodology. *Behavioral Assessment, 10,* 189-196.

Hayes, S. C., Rincover, A., & Solnick, J. V. (1980). The technical drift of applied behavior analysis. *Journal of Applied Behavior Analysis, 13,* 175-185.

Haynes, S. G., & Feinleib, M. (1982). Type A behavior and the incidence of coronary heart disease in the Framingham Heart Study. *Advances in Cardiology, 29*, 85-95.

Haynes, S. G., Feinleib, M., & Kannel, W. B. (1980). The relationship of psychosocial factors to coronary heart disease in the Framingham Study: III. Eight-year incidence of coronary heart disease. *American Journal of Epidemiology, 111*, 37-58.

Haynes, S. G., Levine, S., Scotch, N., Feinleib, M., & Kannel, W. B. (1978). The relationship of psychosocial factors to coronary heart disease in the Framingham Study: I. Methods and risk factors. *American Journal of Epidemiology, 107*, 362-383.

Heffer, R. W., & Kelley, M. L. (1987). Mother's acceptance of behavioral interventions for children: The influence of parent race and income. *Behavior Therapy, 18*, 153-163.

Heiby, E. M., & Carlson, J. G. (1986). The health compliance model. *Journal of Compliance in Health Care, 1*, 135-152.

Heiby, E. M., Onorato, V. A., & Sato, R. A. (in press). A cognitive-behavioral model of adherence to health-related exercise.

Heimberg, R. G. (1989a). Social phobia. *Clinical Psychology Review, 9*, 1-140.

Heimberg, R. G. (1989b). Cognitive and behavioral treatments for social phobia: A critical analysis. *Clinical Psychology Review, 9*, 107-128.

Heimberg, R. G., Klosko, J. S., Dodge, C. S., Shadick, R., Becker, R., & Barlow, D. (1989). Anxiety disorders, depression, and attributional style: A further test of the specificity of depressive attributions. *Cognitive Therapy and Research, 13*, 21-36.

Heimberg, R. G., Vermilyea, J. A., Dodge, C. S., Becker, R. E., & Barlow, D. H. (1987). Attributional style, depression, & anxiety: An evaluation of the specificity of depressive attributions. *Cognitive Therapy and Research, 11*, 537-550.

Henggeler, S. W., Rodick, J. D., Borduin, C. M., Hanson, C. L., Watson, S. M., & Urey, J. R. (1986). Multisystemic treatment of juvenile offenders: Effects on adolescent behavior and family interaction. *Developmental Psychology, 22*, 132-141.

Hennekens, C. H. (1983). Alcohol. In N. M. Kaplan & J. Stamler (Eds.), *Prevention of coronary heart disease* (pp. 130-138). Philadelphia: Saunders.

Herr, S. S. (1984). *Issues in human rights.* New York: JAI Press.

Herr, S. S. (1987, October). *The law on aversive and nonaversive behavioral interventions.* Paper presented at the Fourth Annual Conference on Professional Psychology, Rutgers University.

Hersen, M., & Van Hasselt, V. B. (Eds.). (1987). *Behavior therapy with children and adolescents.* New York: Wiley.

Hester, R. K., & Miller, W. R. (Eds.). (1989). *Handbook of alcoholism treatment approaches: Effective alternatives.* New York: Pergamon Press.

Hilton, M. E. (1987). Drinking patterns and drinking problems in 1984: Results from a general population survey. *Alcoholism: Clinical and Experimental Research, 11*, 167-175.

Hjermann, I., Holme, I., & Leren, P. (1986). Oslo study diet and antismoking trial: Results after 102 months. *American Journal of Medicine, 80*, 7-11.

Hoier, T. S. (1987). Child sexual abuse: Clinical interventions and new directions. *Journal of Child and Adolescent Psychotherapy, 4*, 179-185.

Holahan, C. J., Wilcox, B. L., Spearly, J. L., & Campbell, M. D. (1979). The ecological perspective in community mental health. *Community Mental Health Review, 4*, 1-9.

Holland, S., Bach, D., & Duff, J. (1985). Balloon therapy for obesity—when the balloon bursts. *Journal of the Canadian Association of Radiology, 36*, 347-349.

Hollinger, J. D. (1987). Social skills for behaviorally disordered children as preparation for mainstreaming: Theory, practice, and new directions. *Remedial and Special Education, 8*, 17–27.

Hollon, S. D., & Flick, S. N. (1988). On the meaning and methods of clinical significance. *Behavioral Assessment, 10*, 197–206.

Hollon, S. D., & Kendall, P. C. (1980). Cognitive self-statements in depression: Development of an Automatic Thought Questionnaire. *Cognitive Therapy and Research, 4*, 383–395.

Hollon, S. D., Kendall, P. C., & Lumry, A. (1986). The specificity of depressotypic cognitions in clinical depression. *Journal of Abnormal Psychology, 95*, 52–59.

Holt, P. E., & Andrews, G. (1989). Provocation of panic: Three elements of the panic reaction in four anxiety disorders. *Behaviour Research and Therapy, 27*, 253–262.

Hopkins, B. L., Conard, R. J., & Smith, M. J. (1986). Effective and reliable behavioral control technology. *American Industrial Hygiene Association Journal, 47*, 783–791.

Hops, H., Wills, J., Patterson, G., & Weiss, R. (1972). *Marital Interaction Coding System*. Eugene: University of Oregon and Oregon Research.

Horan, M. J., & Roccella, E. J. (1988). Nonpharmacologic treatment of hypertension in the United States. *Health Psychology, 7*, 267–282.

Horn, W. F., Ialongo, N., Popovich, S., & Peradotto, D. (1987). Behavioral parent training and cognitive-behavioral self-control therapy with ADD-H children: Comparative and combined effects. *Journal of Clinical Child Psychology, 16*, 57–68.

Horner, R. H., Dunlap, G., & Koegel, R. L. (Eds.). (1988). *Generalization and maintenance: Life-style changes in applied settings*. Baltimore: Paul H. Brookes.

Horowitz, L. M., Rosenberg, S. E., Baer, B., Ureno, G., & Villasenor, V. S. (1988). Inventory of Interpersonal Problems: Psychonetic properties and clinical applications. *Journal of Consulting and Clinical Psychology, 56*, 885–892.

Hovell, M. F. (1982). The experimental evidence for weight loss treatment of essential hypertension: A critical review. *American Journal of Public Health, 72*, 359–368.

Howard, A. N., & McLean Baird, I. (1977). A long-term evaluation of very low calorie semi-synthetic diets: An inpatient/outpatient study with egg albumin as the protein source. *International Journal of Obesity, 1*, 63–78.

Hugdahl, K. (1987). Pavlovian conditioning and hemispheric asymmetry: A perspective. In G. Davey (Ed.), *Cognitive processes and Pavlovian conditioning in humans*. New York: Wiley.

Hugdahl, K., & Johnsen, B. H. (1989). Preparedness and electrodermal fear-conditioning: Ontogenetic vs. phylogenetic explanations. *Behaviour Research and Therapy, 27*, 269–278.

Humphrey, L. L. (1982). Children's and teacher's perspectives on children's self-control: The development of two rating scales. *Journal of Consulting and Clinical Psychology, 50*, 624–633.

Ingram, R. E., & Kendall, P. C. (1987). The cognitive side of anxiety. *Cognitive Therapy and Research, 11*, 523–536.

Ingram, R. E., & Wisnicki, K. S. (1988). Assessment of positive automatic cognition. *Journal of Consulting and Clinical Psychology, 56*, 898–902.

Innes, J. A., Campbell, I. W., Campbell, C. J., Needle, A. L., & Munro, J. F. (1974). Long-term follow-up of therapeutic starvation. *British Medical Journal, 2*, 356–359.

Izard, C. E., Kagan, J., & Zajonc, R. B. (Eds.). (1984). *Emotions, cognition, and behavior*. New York: Cambridge University Press.

REFERENCES

Jacob, R. G., Shapiro, A. P., Reeves, R. A., Johnsen, A. M., McDonald, R. H., & Coburn, P. C. (1986). Relaxation therapy for hypertension: Comparison of effects with concomitant placebo, diuretic, and beta blocker. *Archives of Internal Medicine, 146,* 2335-2340.

Jacobson, N. S. (1987a). Clinical practice: An introduction. In N. S. Jacobson (Ed.), *Psychotherapists in clinical practice: Cognitive and behavioral perspectives* (pp. 1-9). New York: Guilford Press.

Jacobson, N. S. (Ed.). (1987b). *Psychotherapists in clinical practice: Cognitive and behavioral perspectives.* New York: Guilford Press.

Jacobson, N. S. (1988). Defining clinically significant change: An introduction. *Behavioral Assessment, 10,* 131-132.

Jacobson, N. S. (1989a). The maintenance of treatment gains following social learning-based marital therapy. *Behavior Therapy, 20,* 325-336.

Jacobson, N. S. (1989b). The therapist-client relationship in cognitive behavior therapy: Implications for treating depression. *Journal of Cognitive Psychotherapy, 3,* 85-96.

Jacobson, N. S., Follette, W. C., & Revenstorf, D. (1984). Psychotherapy outcome research: Methods for reporting variability and evaluating clinical significance. *Behavior Therapy, 15,* 336-352.

Jacobson, N. S., & Revenstorf, D. (1988). Statistics for assessing the clinical significance of psychotherapy techniques: Issues, problems, and new developments. *Behavioral Assessment, 10,* 133-145.

Jarvis, M. J. (1986). Nasal nicotine solution: Its potential in smoking cessation and as a research tool. In J. K. Ockene (Ed.), *The pharmacologic treatment of tobacco dependence: Proceedings of the World Congress* (pp. 167-173). Cambridge, MA: Institute for the Study of Smoking Behavior and Policy.

Jay, S. M., Elliot, C. H., Katz, E., & Siegel, S. E. (1987). Cognitive-behavioral and pharmacologic interventions for children's distress during painful medical procedures. *Journal of Consulting and Clinical Psychology, 55,* 860-865.

Jeffery, R. W., Forster, J. L., & Schmid, T. L. (1989). Worksite health promotion: Feasibility testing of repeated weight control and smoking cessation classes. *American Journal of Health Promotion, 3,* 11-16.

Jenkins, C. D., Rosenman, R. H., & Friedman, M. (1967). Development of an objective psychological test for the determination of the coronary-prone behavior pattern in employed men. *Journal of Chronic Diseases, 20,* 371-379.

Jenkins, C. D., Rosenman, R. H., & Zyzanski, S. J. (1974). Prediction of clinical coronary heart disease by a test for the coronary prone behavior pattern. *New England Journal of Medicine, 23,* 1271-1275.

Jesness, C. F., Allison, T. F., McCormick, P. M., Wedge, R. F., & Young, M. L. (1975). *The Cooperative Behavior Demonstration Project.* Final report to the Office of Criminal Justice. Sacramento, CA: California Youth Authority.

Johnson, P. L., & O'Leary, K. D. (1987). Parental behavior patterns and conduct disorder in girls. *Journal of Abnormal Child Psychology, 15,* 573-581.

Johnson, S. B., & Melamed, B. G. (1979). Assessment and treatment of children's fears. In B. B. Lahey & A. E. Kazdin (Eds.), *Advances in clinical child psychology* (Vol. 2, pp. 107-139). New York: Plenum Press.

Johnston, L. D., O'Malley, P. M., & Bachman, J. G. (1986). *Drug use among American high school students, college students, and other young adults: National trends through 1985* (DHHS Publication No. ADM 86-1450). Rockville, MD: U.S. Department of Health and Human Services.

Jones, M. L., Lattimore, J., Ulicny, G. R., & Risley, T. R. (1986). Ecobehavioral design:

Programming for engagement. In R. P. Barrett (Ed.), *Severe behavior disorders in the mentally retarded: Non-drug approaches to treatment* (pp. 123-155). New York: Plenum Press.

Joseph, J. G., Montgomery, S., Kirscht, J., Kessler, R., Ostrow, D., Wortman, C., Brian, K., Eller, M., & Eshlem, S. (1987). Perceived risk of AIDS: Assessing the behavioral and psychosocial consequences in a cohort of gay men. *Journal of Applied Psychology, 17,* 231-250.

Kahana, E. F., & Kiyak, H. A. (1984). Attitudes and behavior of staff in facilities for the aged. *Research on Aging, 6,* 395-416.

Kamarck, T. W., & Lichtenstein, E. (1988). Program adherence and coping strategies as predictors of success in a smoking treatment program. *Health Psychology, 7,* 557-574.

Kannel, W., Brand, N., Skinner, J., Dawber, T., & McNamara, P. (1967). Relation of adiposity to blood pressure and development of hypertension: The Framingham study. *Annals of Internal Medicine, 67,* 48-59.

Kantor, J. R. (1959). *Interbehavioral psychology.* Granville, OH: Principia Press.

Kaplan, S. J. (1986). *The private practice of behavior therapy.* New York: Plenum Press.

Kaufmann, P. G., Jacob, R. G., Ewart, C. K., Chesney, M. A., Muenz, L. R., Doub, N., Mercer, W., & HIPP Investigators. (1988). Hypertension intervention pooling project. *Health Psychology, 7,* 209-224.

Kavanagh, D. J., & Wilson, P. H. (1989). Prediction of outcome with group cognitive therapy for depression. *Behaviour Research and Therapy, 27,* 333-344.

Kazdin, A. E. (1977). Assessing the clinical or applied significance of behavior change through social validation. *Behavior Modification, 1,* 427-452.

Kazdin, A. E. (1978). *History of behavior modification.* Baltimore: University Park Press.

Kazdin, A. E. (1984). Integration of psychodynamic and behavioral psychotherapies: Conceptual versus empirical syntheses. In H. Arkowitz & S. B. Messer (Eds.), *Psychoanalytic therapy and behavior therapy: Is integration possible?* New York: Plenum Press.

Kazdin, A. E. (1987). *Conduct disorders in childhood oand adolescence.* Newbury Park, CA: Sage.

Kazdin, A. E., Esveldt-Danson, K., French, N., & Unis, A. (1987). Problem-solving skills training and relationship therapy in the treatment of antisocial child behavior. *Journal of Consulting and Clinical Psychology, 55,* 76-85.

Kazdin, A. E., & Wilson, G. T. (1978). *Evaluation of behavior therapy: Issues, evidence and research strategies.* Cambridge, MA: Ballinger.

Kelly, J. A., & St. Lawrence, J. S. (1988). *The AIDS health crisis: Psychological and social interventions.* New York: Plenum Press.

Kenardy, J., Evans, L., & Oei, T. (1988). The importance of cognitions in panic attacks. *Behavior Therapy, 19,* 471-483.

Kendall, P. C. (1977). On the efficacious use of verbal self-instructional procedures with children. *Cognitive Therapy and Research, 1,* 331-341.

Kendall, P. C. (1981). Assessing generalization and the single-subject strategies. *Behavior Modification, 5,* 307-319.

Kendall, P. C. (1982). Cognitive processes and procedures in behavior therapy. In C. M. Franks, G. T. Wilson, P. C. Kendall, & K. D. Brownell, *Annual review of behavior therapy: Theory and practice* (Vol. 8, pp. 120-155). New York: Guilford Press.

Kendall, P. C. (1984). Behavioral assessment and methodology. In G. T. Wilson, C. M. Franks, K. D. Brownell, & P. C. Kendall, *Annual review of behavior therapy: Theory and practice* (Vol. 9, pp. 47-86). New York: Guilford Press.

REFERENCES

Kendall, P. C. (1985a). Behavioral assessment and methodology. In C. M. Franks, G. T. Wilson, P. C. Kendall, & K. D. Brownell, *Annual review of behavior therapy* (Vol. 10, pp. 47-86). New York: Guilford Press.

Kendall, P. C. (1985b). Toward a cognitive-behavioral model of child psychopathology and a critique of related interventions. *Journal of Abnormal Child Psychology, 13*, 357-372.

Kendall, P. C. (1987). Behavioral assessment and methodology. In G. T. Wilson, C. M. Franks, P. C. Kendall, & J. Foreyt, *Review of behavior therapy* (Vol. 11, pp. 40-83). New York: Guilford Press.

Kendall, P. C. (1989a). *Stop and think workbooks*. (Available from 238 Meeting House Lane, Merion Station, PA 19066)

Kendall, P. C. (1989b). The generalization and maintenance of behavior change: Comments, considerations, and the "no-cure" criticism. *Behavior Therapy, 20*, 357-364.

Kendall, P. C. (1991). Child and adolescent therapy: Guiding theory. In P. C. Kendall (Ed.), *Child and adolescent therapy: Cognitive-behavioral procedures*. New York: Guilford Press.

Kendall, P. C., & Bacon, S. F. (1988). Cognitive behavior therapy. In D. B. Fishman, F. Rotgers, & C. M. Franks (Eds.), *Paradigms in behavior therapy: Present and promise* (pp. 141-167). New York: Springer Publishing Co.

Kendall, P. C., & Braswell, L. (1985). *Cognitive-behavioral therapy for impulsive children*. New York: Guilford Press.

Kendall, P. C., Cantwell, D., & Kazdin, A. E. (1989). Depression in children and adolescents: Assessment issues and recommendations. *Cognitive Therapy and Research, 13*, 109-146.

Kendall, P. C., & Epps, J. (1990). Medical treatments. In M. Johnson & L. Wallace (Eds.), *Stress and medical procedures*. Oxford: Oxford University Press.

Kendall, P. C., & Grove, W. M. (1988). Normative comparisons in therapy outcome. *Behavioral Assessment, 10*, 147-158.

Kendall, P. C., & Hollon, S. D. (1981). Assessing self-referent speech: Methods in the measurement of self-statements. In P. C. Kendall & S. D. Hollon (Eds.), *Assessment strategies for cognitive-behavioral interventions* (pp. 85-118). New York: Academic Press.

Kendall, P. C., & Hollon, S. D. (1983). Calibrating therapy: Collaborative archiving of tape samples from therapy outcome trials. *Cognitive Therapy and Research, 7*, 199-204.

Kendall, P. C., & Hollon, S. D. (1989). Anxious self-talk: Development of the Anxious Self-Statement Questionnaire. *Cognitive Therapy and Research, 13*, 81-93.

Kendall, P. C., Hollon, S. D., Beck, A. T., Hammen, C. L., & Ingram, R. E. (1987). Issues and recommendations regarding use of the Beck Depression Inventory. *Cognitive Therapy and Research, 11*, 289-299.

Kendall, P. C., Howard, B., & Epps, J. (1989). The anxious child: Cognitive-behavioral treatment strategies. *Behavior Modification, 12*, 281-310.

Kendall, P. C., Howard, B., & Hays, R. C. (1989). Self-referent speech and psychopathology: The balance of positive and negative thinking. *Cognitive Therapy and Research, 13*, 583-598.

Kendall, P. C., & Ingram, R. E. (1987). The future for cognitive assessment of anxiety: Let's get specific. In L. Michelson & L. M. Ascher (Eds.), *Anxiety and stress disorders: Cognitive-behavioral assessment and treatment* (pp. 89-104). New York: Guilford Press.

Kendall, P. C., & Ingram, R. (1989). Cognitive-behavioral perspectives: Theory and research on depression and anxiety. In P. C. Kendall & D. Watson (Eds.), *Anxiety and depression: Distinctive and overlapping features* (pp. 27-54). New York: Academic Press.

Kendall, P. C., Kane, M., Howard, B., & Siqueland, L. (1989). *Cognitive-behavioral therapy for anxious children: Treatment manual.* (Available from 238 Meeting House Lane, Merion Station, PA 19066)

Kendall, P. C., & Norton-Ford, J. D. (1982). Therapy outcome research methods. In P. C. Kendall & J. N. Butcher (Eds.), *Handbook of research methods in clinical psychology* (pp. 429-460). New York: Wiley.

Kendall, P. C., Reber, M., McLeer, S., Epps, J., & Ronan, K. (1990). Cognitive-behavioral treatment of conduct-disordered children. *Cognitive Therapy and Research.*

Kendall, P. C., & Watson, D. (1981). Psychological preparation for stressful medical procedures. In L. A. Bradley & C. K. Prokop (Eds.), *Medical psychology: Contributions to behavioral medicine* (pp. 198-223). New York: Academic Press.

Kendall, P. C., & Watson, D. (Eds.). (1989). *Anxiety and depression: Distinct and overlapping features.* New York: Academic Press.

Kendall, P. C., & Wilcox, L. E. (1979). Self-control in children: The development of a rating scale. *Journal of Consulting and Clinical Psychology, 47,* 1020-1030.

Kerr, M. M. (1986). Teacher and school personnel training. In R. P. Barrett (Ed.), *Severe behavior disorders in the mentally retarded: Nondrug approaches to treatment* (pp. 273-295). New York: Plenum Press.

Kiesler, C. A. (1985). Policy implications of research on social support and health. In S. Cohen & S. L. Syme (Eds.), *Social support and health* (pp. 347-365). New York: Academic Press.

Kipnis, D. (1987). Psychology and behavioral technology. *American Psychologist, 42,* 30-36.

Kirby, D. F., Mills, P. R., Kellum, J. M., Messmer, J. M., & Sugerman, H. J. (1987). Incomplete small bowel obstruction by the Garren-Edwards gastric bubble necessitating surgical intervention. *American Journal of Gastroenterology, 82,* 251-253.

Kirn, T. F. (1987). Laws ban minors' tobacco purchases, but enforcement is another matter. *Journal of the American Medical Association, 257,* 3323-3324.

Klein, D. F., Rabkin, J. G., & Gorman, J. M. (1985). Etiological and pathophysiological inferences from the pharmacological treatment of anxiety. In A. H. Tuma & J. D. Maser (Eds.), *Anxiety and the anxiety disorders.* Hillsdale, NJ: Erlbaum.

Klein, D. F., Ross, D. C., & Cohen, P. (1987). Panic and avoidance in agoraphobia. *Archives of General Psychiatry, 44,* 377-385.

Klerman, G. L. (1989). Treatment of alcoholism. *New England Journal of Medicine, 320,* 394-395.

Klerman, G. L. (1990). The psychiatric patient's right to effective treatment: Implications of *Osheroff vs. Chestnut Lodge. American Journal of Psychiatry, 147,* 409-418.

Klerman, G., Weissman, M., Rounsaville, B., & Chevron, E. (1984). *Interpersonal psychotherapy of depression.* New York: Basic Books.

Klesges, R. C., & Cigrang, J. A. (1988). Worksite smoking cessation programs: Clinical and methodological issues. In M. Hersen, R. M. Eisler, & P. M. Miller (Eds.), *Progress in behavior modification* (Vol. 23, pp. 36-61). Newbury Park, CA: Sage.

Kneedler, R. D., & Meese, R. L. (1988). Learning-disabled children. In J. C. Witt, S. N. Elliott, & F. M. Gresham (Eds.), *Handbook of behavior therapy in education* (pp. 601-629). New York: Plenum Press.

Koegel, R. L., & Mentis, M. (1985). Motivation in childhood autism: Can they or won't they? *Journal of Child Psychology and Psychiatry, 26,* 185-191.
Kohlenberg, R. J., & Tsai, M. (1987). Functional analytic psychotherapy. In N. S. Jacobson (Ed.), *Psychotherapists in clinical practice: Cognitive and behavioral perspectives* (pp. 388-443). New York: Guilford Press.
Kohr, M. A., Parrish, J. M., Neef, N. A., Driessen, J. R., & Hallinan, P. C. (1988). Communication skills training for parents: Experimental and social validation. *Journal of Applied Behavior Analysis, 21,* 21-30.
Kornitzer, M., Magotteau, V., Degre, C., Kittel, F., Struyven, J., & van Thiele, E. (1982). Angiographic findings and the Type A pattern assessed by means of the Bortner scale. *Journal of Behavioral Medicine, 5,* 313-320.
Kozloff, M. A., Helm, D. T., & Cutler, B. C. (1987). Parent training: Working to increase normalization and prevent institutionalization. In J. A. Mulick & R. F. Antorak (Eds.), *Transitions in mental retardation. Vol. 2. Issues in therapeutic intervention* (pp. 70-93). Norwood, NJ: Ablex.
Kozloff, M. A., Helm, D. T., Cutler, B. C., Douglas-Steele, D., Wells, A., & Scampini, L. (1988). Training programs for families of children with autism or other handicaps. In R. DeV. Peters & R. J. McMahon (Eds.), *Social learning and systems approaches to marriage and the family* (pp. 217-250). New York: Brunner/Mazel.
Kozlowski, L. T., Wilkinson, A., Skinner, W., Kent, C., Franklin, T., & Pope, M. (1989). Comparing tobacco cigarette dependence with other drug dependencies: Greater or equal difficulty quitting and urges to use, but less pleasure from cigarettes. *Journal of the American Medical Association, 261,* 898-901.
Kramer, F. M., Jeffery, R. W., Forster, J. L., & Snell, M. K. (1989). Long-term follow-up of behavioral treatment for obesity: Patterns of weight regain among men and women. *International Journal of Obesity, 13,* 123-136.
Krantz, D. S., Davia, J. E., Dembroski, T. M., MacDougall, J. M., Shaffer, R. T., & Schaeffer, M. A. (1981). Extent of coronary atherosclerosis, Type A behavior, and cardiovascular response to social interaction. *Psychophysiology, 18,* 654-664.
Krasner, L. (1988). Paradigms lost: On a historical/sociological/economic perspective. In D. B. Fishman, F. Rotgers, & C. M. Franks (Eds.), *Paradigms in behavior therapy: Present and promise* (pp. 23-44). New York: Springer Publishing Co.
Kuhn, T. S. (1970). *The structure of scientific revolution* (2nd ed.). Chicago: University of Chicago Press.
Kuiper, N. A., & Olinger, L. J. (1986). Dysfunctional attitudes and a self-worth contingency model of depression. In P. C. Kendall (Ed.), *Advances in cognitive-behavioral research and therapy* (Vol. 5, pp. 115-142). New York: Academic Press.
Kuiper, N. A., Olinger, L. J., & MacDonald, M. R. (1988). Vulnerability and episodic cognitions in a self-worth contingency model of depression. In L. Alloy (Ed.), *Cognitive processes in depression* (pp. 289-309). New York: Guilford Press.
Kurdek, L. A., & Berg, B. (1987). Children's Beliefs about Parental Divorce Scale: Psychometric characteristics and concurrent validity. *Journal of Consulting and Clinical Psychology, 55,* 712-718.
Labs, S. M., & Wurtele, S. K. (1986). Fetal Health Locus of Control Scale: Development and validation. *Journal of Consulting and Clinical Psychology, 54,* 814-819.
Lambert, M. E. (1987a). A computer simulation model for behavior therapy training. *Journal of Behavior Therapy and Experimental Psychiatry, 18,* 245-248.
Lambert, M. E. (1987b). Mr. Howard: A behavior therapy simulation. *the Behavior Therapist, 10,* 139-140.

Lambert, M. E., Intrieri, R. C., & Hollandsworth, R. J. (1986). Development of a computerized reference retrieval system: A behavior therapy training tool. *Journal of Behavior Therapy and Experimental Psychiatry, 17*, 167-169.

Landesman, S., & Butterfield, E. C. (1987). Normalization and deinstitutionalization of mentally retarded individuals. *American Psychologist, 42*, 809-816.

Landesman-Dwyer, S., & Knowles, M. (1987). Ecological analysis of staff training in residential settings. In J. Hogg & P. J. Mittler (Eds.), *Staff training in mental handicap* (pp. 3-30). London: Croom Helm.

Lando, H. A. (1981). Effects of preparation, experimenter contact and a maintained reduction alternative on a broad-spectrum program for eliminating smoking. *Addictive Behaviors, 7*, 143-154.

Lane, T. W., & Murakami, J. (1987). School programs for delinquency prevention and intervention. In E. K. Morris & C. K. Braukmann (Eds.), *Behavioral approaches to crime and delinquency: A handbook of application, research and concepts* (pp. 305-327). New York: Plenum Press.

Lang, P. J. (1985). The cognitive psychophysiology of emotion: Fear and anxiety. In A. H. Tuma & J. D. Maser (Eds.), *Anxiety and the anxiety disorders* (pp. 131-170). Hillsdale, NJ: Erlbaum.

Langford, H. G., Blaufox, M. D., Oberman, A., Hawkins, C. M., Curb, J. D., Cutter, G. R., Wassertheil-Smoller, S., Pressel, S., Babcock, C., Abernethy, J. D., Hotchkiss, J., & Tyler, M. (1985). Dietary therapy slows the return of hypertension after stopping prolonged medication. *Journal of the American Medical Association, 253*, 657-664.

Laws, H. L., & Piantadosi, S. (1981). Superior gastric reduction procedure for morbid obesity: A prospective, randomized trial. *Annals of Surgery, 193*, 334-336.

Lazarus, A. A. (1971). Where do behavior therapists take their troubles? *Psychological Reports, 28*, 349-350.

Lazarus, A. A. (1988). Eclecticism in behaviour therapy. In P. M. G. Emmelkamp, W. T. A. M. Everaerd, F. Kraaimaat, & M. van Son (Eds.), *Advances in theory and practice in behaviour therapy* (pp. 63-70). Amsterdam: Swets & Zeitlinger.

Lazarus, A. A. (1989a). The practice of rational-emotive therapy. In M. E. Bernard & R. DiGiuseppe (Eds.), *Inside rational-emotive therapy: A critical appraisal of the theory and therapy of Albert Ellis* (pp. 95-112). San Diego: Academic Press.

Lazarus, A. A. (1989b). *The practice of multimodal therapy*. Baltimore: Johns Hopkins University Press. (Updated paperback edition)

Lazarus, A. A. (1989c). *If this be research....* Unpublished manuscript, Rutgers University.

Lazarus, A. A. (1989d). Why I am an eclectic (not an integrationist). *British Journal of Guidance and Counseling, 17*, 248-258.

Lazarus, A. A., & Fay, A. (1984). Behavior therapy. In T. B. Karasu (Ed.), *The psychiatric therapies*. Washington, DC: American Psychiatric Association.

Lazarus, R. S. (1989). Cognition and emotion from the RET viewpoint. In M. E. Bernard & R. DiGiuseppe (Eds.), *Inside rational-emotive therapy: A critical appraisal of the theory and therapy of Albert Ellis* (pp. 47-68). San Diego: Academic Press.

Lazarus, R. S., & Folkman, S. (1984). *Stress, appraisal, and coping*. New York: Springer Publishing Co.

Lechner, G. W., & Callender, A. K. (1981). Subtotal gastric exclusion and gastric partitioning: A randomized prospective comparison of one hundred patients. *Surgery, 90*, 637-644.

Lennon, S. J. (1984). Consumer spending on designer jeans: A classical conditioning model. *Journal of Consumer Studies and Home Economics, 8*, 145-151.

REFERENCES

Leventhal, H., & Cameron, L. (1987). Behavioral theories and the problem of compliance. *Patient Educational Counseling, 10,* 117-138.
Leventhal, H., Nerenz, D. R., & Steele, D. J. (1984). Illness representations and coping with health threats. In N. B. Baum & J. Singer (Eds.), *Handbook of psychology and health* (pp. 219-252). Hillsdale, NJ: Erlbaum.
Levin, A. P., Schneier, F. R., & Liebowitz, M. (1989). Social phobia: Biology and pharmacology. *Clinical Psychology Review, 9,* 129-140.
Levin, H., Glass, G., & Meister, G. (1984). *Cost-effectiveness of four educational interventions* (Report #84-A11). Stanford, CA: Institute for Research in Educational Finance and Governance (IFG), Stanford University.
Levis, D. J. (1988). Observations and experience from clinical practice: A critical ingredient for advancing behavioral theory and therapy. *the Behavior Therapist, 11,* 95-100.
Levis, D. L., & Malloy, P. F. (1982). Research in infrahuman and human conditioning. In G. M. Franks & G. T. Wilson (Eds.), *Contemporary behavior therapy: Conceptual and empirical foundations* (pp. 65-118). New York: Guilford Press.
Levy, R. L. (1986). Social support and compliance: Salient methodological problems in compliance research. *Journal of Compliance in Health Care, 1,* 189-198.
Lewinsohn, P. M. (1974). A behavioral approach to depression. In R. J. Friedman & M. M. Katz (Eds.), *The psychology of depression: Contemporary theory and research.* New York: Wiley.
Lewinsohn, P. M., Munoz, R., Youngren, M. A., & Zeiss, A. (1986). *Control your depression.* Englewood Cliffs, NJ: Prentice-Hall.
Ley, P. (1986). Cognitive variables and non-compliance. *Journal of Compliance in Health Care, 1,* 171-188.
Ley, P. (1988). *Communicating with patients. Improving communication, satisfaction and compliance.* London: Croom Helm.
Liberman, R. P. (1980). Review of Paul and Lentz's psychological treatment for chronic mental patients: Milieu versus social learning programs. *Journal of Applied Behavior Analysis, 13,* 367-371.
Liebowitz, M. R., Gorman, J. M., Fyer, A. J., & Klein, D. F. (1985). Social phobia: Review of a neglected anxiety disorder. *Archives of General Psychiatry, 42,* 729-736.
Lindsay, W., Gamsu, C., McLaughlin, E., Hood, E., & Espie, C. (1987). A controlled trial of treatment for generalized anxiety. *British Journal of Clinical Psychology, 26,* 3-16.
Linn, M. W. (1986). Modifiers and Perceived Stress Scale. *Journal of Consulting and Clinical Psychology, 54,* 507-513.
Linner, J. H. (1982). Comparative effectiveness of gastric bypass and gastroplasty. *Annals of Surgery, 117,* 695-700.
Lipid Research Clinics Program. (1984a). The lipid research clinics coronary primary prevention trial results: I. Reduction in incidence of coronary heart disease. *Journal of the American Medical Association, 251,* 351-364.
Lipid Research Clinics Program. (1984b). The lipid research clinics coronary primary prevention trial results: II. The relationship of reduction in incidence of coronary heart disease to cholesterol lowering. *Journal of the American Medical Association, 251,* 365-374.
Locke, E. A. (Ed.). (1986). *Generalizing from laboratory to field settings: Research findings from industrial-organizational psychology, organizational behavior, and human resource management.* Lexington, MA: Lexington.
Luborsky, L. (1987). Research can now affect clinical practice—a happy turnaround. *The Clinical Psychologist, 40,* 56-59.

Luborsky, L., Singer, B., & Luborsky, L. (1975). Comparative studies of psychotherapies: Is it true that everyone has won and all must have prizes? *Archives of General Psychiary, 32*, 995-1008.

Lui, K. J., Darrow, W. W., & Rutherford, G. W., III. (1988). A model-based estimate of the mean incubation period for AIDS in homosexual men. *Science, 240*, 1333-1335.

Lutzker, J. R., & Rice, J. M. (1987). Using recidivism data to evaluate project 12-ways: An ecobehavioral approach to the treatment and prevention of child abuse and neglect. *Journal of Family Violence, 2*, 283-290.

MacCuish, A. C., Munro, J. F., & Duncan, L. J. P. (1968). Follow-up study of refractory obesity treated by fasting. *British Medical Journal, 1*, 91-92.

MacGregor, G. A., Markandu, N. D., Best, F. E., Elder, D. M., Cam, J. M., Sagnella, G. A., & Squires, M. (1982). Double-blind randomized crossover trial of moderate sodium restriction in essential hypertension. *Lancet, 1*, 351-355.

MacMahon, S. W., Blacket, R. B., MacDonald, G. J., & Hall, W. (1984). Obesity, alcohol consumption and blood pressure in Australian men and women: The National Heart Foundation of Australia Risk Factor Prevalence Study. *Journal of Hypertension, 2*, 85-91.

Maher, C. A., & Forman, S. G. (Eds.). (1987). *A behavioral approach to education of children and youth.* Hillsdale, NJ: Erlbaum.

Mahoney, M. J. (1988). *Human change processes: Notes on the facilitation of personal development.* New York: Basic Books.

Mahoney, M. J., Lyddon, W. J., & Alford, D. J. (1989). An evaluation of the rational-emotive therapy of psychotherapy. In M. M. Bernard & R. DiGiuseppe (Eds.), *Inside rational-emotive therapy: A critical appraisal of the theory and therapy of Albert Ellis* (pp. 69-94). San Diego: Academic Press.

Malouf, J. M., & Schutte, N. S. (1986). Development and validation of a measure of irrational belief. *Journal of Consulting and Clinical Psychology, 54*, 860-862.

Maltzman, I. (1989). A reply to Cook, "Craftsman versus professional: Analysis of the controlled drinking controversy." *Journal of Studies of Alcohol, 50*, 466-472.

Manninen, V., Elo, M. O., Frick, M. H., Haapa, K., Heinonen, O. P., Heinsalmi, P., Helo, P., Huttunen, J. K., Kaitaniemi, P., Koskinen, P., Maenpaa, H., Malkonen, M., Manttari, M., Norola, S., Pasternack, A., Pikkarainen, J., Romo, M., Sjoblom, T., & Nikkila, E. A. (1988). Lipid alterations and decline in the incidence of coronary heart disease in the Helsinki heart study. *Journal of the American Medical Association, 260*, 641-651.

Marks, I. (1987). Comment on S. Lloyd Williams' "On anxiety and phobia." *Journal of Anxiety Disorders, 1*, 181-196.

Marks, I., & O'Sullivan, G. (1988). Drugs and psychological treatments for agoraphobia/panic and obsessive-compulsive disorders: A review. *British Journal of Psychiatry, 153*, 650-658.

Marlatt, G. A. (1985). Relapse prevention: Theoretical rationale and overview of the model. In G. A. Marlatt & J. R. Gordon (Eds.), *Relapse prevention: Maintenance strategies in the treatment of addictive behaviors* (pp. 3-70). New York: Guilford Press.

Marlatt, G. A., & Gordon, J. R. (Eds.). (1985). *Relapse prevention: Maintenance strategies in the treatment of addictive behaviors.* New York: Guilford Press.

Martens, B. K., Muir, K. A., & Meller, P. J. (1988). Rewards common to the classroom setting: A comparison of regular and self-contained room ratings. *Behavioral Disorders, 13*, 169-174.

Martens, B. K., & Witt, J. C. (1988). Ecological behavior analysis. In M. Hersen, R. M.

Eisler, & P. M. Miller (Eds.), *Progress in behavior modification* (Vol. 22, pp. 115-140). Newbury Park, CA: Sage.

Martin, I. (1987). Concluding comments on theoretical foundations and requirements in behavior therapy. In H. J. Eysenck & I. Martin (Eds.), *Theoretical foundations of behavior therapy* (pp. 451-464). New York: Springer Publishing Co.

Marzillier, J. S. (1989). Special review of L. Michelson and L. M. Ascher: Anxiety and stress disorders: Cognitive-behavioral assessment and treatment. *Behaviour Research and Therapy, 27*, 211-212.

Mason, E. E. (1982). Vertical banded gastroplasty for obesity. *Archives of Surgery, 117*, 695-700.

Mason, E. E., & Ito, C. (1967). Gastric bypass in obesity. *Surgical Clinics of North America, 47*, 1345-1351.

Mastropieri, M. I., Jenkins, V., & Scruggs, T. E. (1985). Academic and intellectual characteristics of behaviorally disordered children and youth. In R. B. Rutherford (Ed.), *Severe behavior disorders of children and youth* (Vol. 8, pp. 86-104). Reston, VA: Council for Children with Behavioral Disorders.

Matarazzo, J., Best, J. A., Belar, C., Clayman, K. D., Jansen, M., Jones, P., Russo, D., & Sheridan, E. (1983). Working Group on Postdoctoral Training for the Health Psychology Service Provider. *Health Psychology, 2*(Suppl.), 141-145.

Mathews, A. M., Gelder, M. G., & Johnston, D. W. (1981). *Agoraphobia: Nature and treatment.* New York: Guilford Press.

Matson, J. L. (1987). Trends and developments in behavioral assessment and treatment of mentally retarded persons. *School Psychology Review, 16*, 566-581.

Matson, J. L., & Schaughency, E. A. (1988). Mild and moderate mental retardation. In J. C. Witt, S. N. Elliott, & F. M. Gresham (Eds.), *Handbook of behavior therapy in education* (pp. 631-652). New York: Plenum Press.

Mattick, R., Peters, L., & Clarke, C. (1989). Exposure and cognitive restructuring for social phobia: A controlled study. *Behavior Therapy, 20*, 3-24.

Mayer, G. R., Butterworth, T., Nafpaktitis, M., & Sulzer-Azaroff, B. (1983). Preventing school vandalism and improving discipline: A three-year study. *Journal of Applied Behavior Analysis, 16*, 355-369.

McCaffrey, R. J., & Blanchard, E. B. (1985). Stress management approaches to the treatment of essential hypertension. *Annals of Behavioral Medicine, 7*, 5-12.

McCauley, E., Mitchell, J. R., Burke, P., & Moss, S. (1988). Cognitive attributes of depression in children and adolescents. *Journal of Consulting and Clinical Psychology, 56*, 903-908.

McClannahan, L. E., Bailey, J. G., MacDuff, G. S., MacDuff, M. A., Tyhurczy, M. J., & Krantz, P. J. (1987). Facilitating community acceptance of group homes. In M. D. Powers (Ed.), *Expanding systems of service delivery for persons with developmental disabilities* (pp. 113-125). Baltimore: Paul H. Brookes.

McCuller, G. L., Salzberg, C. L., & Lignugaris-Kraft, B. (1987). Producing generalized job initiative in severely mentally retarded sheltered workers. *Journal of Applied Behavior Analysis, 20*, 413-420.

McEvoy, M. A., & Odom, S. L. (1987). Social interaction training for preschool children with behavioral disorders. *Behavioral Disorders, 12*, 242-251.

McKusick, L., Horstman, W., & Coates, T. (1985). AIDS and sexual behavior reported by gay men in San Francisco. *American Journal of Public Health, 75*, 493-496.

McKusker, J., Stoddard, A. M., Mayer, K. H., Zapka, J., Morussen, C., & Saltzman, M. S. (1988). Effect of HIV antibody test knowledge on subsequent sexual behaviors in a cohort of homosexual men. *American Journal of Public Health, 78*, 462-467.

McNamara, J. R. (1986). Personal therapy in the training of behavior therapists. *Psychotherapy, 23*, 370-374.

Meichenbaum, D. (1986). *Stress inoculation training.* New York: Pergamon Press.

Meichenbaum, D., & Cameron, R. (1982). Cognitive-behavior therapy. In G. T. Wilson & C. M. Franks (Eds.), *Contemporary behavior therapy: Conceptual and empirical foundations* (pp. 310-337). New York: Guilford Press.

Meisel, C. J. (Ed.). (1986). *Mainstreaming handicapped children: Outcomes, contraversies, and new directions.* Hillsdale, NJ: Erlbaum.

Merckelbach, H., Van Hout, W., Van den Hout, M., & Mersch, P. (1989). Psychophysiological and subjective reactions of social phobics and normals to facial stimuli. *Behaviour Research and Therapy, 27*, 289-294.

Merrett, F., & Wheldall, K. (1987). British teachers and the behavioural approach to teaching. In K. Wheldall (Ed.), *The behaviourist in the classroom* (pp. 18-49). London: Allen & Unwin.

Meshkinpour, H., Hsu, D., & Farivar, S. (1988). Effect of gastric bubble as a weight reduction device: A controlled, crossover study. *Gastroenterology, 95*, 589-592.

Meunier, G. F. (1988). Behavior therapy and the institutionalized elderly. *the Behavior Therapist, 11*, 19-20.

Michela, J. L., & Wood, J. V. (1986). Causal attributions in health and illness. In P. C. Kendall (Ed.), *Advances in cognitive-behavioral research and therapy* (Vol. 5, pp. 179-236). New York: Academic Press.

Michelson, L., & Ascher, L. M. (Eds.). (1987). *Anxiety and stress disorders: Cognitive-behavioral assessment and treatment.* New York: Guilford Press.

Miller, I. W., Norman, W. H., Bishop, S. B., & Dow, M. G. (1986). The modified Scale for Suicidal Ideation: Reliability and validity. *Journal of Consulting and Clinical Psychology, 54*, 724-725.

Miller, I. W., Norman, W., & Keitner, G. I. (1989, June). *Validation of a high cognitive dysfunction subgroup of depressed patients.* Paper presented to the World Congress on Cognitive Therapy, Oxford University, Oxford, England.

Miller, S. M., Leinbach, A., & Brody, D. S. (1989). Coping style in hypertensive patients: Nature and consequences. *Journal of Consulting and Clinical Psychology, 57*, 333-337.

Miller, W. R., & Hester, R. K. (1986). The effectiveness of alcoholism research: What research reveals. In W. R. Miller & N. Heather (Eds.), *Treating addictive behaviors: Processes of change* (pp. 121-174). New York: Plenum Press.

Miller, W. R., & Hester, R. K. (1989). Treating alcohol problems: Toward an informed eclecticism. In R. K. Hester & W. R. Miller (Eds.), *Handbook of alcoholism treatment approaches: Effective alternatives* (pp. 3-13). New York: Pergamon Press.

Miller-Perrin, C. L., & Wurtele, S. K. (1988). The child sexual abuse prevention movement: A critical analysis of primary and secondary approaches. *Clinical Psychology Review, 8*, 313-329.

Milne, D. (1986). *Training behaviour therapists: Methods, evaluation and implementation with parents, nurses and teachers.* London: Croom Helm.

Milner, J. S., Gold, R. G., & Wimberley, R. C. (1986). Prediction and explanation of child abuse potential inventory. *Journal of Consulting and Clinical Psychology, 54*, 865-866.

Mischel, W., & Peake, P. (1982). Beyond déjà vu in the search for cross-situational consistency. *Psychological Review, 89*, 730-755.
Mitchell, J. (1988). Preliminary results of a comparison treatment trial of bulimia nervosa. In K. M. Pirke, W. Vandereycken, & D. Ploog (Eds.), *The psychobiology of bulimia nervosa*. New York: Springer-Verlag.
Moore, T. J. (1989). *Heart failure*. New York: Random House.
Morris, E. K., & Braukmann, C. J. (Eds.). (1987). *Behavioral approaches to crime and delinquency: A handbook of application, research, and concepts*. New York: Plenum Press.
Morris, E. K., & Hursh, D. E. (1979, September). *Some basic considerations and concepts*. Paper presented at a symposium entitled "Behavior Analysis and Developmental Psychology," American Psychological Association Annual Convention, New York.
Morris, R. J., & Kratochwill, T. R. (1983). *Treating children's fears and phobias: A behavioral approach*. New York: Pergamon Press.
Mosher-Ashley, P. M. (1987). Procedural and methodological parameters in behavioral-gerontological research: A review. *International Journal of Aging and Human Development, 24*, 189-229.
Mowrer, O. H. (1960). *Learning and behavior*. New York: Wiley.
Muller, J. D. (1982). Intragastric prosthesis for management of obesity. *World Journal of Surgery, 6*, 492-496.
Murphy, G. C. (1985). Designing an organizational environment supportive of in-service training programs: A comment on Wheldall and Merrett. *Behaviour Change, 2*, 33-35.
Myers, J. K., Weissman, M. M., Tischler, C. E., Holzer, C. E., III, Orvaschel, H., Anthony, J. C., Boyd, J. H., Burke, J. D., Jr., Kramer, M., & Stoltzman, R. (1984). Six-month prevalence of psychiatric disorders in three communities. *Archives of General Psychiatry, 41*, 959-967.
Nathan, P. E. (1986). Outcomes of treatment for alcoholism: Current data. *Annals of Behavioral Medicine, 8*, 40-46.
Nathan, P. E. (1989). A prefatory comment. *Journal of Studies on Alcohol, 50*, 465.
Nathan, P. E., & Skinstad, A. H. (1987). Outcomes of treatment for alcohol problems: Current methods, problems, and results. *Journal of Consulting and Clinical Psychology, 55*, 332-340.
National Center for Health Statistics. (1987a). Trends in serum cholesterol levels among U.S. adults aged 20 to 74 years: Data from the National Health and Nutrition Examination Surveys, 1960 to 1980. *Journal of the American Medical Association, 257*, 937-942.
National Center for Health Statistics. (1987b). *Anthropometric reference data and prevalence of overweight. United States 1976-1980* (DHHS Publicatoin No. PHS 87-1688). Hyattsville, MD: U.S. Department of Health and Human Services, Public Health Service.
National Center for Health Statistics. (1988). *Health, United States, 1987* (DHHS Publication No. PHS 88-1232). Washington, DC: U.S. Government Printing Office.
National Center for Health Statistics. (1989). *Annual summary of births, marriages, divorces, and deaths: United States, 1988* (DHHS Publication No. PHS 89-1220). Washington, DC: U.S. Government Printing Office.
National Commission on Excellence in Education. (1983). *A nation at risk: The imperative for educational reform*. Washington, DC: U.S. Government Printing Office.
National Institute on Alcohol Abuse and Alcoholism, Alcohol Epidemiologic Data System. (1985). *U.S. apparent consumption of alcoholic beverages based on state*

sales, taxation, or receipt data. U.S. alcohol epidemiologic data reference manual (Vol. 1). Rockville, MD: National Institute on Alcohol Abuse and Alcoholism.

National Research Council. (1989). *Diet and health: Implications for reducing chronic disease risk.* Washington, DC: National Academy Press.

Neef, N. A., Iwata, B. A., & Page, T. J. (1986). Ethical standards in behavioral research: A historical analysis and review of publication practices. In A. Poling & R. W. Fugua (Eds.), *Research methods in applied behavior analysis: Issues and advances* (pp. 233-263). New York: Plenum Press.

Neef, N. A., Parrish, J. M., Egel, A. L., & Sloan, M. E. (1986). Training respite care providers for families with handicapped children: Experimental analysis and validation of an instructional package. *Journal of Applied Behavior Analysis, 19,* 105-124.

Neel, R. S., Meadows, N., Levine, P., & Edgar, E. B. (1988). What happens after special education: A statewide follow-up study of secondary students who have behavioral disorders. *Behavioral Disorders, 13,* 209-216.

Nehemkis, A. M., & Gerber, K. E. (1986). Compliance and the quality of survival. In K. E. Gerber & A. M. Nehemkis (Eds.), *Compliance: The dilemma of the chronically ill* (pp. 73-97). New York: Springer Publishing Co.

Nevid, J. S., Lavi, B., & Primavera, L. H. (1986). Cluster analysis of training orientations in clinical psychology. *Professional Psychology: Research and Practice, 17,* 367-370.

Nevid, J. S., Lavi, B., & Primavera, L. H. (1987). Principal components analysis of therapeutic orientations of doctoral programs in clinical psychology. *Journal of Clinical Psychology, 43,* 723-729.

Nezu, A. M., Nezu, C. M., & Perri, M. G. (1989). *Problem-solving therapy for depression: Theory, research, and clinical guidelines.* New York: Wiley.

Nezu, A. M., & Perri, M. G. (1989). Social problem-solving therapy for unipolar depression: An initial dismantling investigation. *Journal of Consulting and Clinical Psychology, 57,* 408-413.

Nieben, O., & Harboe, H. (1982). Intragastric balloon as an artificial bezoar for the treatment of obesity. *Lancet, 1,* 198-201.

Nietzel, M. T., Russell, R. L., Hemmings, K. A., & Gretter, M. L. (1987). Clinical significance of psychotherapy for unipolar depression: A meta-analytic approach to social comparison. *Journal of Consulting and Clinical Psychology, 55,* 156-161.

Nietzel, M. T., & Trull, J. J. (1988). Meta-analytic approaches to social comparisons: A method for measuring clinical significance. *Behavioral Assessment, 10,* 159-169.

Nisbett, R., & Ross, L. (1980). *Human inference.* Englewood Cliffs, NJ: Prentice-Hall.

Norcross, J. C. (Ed.). (1986). *Handbook of eclectic psychotherapy.* New York: Brunner/Mazel.

Norcross, J. C., & Prochaska, J. O. (1984). Where do behavior (and other) therapists take their troubles? *the Behavior Therapist, 7,* 26-27.

O'dell, S. L., Tarler-Benlolo, L., & Flynn, J. M. (1979). An instrument to measure knowledge of behavioral principles as applied to children. *Journal of Behavior Therapy and Experimental Psychiatry, 10,* 29-34.

O'Donnell, C. R. (1987). Childhood aggression and violence: Individual and system approaches. In D. H. Crowell, I. M. Evans, & C. R. O'Donnell (Eds.), *Childhood aggression and violence: Sources of influence, prevention, and control* (pp. 285-294). New York: Plenum Press.

O'Donnell, C. R., Manos, M. J., & Chesney-Lind, M. (1987). Diversion and neighbor-

REFERENCES

hood delinquency programs in open settings: A social network interpretation. In E. K. Morris & C. J. Braukmann (Eds.), *Behavioral approaches to crime and delinquency: A handbook of application, research, and concepts* (pp. 251-269). New York: Plenum Press.

O'Donohue, W., Fisher, J., & Krasner, L. (1986). Behavior therapy and the elderly: A conceptual and ethical analysis. *International Journal of Aging and Human Development, 23,* 1-15.

Office of the Assistant Secretary for Health. (1988). Report of the second Public Health Service AIDS prevention and control conference. *Public Health Reports, 103*(Suppl.), 3.

Office of Medical Applications of Research, National Institutes of Health. (1985). Lowering blood cholesterol to prevent heart disease. *Journal of the American Medical Association, 253,* 2080-2086.

Ohman, A. (1986). Face the beast and fear the face: Animal and social fears as prototypes for evolutionary analyses of emotion. *Psychophysiology, 23,* 123-145.

O'Leary, A. (1985). Self-efficacy and health. *Behaviour Research and Therapy, 23,* 437-451.

O'Leary, A. (1989). *Effects of stress on immune function: Human studies.* Unpublished manuscript, Rutgers University.

O'Leary, K. D., & Borkovec, T. D. (1978). Conceptual, methodological, and ethical problems of placebo groups in psychotherapy research. *American Psychologist, 33,* 821-830.

O'Leary, K. D., & O'Leary, S. G. (1977). Behavior modification with children. In K. D. O'Leary & S. G. O'Leary (Eds.), *Classroom management: The successful use of behavior modification* (2nd ed., pp. 48-59). New York: Pergamon Press.

O'Leary, K. D., & Wilson, G. T. (1987). *Behavior therapy: Application and outcome* (2nd ed.). Englewood Cliffs, NJ: Prentice-Hall.

Olinger, L. J., Kuiper, N. A., & Shaw, B. F. (1987). Dysfunctional attitudes and stressful life events: An interactive model of depression. *Cognitive Therapy and Research, 11,* 25-40.

Ollendick, T. H., & Cerny, J. A. (1981). *Clinical behavior therapy with children.* New York: Plenum Press.

O'Neill, J., Brown, M., Gordon, W., & Schonhorn, R. (1985). The impact of deinstitutionalization on activities and skills of severely/profoundly mentally retarded multiply-handicapped adults. *Applied Research in Mental Retardation, 6,* 361-371.

Ost, L. (1988). Applied relaxation versus progressive relaxation in the treatment of panic disorder. *Behaviour Research and Therapy, 26,* 13-22.

Ost, L. (1989). A maintenance program for behavioral treatment of anxiety disorders. *Behaviour Research and Therapy, 27,* 123-130.

Ost, L., & Gotestam, K. G. (1976). Behavioral and pharmacological treatments for obesity: An experimental comparison. *Addictive Behaviors, 1,* 331-338.

Ozer, E. M., & Bandura, A. (1989). *Mechanisms governing empowerment effects: A self-efficacy analysis.* Unpublished manuscript, Stanford University.

Pace, W. G., Martin, E. W., Tetirick, T., Fabri, P. J., & Carey, L. C. (1979). Gastric partitioning for morbid obesity. *Annals of Surgery, 190,* 392-400.

Paffenbarger, R. S., Jr., Thorne, M. C., & Wing, A. L. (1968). Chronic disease in former college students: VIII. Characteristics in youth predisposing to hypertension in later years. *American Journal of Epidemiology, 88,* 25-32.

Paine, S. C., Bellamy, G. T., & Wilcox, B. (1984). *Human services that work.* Baltimore: Paul H. Brookes.

Parloff, M. B., Waskow, E. E., & Wolfe, B. E. (1978). Research on therapist variables in relation to process and outcome. In S. L. Garfield & A. E. Bergin (Eds.), *Handbook of psychotherapy and behavior change: An empirical analysis* (2nd ed.). New York: Wiley.

Patterson, G. R. (1982). *Coercive family processes.* Eugene, OR: Castalia.

Patterson, G. R. (1986). Performance models for antisocial boys. *American Psychologist, 41,* 1–13.

Patterson, G. R., & Reid, J. B. (1984). Social interactional processes in the family: The study of the moment by moment family transactions in which human social development is embedded. *Journal of Applied Developmental Psychology, 5,* 237–262.

Paul, G. L. (1985). Can pregnancy be a placebo effect? Terminology, designs, and conclusions in the study of psychosocial and pharmacological treatments of behavioral disorders. In L. White, B. Tursky, & G. E. Schwartz (Eds.), *Placebo: Theory, research, and mechanisms* (pp. 137–163). New York: Guilford Press.

Paul, G. L. (Ed.). (1986). *Assessment in residential treatment settings: Principles and methods to support cost-effective quality operations.* Champaign, IL: Research Press.

Paul, G. L., & Lentz, R. J. (1977). *Psychosocial treatment of chronic mental patients: Milieu versus social-learning programs.* Cambridge, MA: Harvard University Press.

Pavlou, K. N., Krey, S., & Steffee, W. P. (1989). Exercise as an adjunct to weight loss and maintenance in moderately obese subjects. *American Journal of Clinical Nutrition, 49,* 1115–1123.

Payne, J. H., DeWind, L., Schwab, C. E., & Kern, W. H. (1973). Surgical treatment of morbid obesity: Sixteen years of experience. *Archives of Surgery, 106,* 432–437.

Pechacek, T. F. (1979). Modification of smoking behavior. In N. A. Kresnegor (Ed.), *The behavioral aspects of smoking* (NIDA Research Monograph No. 26, pp. 127–188). Washington, DC: U.S. Department of Health, Education and Welfare.

Peck, C., & King, N. J. (1988). Medical compliance. In N. J. King & A. Remeny (Eds.), *Compliance: A behavioural approach* (pp. 185–194). Sydney, Australia: Grune & Stratton.

Pellegrini, D. (1985). Training in social problem-solving. In M. Rutter & L. Hersov (Eds.), *Child and adolescent psychiatry: Modern approaches* (2nd ed.). London: Blackwell.

Pellgrini, D., & Urbain, E. S. (1985). An evaluation of interpersonal cognitive problem solving training with children. *Journal of Child Psychology and Psychiatry, 26,* 17–41.

Pelosi, N. (1988). AIDS and public policy: A legislative view. *American Psychologist, 43,* 843–845.

Pendery, M. L., Maltzman, I. M., & West, L. J. (1982). Controlled drinking by alcoholics: New findings and a reevaluation of a major affirmative study. *Science, 217,* 169–175.

Percival, M. L. (1984). "The balloon diet": A noninvasive treatment for morbid obesity; preliminary report of 108 patients. *Canadian Journal of Surgery, 27,* 135–136.

Perri, M. G., Nezu, A. M., Patti, E. T., & McCann, K. L. (1989). Effect of length of treatment on weight loss. *Journal of Consulting and Clinical Psychology, 57,* 450–452.

Perry, N. W. (1987). The new Boulder model: Critical element. *The Clinical Psychologist, 40,* 9–11.

Peterson, C. (1988). Explanatory style as a risk factor for illness. *Cognitive Therapy and Research, 12,* 119–122.

REFERENCES

Peterson, D. R. (1987). Education for practice. *The Clinical Psychologist, 40*, 7-9.
Phillips, E. L., Phillips, E. A., Fixsen, D. A., & Wolf, M. M. (1974). *The teaching-family handbook.* Lawrence, KS: University of Kansas.
Pierce, J. P., Fiore, M. C., Novotny, T. E., Hatziandreu, E. J., & Davis, R. M. (1989a). Trends in cigarette smoking in the United States: Educational differences are increasing. *Journal of the American Medical Association, 261*, 56-60.
Pierce, J. P., Fiore, M. C., Novotny, T. E., Hatziandreu, E. J., & Davis, R. M. (1989b). Trends in cigarette smoking in the United States: Projections to the year 2000. *Journal of the American Medical Association, 261*, 61-65.
Pieters, R. S. M., & Verhallen, T. M. M. (in press). Participation in source separation projects: Design characteristics and perceived costs and benefits. *Resource and Conservation.*
Plas, J. M. (1986). *Systems psychology in the schools.* New York: Pergamon Press.
Polansky, N. A., & Gaudin, J. M. (1983). Social distancing of the neglectful family. *Social Science Review, 57*, 196-208.
Pories, W. J., Flickinger, E. G., Meelheim, D., VanRij, A. M., & Thomas, F. T. (1982). The effectiveness of gastric bypass over gastric partition in morbid obesity: Consequence of distal gastric and duodenal exclusion. *Annals of Surgery, 196*, 389-399.
Power, K. G., Jerrom, D., Simpson, R., Mitchell, M., & Swanson, V. (1989). A controlled comparison of cognitive-behavior therapy, diazepam, and placebo in the management of generalized anxiety. *Behavioural Psychotherapy, 17*, 1-14.
Power, T. J., & Bartholomew, K. W. (1985). Getting caught in the middle: A case-study in family-school consultation. *School Psychology Review, 14*, 222-229.
Powers, M. D. (Ed.). (1987). *Expanding systems of service delivery for persons with developmental disabilities.* Baltimore: Paul H. Brookes.
Powers, M. D., & Franks, C. M. (1988). Behavior therapy and the education process. In J. C. Witt, S. N. Elliott, & F. M. Gresham (Eds.), *Handbook of behavior therapy in education* (pp. 3-36). New York: Plenum Press.
Rachlin, H. (1988). Molar behaviorism. In D. B. Fishman, F. Rotgers, & C. M. Franks (Eds.), *Paradigms in behavior therapy: Present and promise* (pp. 77-105). New York: Springer Publishing Co.
Rachman, S. (1983). Irrational thinking, with special reference to cognitive therapy. *Advances in Behaviour Research and Therapy, 5*, 63-88.
Rachman, S. (1989). The return of fear: Review and prospect. *Clinical Psychology Review, 9*, 147-168.
Rachman, S. (1990). *Fear and courage* (2nd ed.). New York: Freeman.
Rachman, S., & Levitt, K. (1988). Panic, fear reduction and habituation. *Behaviour Research and Therapy, 26*, 199-206.
Rachman, S., Lopatka, C., & Levitt, K. (1988). Experimental analyses of panic: II. Panic patients. *Behaviour Research and Therapy, 26*, 33-40.
Rachman, S., & Maser, J. D. (Eds.). (1988). *Panic: Psychological perspectives.* Hillsdale, NJ: Erlbaum.
Ramsey, E., & Walker, H. M. (1988). Family management correlates of antisocial behavior among middle school boys. *Behavioral Disorders, 13*, 187-201.
Rapee, R. M. (1985). A distinction between panic disorder and generalized anxiety disorder: Clinical presentation. *Australia and New Zealand Journal of Psychiatry, 19*, 227-232.
Raps, C. S., Peterson, C., Reinhard, K. E., Abramson, L. Y., & Seligman, M. (1982). Attributional style among depressed patients. *Journal of Abnormal Psychology, 91*, 102-108.

Reeves, R. S., Foreyt, J. P., Scott, L. W., Mitchell, R. E., Wohlleb, J., & Gotto, A. M., Jr. (1983). Effects of a low cholesterol eating plan on plasma lipids: Results of a three-year community study. *American Journal of Public Health, 73*, 873-877.

Rehm, L. P., Kaslow, N. J., & Rabin, A. S. (1987). Cognitive and behavioral targets in a self-control therapy program for depression. *Journal of Consulting and Clinical Psychology, 87*, 60-67.

Reid, D. H., & Schepis, M. M. (1986). Direct care staff training. In R. P. Barrett (Ed.), *Severe behavior disorders in the mentally retarded: Nondrug approaches to treatment* (pp. 297-322). New York: Plenum Press.

Reimers, T. M., Wacker, D. P., & Koeppl, G. (1987). Acceptability of behavioral interventions: A review of the literature. *School Psychology Review, 16*, 212-227.

Remington, B., & Remington, M. (1987). Behavior modification in probation work: A review and evaluation. *Criminal Justice and Behavior, 14*, 156-174.

Rescorla, R. A. (1988). Pavlovian conditioning: It's not what you think. *American Psychologist, 43*, 151-160.

Reynolds, W. M., & Coats, K. I. (1986). A comparison of cognitive-behavioral therapy and relaxation training for the treatment of depression in adolescents. *Journal of Consulting and Clinical Psychology, 54*, 653-660.

Richards, A. M., Nicholls, M. G., Espiner, E. A., Ikram, H., Maslowski, A. H., Hamilton, E. J., & Wells, J. E. (1984). Blood-pressure response to moderate sodium restriction and to potassium supplementation in mild essential hypertension. *Lancet, 1*, 757-761.

Rickard, K. M., Graziano, W., & Forehand, R. (1984). Parental expectations and childhood deviance in clinic-referred and non-clinic children. *Journal of Clinical Child Psychology, 13*, 179-186.

Riley, D. M., Sobell, L. C., Leo, G. I., Sobell, M. B., & Klajner, F. (1987). Behavioral treatment of alcohol problems: A review and a comparison of behavioral and nonbehavioral studies. In M. Cox (Ed.), *Treatment and prevention of alcohol problems: A resource manual* (pp. 73-115). New York: Academic Press.

Rimland, B. (1964). *Infantile autism*. New York: Appleton-Century-Crofts.

Riskind, J. H., Castellon, C. S., & Beck, A. T. (1989). Spontaneous causal explanations in unipolar depression and generalized anxiety: Content analysis of dysfunctional-thought diaries. *Cognitive Therapy and Research, 13*, 97-108.

Robins, L. (1966). *Deviant children grown up*. Baltimore: William & Wilkins.

Roccella, E. J., & Horan, M. J. (1988). The National High Blood Pressure Education Program: Measuring progress and assessing its impact. *Health Psychology, 7*, 297-303.

Rodin, J., Elias, M., Silberstein, L. R., & Wagner, A. (1988). Combined behavioral and pharmacologic treatment for obesity: Predictors of successful weight maintenance. *Journal of Consulting and Clinical Psychology, 56*, 399-404.

Roehling, P. V., & Robin, A. L. (1986). Development and validation of the Family Beliefs Inventory: A measure of unrealistic beliefs among parents and adolescents. *Journal of Consulting and Clinical Psychology, 54*, 693-697.

Rogers, C. R. (1957). The necessary and sufficient conditions of therapeutic personality change. *Journal of Consulting Psychology, 21*, 95-103.

Romanczyk, R. G. (1986). Self-injurious behavior: Conceptualization, assessment and treatment. In K. D. Gacloe (Ed.), *Advances in learning and behavioral disabilities* (pp. 86-102). Greenwich, CT: JAI Press.

Rook, K. S. (1984). The negative side of social interaction: Impact on psychological well-being. *Journal of Personality and Social Psychology, 46*, 1097-1108.

REFERENCES

Rorer, L. G. (1989). Rational-emotive therapy: I. An integrated psychological and philosophical basis. *Cognitive Therapy and Research, 13,* 475-492.

Rose, J. E. (1986). Transdermal nicotine as a strategy for nicotine replacement. In J. K. Ockene (Ed.), *The pharmacologic treatment of tobacco dependence: Proceedings of the World Congress* (pp. 158-166). Cambridge, MA: Institute for the Study of Smoking Behavior and Policy.

Rose, J. E., Herskovic, J. E., Trilling, Y., & Jarvik, M. E. (1985). Transdermal nicotine reduces cigarette craving and nicotine preference. *Clinical Pharmacology and Therapeutics, 38,* 450-456.

Rose, J. E., Jarvik, M. E., & Rose, K. D. (1984). Transdermal administration of nicotine. *Drug and Alcohol Dependence, 13,* 209-213.

Rosen, R. C., & Beck, J. G. (1988). *Patterns of sexual arousal: Psychophysiological processes and clinical applications.* New York: Guilford Press.

Rosenfarb, I. S. (1987). A note from the chair. *The Issues: A Publication of the Theoretical and Philosophical Issues SIG of the AABT, 1,* 1.

Rosenman, R. H., Brand, R. J., Jenkins, C. D., Friedman, M., Straus, R., & Wurm, M. (1975). Coronary heart disease in the Western Collaborative Group Study: Final follow-up experience of 8½ years. *Journal of the American Medical Association, 233,* 872-877.

Rosenman, R. H., Friedman, M., Straus, R., Wurm, M., Kositchek, R., Hahn, W., & Werthessen, N. T. (1964). A predictive study of coronary heart disease: The Western Collaborative Group Study. *Journal of the American Medical Association, 189,* 113-120.

Rosenman, R. H., Swan, G. E., & Carmelli, D. (1988). Definition, assessment, and evolution of the Type A behavior pattern. In B. K. Houston & C. R. Snyder (Eds.), *Type A behavior pattern: Research, theory, and intervention* (pp. 8-31). New York: Wiley.

Ross, A. O. (1985). To form a more perfect union: It is time to stop standing still. *Behavior Therapy, 16,* 195-204.

Rossiter, E., Agras, W. S., Telch, M., & Losch, M. (1988). Changes in self-reported food intake in bulimics as a consequence of antidepressant treatment. *International Journal of Eating Disorders, 7,* 779-784.

Rotgers, F. (1988). Social-learning theory, philosophy of science, and the identity of behavior therapy. In D. B. Fishman, F. Rotgers, & C. M. Franks (Eds.), *Paradigms in behavior therapy: Present and promise* (pp. 187-210). New York: Springer Publishing Co.

Ruben, D. H. (1986). The "interbehavioral" approach to treatment. *Journal of Contemporary Psychotherapy, 16,* 62-71.

Ruben, D. H., & Delprato, D. J. (Eds.). (1987). *New ideas in therapy: Introduction to an interdisciplinary approach.* Westport, CT: Greenwood Press.

Rubin, K. H., & Mills, R. S. L. (1988). The many faces of social isolation in childhood. *Journal of Consulting and Clinical Psychology, 56,* 916-924.

Runcie, J., & Thomson, T. J. (1970). Prolonged starvation—dangerous procedure? *British Medical Journal, 3,* 432-435.

Rusch, F. R., Chadsey-Rusch, J., White, D., & Gifford, J. L. (1985). Programs for severely mentally retarded adults: Perspectives and methodology. In D. Bricker & J. Filler (Eds.), *Severe mental retardation: From theory to practice* (pp. 119-140). Lancaster, PA: Lancaster Press.

Russell, G. F. M., Szmukler, G. I., Dare, C., & Eisler, I. (1987). An evaluation of family therapy in anorexia nervosa and bulimia nervosa. *Archives of General Psychiatry, 44,* 1047-1056.

Russell, M. A. H., Jarvis, M. J., Feyerabend, C., & Ferno, O. (1983). Nasal nicotine solution: A potential aid to giving up smoking? *British Medical Journal, 286,* 683-684.

Russo, D. C. (1987). American Board of Behavior Therapy formed at Chicago convention. *the Behavior Therapist, 10,* 73.

Russo, D. C., & Budd, K. S. (1987). Limitations of operant practice in the study of disease. *Behavior Modification, 11,* 264-285.

Rychtarik, R. G., Foy, D. W., Scott, T., Lokey, L., & Prue, D. M. (1987). Five-six-year follow-up of broad spectrum behavioral treatment for alcoholism: Effects of training controlled drinking skills. *Journal of Consulting and Clinical Psychology, 55,* 106-108.

Sallis, J. F., Hill, R. D., Fortmann, S. P., & Flora, J. A. (1986). Health behavior change at the worksite: Cardiovascular risk reduction. In M. Hersen, R. M. Eisler, & P. M. Miller (Eds.), *Progress in behavior modification* (Vol. 20, pp. 161-197). New York: Academic Press.

Salzberg, C. L., Agran, M., & Lignugaris-Kraft, B. (1986). Behaviors that contribute to entry-level employment: A profile of five jobs. *Applied Research in Mental Retardation, 7,* 299-314.

Salzberg, C. L., Lignugaris-Kraft, B., & McCuller, G. L. (1988). Reasons for job loss: A review of employment termination studies of mentally retarded workers. *Research in Developmental Disabilities, 9,* 263-281.

Salzberg, C. L., Likins, M., McConaughy, E. K., & Lignugaris-Kraft, B. (1986). Social competence and employment of retarded persons. *International Review of Research in Mental Retardation, 14,* 225-257.

Sanchez-Craig, M., Annis, H. M., Bornet, A. R., & MacDonald, K. R. (1984). Random assignment to abstinence and controlled drinking: Evaluation of a cognitive-behavioral program for problem drinkers. *Journal of Consulting and Clinical Psychology, 52,* 390-403.

Sarason, I. G. (1980). Introduction to the study of test anxiety. In I. G. Sarason (Ed.), *Test anxiety: Theory, research, and applications* (pp. 3-14). Hillsdale, NJ: Erlbaum.

Saunders, S. M., Howard, K. I., & Newman, F. I. (1988). Evaluating the clinical significance of treatment effects: Norms and normality. *Behavioral Assessment, 10,* 209-218.

Schachar, R., Sandberg, S., & Rutter, M. (1986). Agreement between teachers' ratings and observations of hyperactivity, inattentiveness, and defiance. *Journal of Abnormal Child Psychology, 14,* 331-345.

Schechter, M. T., Carib, K. J. P., Math, M., Willoughby, B., Douglas, B., McLeod, W. A., Maynard, M., Constance, P., & O'Shaughnessy, M. (1988). Patterns of sexual behavior and condom use in a cohort of homosexual men. *American Journal of Public Health, 78,* 1535-1538.

Scherwitz, L., McKelvain, R., & Laman, C. (1983). Type A behavior, self-involvement, and coronary atherosclerosis. *Psychosomatic Medicine, 45,* 47-57.

Schilling, R. F., & Schinke, S. P. (1988). Behavioral interventions with families of developmentally disabled children. In M. Hersen, R. M. Eisler, & P. M. Miller (Eds.), *Progress in behavior modification* (Vol. 22, pp. 88-114). Newbury Park, CA: Sage.

Schnaitter, R. (1987). Behaviorism is not cognitive and cognitism is not behavioral. *Behaviorism, 15,* 1-10.

REFERENCES

Schopler, E., & Mesibov, G. B. (Eds.). (1986). *Social behavior in autism*. New York: Plenum Press.
Schotte, D. E., & Clum, G. A. (1987). Problem-solving skills in suicidal psychiatric patients. *Journal of Consulting and Clinical Psychology, 55*, 49-54.
Schreibman, L. (1988). Parent training as a means of facilitating generalization of autistic children. In R. H. Horner, S. Dunlap, & R. L. Koegel (Eds.), *Generalization and maintenance: Life-style changes in applied settings* (pp. 21-40). Baltimore: Paul H. Brookes.
Schreibman, L., Koegel, R. L., Mills, D. L., & Burke, J. C. (1984). Training parent-child interactions. In E. Schopler & G. B. Mesibov (Eds.), *The effects of autism on the family* (pp. 187-205). New York: Plenum Press.
Schreibman, L., O'Neill, R. E., & Koegel, R. L. (1983). Behavioral training for siblings of autistic children. *Journal of Applied Behavior Analysis, 16*, 129-138.
Schucker, B., Bailey, K., Heimbach, J. T., Mattson, M. E., Wittes, J. T., Haines, C. M., Gordon, D. J., Cutler, J. A., Keating, V. S., Goor, R. S., & Rifkind, B. M. (1987). Change in public perspective on cholesterol and heart disease: Results from two national surveys. *Journal of the American Medical Association, 258*, 3527-3531.
Schunk, D. H. (1987). Peer models and children's behavioral change. *Review of Educational Research, 57*, 149-174.
Schwartz, G. E. (1988). From behavior therapy to cognitive behavior therapy to systems therapy: Toward an integrative health science. In D. B. Fishman, F. Rotgers, & C. M. Franks (Eds.), *Paradigms in behavior therapy: Present and promise* (pp. 292-320). New York: Springer Publishing Co.
Schwartz, H. J. (Ed.). (1988). *Bulimia: Psychoanalytic treatment and theory*. Madison, CT: International Universities Press.
Schwartz, J. L. (1987). *Review and evaluation of smoking cessation methods: The United States and Canada, 1978-1985* (NIH Publication No. 87-2940). Washington, DC: U.S. Department of Health and Human Services.
Schwartz, R. C., Barrett, M. J., & Saba, G. (1985). Family therapy for bulimia. In D. M. Garner & P. E. Garfinkel (Eds.), *Handbook of psychotherapy for anorexia nervosa and bulimia* (pp. 280-307). New York: Guilford Press.
Schwartz, R. M., & Garamoni, G. L. (1986). A structural model of positive and negative states of mind: Asymmetry in the internal dialogue. In P. C. Kendall (Ed.), *Advances in cognitive-behavioral research and therapy* (Vol. 5, pp. 1-62). Orlando, FL: Academic Press.
Schwartz, R. M., & Garamoni, G. L. (1989). Cognitive balance and psychopathology: Evaluation of an information processing model of positive and negative states of mind. *Clinical Psychology Review, 9*, 271-294.
Schwartz, R. M., & Michelson, L. (1987). States-of-mind model: Cognitive balance in the treatment of agoraphobia. *Journal of Consulting and Clinical Psychology, 55*, 557-565.
Schwartz, S., & Johnson, J. H. (1985). *Psychopathology of childhood: A clinical-experimental approach* (2nd ed.). New York: Pergamon Press.
Scogin, F., Hamblin, D., & Beutler, L. E. (1987). Bibliotherapy for depressed older adults: A self-help alternative. *Gerontologist, 27*, 383-387.
Scogin, F., Jamison, C., & Gochneaur, K. (1989). Cooperative efficacy of cognitive and behavioral bibliotherapy for mildly and moderately depressed older adults. *Journal of Consulting and Clinical Psychology, 57*, 403-407.
Scott, H. W., Dean, R., Shull, J. H., Abram, H. S., Weeb, W., & Younger, R. K. (1973).

New considerations in use of jejunoileal bypass in patients with morbid obesity. *Annals of Surgery, 177,* 723-735.

Scott, M. J., & Stradling, S. G. (1987). Evaluation of a group programme for parents of problem children. *Behavioural Psychotherapy, 15,* 224-239.

Scruggs, T. E., Mastropieri,M., Tolfa Veit, D., & Osguthorpe, R. T. (1986). Behaviorally disordered students as tutors: Effects on social behavior. *Behavior Disorders, 12,* 36-44.

Secretary of Health and Human Services. (1987). *Sixth special report to the U.S. Congress on alcohol and health* (DHHS Publication No. ADM 87-1519). Rockville, MD: U.S. Department of Health and Human Services.

Seekins, T., Mathews, R. M., & Fawcett, S. B. (1984). Enhancing leadership skills for community self-help organizations through behavioral instruction. *Journal of Community Psychology, 12,* 155-163.

Segal, Z., & Shaw, B. (1989, June). *Empirical findings from a twelve month prospective follow-up of remitted depressed patients.* Paper presented to World Congress of Cognitive Therapy, Oxford University, Oxford, England.

Seligman, M. E. P. (1971). Phobias and preparedness. *Behavior Therapy, 2,* 307-320.

Seligman, M. E. P. (1988). Competing theories of panic. In S. Rachman & J. Maser (Eds.), *Panic: Psychological perspectives* (pp. 321-330). Hillsdale, NJ: Erlbaum.

Sempos, C., Fulwood, R., Haines, C., Carroll, M., Anda, R., Williamson, D. F., Remington, P., & Cleeman, J. (1989). The prevalence of high blood cholesterol levels among adults in the United States. *Journal of the American Medical Association, 262,* 45-52.

Shafer, M. S. (1987). Competitive employment for workers with mental retardation. In M. Hersen, R. M. Eisler, & P. M. Miller (Eds.), *Progress in behavior modification* (Vol. 21, pp. 86-107). Newbury Park, CA: Sage.

Shapiro, D. A., & Shapiro, D. (1982). Meta-analysis of comparative therapy outcome studies: A replication and refinement. *Psychological Bulletin, 92,* 581-604.

Shekelle, R. B., Billings, J. H., Borhani, N. O., Gerace, T. A., Hulley, S. B., Jacobs, D. R., Lasser, N. L., Mittlemark, M. B., Neaton, J. D., & Stamler, J. (1985). The MRFIT behavior pattern study: II. Type A behavior and incidence of coronary heart disease. *American Journal of Epidemiology, 122,* 559-570.

Shekelle, R. B., Gale, M., & Norusis, M. (1985). Type A score (Jenkins Activity Survey) and risk of recurrent coronary heart disease in the Aspirin Myocardial Infarction Study. *American Journal of Cardiology, 56,* 221-225.

Sheldon, J. (1987). Legal and ethical issues in the behavioral treatment of juvenile and adult offenders. In E. K. Morris & C. J. Braukmann (Eds.), *Behavioral approaches to crime and delinquency: A handbook of application, research, and concepts* (pp. 543-575). New York: Plenum Press.

Sheridan, E. P., Matarazzo, J. D., Boll, T. J., Perry, N. W., Jr., Weiss, S. M., & Belar, C. D. (1988). Postdoctoral education and training for clinical service providers in health psychology. *Health Psychology, 7,* 1-17.

Sherman, J., Jorenby, D., & Baker, T. (1988). Classical conditioning with alcohol. In C. D. Chaudron & A. Wilkinson (Eds.), *Theories on alcoholism* (pp. 173-238). Toronto: Addiction Research Foundation.

Shoham-Salomon, V., & Rosenthal, R. (1987). Paradoxical interventions: A meta-analysis. *Journal of Consulting and Clinical Psychology, 57,* 414-419.

Siegel, K., Bauman, L. J., Christ, G. H., & Krown, S. (1988). Patterns of change in sexual behavior among gay men in New York City. *Archives of Sexual Behavior, 17,* 481-497.

Sikand, G., Kondo, A., Foreyt, J. P., Jones, P. H., & Gotto, A. M., Jr. (1988). Two-year

REFERENCES

follow-up of patients treated with a very-low-calorie diet and exercise training. *Journal of the American Dietetic Association, 88,* 487-488.

Simon, D. J., & Johnston, J. C. (1987). Working with families. The missing link in behavior disorder interventions. In R. B. Rutherford, C. M. Nelson, & S. R. Forness (Eds.), *Severe behavior disorders of children and youth* (pp. 82-92). Boston: College-Hill Press.

Simons, A. D., Garfield, S. L., & Murphy, G. (1984). The process of change in cognitive therapy and pharmacotherapy for depression. *Archives of General Psychiatry, 41,* 45-51.

Simpson, R. G., & Halpin, G. (1986). Agreement between parents and teachers in using the revised Behavior Problem Checklist to identify deviant behavior in children. *Behavior Disorders, 12,* 54-59.

Singh, N. N., & Katz, R. C. (1985). On the modification of acceptability ratings for alternative child treatments. *Behavior Modification, 9,* 375-386.

Skinner, B. F. (1953). *Science and human behavior.* New York: Macmillan.

Skinner, B. F. (1986). What is wrong with daily life in the Western world? *American Psychologist, 41,* 568-574.

Skolnick, A. S., & Skolnick, J. H. (1989). *Family in transition* (6th ed.). Glenview, IL: Scott, Foresman.

Skrtic, T. M. (1987). Social consequences of P.L. 94-142 and the new mainstreaming debate. Review of C. J. Meisel's "Mainstreaming handicapped children: Outcomes, controversies, and new directions." *Contemporary Psychology, 32,* 419.

Skutle, A., & Berg, G. (1987). Training in controlled drinking for early-stage drinkers. *British Journal of Addiction, 82,* 493-501.

Slate, J. R., & Saudargas, R. A. (1986). Differences in the classroom behavior of behaviorally disordered and regular class children. *Behavior Disorders, 12,* 45-53.

Smith, J., & Tawney, J. W. (1983). Compliance monitoring: A dead or critical issue. *Exceptional Children, 50,* 119-127.

Smith, M. L., & Glass, G. V. (1977). Meta-analysis of psychotherapy outcome studies. *American Psychologist, 32,* 752-760.

Smith, M. L., Glass, G., & Miller, T. (1980). *The benefits of psychotherapy.* Baltimore: Johns Hopkins University Press.

Smith, T. (1982). *Critique of rational-emotive therapy.* Unpublished manuscript.

Snyder, D. K., Wills, R. M., & Faither, S. L. (1988). Distinguishing specific from nonspecific interventions in comparative outcome studies: Reply to Collins and Thompson. *Journal of Consulting and Clinical Psychology, 56,* 934-935.

Sobell, L. C., Toneatto, A., & Sobell, M. B. (1990). Behavior therapy (alcohol and other substance abuse) 1990. In A. S. Bellack & M. Hersen (Eds.), *Handbook of comparative treatments for adult disorders* (pp. 479-505). New York: Wiley.

Sobell, M. B., & Sobell, L. C. (1973a). Alcoholics treated by individualized behavior therapy: One year treatment outcome. *Behaviour Research and Therapy, 11,* 599-618.

Sobell, M. B., & Sobell, L. C. (1973b). Individualized behavior therapy for alcoholics. *Behavior Therapy, 4,* 49-72.

Sobell, M. B., & Sobell, L. C. (1976). Second year treatment outcome of alcoholics treated by individualized behavior therapy: Results. *Behaviour Research and Therapy, 14,* 195-215.

Sobell, M. B., & Sobell, L. C. (1989). Moratorium on Maltzman: An appeal to reason. *Journal of Studies on Alcohol, 50,* 473-480.

Sobell, M. B., Wilkinson, D. A., & Sobell, L. C. (in press). Alcohol and drug problems. In

A. S. Bellack, M. Hersen, & A. E. Kazdin (Eds.), *International handbook of behavior modification and therapy*. New York: Plenum Press.
Society of Behavioral Medicine. (1989). *Bylaws of the Society of Behavioral Medicine*. Washington, DC: Society of Behavioral Medicine.
Solomon, P. (1983). Analyzing opposition to community residential facilities for troubled adolescents. *Child Welfare, 62*, 361-366.
Spencer, I. O. B. (1968). Death during therapeutic starvation for obesity. *Lancet, 1*, 1288-1290.
Spivack, G., Platt, J., & Shure, M. (1976). *The problem solving approach to adjustment*. San Francisco: Jossey-Bass.
Spring, B. (1988). Cognition: The experimental psychology of subjective thought. *Current Opinion in Psychiatry, 1*, 713-718.
Staats, A. W. (1975). *Social behaviorism*. Homewood, IL: Dorsey Press.
Staats, A. W. (1988). Paradigmatic behaviorism, unified positivism, and paradigmatic behavior therapy. In D. B. Fishman, F. Rotgers, & C. M. Franks (Eds.), *Paradigms in behavior therapy: Present and promise* (pp. 211-253). New York: Springer Publishing Co.
Stall, R. D., Coates, T. J., & Hoff, C. (1988). Behavioral risk reduction for HIV infection among gay and bisexual men: A review of results from the United States. *American Psychologist, 43*, 878-885.
Stall, R. D., & Ostrow, D. (1989). Intravenous drug use, the combination of drugs and sexual activity and HIV infection among gay and bisexual men: The San Francisco men's health study. *Journal of Drug Issues, 19*, 57-73.
Stall, R. D., Wiley, J. A., McKusick, L., Coates, T. J., & Ostrow, D. (1986). Alcohol and drug use during sexual activity and compliance with safe sex guidelines for AIDS: The AIDS behavioral research project. *Health Education Quarterly, 13*, 359-371.
Stiles, W. B., Shapiro, D. A., & Firth-Cozens, J. A. (1988). Verbal response mode used in contrasting psychotherapies: A within-subjects comparison. *Journal of Consulting and Clinical Psychology, 56*, 727-733.
Stokes, T. F., & Osnes, P. G. (1988). The developing applied technology of generalizations and maintenance. In R. H. Horner, G. Dunlap, & R. L. Koegel (Eds.), *Generalization and maintenance: Life-style changes in applied settings* (pp. 5-19). Baltimore: Paul H. Brookes.
Stokes, T. F., & Osnes, P. G. (1989). An operant pursuit of generalization. *Behavior Therapy, 20*.
Stone, G. C. (1983). Proceedings of the National Working Conference on Education and Training in Health Psychology, May 23-27, 1983, Arden House, Harriman, New York. *Health Psychology, 2*(Suppl.), 1-153.
Strauss, C. C., Lahey, B. B., Frick, P., Frame, C. L., & Hynd, G. W. (1988). Peer social status of children with anxiety disorders. *Journal of Consulting and Clinical Psychology, 56*, 137-141.
Strauss, C. C., Last, C. G., Hersen, M., & Kazdin, A. E. (1988). Association between anxiety and depression in children and adolescents with anxiety disorders. *Journal of Abnormal Child Psychology, 16*, 56-78.
Strauss, C. C., Lease, C., Last, C., & Francis, G. (1988). Overanxious disorder: An examination of developmental differences. *Journal of Abnormal Child Psychology, 16*, 433-443.
Strickland, B. R., Follick, M., Altman, D., Cahn, J., Dingus, C. M., Kurz, R., Temoshok, L., & Trickett, E. (1983). Working Group on Apprenticeship. *Health Psychology, 2*(Suppl.), 131-134.

REFERENCES

Strupp, H. H. (1989). Psychotherapy: Can the practitioner learn from the researcher? *American Psychologist, 44,* 717-724.

Stumphauzer, J. S. (1986). *Helping delinquents change: A treatment manual of social learning approaches.* New York: Haworth Press.

Stunkard, A. J. (1989). Review of Schwartz, H. J. (Ed.), *Bulimia: Psychoanalytic treatment and theory.* Madison, CT: International Universities Press, 1988. *Psychiatric Annals, 19,* 279.

Sturmey, P., Newton, T., Milne, D., & Burdett, C. (1987). Parallel forms of the Knowledge of Behavioral Principles as Applied to Children questionnaire: An independent, multi-centred, British replication. *Journal of Behavior Therapy and Experimental Psychiatry, 18,* 223-227.

Subcommittee on Definition and Prevalence of the 1984 Joint National Committee. (1985). Hypertension prevalence and the status of awareness, treatment, and control in the United States. Final report of the Subcommittee on Definition and Prevalence of the 1984 Joint National Committee. *Hypertension, 7,* 457-468.

Suelzle, M., & Keenan, V. (1984). Parents as advocates for social change in the 1980s?: Untapped resources for social change in the 1980s. In M. L. Henninger & E. M. Nesselroad (Eds.), *Working with parents of handicapped children* (pp. 485-502). New York: University Press of America.

Sugerman, H. J. (1987). Gastric surgery for morbid obesity. *Problems in General Surgery, 4,* 258-269.

Sugerman, H. J., Londrey, G. L., Kellum, J. M., Wolf, L., Liszka, T., Engle, K. M., Birkenhauer, R., & Starkey, J. V. (1989). Weight loss with vertical banded gastroplasty and Roux-Y gastric bypass for morbid obesity with selective versus random assignment. *American Journal of Surgery, 157,* 93-102.

Sugerman, H. J., Starkey, J. V., & Birkenhauer, R. (1987). A randomized prospective trial of gastric bypass versus vertical banded gastroplasty for morbid obesity and their effects on sweets versus non-sweets eaters. *Annals of Surgery, 205,* 613-624.

Suinn, R. (1974). Anxiety management training for general anxiety. In R. Suinn & R. Weigel (Eds.), *The innovative therapies: Critical and creative contributions.* New York: Harper & Row.

Suinn, R. M., & Richardson, F. (1971). Anxiety management training: A nonspecific behavior therapy program for anxiety control. *Behavior Therapy, 2,* 498-510.

Sullivan, A. C., Hogan, S., & Triscari, J. (1987). New developments in pharmacological treatments for obesity. In R. J. Wurtman & J. J. Wurtman (Eds.), *Human obesity* (pp. 269-276). New York: New York Academy of Sciences.

Sulzer-Azaroff, B. (1985). A behaviorist's response to the report of the National Commission on Excellence in Education. *The Behavior Analyst, 8,* 29-38.

Sulzer-Azaroff, B. (1986). Behavior analysis and education: Crowning achievements and crying needs. *Division 25 Recorder, 21,* 55-65.

Sulzer-Azaroff, B., & Mayer, G. R. (1986). *Achieving educational excellence using behavioral strategies.* New York: Holt, Rinehart & Winston.

Tarnowski, K. J., Kelly, P. A., & Mendlowitz, D. R. (1987). Acceptability of behavioral pediatric interventions. *Journal of Consulting and Clinical Psychology, 55,* 435-436.

Taylor, C. B., & Arnow, B. (1988). *The nature and treatment of anxiety disorders.* New York: Free Press.

Taylor, C. B., Sheikh, J., Agras, W. S., Roth, W. T., Margraf, J., Ehlers, A., Maddock, R. J., & Gossard, D. (1986). Self-report of panic attacks: Agreement with heart rate changes. *American Journal of Psychiatry, 143,* 478-482.

Taylor, T. V., & Pullan, B. R. (1983). Initial experience with a free floating intragastric balloon in the treatment of morbid obesity. *Gut, 24,* A979. (Abstract)
Teasdale, J. (1989, June). *Discussant's comments.* Paper session, cognitive vulnerability, at World Congress of Cognitive Therapy, Oxford University, Oxford, England.
Telch, M. J., Agras, W. S., Taylor, C. B., Roth, W. T., & Gallen, C. (1985). Combined pharmacological and behavioural treatment for agoraphobia. *Behaviour Research and Therapy, 23,* 325-335.
Telch, M. J., Brouillard, M., Telch, C., Agras, W. S., & Taylor, C. B. (1989). Role of cognitive appraisal in panic-related avoidance. *Behaviour Research and Therapy, 27,* 373-384.
Temoshok, L., Sweet, D. M., & Zich, J. (1987). A three city comparison of the public's knowledge and attitudes about AIDS. *Psychology and Health, 1,* 43-60.
Terborg, J. R. (1986). Health promotion at the worksite: A research challenge for personnel and human resources management. In K. H. Rowland & G. R. Ferris (Eds.), *Research in personnel and human management* (pp. 225-267). Greenwich, CT: JAI Press.
Tertinger, D. A., Greene, B. F., & Lutzker, J. R. (1984). Home safety: Development and validation of one component of an ecobehavioral treatment program for abused and neglected children. *Journal of Applied Behavior Analysis, 17,* 159-174.
Thompson, L. W., Gallagher, D., & Breckenridge, J. S. (1987). Comparative effectiveness of psychotherapies for depressed elderly. *Journal of Consulting and Clinical Psychology, 55,* 385-390.
Thurman, S. K. (1977). Congruence of behavioral ecologies: A model for special education. *Journal of Special Education, 11,* 329-333.
Thyer, B. A. (1987). Behavioral social work: An overview. *the Behavior Therapist, 10,* 131-134.
Tiffany, S. T., Martin, E. M., & Baker, T. B. (1986). Treatments for cigarette smoking: An evaluation of the contributions of aversion and counseling procedures. *Behaviour Research and Therapy, 24,* 437-452.
Todd, J. T., & Morris, E. K. (1983). Misconceptions and miseducation: Presentations of radical behaviorism in psychology textbooks. *The Behavior Analyst, 6,* 153-160.
Tonnesen, P., Fryd, V., Hansen, M., Helsted, J., Gunnersen, A. B., Forchammer, H., & Stockner, M. (1988). Two and four mg nicotine chewing gum and group counseling in smoking cessation: An open, randomized, controlled trial with a 22 month follow-up. *Addictive Behaviors, 13,* 17-27.
Triscari, J., & Sullivan, A. C. (1984a). Antiobesity effects of a novel lipid synthesis inhibitor (Ro 22-0654). *Life Sciences, 34,* 2433-2442.
Triscari, J., & Sullivan, A. C. (1984b). Anti-obesity activity of a novel lipid synthesis inhibitor. *International Journal of Obesity, 8*(Suppl. 1), 227-239.
Turk, D. C., Salovey, P., & Litt, M. D. (1986). Adherence: A cognitive-behavioral perspective. In K. E. Gerber & A. M. Nehemkis (Eds.), *Compliance: The dilemma of the chronically ill* (pp. 44-72). New York: Springer Publishing Co.
Turkat, I. D., Harris, R. C., & Forehand, R. (1979). An assessment of the public reaction to behavior modification. *Journal of Behavior Therapy and Experimental Psychiatry, 10,* 101-103.
Turnbull, A. P., Summers, J. A., & Brotherson, M. J. (1984). *Family systems theory: A guide for research and intervention.* Lawrence, KS: Research and Training Center on Independent Living, University of Kansas.
Turner, S., Beidel, D., & Larkin, K. (1986). Situational determinants of social anxiety in clinic and nonclinic samples: Physiological and cognitive correlates. *Journal of Consulting and Clinical Psychology, 54,* 523-527.

REFERENCES

U.S. Department of Health and Human Services. (1986). *Cancer control objectives feor the nation 1985-2000* (NIH Publication No. 86-2880). Washington, DC: U.S. Government Printing Office.

U.S. Department of Health and Human Services. (1988a). *Report of the expert panel on detection, evaluation, and treatment of high blood cholesterol in adults* (NIH Publication No. 88-2925). Washington, DC: U.S. Government Printing Office.

U.S. Department of Health and Human Services. (1988b). *The Surgeon General's report on nutrition and health* (DHHS Publication No. PHS 88-50210). Washington, DC: U.S. Government Printing Office.

U.S. Department of Health and Human Services. (1988c). *The health consequences of smoking: Nicotine addiction. A report of the Surgeon General, 1988* (DHHS Publication No. CDC 88-8406). Washington, DC: U.S. Government Printing Office.

U.S. Department of Health and Human Services (1989a). *Health and behavior research initiatives by the National Institutes of Health.* Washington, DC: U.S. Government Printing Office.

U.S. Department of Health and Human Services. (1989b). *Reducing the health consequences of smoking: 25 years of progress. A report of the Surgeon General. Executive summary* (DHHS Publication No. CDC 89-8411). Washington, DC: U.S. Government Printing Office.

U.S. Department of Health and Human Services. (1989c). *NHLBI kit '89.* Washington, DC: U.S. Government Printing Office.

U.S. Public Health Service. (1964). *Smoking and health. Report of the Advisory Committee to the Surgeon General of the Public Health Service* (PHS Publication No. 1103). Washington, DC: U.S. Government Printing Office, U.S. Department of Health, Education, and Welfare, Public Health Service, Centers for Disease Control.

Vandenbos, G. R. (1986). Psychotherapy research: A special issue. *American Psychologist, 41,* 111-112.

van Griensven, G. J. P., de Vroome, E. M. M., Tielman, R. A. P., Goudsmit, J., van der Noorda, J., de Wolf, F., & Coutinho, R. A. (1988). Impact of HIV antibody testing on changes in sexual behavior among homosexual men in The Netherlands. *American Journal of Public Health, 78,* 1575-1577.

Verhallen, T. M., & DeNooij, G. J. (1982). Retail attribute sensitivity and shopping patron age. *Journal of Economic Psychology, 2,* 39-55.

Verhallen, T. M. M., & Robben, H. S. J. (1984). *Gift evaluation and behavioural costs.* Paper presented at the IAREP Colloquium, Tilburg, Holland.

Verhallen, T. M. M., & van Raaij, W. F. (1986). How consumers trade off behavioral costs and benefits. *European Journal of Marketing, 20,* 19-34.

Voeltz, L. M., & Evans, I. M. (1982). The assessment of behavioral interrelations in child behavior-therapy. *Behavioral Assessment, 4,* 131-165.

Voeltz, L. M., & Evans, I. M. (1983). Educational validity: Procedures to evaluate outcomes in programs for severely handicapped learners. *Journal of the Association for the Severely Handicapped, 8,* 3-15.

Wachtel, P. (1977). *Psychoanalysis and behavior therapy: Toward an integration.* New York: Basic Books.

Wachtel, P. (1987). *Action and insight.* New York: Guilford Press.

Wacker, D. P. & Berg, W. K. (1988). Behavioral habilitation of students with severe handicaps. In J. C. Witt, S. N. Elliott, & F. M. Gresham (Eds.), *Handbook of behavior therapy in education* (pp. 719-737). New York: Plenum Press.

Wadden, T. A., & Stunkard, A. J. (1986). Controlled trial of very low calorie diet, behavior therapy, and their combination in the treatment of obesity. *Journal of Consulting and Clinical Psychology, 54,* 482-488.

Wadden, T. A., Stunkard, A. J., & Liebschutz, J. (1988). Three-year follow-up of the treatment of obesity by very low calorie diet, behavior therapy, and their combination. *Journal of Consulting and Clinical Psychology, 56,* 925-928.

Wahler, R. G., & Dumas, J. E. (1984). Changing the observational coding styles of insular and noninsular mothers: A step toward maintenance of parent training effects. In R. F. Dangel & R. A. Polster (Eds.), *Parent training: Foundations of research and practice* (pp. 379-416). New York: Guilford Press.

Wahler, R., & Dumas, J. E. (1986). "A chip off the old block." Some interpersonal characteristics of coercive children across generations. In P. Strain, M. Grolnick, & H. Walker (Eds.), *Children's social behavior* (pp. 146-162). New York: Academic Press.

Wahler, R. G., & Hann, D. M. (1986). A behavioral systems perspective in childhood psychopathology: Expanding the three-term operant contingency. In N. A. Krasnegor, J. D. Arasteh, & M. F. Cataldo (Eds.), *Child health behavior: A behavioral pediatrics perspective* (pp. 146-167). New York: Wiley.

Ward, C. I., & McFall, R. M. (1986). Further validation of the Problem Inventory for Adolescent Girls: Comparing caucasian and black delinquents and nondelinquents. *Journal of Consulting and Clinical Psychology, 54,* 732-736.

Warren, R., & McLellarn, R. W. (1987). What do RET therapist think they are doing? An international survey. *Journal of Rational-Emotive Therapy, 5,* 71-91.

Warren R., McLellarn, R., & Ponzoha, C. (1988). Rational-emotive therapy vs. general cognitive-behavior therapy in the treatment of low self-esteem and related emotional disturbances. *Cognitive Therapy and Research, 12,* 21-38.

Watkins, C. E., Campbell, V. L., Lopez, F. G., & Himmel, C. D. (1987). Where do behavioral (and other) counseling psychologists take their troubles? *the Behavior Therapist, 10,* 231-232.

Watkins, J. D. (1988). Responding to the HIV epidemic: A national strategy. *American Psychologist, 43,* 849-851.

Watson, D., & Kendall, P. C. (1989a). Common and differentiating features of anxiety and depression: Current findings and future directions. In P. C. Kendall & D. Watson (Eds.), *Anxiety and depression: Distinctive and overlapping features* (pp. 493-508). New York: Academic Press.

Watson, D., & Kendall, P. C. (1989b). Understanding anxiety and depression: Their relation to negative and positive affective states. In P. C. Kendall & D. Watson (Eds.), *Anxiety and depression: Distinctive and overlapping features* (pp. 3-26). New York: Academic Press.

Weber, J. L., & Stoneman, Z. (1986). Parental nonparticipation in program planning for mentally retarded children: An empirical investigation. *Applied Research in Mental Retardation, 7,* 359-369.

Wedding, D., Horton, A. M., & Webster, J. (1987). *The neuropsychology handbook: Behavioral and clinical perspectives.* New York: Springer Publishing Co.

Wedding, D. (1986). Screening for cognitive dysfunction in behavior therapy practice. *the Behavior Therapist, 5,* 97-98.

Weinberg, R. S., Gould, D., & Jackson, A. (1979). Expectations and performance: An empirical test of Bandura's self-efficacy theory. *Journal of Sport Psychology, 1,* 320-331.

Weissberg, R. P., Caplan, M., & Bennetto, L. (1988). *The Yale-New Haven social problem solving program for young adolescents.* (Available from the author, Department of Psychology, Yale University)

REFERENCES

Weissman, M. M., Jarrett, R. B., & Rush, A. J. (1987). Psychotherapy and its relevance to the pharmacotherapy of major depression. In H. Y. Meltzer (Ed.), *Psychopharmacology: The third generation of progress*. New York: Raven Press.

Weisz, J. R., Weiss, B., Alicke, M. D., & Klotz, M. L. (1987). Effectiveness of psychotherapy with children and adolescents: A meta-analysis for clinicians. *Journal of Consulting and Clinical Psychology, 55*, 542-549.

Wells, J. K., Howard, G. S., Nowlin, W. F., & Vargas, M. (1988). Pain and adjustment: Effects of a stress inoculation procedure on presurgical anxiety and post surgical adjustment. *Journal of Consulting and Clinical Psychology, 54*, 831-835.

Wells, K. C., & Virtulano, L. A. (1984). Anxiety disorders in childhood. In S. E. Turner (Ed.), *Behavioral theories and treatment of anxiety*. New York: Plenum Press.

Werry, J. S. (1986). Diagnosis and assessment. In R. Gittelman (Ed.), *Anxiety disorders of childhood* (pp. 73-100). New York: Guilford Press.

Westen, D. (1988). Transference and information processing. *Clinical Psychology Review, 8*, 161-179.

Westling, H. (1976). Experience with nicotine-containing chewing gum in smoking cessation. *Lakartioningar, 73*, 2549-2553.

Wheldall, K. (Ed.). (1987). *The behaviourist in the classroom*. London: Allen & Unwin.

Wheldall, K., & Merrett, F. (1987). Training teachers to use the behavioural approach to classroom management: The development of BATPACK. In K. Wheldall (Ed.), *The behaviourist in the classroom* (pp. 130-168). London: Allen & Unwin.

White, M. A. (1975). Natural rates of teacher approval and disapproval in the classroom. *Journal of Applied Behavior Analysis, 8*, 367-372.

Whittaker, J. K., Garbarino, J., & Associates (1983). *Social support networks: Informal helping in the human services*. New York: Aldine.

Whittaker, J. K., Schinke, S. P., & Gilchrist, L. D. (1986). The ecological paradigm in child, youth, and family services: Implications for policy and practice. *Social Service Review, 60*, 483-503.

Who needs an intragastric balloon for weight reduction? (Editorial). (1988). *Lancet, 2*, 664.

Will, M. C. (1985). *Educating children with learning problems: A shared responsibility*. Unpublished manuscript.

Williams, G. D., Doernber, D., Stinson, F., & Noble, J. (1986). National, state, and regional trends in apparent per capital consumption of alcohol. *Alcohol Health and Research World, 10*, 60-63.

Williams, G. D., Stinson, F. S., Parker, D., Harford, T., & Noble, J. (1987). Demographic trends, alcohol abuse and alcoholism, 1985-1995. *Alcohol Health and Research World, 11*, 80-83, 91.

Williams, R. B., Jr., & Barefoot, J. C. (1988). Coronary-prone behavior: The emerging role of the hostility complex. In B. K. Houston & C. R. Snyder (Eds.), *Type A behavior pattern: Research, theory, and intervention* (pp. 189-211). New York: Wiley.

Williams, R. L., & Long, J. D. (1983). *Toward a self-managed life-style*. Boston: Houghton Mifflin.

Williams, S. L. (1987). On anxiety and phobia. *Journal of Anxiety Disorders, 1*, 161-180.

Williams, S. L., Dooseman, G., & Kleifield, E. (1984). Comparative power of guided mastery and exposure treatments for intractable phobias. *Journal of Consulting and Clinical Psychology, 52*, 505-518.

Williams, S. L., Kinney, P. J., & Falbo, J. (1989). Generalization of therapeutic changes in agoraphobia: The role of perceived self-efficacy. *Journal of Consulting and Clinical Psychology, 57*, 336-442.

Williams, S. L., Turner, S. M., & Peer, D. F. (1985). Guided mastery and performance desensitization treatments for severe acrophobia. *Journal of Consulting and Clinical Psychology, 53,* 237-247.

Williams, S. L., & Zane, G. (1989). Guided mastery and stimulus exposure treatments for severe performance anxiety in agoraphobics. *Behaviour Research and Therapy, 27,* 237-246.

Wills, R. M., Faitler, S. L., & Snyder, D. K. (1987). Distinctiveness of behavioral versus insight-oriented marital therapy: An empirical analysis. *Journal of Consulting and Clinical Psychology, 55,* 685-690.

Wilson, G. T. (1982a). Clinical issues and strategies in the practice of behavior therapy. In C. M. Franks, G. T. Wilson, P. C. Kendall, & K. D. Brownell, *Annual review of behavior therapy: Theory and practice* (Vol. 8, pp. 305-345). New York: Guilford Press.

Wilson, G. T. (1982b). Fear reduction methods and the treatment of anxiety disorders. In C. M. Franks, G. T. Wilson, P. C. Kendall, & K. D. Brownell, *Annual review of behavior therapy: Theory and practice* (Vol. 8, pp. 82-119). New York: Guilford Press.

Wilson, G. T. (1982c). Psychotherapy process and procedure: The behavioral mandate. *Behavior Therapy, 13,* 291-312.

Wilson, G. T. (1984). Fear reduction methods and the treatment of anxiety disorders. In G. T. Wilson, C. M. Franks, K. D. Brownell, & P. C. Kendall, *Annual review of behavior therapy: Theory and practice* (Vol. 9). New York: Guilford Press.

Wilson, G. T. (1985a). Fear reduction methods and the treatment of anxiety disorders. In C. M. Franks, G. T. Wilson, P. C. Kendall, & K. D. Brownell, *Annual review of behavior therapy: Theory and practice* (Vol. 10, pp. 87-122). New York: Guilford Press.

Wilson, G. T. (1985b). Limitations of meta-analysis in the evaluation of the effects of psychological therapy. *Clinical Psychology Review, 5,* 35-47.

Wilson, G. T. (1987a). Clinical issues and strategies in the practice of behavior therapy. In G. T. Wilson, C. M. Franks, P. C. Kendall, & J. P. Foreyt, *Review of behavior therapy: Theory and practice* (Vol. 11, pp. 288-317). New York: Guilford Press.

Wilson, G. T. (1987b). Fear reduction methods and the treatment of anxiety disorders. In G. T. Wilson, C. M. Franks, P. C. Kendall, & J. P. Foreyt, *Review of behavior therapy* (Vol. 11, pp, 84-113). New York: Guilford Press.

Wilson, G. T. (1987c). Psychosocial treatment of anxiety disorders. In B. Shaw, F. Cashman, Z. Segal, & M. Vallis (Eds.), *Anxiety disorders: Theory, diagnosis, and treatment* (pp. 149-164). New York: Plenum Press.

Wilson, G. T., & Evans, I. M. (1977). The therapist-client relationship in behavior therapy. In R. S. Gurman & A. M. Razin (Eds.), *The therapist's contribution to effective psychotherapy: An empirical approach* (pp. 544-565). New York: Pergamon Press.

Wilson, G. T., & Rachman, S. J. (1983). Meta-analysis and the evaluation of psychotherapy outcome: Limitations and liabilities. *Journal of Consulting and Clinical Psychology, 51,* 54-64.

Wilson, G. T., Rossiter, E., Kleifield, E., & Lindholm, L. (1986). Cognitive-behavioral treatment of bulimia: A controlled evaluation. *Behaviour Research and Therapy, 24,* 277-288.

Wilson, G. T., & Smith, D. (1987). Cognitive-behavioral treatment of bulimia nervosa. *Annals of Behavior Medicine, 9,* 12-17.

Wilson, J. Q., & Herrnstein, R. J. (1985). *Crime and human nature.* New York: Simon & Schuster.

REFERENCES

Wing, R. R., & Jeffery, R. W. (1979). Outpatient treatment of obesity: A comparison of methodology and clinical results. *International Journal of Obesity, 3,* 261-279.

Witt, J. C. (1986). Teachers' resistance to the use of school-based interventions. *Journal of School Psychology, 24,* 37-44.

Witt, J. C., & Elliott, S. N. (1985). Acceptability of classroom management strategies. In R. R. Kratochwill (Ed.), *Advances in school psychology* (Vol. 4, pp. 251-288). Hillsdale, NJ: Erlbaum.

Witt, J. C., Elliott, S. N., & Gresham, F. M. (Eds.). (1988). *Handbook of behavior therapy in education.* New York: Plenum Press.

Wolf, M. M. (1978). Social validity: The case for subjective measurement, or how applied behavior analysis is finding its heart. *Journal of Applied Behavior Analysis, 11,* 203-211.

Wolf, M. M., Braukmann, C. J., & Ramp, K. A. (1987). Serious delinquent behavior as part of a significantly handicapping condition: Cures and supportive environments. *Journal of Applied Behavior Analysis, 20,* 347-359.

Wolfe, D. A. (1987). *Child abuse: Implications for child development and psychopathology.* Newbury Park, CA: Sage.

Wolfe, D. A., Edwards, B., Manion, I., & Koverola, C. (1988). Early intervention for parents at risk of child abuse and neglect: A preliminary investigation. *Journal of Consulting and Clinical Psychology, 56,* 40-47.

Wolpe, J. (1958). *Psychotherapy by reciprocal inhibition.* Stanford, CA: Stanford University Press.

Wolpe, J. (1973). *The practice of behavior therapy.* New York: Pergamon Press.

Wolpe, J. (1986). Misconceptions about behaviour therapy: Their sources and consequences. *Behaviour Change, 3,* 9-15.

Wolpe, J. (1988). A dilemma at the Journal's inception. *Behaviour Research and Therapy, 26,* vii.

Wolpe, J., & Rowan, V. C. (1988). Panic disorder: A product of classical conditioning. *Behaviour Research and Therapy, 26,* 441-450.

Wood, G., Green, L., & Bry, B. H. (1982). The impact of behavioral training upon the knowledge and effectiveness of juvenile probation officers and volunteers. *Journal of Community Psychology, 10,* 133-141.

Wood, J. R. A. (1986). Observation in training parents of handicapped children: A review. *Behavioural Psychotherapy, 14,* 99-114.

Wood, P. D., Stefanick, M. L., Dreon, D. M., Frey-Hewett, B., Garay, S. C., Williams, P. T., Superko, H. R., Fortmann, S. P., Albers, J. J., Vranizan, K. M., Ellsworth, N. M., Terry, R. B., & Haskell, W. L. (1988). Changes in plasma lipids and lipoproteins in overweight men during weight loss through dieting as compared with exercise. *New England Journal of Medicine, 319,* 1173-1179.

Wood, R. E., & Bandura, A. (1989). Impact of conceptions of ability of self-regulatory mechanisms and complex decision-making. *Journal of Personality and Social Psychology 56,* 407-415.

Woolfolk, R. L. (1988). The self in cognitive behavior therapy. In D. B. Fishman, F. Rotgers, & C. M. Franks (Eds.), *Paradigms in behavior therapy: Present and promise* (pp. 168-184). New York: Springer Publishing Co.

Woolfolk, R. L., & Sass, L. A. (1989). Philosophical foundations of rational-emotive therapy. In M. E. Bernard & R. DiGiuseppe (Eds.), *Inside rational-emotive therapy: A critical appraisal of the theory and therapy of Albert Ellis* (pp. 9-26). San Diego: Academic Press.

Work, W. C., Hightower, A. D., Fantuzzo, J. W., & Rohrbeck, C. A. (1987). Replication and extension of the Teacher Self-Control Rating Scale. *Journal of Consulting and Clinical Psychology, 55*, 115-116.

Wyatt, G. E., & Powell, G. J. (Eds.). (1988). *Lasting effects of child sexual abuse.* Newbury Park, CA: Sage.

Wyatt, W. J., & Hawkins, R. P. (1987). Rates of teachers verbal approval and disapproval. Relationship to grade level, classroom activity, student behavior, and teacher characteristics. *Behavior Modification, 11*, 27-51.

Wyatt, W. J., Hawkins, R. P., & Davis, P. (1986). Behaviourism: Are reports of its death exaggerated? *The Behavior Analyst, 9*, 101-105.

Wyatt v. Stickney. (1972). 344 F Supp. 387, 395-407, Middle District of Alabama.

Yontef, G., & Simkin, J. (1989). Gestalt therapy. In R. Corsini & D. Wedding (Eds.), *Current psychotherapies* (4th ed.). Itasca, IL: Peacock.

Zeiss, A. M., Lewinsohn, P. M., & Munoz, R. F. (1979). Nonspecific improvement effects in depression using interpersonal skills training, pleasant activity schedules, or cognitive training. *Journal of Consulting and Clinical Psychology, 47*, 427-438.

Ziegler, D. J. (1989). A critique of rational-emotive theory of personality. In M. E. Bernard & R. DiGiuseppe (Eds.), *Inside rational-emotive therapy: A critical appraisal of the theory and therapy of Albert Ellis* (pp. 27-46). San Diego: Academic Press.

Zimmerman, M., & Coryell, W. (1987). The Inventory to Diagnose major depressive disorder. *Journal of Consulting and Clinical Psychology, 55*, 55-59.

Zitrin, C. M., Klein, D. F., & Woerner, M. G. (1980). Treatment of agoraphobia with group exposure *in vivo* and imipramine. *Archives of General Psychiatry, 37*, 63-72.

Zitrin, C. M., Klein, D. F., Woerner, M. G., & Ross, D. C. (1983). Treatment of phobias: I. Comparison of imipramine hydrochloride and placebo. *Archives of General Psychiatry, 40*, 125-138.

Zuriff, G. E. (1985). *Behaviorism: A conceptual reconstruction.* New York: Columbia University Press.

AUTHOR INDEX

Abel, G. G., 154, 308
Abramson, L. Y., 53, 339
Achenbach, T. M., 127, 303
Adams, H., 44, 303
Addington, H. J., 215, 310
Adler, C. M., 82, 303
Adlington, F. M., 227, 240, 313
Affleck, G., 132, 303
Agran, M., 26, 342
Agras, W. S., 43, 82, 97, 155, 283, 286, 292, 293, 298, 301, 303, 348
Aivazyan, T. A., 155, 303
Albin, J., 240, 315
Alden, L., 219, 303
Alderman, M. H., 173, 303
Alford, D. J., 112, 332
Alicke, M. D., 63, 351
Allen, D. D., 14, 307
Allison, T. F., 37, 325
Alloy, L. B., 105, 303
Altman, D. G., 211, 212, 303
Amaral, P. L., 40, 304
American Humane Association, 248, 304
American Psychiatric Association, 72, 304
American Psychological Association, 138, 304
Amies, P., 90, 310
Anastasiades, P., 91, 310
Anderson, T. K., 254, 255, 304
Andrasik, F., 68, 307
Andrews, G., 98, 99, 324

Anger, W. K., 35, 318
Annis, H. M., 219, 342
Arkowitz, H., 272, 304
Arnkoff, D. B., 57, 275, 286, 290, 304
Arnow, B., 72, 89, 100, 347
Ascher, L. M., 72, 334
Auerbach, S. M., 135, 304
Axelsson, S., 204, 304
Azar, S. T., 45, 260, 304, 316

Bach, D., 195, 323
Bachman, J. G., 214, 216, 325
Bacon, S. F., 3, 327
Baer, B., 45, 324
Baer, D. M., 67, 256, 304, 307
Baeyens, F., 74, 304
Bailar, J. C. III, 162, 304
Bailey, J. S., 34, 304
Baker, T., 74, 217, 305, 344
Baker, T. B., 207, 309
Ballard, K. D., 258, 305
Baltes, M. M., 41, 305
Bandura, A., 40, 75, 76, 77, 78, 79, 80, 80n, 81, 83, 85, 86, 100, 288, 305, 337, 353
Bank, L., 36, 242, 305
Barber, K., 30, 305
Barber, M., 30, 305
Barchas, J. D., 79, 305
Barefoot, J. C., 161, 351
Barkley, R. A., 242, 305

Barlow, D. H., 49, 54, 72, 73, 80, 80n, 82, 83, 84, 85, 86, 89n, 96, 97, 100, 101, 120, 277n, 295, 296, 297, 298, 303, 305, 323
Barofsky, I., 15, 305
Barone, V. J., 252, 305
Barrett, E. T., 45, 305
Barrett, M. J., 294, 343
Barrett, R. P., 18, 305
Barsky, A. J., 142, 305
Bartholomew, K. W., 227, 339
Bass, C., 160, 305
Bauman, L. J., 169, 344
Baumeister, A. A., 22, 309
Bays, K., 42, 306
Beach, S. R. H., 131, 317
Beck, A. T., 45, 50, 51, 53, 54, 58, 60, 61, 91, 92, 93, 95, 101, 104, 105, 120, 121, 122, 282, 284, 288, 289, 292, 295, 306, 327, 340
Beck, J. G., 298, 341
Becker, M. H., 169, 306
Becker, R. E., 54, 56, 314, 323
Bedell, J. R., 134, 318
Behrens, B. C., 230, 313
Beidel, D., 48, 348
Beidel, D. C., 4, 124, 306
Beitman, B. D., 280, 281, 292, 306
Bellamy, G. T., 38, 337
Belsky, J., 252, 306
Bemis, K., 108, 284, 314
Benjamin, S. B., 193, 194, 306
Bennett, W., 179, 197, 198, 306
Bennetto, L., 135, 350
Bennun, I., 11, 306
Benowitz, N., 205, 322
Benowitz, N. L., 205, 322
Berg, B., 45, 329
Berg, G., 219, 345
Berg, W. K., 266, 349
Bergan, J. R., 255, 304
Berger, M., 254, 306
Berkman, L., 40, 307
Berman, J. S., 63, 311
Bernard, D. L., 189, 320
Bernard, M. E., 112, 116, 307

Bernstein, D., 92, 307
Best, J. A., 16, 310
Beutler, L. E., 109, 110, 307, 343
Bibeau, D. L., 171, 307
Bien, N. Z., 264, 307
Biever, J. L., 56, 320
Bigelow, G. E., 192, 307
Bijou, S. W., 226, 307
Billings, J. H., 160, 344
Birbaumer, N., 97, 315
Birkenhauer, R., 195, 347
Bishop, S. B., 45, 334
Bistrian, B. R., 189, 307
Black, D. R., 14, 307
Black, G. W., 155, 312
Blackburn, G. L., 189, 307
Blacket, R. B., 154, 332
Blair, L. W., 133, 322
Blair, S. N., 154, 307
Blanchard, E. B., 67, 68, 154, 155, 298, 307, 308, 333
Blankenhorn, D. H., 151, 308
Blinde, L., 14, 307
Block, P. C., 160, 314
Bloom, W. L., 188, 308
Blowers, C., 92, 93, 308
Bohnert, M., 91, 306
Boivin, M. J., 8, 308
Boll, T., 176, 308
Bommer, M., 33, 308
Bonneson, C. I., 45, 308
Borkovec, T. D., 77, 92, 93, 94, 107, 122, 125, 307, 308, 337
Bornet, A. R., 219, 342
Bortner, R. W., 159, 308
Boudewyns, P. A., 27, 308
Bower, G. H., 277, 296, 308
Braith, J., 113, 309
Branch, M. N., 4, 308
Brand, N., 153, 326
Brand, R. J., 159, 309
Brandon, T. H., 207, 309
Brantmark, B., 204, 304
Braswell, L., 64, 113, 126, 127, 309, 327
Braukmann, C. J., 36, 38, 309, 317, 335, 353

AUTHOR INDEX

Breckenridge, J. S., 110, 348
Breiner, J., 244, 318
Breslow, L., 164, 309
Brewin, C., 100, 309
Brody, D. S., 135, 334
Brooks, P. H., 22, 309
Brotherson, M. J., 228, 348
Brouillard, M., 82, 348
Brouillard, M. E., 79, 305
Brown, F. A., 269, 316
Brown, G., 45, 51, 54, 306
Brown, M., 21, 337
Browne, A., 250, 309
Browne, M. A., 6, 309
Brownell, K. D., 176, 192, 215, 297, 309
Brunk, M., 250, 251, 309
Bry, B. H., 37, 264, 265, 307, 309, 310, 353
Budd, K. S., 4, 5, 241, 310, 342
Burchard, J. D., 37, 38, 310
Burchard, S. N., 37, 310
Burdett, C., 12, 347
Burgess, R. L., 253, 310
Burgio, K. L., 39, 310
Burgio, L. D., 39, 310
Burke, J. C., 247, 343
Burke, P., 54, 333
Burns, D., 110, 310
Bushell, D., 256, 304
Butcher, J. N., 51, 310
Butler, G., 87, 90, 90n, 91, 92, 93, 310
Butrum, R. R., 166, 310
Butterfield, E. C., 20, 330
Butterworth, T., 264, 333

Caddy, G. R., 215, 310
Callender, A. K., 195, 330
Calvert, S. C., 238, 310
Cameron, L., 17, 331
Cameron, R., 16, 296, 297, 310, 334
Campbell, M. D., 225, 323
Campbell, V. L., 9, 350
Camper, P. M., 132, 311
Cane, D. B., 50, 52, 321
Canner, P. L., 150, 311

Cantwell, D., 50, 327
Caplan, M., 135, 350
Carey, L. C., 195, 337
Carey, M. P., 50, 113, 311
Carlson, C. L., 266, 311
Carlson, J. G., 17, 323
Carlson, L. A., 151, 311
Carmelli, D., 158, 341
Carsrud, A. L., 19, 311
Carstensen, L. L., 40, 41, 311
Casat, C. D., 124, 317
Case, N. B., 160, 311
Case, R. B., 160, 311
Casey, R. J., 63, 311
Castellon, C. S., 53, 340
Cataldo, M. F., 171, 311
Center, D. B., 267, 311
Centers for Disease Control, 144, 167, 168, 179, 180, 183, 311
Cerny, J. A., 96, 101, 123, 295, 305, 337
Chadsey-Rusch, J., 22, 23, 311
Chambers, A., 125, 308
Chesney, M. A., 155, 312
Chesney-Lind, M., 39, 336
Chevron, E., 283, 328
Christ, G. H., 169, 344
Christensen, A. P., 227, 240, 313
Christensen, L., 65, 312
Christian, W. P., 27, 319
Cigrang, J. A., 171, 328
Cioffi, D., 79, 305
Clabby, J. F., 135, 315
Clark, D. A., 57, 91, 97, 99, 100, 101, 121, 297, 312
Clark, H. B., 30, 305
Clark, L., 49, 50, 312
Clarke, C., 88, 333
Clifford, C. K., 166, 310
Clum, G. A., 136, 343
Coates, T., 169, 333
Coates, T. J., 169, 171, 311, 312, 346
Coats, K. I., 111, 340
Cobb, J., 92, 308
Cohen, J., 261, 312
Cohen, J. B., 160, 312
Cohen, P., 97, 328

Cohn, A. W., 37, 312
Collins, F. L., 108, 312
Committee on the Review of Medicine, 89, 312
Communications Technologies, Inc., 170, 312
Compas, B. E., 45, 131, 312
Conard, R. J., 35, 324
Condiotti, M. M., 78, 312
Cone, J. D., 227, 312, 313
Cook, D. R., 217, 313
Cook, E. F., 140, 321
Cook, E. W., 48, 313
Cooper, K. H., 154, 307
Correo, J., 254, 313
Coryell, W., 45, 354
Cosper, M., 258, 313
Costello, E. J., 123, 313
Council on Scientific Affairs, 187, 313
Craighead, L. W., 191, 313
Craske, M., 82, 303
Craske, M. G., 83, 313
Crombez, G., 74, 304
Croog, S., 132, 303
Crooks, T. J., 258, 305
Cubberley, P. T., 189, 313
Cullari, S., 28, 317
Cullinan, D., 258, 316
Cullington, A., 90, 90n, 91, 92, 93, 310
Cumberland, W. G., 164, 309
Cummings, C., 16, 313
Cupples, L. A., 152, 313
Cuthbert, B. N., 48, 313
Cutler, B. C., 235, 329

Dadds, M. R., 227, 229, 230, 231, 240, 242, 313
D'Agostino, R. B., 152, 313
Dahlstrom, G., 51, 310
Dare, C., 294, 341
Darrow, W. W., 168, 330
Davies, G., 244, 318
Davis, G. E., 45, 312
Davis, P., 43, 354
Davis, R. M., 201, 339

Davison, G. C., 7, 115, 298, 299, 313, 314, 321
Dawber, T., 153, 326
Dawber, T. R., 153, 314
DeBacker, G., 159, 314
DeBakey, M. E., 193, 314
Deitz, S. M., 2, 314
deKock, V., 21, 317
Delprato, D. J., 5, 6, 314, 341
DeNooij, G. J., 34, 349
Derry, P., 277, 314
DeRubeis, R., 108, 284, 314
De Silva, P., 76, 314
Des Jarlais, D. C., 169, 314
DeWind, L., 195, 338
DiFranza, J. R., 211, 314
DiGiuseppe, R., 112, 116, 307
Dimsdale, J. E., 160, 314
Dixen, J., 249, 314
Dobson, K. S., 60, 61, 107, 108, 109, 314
Dodge, C. S., 54, 56, 314, 323
Doernber, D., 213, 351
Doll, R., 165, 314
Donovan, D. M., 218, 314
Dooseman, G., 77, 351
Dorenberg, D., 214
Dorfman, D. D., 45, 317
Dow, M. G., 45, 334
Dramaix, M., 159, 314
Drenick, E. J., 188, 314
Driessen, J. R., 241, 329
Druckman, D., 174, 175, 176, 315
Duff, J., 195, 323
Dumas, J. E., 226, 229, 231, 239, 240, 315, 350
Duncan, L. J. P., 188, 332
Dunlap, G., 244, 324
Durand, V. M., 254, 315
Durham, R. C., 94, 315
Dush, D. M., 63, 64, 315
Dustan, H., 153, 315
D'Zurilla, T., 135, 315

Ebrahimi, S., 125, 308
Edelbrock, C. S., 127, 303

AUTHOR INDEX

Edelstein, B. A., 11, 70, 108, 315
Edgar, E. B., 269, 336
Edwards, B., 251, 353
Eelen, P., 3, 74, 315
Egel, A. L., 237, 246, 315, 336
Ehlers, A., 97, 98, 315
Eisler, I., 294, 341
Elias, M., 135, 192, 315, 340
Elliot, C. H., 134, 325
Elliott, S. N., 227, 254, 315, 353
Ellis, A., 112, 114, 116, 119, 120, 315
Emerson, C., 28, 315
Emerson, E., 28, 315
Emery, G., 60, 92, 93, 95, 104, 120, 121, 122, 306
Emmelkamp, P. M. G., 118, 119, 295, 315, 318
Emmons, C. A., 169, 316
Enyart, P., 50, 311
Epps, J., 128, 133, 327
Epstein, J. A., 133, 322
Epstein, M., 258, 316
Epstein, N., 45, 51, 306
Erickson, M., 258, 313
Erickson, R. J., 41, 311
Erwin, E., 2, 3, 316
Espie, C., 92, 331
Esveldt-Dawson, K., 126, 326
Evans, I. M., 23, 227, 269, 281, 316, 349, 352
Evans, L., 99, 326
Evans, M., 108, 284, 314
Expert Panel on Detection, Evaluation, and Treatment of High Blood Cholesterol in Adults, 144, 316
Eyberg, S., 235, 316
Eysenck, H. J., 2, 3, 73, 316

Fabre, T. R., 267, 316
Fabri, P. J., 195, 337
Fabry, P. L., 241, 310
Fagerstrom, K. O., 204, 316
Fairburn, C. G., 284, 285, 293, 294, 295, 298, 316
Faitler, S. L., 198, 345, 352

Falbo, J., 78, 351
Fantuzzo, J. W., 46, 260, 316
Faraone, S. V., 45, 317
Farivar, S., 194, 334
Faulstich, M. E., 50, 311
Fawcett, S. B., 29, 38, 317, 344
Fay, A., 281, 330
Feinleib, M., 159, 322, 323
Felce, D., 21, 317
Feldman, M. A., 237, 317
Fellner, D. J., 35, 317
Ferguson, D. G., 28, 317
Ferno, O., 205, 342
Ferster, C. B., 289, 317
Festinger, L., 261, 317
Feyerabend, C., 205, 342
Finch, A. J., 124, 317
Fincham, F. D., 131, 317
Finkelhor, D., 248, 249, 250, 309, 317
Fiore, M. C., 200, 201, 317
Firth-Cozens, J. A., 108, 346
Fischler, G. L., 136, 317
Fisher, A. H., 193, 319
Fisher, J., 39, 337
Fishman, D. B., 3, 317
Fixsen, D. A., 30, 339
Flatt, J. P., 189, 307
Flick, S. N., 66, 67, 324
Flickinger, E. G., 195, 339
Flora, J. A., 171, 342
Floyd, F. J., 47, 317, 318
Flynn, J. M., 12, 336
Foa, E. B., 122, 126, 295, 318
Foley, F. W., 134, 318
Folkman, S., 82, 85, 100, 330
Follette, W. C., 65, 325
Fontaine, O., 3, 315
Ford, J., 189, 320
Forehand, R., 8, 233, 238, 241, 244, 318, 340, 348
Foreyt, J. P., 147, 172, 178, 191, 207, 211, 215, 216, 222, 297, 309
Forman, S. G., 254, 332
Forster, J. L., 171, 199, 325
Forsythe, C. J., 45, 131, 312
Fortmann, S. P., 171, 342

Foshee, V., 171, 307
Foster, V., 211, 303
Fowler, S. A., 262, 318
Fox, D. K., 35, 318
Fox, J., 229, 318
Foxall, D. J., 33, 34, 318, 319
Foxall, G. R., 33, 34, 319
Foy, D. W., 219, 319
Frame, C. L., 125, 346
Francis, G., 123, 124, 346
Frank, B. B., 193, 319
Frank, C. M., 1, 3, 5, 73, 225, 226, 227, 256, 297, 317, 319, 339
French–Belgian Collaborative Group, 159, 319
French, N., 126, 326
Frick, M. H., 147, 319
Frick, P., 125, 346
Friedman, G. D., 154, 319
Friedman, M., 158, 319, 325
Friedman, S. R., 169, 314
Fry, T. J., 27, 308
Fuoco, F. J., 27, 319
Furtkamp, E., 12, 319
Fyer, A. J., 87, 331

Gale, M., 160, 344
Gallagher, D., 110, 348
Gallen, C., 97, 293, 348
Gamser, C., 92, 331
Garamoni, G. L., 58, 59, 60, 343
Garbarino, J., 226, 351
Garfield, S. L., 115, 272, 278, 293, 320, 345
Garfinkel, P. E., 298, 320
Garner, D. M., 285, 294, 298, 320
Garner, D. W., 211, 314
Garnett, E. S., 189, 320
Garren, L. R., 193, 320
Garren, M., 193, 320
Gaudin, J. M., 226, 339
Gelder, M., 90, 91, 310
Gelder, M. G., 102, 333
Geller, E. S., 32, 320
Gendreau, P., 37, 320

Genuth, S., 189, 320
George, F. E., 264, 310
Gerber, K. E., 15, 320, 336
Gesten, E. L., 32, 320
Gibbons, L. W., 154, 307
Gifford, D., 12, 319
Gifford, J. L., 23, 341
Gilchrist, L. D., 225, 351
Ginsberg, D., 205, 322
Giordano, F., 193, 320
Glanz, K., 171, 172, 320
Glasgow, R. E., 171, 172, 320
Glass, C. R., 56, 320
Glass, G., 263, 331
Glass, G. V., 60, 97, 278, 345
Gleser, G. C., 45, 305
Glynn, T., 243, 254, 320
Gochneaur, K., 110, 343
Gold, R. G., 45, 334
Goldberg, M., 47, 318
Goldfried, M. R., 272, 275, 276, 278, 279, 280, 282, 285, 298, 306, 313, 320
Goldiamond, I., 5, 321
Goldman, L., 140, 321
Goldstein, I. B., 155, 321
Goodbody, R. A., 189, 320
Goodrick, G. K., 222, 318
Goodyear, N. N., 154, 307
Gordon, J. R., 218, 332
Gordon, W., 21, 337
Gorman, J. M., 87, 96, 328, 331
Gotestam, K. G., 192, 337
Gotlib, I. H., 50, 52, 321
Gottlieb, J., 18, 321
Gotto, A. M., 172, 222, 318
Gotto, A. M., Jr., 147, 191, 318, 344
Gould, D., 79, 350
Graber, R. A., 219, 321
Gradel, K., 246, 315
Graham, J., 51, 310
Gratto, C., 33, 308
Gravender, J., 33, 308
Gray, M., 40, 321
Graziano, W., 233, 340
Green, L., 32, 37, 321, 353
Green, L. W., 171, 307

AUTHOR INDEX

Greene, B. F., 252, 305, 348
Greenwood, C. R., 263, 321
Gresham, F. M., 50, 254, 353
Gretter, M. L., 61, 336
Griest, D. L., 229, 321
Griffiths, R. R., 192, 307
Gross, J., 45, 321
Grove, W. M., 61, 66, 67, 128, 327
Gruenberg, D. L., 143, 321
Guarnieri, P., 68, 307

Haaga, D., 275, 321
Haaga, D. A. F., 115, 321
Haas, J. R., 2, 67, 321, 322
Hackett, T. P., 160, 314
Hahlweg, K., 11, 306
Halford, W. K., 132, 321
Hall, G. C., 48, 321
Hall, S. M., 205, 207, 322
Hall, W., 154, 332
Hallinan, P. C., 241, 329
Halpin, G., 259, 345
Hamblin, D., 110, 343
Hammen, C., 52, 322
Hammen, C. L., 50, 61, 105, 327
Handleman, J. S., 245, 322
Hann, D. M., 5, 350
Harackiewicz, J. M., 133, 322
Harboe, H., 193, 336
Harford, T., 213, 351
Harris, R. C., 8, 348
Harris, S. L., 227, 245, 322
Hartlage, L. C., 9, 42, 322
Hartsough, D. M., 45, 308
Hatch, J. P., 155, 322
Hatziandreu, E. J., 201, 339
Haugaard, J. J., 248, 322
Hawkins, R. P., 43, 260, 354
Hayashida, M., 223, 322
Hayes, B., 132, 322
Hayes, S. C., 2, 67, 275, 286, 287, 287n, 288, 289, 297, 321, 322
Haynes, M. R., 154, 308
Haynes, S. G., 159, 322, 323
Hays, R. C., 45, 55, 56, 59, 327

Heffer, R. W., 231, 323
Heiby, E. M., 17, 323
Heimberg, R. G., 53, 54, 56, 87, 314, 323
Heller, S. S., 160, 311
Helm, D. T., 235, 329
Hemmings, K. A., 61, 336
Henggeler, S. W., 250, 309, 323
Hennekens, C. H., 154, 323
Herr, S. S., 43, 323
Herrnstein, R. J., 36, 352
Hersen, M., 124, 228, 323, 346
Herskovic, J. E., 206, 341
Hesketh, B., 132, 322
Hester, R. K., 217, 218, 221, 222, 323, 334
Hibbert, G., 90, 91, 310
Hightower, A. D., 46, 353
Hill, R. D., 171, 342
Hilton, M. E., 214, 323
Himmell, C. D., 9, 350
Hirt, M. L., 63, 315
Hjermann, I., 150, 323
Hoekstra, R. J., 119, 315
Hoff, C., 169, 170, 346
Hogan, S., 192, 347
Hoier, T. S., 227, 249, 312, 318, 323
Holahan, C. J., 225, 323
Holland, S., 195, 323
Hollandsworth, R. J., 12, 330
Hollinger, J. D., 268, 324
Hollon, S., 108, 284, 314
Hollon, S. D., 45, 50, 55, 56, 57, 58, 61, 66, 67, 107, 108, 324, 327
Holme, I., 150, 323
Holt, P. E., 98, 99, 324
Holtzworth-Munroe, A., 132, 311
Hood, E., 92, 331
Hope, D. A., 56, 314
Hopkins, B. L., 35, 318, 324
Hops, H., 46, 324
Horan, M. J., 152, 153, 154, 324, 340
Horn, W. F., 243, 324
Horner, R. H., 244, 324
Horowitz, L. M., 45, 324
Horstman, W., 169, 333
Horton, A. M., 9, 350
Hovell, M. F., 153, 324

Howard, A. N., 189, 324
Howard, B., 45, 55, 56, 59, 123, 327
Howard, G. S., 133, 351
Howard, K. I., 66, 342
Hsu, D., 194, 334
Hugdahl, K., 74, 87n, 324
Humphrey, L. L., 46, 324
Hursh, D. E., 226, 335
Hutter, A. M., 160, 314
Hynd, G. W., 125, 346

Ingram, R. E., 45, 50, 53, 55, 56, 61, 121, 122, 324, 327
Innes, J. A., 188, 324
Intrieri, R. C., 12, 330
Ito, C., 195, 333
Iwata, B. A., 7, 336
Izard, C. E., 83, 324

Jackson, A., 79, 350
Jacob, R. G., 155, 325
Jacobson, N. S., 65, 67, 71, 108, 132, 281, 287, 288, 289, 295, 325
James, J. E., 242, 313
Jamison, C., 110, 343
Jarrett, R. B., 292, 351
Jarvik, M. E., 206, 341
Jarvis, M. J., 205, 342
Jason, L. A., 32, 320
Jay, S. M., 134, 325
Jeffery, R. W., 171, 172, 197, 199, 325, 353
Jenkins, C. D., 158, 159, 160, 309, 325
Jenkins, J. O., 249, 314
Jenkins, V., 268, 333
Jerrom, D., 94, 339
Jesness, C. F., 37, 325
Johnsen, B. H., 87n, 324
Johnson, J. H., 244, 343
Johnson, P. L., 231, 325
Johnson, S. B., 49, 325
Johnston, D. W., 102, 333
Johnston, J. C., 226, 345
Johnston, L. D., 214, 215, 216, 325
Jones, M. L., 24, 325

Jones, P. H., 191, 344
Jones, R. T., 205, 207, 322
Jorendy, D., 74, 344
Joseph, J. G., 169, 170, 306, 326

Kagan, A., 160, 312
Kagan, J., 83, 324
Kagel, J. H., 32, 321
Kahana, E. F., 42, 326
Kaliszak, J. E., 192, 307
Kamarck, T. W., 207, 326
Kane, M., 123, 328
Kannel, W., 153, 326
Kannel, W. B., 159, 323
Kantor, J. R., 6, 326
Kaplan, S. J., 2, 67, 326
Kaslow, N. J., 109, 340
Katz, E., 134, 325
Katz, R. C., 227, 345
Kauffman, J., 258, 316
Kaufmann, P. G., 155, 326
Kavanagh, D. J., 79, 326
Kazdin, A. E., 1, 50, 65, 124, 126, 127, 128, 129, 228, 279, 280, 292, 326, 327, 346
Keenan, V., 234, 347
Kelley, M. L., 231, 323
Kellum, J. M., 195, 328
Kelly, J. A., 168, 326
Kelly, P. A., 227, 347
Kenardy, J., 99, 326
Kendall, P. C., 3, 44, 45, 46, 47, 49, 50, 51, 52, 53, 55, 56, 57, 58, 59, 60, 61, 64, 65, 66, 67, 70, 71, 103, 107, 108, 112, 113, 114, 118, 120, 121, 122, 123, 126, 127, 128, 129, 130, 131, 133, 135, 136, 317, 324, 326, 327, 328, 350
Kern, W. H., 195, 338
Kerr, M. M., 267, 328
Kessler, R. C., 169, 316
Khramelashvili, V. V., 155, 307
Kiesler, C. A., 226, 328
Kilmann, P. R., 135, 304
Kindermann, T., 41, 305

AUTHOR INDEX

King, N., 42, 306
King, N. J., 14, 338
Kinney, P. J., 78, 351
Kipnis, D., 7, 328
Kirby, D. F., 195, 328
Kirn, T. F., 211, 328
Kirshenbaum, S., 82, 303
Kittel, F., 159, 314
Kiyak, H. A., 42, 326
Klajner, F., 218, 340
Klatsky, A. L., 154, 319
Kleifield, E., 77, 285, 351
Klein, D. F., 87, 96, 97, 331, 354
Klerman, G. L., 222, 223, 283, 284, 291, 292, 294, 328
Klesges, R. C., 171, 328
Klimes, I., 90, 91, 310
Klotz, M. L., 63, 351
Kneedler, R. D., 266, 328
Knowles, M., 13, 330
Koegel, R. L., 244, 245, 247, 324, 329, 343
Koeppl, G., 227, 340
Kohlenberg, R. J., 278, 289, 290, 329
Kohr, M. A., 241, 329
Kondo, A., 191, 344
Kornitzer, M., 159, 160, 329
Koverola, C., 251, 353
Kozak, M. J., 122, 126, 318
Kozloff, M. A., 235, 236, 246, 329
Kozlowski, L. T., 202, 329
Kraemer, H. C., 155, 303
Kramer, F. M., 199, 200, 329
Krantz, D. S., 160, 329
Krasner, L., 3, 39, 298, 313, 337
Kratochwill, T. R., 123, 254, 255, 304, 335
Krey, S., 199, 338
Krown, S., 169, 344
Kuhn, T. S., 3, 225, 329
Kuiper, N., 277, 314
Kuiper, N. A., 105, 329, 337
Kurdek, L. A., 45, 329
Kurtz, R., 272, 320

Labs, S. M., 45, 329
Lahey, B. B., 125, 266, 311, 346

Lalongo, N., 243, 324
Laman, C., 160, 342
Lambert, M. E., 11, 12, 329, 330
Landesman, S., 20, 330
Landesman-Dwyer, S., 13, 330
Lando, H. A., 210, 330
Lane, T. W., 263, 330
Lang, P. J., 48, 330
Langford, H. G., 154, 330
Langlotz, M., 11, 306
Lanza, E., 166, 310
Larkin, K., 48, 348
LaRocca, N. G., 134, 318
Larsen, K. H., 56, 320
Last, C., 123, 124, 346
Last, C. G., 124, 346
Lattimore, J., 24, 325
Laude, R., 91, 306
Lavi, B., 9, 336
Laws, H. L., 195, 330
Lazarus, A. A., 2, 9, 115, 116, 273, 274, 275, 278, 280, 281, 282, 286, 287, 292, 330
Lazarus, R. S., 82, 85, 100, 114, 330
Lease, C., 123, 124, 346
Lechner, G. W., 195, 330
Leinbach, A., 135, 334
Leitenberg, H., 45, 321
Lennon, S. J., 34, 330
Lentz, R. J., 27, 338
Leo, G. I., 218, 340
Leren, P., 150, 323
Leventhal, H., 17, 18, 331
Levin, A. P., 88, 331
Levin, H., 263, 331
Levine, P., 269, 336
Levine, S., 132, 159, 303
Levis, D. J., 75, 295, 296, 331
Levitt, K., 99, 309
Levy, R. L., 16, 331
Lewinsohn, P. M., 109, 110, 292, 331, 354
Ley, P., 14, 331
Liberman, R. P., 291, 331
Lichtenstein, E., 79, 207, 312, 326
Liebowitz, M. R., 87, 88, 331
Liebschutz, J., 190, 350

Liebson, I., 192, 307
Lignugaris-Kraft, B., 25, 26, 333, 342
Likins, M., 25, 342
Lindholm, L., 285, 352
Lindsay, W., 92, 331
Linn, M. W., 45, 331
Linner, J. H., 195, 331
Lipid Research Clinics Program, 143, 150, 331
Lipovsky, J. A., 124, 317
Litt, M. D., 15, 348
Locke, E. A., 5, 331
Lokey, L., 219, 342
Long, J. D., 10, 351
Lopatka, C., 99, 339
Lopez, F. G., 9, 350
Losch, M., 298, 341
Luborsky, L., 280, 286, 295, 331, 332
Lui, K. J., 168, 332
Lumry, A., 58, 324
Lutzker, J. R., 252, 305, 332, 348
Lyddon, W. J., 112, 332
Lynch, M. E., 189, 307
Lytle, R., 125, 308

MacCuish, A. C., 188, 332
MacDonald, G. J., 154, 332
MacDonald, K. R., 219, 342
MacDonald, M. R., 105, 329
MacGregor, G. A., 153, 332
MacMahon, S. W., 154, 332
Madonna, M. R., 14, 307
Maher, C. A., 254, 332
Mahoney, M. J., 6, 112, 113, 114, 309, 332
Malloy, P. F., 296, 331
Malouf, J. M., 45, 332
Maltzman, I., 215, 332
Maltzman, I. M., 215, 338
Manion, I., 251, 353
Manninen, V., 147, 332
Manos, M. J., 39, 336
Margraf, J., 97, 315
Markman, H., 47, 317
Marks, I., 77, 79, 80, 87, 100, 332

Marlatt, G. A., 102, 218, 314, 332
Martens, B. K., 2, 268, 332
Martin, E. W., 195, 337
Martin, I., 2, 316, 333
Marzillier, J. S., 296, 333
Maser, J. D., 96, 100, 297, 339
Mason, E. E., 195, 333
Mastropieri, M., 268, 344
Mastropieri, M. I., 268, 333
Matarazzo, J., 176, 333
Mathews, A., 92, 93, 94, 102, 125, 308
Mathews, A. M., 125, 295, 308, 333
Mathews, R. M., 29, 344
Matson, J. L., 235, 266, 333
Mattick, R., 88, 333
Mauderlink, G., 133, 322
Mayer, G. R., 254, 258, 264, 333, 347
McCaffrey, R. J., 154, 333
McCann, K. L., 198, 338
McCann, U., 293, 303
McCauley, E., 54, 333
McClannahan, L. E., 29, 333
McConaughy, E. K., 25, 342
McCormick, P. M., 37, 325
McCuller, G. L., 25, 26, 333, 342
McEvoy, M. A., 268, 333
McFall, R. M., 45, 350
McKelvain, R., 160, 342
McKusick, L., 169, 170, 312, 333
McKusker, J., 169, 333
McLaughlin, E., 92, 331
McLean Baird, I., 189, 324
McLeer, S., 128, 328
McLellarn, R., 119, 350
McLellarn, R. W., 117, 350
McLeroy, K. R., 171, 307
McMahon, R. J., 238, 244, 310, 318
McNamara, J. R., 10, 11, 334
McNamara, P., 153, 326
McNeil, D. W., 48, 313
Meadows, N., 269, 336
Meelheim, D., 195, 339
Meese, R. L., 266, 328
Mefford, I. N., 79, 305
Meichenbaum, D., 122, 133, 296, 297, 334
Meisel, C. J., 267, 334

AUTHOR INDEX

Meister, G., 263, 331
Melamed, B. G., 48, 49, 325
Meller, P. J., 268, 332
Melton, G. B., 254, 313
Mendlowitz, D. R., 227, 347
Mendoza, J. L., 65, 312
Mentis, M., 245, 329
Merckelbach, H., 87, 334
Merluzzi, T. V., 56, 320
Merrett, F., 254, 255, 334, 351
Mersch, P., 87, 334
Meshkinpour, H., 194, 334
Mesibov, G. B., 244, 343
Messer, S. B., 272, 304
Messmer, J. M., 195, 328
Meunier, G. F., 39, 334
Michela, J. L., 132, 334
Michelson, L., 58, 59, 72, 334, 343
Miller, I. W., 45, 334
Miller, S. M., 135, 334
Miller, S. T., 154, 308
Miller, T., 97, 278, 345
Miller, W. R., 217, 218, 219, 221, 222, 321, 323, 354
Miller-Perrin, C. L., 249, 334
Mills, D. L., 247, 343
Mills, P. R., 195, 328
Mills, R. S. L., 124, 341
Milne, D., 12, 13, 334, 347
Milner, J. S., 45, 334
Mischel, W., 278, 335
Mitchell, J., 293, 335
Mitchell, J. R., 54, 333
Mitchell, M., 95, 339
Mitchell, R. E., 147, 318
Montgomery, S., 169, 316
Moore, T. J., 151, 335
Morin, S. F., 169, 312
Morris, E. K., 7, 36, 38, 226, 335, 348
Morris, R. J., 123, 335
Mosher-Ashley, P. M., 40, 335
Moss, A. J., 160, 311
Moss, S., 54, 333
Mowrer, O. H., 296, 335
Muir, K. A., 268, 332
Mullen, K. D., 171, 307

Muller, J. D., 193, 335
Mundy, M., 90, 310
Munoz, R., 110, 331
Munoz, R. F., 109, 354
Munro, J. F., 188, 332
Murakami, J., 263, 330
Murphy, G., 293, 345
Murphy, G. C., 254, 335
Myers, J. K., 96, 335

Nafpaktitis, M., 264, 333
Nathan, P. E., 215, 222, 335
National Center for Health Statistics, 140, 141, 142, 143, 162, 168, 179, 180, 335
National Commission on Excellence in Education, 263, 335
National Institute on Alcohol Abuse and Alcoholism, Alcohol Epidemiologic Data System, 214, 335
National Research Council, 186, 336
Neef, N. A., 7, 237, 241, 329, 336
Neel, R. S., 269, 336
Neff, D., 68, 307
Nehemkis, A. M., 15, 16, 313, 320, 336
Nelson, G. M., 48, 321
Nelson, R., 125, 308
Nerenz, D. R., 18, 331
Nevid, J. S., 9, 10, 336
Newman, F. I., 66, 342
Newton, T., 12, 347
Nezu, A. M., 135, 136, 198, 336
Nezu, C. M., 135, 336
Nieben, O., 193, 336
Nietzel, M. T., 61, 66, 67, 336
Nisbett, R., 79, 336
Noble, J., 213, 214, 351
Norcross, J. C., 9, 272, 273, 280, 306, 336
Norman, W. H., 45, 334
Norton-Ford, J. D., 65, 66, 328
Norusis, M., 160, 344
Norwood, B. D., 211, 314
Novotny, T. E., 201, 339
Nowlin, W. F., 133, 351
Nunn, L. B., 219, 319

O'Brien, R. M., 191, 313
Ochsner, A., 193, 314
O'dell, S. L., 12, 336
Odom, S. L., 268, 333
O'Donnell, C. R., 39, 336
O'Donohue, W., 36, 337
Oei, T., 99, 326
O'Farrell, T., 47, 318
Office of the Assistant Secretary of Health, 168, 337
Office of Medical Applications of Research, National Institutes of Health, 143, 337
Ohman, A., 87, 87n, 337
O'Leary, A., 79, 337
O'Leary, K. D., 107, 231, 260, 282, 325, 337
O'Leary, S. G., 260, 337
Olinger, L. J., 105, 329, 337
Ollendick, T. H., 123, 337
O'Malley, P. M., 214, 216, 325
O'Neill, J., 21, 337
O'Neill, R. E., 247, 343
Onorato, V. A., 17, 323
Osguthorpe, R. T., 268, 344
Osnes, P. G., 70, 108, 244, 346
Ost, L., 80, 101, 102, 192, 337
Ostrow, D., 169, 170, 346
O'Sullivan, G., 100, 332
Owen, V. E., 269, 316
Ozer, E. M., 81, 337

Pace, W. G., 195, 337
Paffenbarger, R. S., Jr., 154, 337
Page, T. J., 7, 336
Paine, S. C., 38, 337
Parker, D., 213, 351
Parloff, M. B., 10, 338
Parrish, J. M., 237, 241, 336
Patrusheva, I. F., 155, 303
Patterson, G., 46, 324
Patterson, G. R., 36, 229, 242, 305, 338
Patti, E. T., 198, 338
Paul, G. L., 27, 280, 338
Pavlou, K. N., 199, 338

Payne, J. H., 195, 338
Peake, P., 278, 335
Pechacek, T. F., 210, 338
Peck, C., 14, 338
Peer, D. F., 77, 352
Pellegrini, D., 135, 338
Pelosi, N., 168, 338
Pendery, M. L., 215, 338
Peradotto, D., 243, 324
Percival, M. L., 193, 338
Perkins, D., 215, 310
Perri, M. G., 135, 136, 198, 336, 338
Perry, N. W., 299, 338
Peters, L., 88, 333
Peterson, C., 53, 132, 338, 339
Peterson, D. R., 299, 339
Peto, R., 165, 314
Phillips, E. A., 30, 339
Phillips, E. L., 30, 339
Piantadosi, S., 195, 330
Pierce, J. P., 201, 339
Pieters, R. S. M., 34, 339
Plas, J. M., 227, 256, 339
Platt, J., 127, 346
Plotzker, R., 193, 320
Polansky, N. A., 226, 339
Polster, S. A., 189, 313
Ponzoha, C., 119, 350
Popovich, S., 243, 324
Pories, W. J., 195, 339
Powell, G. J., 248, 354
Power, K. G., 94, 339
Power, T. J., 227, 339
Powers, M. D., 225, 256, 339
Primavera, L. H., 9, 336
Prochaska, J. O., 9, 336
Proctor, W. C., 48, 321
Prue, D. M., 219, 342
Pullan, B. R., 193, 348

Rabin, A. S., 109, 340
Rabkin, J. G., 96, 328
Rachlin, H., 3, 339
Rachman, S., 72, 76, 83, 96, 97, 99, 100, 296, 297, 314, 339

AUTHOR INDEX

Rachman, S. J., 83, 280, 313, 352
Ramp, K. A., 36, 353
Ramsey, E., 230, 339
Rapee, R. M., 91, 339
Raps, C. S., 53, 339
Rasenick-Dous, L., 211, 303
Reber, M., 128, 328
Reed, D., 160, 312
Reeves, R. S., 147, 340
Rehm, L. P., 109, 340
Reid, D. H., 13, 340
Reid, J. B., 229, 338
Reid, J. R., 36, 242, 305
Reimers, T. M., 227, 340
Reinhard, K. E., 53, 339
Reisenzein, R., 41, 305
Remington, B., 37, 340
Remington, M., 37, 340
Repp, A. C., 21, 317
Reppucci, N. D., 248, 322
Rescorla, R. A., 3, 73, 74, 75, 340
Revenstorf, D., 65, 325
Reynolds, W. M., 111, 340
Reznikoff, M., 134, 318
Rice, J. M., 252, 332
Richards, A. M., 153, 340
Richardson, F., 90, 347
Richardson, R. A., 253, 310
Rickard, K. M., 233, 340
Riley, D. M., 218, 340
Rimland, B., 244, 340
Rincover, A., 297, 322
Riskind, J. H., 53, 54, 306, 340
Risley, T. R., 24, 325
Robben, H. S. J., 34, 349
Robin, A. L., 46, 340
Robins, L., 126, 340
Roccella, E. J., 152, 153, 154, 324, 340
Rodichok, L. D., 68, 307
Rodin, J., 192, 340
Roehling, P. V., 46, 340
Rogers, C. R., 92, 340
Rohrbeck, C. A., 45, 46, 260, 304, 316
Romanczyk, R. G., 235, 340
Ronan, K., 128, 328
Rook, K. S., 41, 340

Rorer, L. G., 112, 341
Rose, J. E., 206, 341
Rose, K. D., 206, 341
Rosen, J. C., 45, 321
Rosen, R. C., 298, 341
Rosenberg, S. E., 45, 324
Rosenfarb, I. S., 2, 321, 341
Rosenhamer, G., 151, 311
Rosenman, R. H., 158, 159, 160, 309, 319, 325, 341
Rosenthal, R., 62, 344
Ross, A. O., 2, 43, 297, 297n, 341
Ross, D. C., 97, 328, 354
Ross, L., 79, 336
Ross, R. R., 37, 320
Rossiter, E., 285, 298, 341
Rotgers, F., 3, 317, 341
Roth, W., 97, 315
Roth, W. T., 97, 293, 348
Rothbaum, B. O., 122, 318
Rounsaville, B., 283, 328
Rowan, V. C., 99, 353
Ruben, D. H., 6, 341
Rubin, K. H., 124, 341
Rugg, D., 205, 207, 322
Ruggiero, L., 50, 311
Runcie, J., 189, 341
Rusch, F. R., 22, 23, 311, 341
Rush, A. J., 60, 104, 292, 306, 351
Russell, G. F. M., 294, 341
Russell, M. A. H., 205, 342
Russell, R. L., 61, 336
Russo, D. C., 2, 4, 5, 342
Rutherford, G. W., III, 168, 332
Rutter, M., 259, 342
Rychtarik, R. G., 219, 319, 342

Saba, G., 294, 343
Safran, J., 272, 275, 276, 278, 279, 282, 285, 320
Salenko, B. B., 155, 303
Sallis, J. F., 171, 342
Salovey, P., 15, 348
Salzberg, C. L., 25, 26, 333, 342
Sambhi, M. P., 155, 321
Sanchez-Craig, M., 219, 342

Sandberg, S., 259, 342
Sanders, M. R., 132, 230, 231, 242, 313, 321
Sarason, I. G., 122, 342
Sass, L. A., 112, 353
Sato, R. A., 17, 323
Saudargas, R. A., 258, 345
Saunders, S. M., 66, 67, 342
Sausone, C., 133, 322
Savelle, S., 229, 318
Schachar, R., 259, 342
Schaughency, E. A., 266, 333
Schechter, M. T., 169, 342
Scheinberg, L. C., 134, 318
Schepis, M. M., 13, 340
Scherwitz, L., 160, 342
Scheuer, A. D., 227, 316
Schiers, W., 12, 319
Schilling, R. F., 228, 342
Schindler, L., 11, 306
Schinke, S. P., 225, 228, 342, 351
Schmaling, K. B., 132, 311
Schmid, T. L., 171, 325
Schmid, U., 41, 305
Schnaitter, R., 4, 342
Schneider, J. A., 155, 303
Schneier, F. R., 88, 331
Schonhorn, R., 21, 337
Schopler, E., 244, 343
Schotte, D. E., 136, 343
Schreibman, L., 244, 247, 343
Schroeder, H. E., 63, 315
Schucker, B., 144, 343
Schulman, C. L., 189, 313
Schunk, D. H., 261, 343
Schutte, N. S., 45, 332
Schwab, C. E., 195, 338
Schwartz, G. E., 3, 343
Schwartz, H. J., 294, 343
Schwartz, J. L., 204, 206, 207, 209, 343
Schwartz, R. C., 244, 294, 343
Schwartz, R. M., 58, 59, 60, 343
Schwartz, S., 230, 231, 313, 343
Schwarz, S. P., 67, 308
Scogin, F., 110, 343
Scotch, N., 159, 323

Scott, H. W., 195, 343
Scott, K., 8, 308
Scott, L. W., 147, 172, 318
Scott, M. J., 236, 344
Scott, T., 219, 342
Scruggs, T. E., 268, 333, 344
Secretary of Health and Human Services, 213, 344
Seekins, T., 29, 38, 317, 344
Seewald-Klein, T. S., 171, 172, 320
Segal, Z., 105, 344
Seligman, M., 53, 339
Seligman, M. E. P., 87, 100, 344
Sempos, C., 145, 344
Shafer, M. S., 25, 344
Shapiro, D., 63, 344
Shapiro, D. A., 63, 108, 344, 346
Shapiro, D. S., 155, 321
Shaw, B., 105, 344
Shaw, B. F., 60, 104, 105, 107, 108, 109, 306, 314, 337
Shekelle, R. B., 160, 344
Sheldon, J., 38, 344
Sheridan, E. P., 177, 344
Sherman, J., 74, 344
Shoham-Salomon, V., 62, 344
Shure, M., 127, 346
Siegel, K., 169, 344
Siegel, S. E., 134, 325
Siegelaub, A. B., 154, 319
Sikand, G., 191, 344
Silberstein, L. R., 192, 340
Simkin, J., 275, 354
Simon, D. J., 226, 345
Simons, A. D., 293, 345
Simpson, R., 94, 339
Simpson, R. G., 259, 345
Singer, B., 280, 332
Singh, N. N., 227, 345
Siqueland, L., 123, 328
Skinner, B. F., 2, 287, 345
Skinner, J., 153, 326
Skinner-Smith, J. D., 14, 307
Skinstad, A. H., 222, 335
Skolnick, A. S., 46, 345
Skolnick, J. H., 46, 345

AUTHOR INDEX

Skrtic, T. M., 266, 345
Skutle, A., 219, 345
Slate, J. R., 258, 345
Sloan, M. E., 237, 336
Smith, D., 293, 352
Smith, E. M., 57, 304
Smith, J., 267, 345
Smith, M. J., 35, 324
Smith, M. L., 60, 97, 278, 280, 281, 292, 345
Smith, R., 188, 314
Smith, R. J., 162, 304
Smith, T., 272, 273, 345
Snell, M. K., 199, 329
Snyder, D. K., 108, 345, 352
Sobell, L. C., 212, 215, 217, 218, 222, 345
Sobell, M. B., 212, 215, 217, 218, 345
Society of Behavioral Medicine, 138, 346
Solnick, J. V., 297, 322
Solomon, P., 28, 346
Southam, M. A., 155, 303
Spearly, J. L., 225, 323
Spencer, I. O. B., 189, 346
Spivack, G., 127, 346
Spring, B., 74, 346
Spry, K. M., 269, 316
St. Lawrence, J. S., 168, 326
Staats, A. W., 3, 227, 346
Stall, R. D., 169, 170, 346
Starkey, J. V., 195, 347
Steele, D. J., 18, 331
Steer, R. A., 45, 51, 54, 306
Steffee, W. P., 199, 338
Stern, W. R., 193, 319
Stiles, W. B., 108, 346
Stinson, F., 213, 214, 351
Stinson, F. S., 213, 351
Stokes, T. F., 70, 108, 244, 346
Stone, G. C., 176, 177, 346
Stoneman, Z., 234, 350
Stradling, S. G., 236, 344
Strauss, C. C., 123, 124, 346
Strickland, B. R., 176, 346
Strupp, H. H., 281, 282, 292, 347
Stuart, R. B., 7, 314
Stumphauzer, J. S., 37, 347

Stunkard, A. J., 189, 190, 191, 192, 294, 309, 313, 347, 349, 350
Sturmey, P., 12, 347
Subcommittee on Definition and Prevalence of the 1984 Joint National Committee, 151, 347
Suelzle, M., 234, 347
Sugerman, H. J., 195, 196, 328, 347
Suinn, R. M., 90, 122, 347
Sullivan, A. C., 192, 347, 348
Sulzer-Azaroff, B., 35, 254, 258, 261, 264, 317, 347
Summers, J. A., 228, 348
Swan, G. E., 155, 158, 341
Swanson, V., 95, 339
Sweell, R. G., 8, 308
Sweet, D. M., 169, 348
Swets, J. A., 174, 175, 176, 315
Syme, S. L., 40, 160, 307
Szmukler, G. I., 294, 341

Tarler-Benlolo, L., 12, 336
Tarnowski, K. J., 227, 347
Tawney, J. W., 267, 345
Taylor, C. B., 72, 79, 82, 89, 97, 98, 99, 100, 293, 347, 348
Taylor, S. B., 155, 303
Taylor, T. V., 193, 348
Teasdale, J., 105, 348
Telch, C., 82, 348
Telch, M., 298, 341
Telch, M. J., 82, 96, 97, 293, 348
Tellegen, A., 51, 310
Temoshok, L., 169, 348
Tennen, H., 132, 303
Terborg, J. R., 171, 172, 320, 348
Tertinger, D. A., 252, 348
Tetirick, T., 195, 337
Thananopavaren, C., 155, 321
Thomas, F. T., 195, 339
Thompson, J. K., 108, 312
Thompson, L. W., 110, 111, 348
Thompson, T. J., 189, 341
Thompson-Skinner, M. F., 14, 307
Thorne, M. C., 154, 337

Thurman, S. K., 24, 348
Thyer, B. A., 300, 348
Tiffany, S. T., 207, 309, 348
Todd, J. T., 7, 348
Tolfa Veit, D., 268, 344
Toneatto, A., 218, 345
Tonnesen, P., 205, 348
Trilling, Y., 206, 341
Triscari, J., 192, 347, 348
Trull, J. J., 66, 67, 336
Tsai, M., 278, 289, 290, 329
Tunstall, C., 205, 207, 322
Turk, D. C., 15, 348
Turkat, I. D., 8, 348
Turnball, A. P., 228, 348
Turner, S., 48, 348
Turner, S. M., 4, 77, 124, 306, 352
Turvey, A. A., 94, 315
Tuttle, M., 33, 308
Tye, J. B., 211, 303, 314

Ulicny, G. R., 24, 325
Unis, A., 126, 326
Urbain, E. S., 136, 338
Ureno, G., 45, 324
U.S. Department of Health and Human Services, 138, 141, 142, 144, 145, 146, 149, 150, 152, 156, 157, 163, 164, 165, 166, 167, 180, 184, 185, 202, 203, 204, 206, 210, 214, 349
U.S. Public Health Service, 156, 349

Van den Bergh, O., 74, 304
Vandenbos, G. R., 279, 292, 349
Van den Hout, M., 87, 334
van Griensven, G. J. P., 169, 349
Van Hasselt, V. B., 228, 323
Van Hout, W., 87, 334
van Raaij, W. F., 34, 349
VanRij, A. M., 195, 339
Vargas, M., 133, 351
Verhallen, T. M. M., 34, 339, 349
Vermilyea, J. A., 54, 323
Villasenor, V. S., 45, 324

Virtulano, L. A., 49, 351
Visser, S., 119, 315
Voeltz, L. M., 23, 227, 349
Vondra, J., 252, 306
Vye, C. S., 113, 309

Wachtel, P., 122, 272, 349
Wacker, D. P., 227, 266, 340, 349
Wadden, T. A., 189, 190, 192, 309, 349, 350
Wade, C., 160, 305
Wagner, A., 192, 340
Wagner, B. M., 45, 131, 312
Wahler, R. G., 5, 226, 229, 231, 315, 350
Walker, H. M., 230, 267, 316, 339
Ward, C. I., 45, 350
Ward, M. M., 155, 312
Warren, R., 117, 119, 120, 350
Wascom, A. M., 267, 311
Waskow, E. E., 10, 338
Watkins, C. E., 9, 350
Watkins, J. D., 169, 170, 350
Watson, D., 49, 52, 121, 135, 328, 350
Weber, J. L., 234, 350
Webitt, W., 193, 320
Webster, J., 9, 350
Wedding, D., 9, 42, 350
Wedge, R. F., 37, 325
Weed, K. A., 269, 316
Weinberg, R. S., 79, 350
Weiss, B., 63, 351
Weiss, R., 47, 324
Weissberg, R. P., 135, 350
Weissman, M., 283, 328
Weisman, M. M., 292, 351
Weisz, J. R., 63, 64, 351
Wells, J. K., 133, 134, 135, 351
Wells, K. C., 49, 229, 321, 351
Werry, J. S., 49, 351
West, L. J., 215, 338
Westen, D., 276, 277, 351
Westling, H., 204, 351
Whelan, J. P., 250, 309
Wheldall, K., 254, 255, 334, 351
White, D., 23, 341

AUTHOR INDEX

White, M. A., 260, 351
Whittaker, J. K., 225, 226, 351
"Who Needs," 194, 351
Wicker, R., 154, 308
Wigley, V., 254, 306
Wilcox, B., 38, 337
Wilcox, B. L., 225, 323
Wilcox, L. E., 46, 129, 328
Wiley, J. A., 170, 346
Wilkinson, D. A., 218, 345
Will, M. C., 266, 351
Williams, G. D., 213, 214, 351
Williams, L. M., 249, 317
Williams, R. B., Jr., 161, 351
Williams, R. L., 10, 351
Williams, S. L., 76, 77, 78, 79, 80, 83, 305, 351, 352
Willmuth, M. E., 45, 321
Wills, J., 46, 324
Wills, R. M., 108, 345, 352
Wilson, G. T., 60, 72, 76, 77, 80, 96, 97, 102, 120, 122, 271, 274, 275, 276, 278, 280, 281, 282, 283, 285, 286, 291, 292, 293, 296, 297, 319, 326, 337, 352
Wilson, J. Q., 36, 352
Wilson, P. H., 79, 326
Wimberley, R. C., 45, 334
Wing, A. L., 154, 337
Wing, R. R., 197, 353
Wisnicki, K. S., 45, 55, 56, 324
Witt, J. C., 2, 227, 254, 261, 332, 353
Woerner, M. G., 97, 354
Wolf, M. M., 30, 36, 65, 309, 339, 353
Wolfe, B. E., 10, 338

Wolfe, D. A., 248, 251, 353
Wolpe, J., 7, 73, 99, 122, 297, 353
Wong, S. L., 189, 307
Wood, G., 37, 353
Wood, J. R. A., 236, 353
Wood, J. V., 132, 334
Wood, P. D., 145, 353
Wood, R. E., 79, 353
Woodhouse, M. A., 189, 320
Woolfolk, R. L., 3, 112, 353
Work, W. C., 46, 353
Wurtele, S. K., 45, 249, 329, 334
Wyatt, G. E., 248, 354
Wyatt, W. J., 43, 260, 354
Wyatt v. Stickney, 24, 354

Yontef, G., 275, 354
Young, M. L., 37, 325
Youngren, M. A., 110, 331
Yule, W., 254, 306
Yurenev, A. P., 155, 303

Zaitsev, V. P., 155, 303
Zajonc, R. B., 83, 324
Zane, G., 80, 352
Zeiss, A., 110, 331
Zeiss, A. M., 109, 354
Zich, J., 169, 348
Ziegler, D. J., 122, 354
Zimmerman, M., 45, 354
Zitrin, C. M., 97, 354
Zuriff, G. E., 4, 354
Zyzanski, S. J., 159, 160, 325

SUBJECT INDEX

Abstinence from drinking, 218-222
Achievement Place model, 35, 36
Addictive disorders, 178-224
Adolescent Perceived Events Scale, 45
Adolescents, 225-270
  cognitive therapy, 111
  interventions, meta analysis, 63, 64
  school settings, delinquency, 263-265
"Adulto-centric" bias, 250
Affective therapy, 85, 86
Age factors, cognitive therapy, 64
Aged
  cognitive therapy, depression, 109-111
  overview, 39-42
Aggression, 128
Agoraphobia
  attribution specificity, 53, 54
  fear reduction methods, 73
  models, 95-100
  pharmacotherapy, 88, 89, 293
  psychophysiology, 48
  self-efficacy theory, 80-83
AIDS, 166-171
Alcohol intake
  and cancer, 165, 166
  and hypertension, 154
Alcoholism, 212-224
  behavioral treatment, 217-222
  controlled drinking, 215-222
  prevalence, 213-215
Alprazolam, 88, 109, 110
Anticipatory anxiety, 82, 83

Antidepressant drugs, 293
Antisocial behavior
  adolescents, 126-131
  family management program, 242
  overview, 35-39
  systems aspects, family, 230, 231
Anxiety (see also Anxiety disorders)
  in children, 122-125
  cognitive component, 82, 85, 86, 120-122
  definition, 84
  depression relationship, 49-55, 124
  developmental differences, 123, 124
  self-efficacy theory, 78-86
  theories, 73-86
  treatment, 72-102, 120-126
Anxiety and Depression (Kendall & Watson), 49
Anxiety and Its Disorders (Barlow), 72, 83
Anxiety and Stress Disorders (Michelson & Ascher), 72
Anxiety disorders (see also Agoraphobia; Panic)
  assessment, 49-55
  attribution specificity, 53-55, 133
  in children, 122-125
  cognitive assessment, 56, 57
  cognitive component, 82, 85, 86
  depression relationship, 49-55, 124
  fear reduction methods, 72-102, 120-126

SUBJECT INDEX

models, 95–100
psychophysiology, 48, 49
symptoms, 50
Anxiety management training
 evaluation, 90–93
 versus nondirective counseling, 92, 93
Anxious apprehension, 83–86
Anxious Self-Statements Questionnaire, 45, 56, 57
Applied relaxation, 101, 102
Approval rates, teachers, 260
Arden House conference on training, 176, 177
Argumentation approach, 113
Army Research Institute report, 174–176
Arousal
 and panic, 98
 treatment effectiveness role, 131
Aspirin Myocardial Infarction Study, 160
Assessment, 44–71
Association for Advancement of Behavior Therapy, 1–3, 301
Attention deficit disorder, 242
Attitudes
 toward behavior therapy, 8, 9
 toward elderly, staff, 42
 toward mentally retarded, 18–20
Attributions, 131–133
 depression versus anxiety, 53–55, 133
 distressed couples, 131, 132
 functional psychotherapy use, 289, 290
Autism
 motivational variables, 245, 246
 parent training, 246, 247
 sibling training, 247, 248
Automatic processes
 anxiety, 122
 and cognitive model, 100
Automatic Thoughts Questionnaire, 45, 55, 56, 59
Avoidance behavior
 anxiety management effect, 91, 92
 in generalized anxiety disorder, 91
 and self-efficacy, anxiety, 82, 83
Avoidant disorder, children, 123–125

Beck Anxiety Inventory, 45, 51, 52
Beck Depression Inventory, 50
 depression and anxiety, 52
 meta analysis, 61, 62
Behavior Modification, 120
Behavior Problem Checklist, 259
Behavior therapists
 perceptions of patients, 11
 psychotherapy of, 9
 training, 9–12, 298–300
Behavior therapy (*see also* Cognitive-behavioral therapy)
 equivalency issue, 281, 282
 meta analysis, 60–64
 and pharmacotherapy, 88, 89, 94, 95, 109, 110, 292–294
Behavior Therapy, 70
Behavior Therapy with Children and Adolescents (Hersen & Van Hasselt), 228
Behavioral Approaches to Teaching Package, 254
Behavioral assessment, 44–71
Behavioral Assessment, 65
Behavioral consultation, schools, 255
Behavioral medicine, 138–177
Behavioral neuropsychology, 9
Behavioral observation (*see* Observational systems)
Behavioral parent training, 235–244
 autism, 246, 247
 child abuse, 251, 252
 and income level, 231–234
 insular mothers, 231, 232
 marital discord effect on, 229–232
 and meeting attendance, 240, 241
 treatment acceptability, 238
Behavioral Residential Treatment, 27
Behavioral social work, 300
Behavioral supervision model, 13
Behavioral technology, 7
Behaviorism, 4
Behaviour Research and Therapy, 297
Belgian Heart Disease Prevention Trial, 159
Benzodiazepines, 88–90

Bibliotherapy, 110
Biofeedback
  Army Research Institute evaluation, 175
  hypertension, 154, 155
Blacks, 140-142
Blood pressure (*see* Hypertension)
Bortner Rating Scale, 159
Breast cancer, 141, 142
Bulimia nervosa, 284, 285, 293, 294
Business, 32-35

Cancer, 162-166
  and diet, 165, 166
  mortality rates, 140-142, 164
  prevention objectives, 161-163
  and smoking, 164, 165
Cardiovascular arousal, 98
Cardiovascular disease (*see* Heart disease)
CAVE technique, 53
Center for Epidemiological Studies Depression Scale, 52
Chestnut Lodge, 291, 292
Child abuse, 248-253
  ecological model, 250
  versus neglect, 250, 251
  parent support model, 253
  parent training, 251, 252
  social situation model, 250
Child Abuse Potential Questionnaire, 45
Child neglect, 250, 251
Children, 225-270
  anxiety, 122-125
  attributional style, depression, 54
  family relationships, 228-235
  interventions, meta analysis, 63, 64
  systems approaches, 225-228
Children's Beliefs about Parental Divorce Scale, 45
Children's ratings, 240
Cholesterol levels, 143-151
  awareness of, 144
  diet-drug trials, 147-151
  treatment guidelines, 144-147
Cholesterol Lowering Atherosclerosis Study, 151

Cigarette smoking
  addictive aspects, 202, 203
  behavior therapy, 209, 210
  cancer relationship, 164, 165
  community programs, 211, 212
  educational status, 201
  pharmacological treatments, 204-207
  prevalence, 200, 201
  prevention, 156-158
  Surgeon General's report, 202, 203
  trends, 201, 202
  worksite cessation programs, 172
Classical conditioning, 3
  anxiety theory, 73-75
  cognitive processes, 74, 75
  panic model, 99, 100
  theoretical advances, 73-75, 296
Classroom setting (*see* Schools)
Claustrophobic panic, 99
Clinic-referred children, 233, 240
Clinical practice, and research, 295-298
Clinical Psychology Review, 60
Clinical significance, 64-68
Clinically relevant behaviors, 289
Clofibrate, 151
Cognitive ability, 64
Cognitive-affective structure, 277, 296
Cognitive assessment
  anxiety, 56, 57
  depression, 55, 56
  validity of, 57, 58
Cognitive-behavioral therapy, 103-137
  age factors, 64
  anxiety, 72-102, 120-126
  conduct disorder, 126-131
  depression, 104-111
  differentiability, 108
  eclecticism, 272, 273
  equivalency issue, 282
  generalized anxiety, 89-95
  integration of, 275-288
  and interpersonal psychotherapy, 284, 285
  meta analysis, 60-64
  panic disorder, 100-102

SUBJECT INDEX

and pharmacotherapy, 60, 61, 88, 89, 94, 95, 109, 110, 292-294
social phobia, 87-89
trends, 3, 4
Cognitive constructs, 276
Cognitive control, 287
Cognitive processes, 103-137
in anxiety, 121, 122
and arousal, 82, 85, 86
in depression, 104-111
panic model, 97-100
Cognitive Status Examination, 45
Cognitive structures, 277, 296
Cognitive therapy (see Cognitive-behavioral therapy)
Cognitive Therapy and Research, 120
Cognitive Therapy Scale, 109
Cognitive vulnerability, 104-106
Colestipol, 151
Communication Skills Test, 47
Community integration
and deinstitutionalization, 27-32
mentally retarded, 23, 24
Compliance, 14-18
cognitive factors, 14, 15
overview, 14-18
and quality of life, 15
self-regulation model, 18
society's role, 16
Components analysis, 107
Computers, 11, 12
Conditioning theory (see also Classical conditioning)
anxiety, 73-75
cognitive processes, 74, 75
panic attacks, 99, 100
Conduct disorder, 126-131 (see also Antisocial behavior; Delinquency)
in girls, 231
systems aspects, family, 229-231
Conduct Disorders in Childhood and Adolescence (Kazdin), 228
Conners Teacher Rating Scale, 259
Constructivist theory, 114
Consultation, schools, 255
Consumer behavior, 32-35

Consumer satisfaction, 238
Content Analysis of Verbatim Explanations technique, 53
Contextual approach, psychotherapy, 286-288
Contiguity principle, conditioning, 74
Control Your Depression (Lewinsohn et al.), 110
Controllability, and anxiety, 85, 86
Controlled cognitive processes, 100
Controlled drinking
controversy, 215-217
effectiveness, 218-222
Coronary Drug Project, 150
Coronary Primary Prevention Trial, 150
Cost-benefit behavioral model, 34
Costello-Comrey Scales, 52
Council on Scientific Affairs Report, 187, 188
Crime, 35-39
Crisis Call Outcome Rating Scale, 45

Deinstitutionalization
community factors, 27-32
evaluation of, retarded, 21, 22
mentally retarded, 18-27
and noncompliance, 16
Delinquency (see also Antisocial behavior)
behavioral therapy, 126-131
overview, 35-39
school settings, 263-265
Demoralization, and treatment, 91
Depression
and anxiety, 49-55, 124
assessment, 49-55
attribution specificity, 53-55, 133
cognitive assessments, 55, 56
problem-solving training, 135-137
symptoms, 50
Detoxification, 222, 223
Developmental interactionism, 5, 6
Diazepam, 95
Diet, and cancer, 165, 166
Dietary fat, 165, 166

Dietary therapy, cholesterol, 145–151
Diethylpropion, 192
Differentiability of treatment, 108
Disapproval rates, teachers, 260
Distressed couples, attributions, 131, 132
Doctoral programs, 9, 10
Drug abuse, and AIDS, 169, 170
Drug treatment
   and behavior therapy, combination, 292–294
   depression, 109, 110
   generalized anxiety, 94, 95
   meta analysis, 60, 61
   obesity, 191–193
   social phobia, 88, 89
Dysfunctional Attitudes Scale, 105, 106
Dysthymic disorder, 53, 54

Eating Attitudes Test, 45
Eclecticism
   psychotherapy, 272–275
   in training programs, 10
Ecological model
   child abuse, 250, 252
   family, 229
Economics, 32–35
Education, 254–270 (*see also* Schools)
Education for All Handicapped Children Act of *1985*, 234, 235, 266, 267
Elderly (*see* Aged)
Electrodermal responses, 48, 49
Employment, mentally retarded, 25
Empty chair technique, 275
Encoded memories, 296
Environmental programming, 24, 25
Ethics
   in business, 33
   overview, 6, 7
Exercise
   cholesterol levels, 145, 146
   hypertension effect, 154
   and obesity, 199
   and resting metabolic rate, 187
   worksite programs, 173

Exposure technique
   conceptual weaknesses, 75–78
   generalization effects, 78
   generalized anxiety treatment, 93
   panic reduction, 97, 101
   social phobia, 88
External attributions, 133
Extinction, 76
Eye contact, 87

Facial cues, 87
Family, systems approach, 228–235
Family Beliefs Inventory, 46
Family therapy, 294
Fasting, 187–189
Fear, 84
Fear and Courage (Rachman), 72, 73
Fear reduction methods, 72–102
Feeling Good (Burns), 110
Fenfluramine, 191, 192
Fetal Health Locus of Control, 45
Fiber, and cancer, 165, 166
Field studies, 5
Follow-up studies, 68, 69
Framingham study, 159
Framingham Type A Scale, 159
French-Belgian Collaborative Study, 159
Frequency count measures, 44, 45
Functional analysis, 65, 67, 68
Functional analytic psychotherapy, 289, 290
Functional exposure, 77
Fusionism, 274

Garren-Edwards gastric bubble, 193–195
Gastric bubble, 193–195
Gastric surgery, obesity, 195–197
Gemfibrozil, 147
General systems theory, 6 (*see also* Systems theory)
Generalization
   autistic children, 247
   exposure treatments, 78
   issues, 70, 71

SUBJECT INDEX

Generalized anxiety disorder, 89-95
  epidemiology, 89
  fear reduction methods, 73-102
  treatment, 89-95, 125, 126
Geriatrics (*see* Aged)
Girls, conduct disorder, 231
Group homes
  community resistance, 28
  juvenile delinquents, 36
Group leadership skills, 29, 30

Habilitation programs, 23, 24
Habituation, 76
Handbook of Behavior Therapy in Education (Witt et al.), 254
Handicapped children
  mainstreaming, 266, 268
  parents, 237, 267
Health compliance model, 17
Health psychology, 138-177
  training in, 176, 177
Health status, 137-177
Heart disease, 143-158
  cholesterol, 143-151
  mortality rates, 140-142
Heart rate
  anxiety disorders, 48, 49
  panic studies, 97, 98
Helsinki Heart Study, 147, 151
High blood pressure (*see* Hypertension)
Holistic perspective, 6
Home-based remedial programs, 243
Honolulu Heart Study, 160
Hopelessness, 54
Hostility, Type A behavior, 161
Hyperactivity, 242
Hypertension, 151-156
  alcohol restriction, 154
  sodium restriction, 153, 154
  stress reduction strategies, 154-156
  weight reduction, 154
  worksite programs, 172, 173
Hypertension Intervention Pooling Project, 155

Imaginal exposure, 77, 78
Imipramine, 90
Impulsivity, 126-128
Income level, and parent training, 231-234
Individual differences, 135
Individualized Educational Plan, 234, 235
Industry, 32-35
Informed consent, 7, 294
Inpatient detoxification, 222, 223
Inside Rational-Emotive Therapy (Bernard & DiGiuseppe), 112, 116
Institutional tours, 18, 19
Insular mothers, 231, 232
Integrationism, psychotherapy, 275-288
Interbehavioral psychology, 6
Interpersonal problem solving, 135-137
Interpersonal psychotherapy, 283-286
Interventionist parents, 240
Inventory of Interpersonal Problems, 45
Inventory of Positive Automatic Thoughts, 45
Inventory to Diagnose Depression, 45

Jejunoileal bypass, 195
Jenkins Activity Survey, 158
Job initiative, 26
Journal of Anxiety Disorders, 73
Journal of Consulting and Clinical Psychology, 60
Journal of Psychopathology and Behavioral Assessment, 44, 45
Journal of Studies on Alcohol, 215
Junior high school students, 264
Juvenile delinquency (*see* Delinquency)

Laboratory studies, 5
Lean body mass, 189
Learning disabilities, 265, 266
Life expectancy, 140-142
Linear analysis, 5, 6
Lipids (*see* Cholesterol levels)

Lung cancer
  mortality rates, 141, 142, 162, 164
  and smoking, 164, 165

Mainstreaming, 266–268
Maintenance of gains
  anxiety disorder treatment, 102
  issues, 70, 71
Management skills, anxiety, 71
Manualization of treatment, 107–109
Marital conflict
  attributions, 131, 132
  parent training effect, 229, 230
Marital Interaction Coding System, 46, 47
Mastery modeling, 81, 82
Measure of Irrational Beliefs, 45
Measurement error, 65
Medical patients, stress, 133–135
Medication (see Drug treatment)
Mental practice, 174, 175
Mental retardation
  attitudes toward, 18–20
  community integration, 23, 24
  and deinstitutionalization, 18–27
  ecological congruence, 24
  mainstreaming, 266, 267
  parent training, 236, 237
  vocational habilitation, 25, 26
Mentally retarded parents, 236, 237
Meta analysis
  behavioral therapies, 60–64
  critique, 278
  and psychotherapy, 278, 280, 281
Microcomputers, 11, 12
Millon Clinical Multiaxial Inventory, 52
Mining injuries, 35
Minnesota Heart Health Program, 211
MMPI, 50, 51
Modified Scale for Suicidal Ideation, 45
Modifiers and Perceived Stress Scale, 45
Mothers
  expectations of, 233, 234
  parent training success, 231–235
Motivation, autistic children, 245, 246

Motivational programs, 38
Multicenter Post-Infarction Program, 160
Multiple Affective Adjective Checklist, 52
Multiple Risk Factor Intervention Trial, 160
Multiple sclerosis, 134

National Cholesterol Education Program, 143, 144
National High Blood Pressure Education Program, 152
National Research Council's Diet and Health Report, 186, 187
Natural reinforcers, 289
Nature and Treatment of Anxiety Disorders, The (Taylor & Arnow), 72
Negative emotions, 113, 114
Negative social interactions, 41
Negative thoughts
  anxiety component, 85, 86
  assessment instruments, 55–57
  and psychopathology, 58–60
Neurolinguistic programming, 175
Neuropsychology, 9
Niacin, 150, 151
Nicotine gum, 204–206
Nicotine patch, 205, 206
Nicotinic acid, 151
"No-cure" criticism, 69–71
Noncompliance (see Compliance)
Nondirective counseling
  versus anxiety management, 92, 93
  versus cognitive therapy, 125
Nonlinear analysis, 5
Nonspecific effects, psychotherapy, 284, 285
Normative comparisons, 65–67
Nurses, training programs, 12
Nutrition education programs, 171, 172

Obesity, 178–200
  behavior therapy, 197–200
  and cancer, 165, 166

SUBJECT INDEX

dietary treatments, 188-191, 197, 198
drug treatment, 191-193
exercise role, 199
gastric bubble, 193-195
and hypertension, 153
long-term follow-up, 199, 200
prevalence, 179-183
Surgeon General's report, 180, 181, 184-186
surgery, 195-197
very-low-calorie diets, 188-191
worksite programs, 171, 172
Observational systems
evaluation, 46, 47
versus teacher ratings, 258, 259
Obsessive-compulsive disorder, 119
Older Adults Pleasant Events Schedule, 110
Ontogenetic explanation, 87n
Operant reinforcement, 289, 290
Oppositional behavior (see also Conduct disorder)
home versus school, 244
systems aspects, family, 229, 230
Organizational behavior, 32-35
Osheroff v. Chestnut Lodge, 291
Oslo Study Diet and Antismoking Trial, 150
Outcome, psychotherapy, 280, 283-286, 290-292
Outpatient detoxification, 222, 223
Overanxious disorder, 123-125

Panic
anxiety management training, 91
definition, 84
fear reduction methods, 73-102, 125, 126
models, 95-100
neurobiology, 96, 97
self-efficacy theory, 80-83
psychological models, 97-100
psychological treatment, 100-102, 125, 126
Paradoxical intervention, 62, 63

Parapsychology, 175
Parent-child interaction therapy, 235
Parent-professional interactions, 241, 242
Parent ratings, 259, 260
Parent training (see Behavioral parent training)
Parental expectations, 233, 234
Parents Anonymous, 253
Partner support training, 230
Path analysis, 97
Patients, perceptions of therapist, 11
Pavlovian conditioning (see Classical conditioning)
Pawtucket Heart Health Project, 211
Pedophilia, 48
Peer-mediated intervention, 260-263, 268
Performance-based exposure, 77, 78
Permissive parents, 240
Personal psychotherapy, 10
Pharmacotherapy (see Drug treatment)
Phenelzine, 88, 89
Phobic disorders (see also Agoraphobia; Panic)
attribution specificity, 53, 54
psychophysiology, 48
self-efficacy theory, 80-83
Phylogenetic explanations, 87n
Physical activity (see also Exercise)
and obesity, 187
Play therapy, 235
Plethysmography, 48
Political considerations, 30-32, 38, 39
Positive reinforcement, 238, 241
Positive thoughts
assessment instruments, 55, 56
and psychopathology, 58-60
Predictability, 85, 86
Preparedness concept, 87
Probation officers, 37
Problem Inventory for Adolescent Girls, 45
Problem-solving training, 135-137
conduct disorder, 126-131
depression, 136
Professional school model, 298, 299

Professional training
  models of, 298–300
  overview, 9–14
  personal therapy controversy, 10
Profile of Mood States, 52
Progressive relaxation, 101, 102
Project 12-Ways, 252
Protein levels, 166
Psychoanalytic training, 10
Psychodynamic therapy
  versus cognitive therapy, 110, 111
  eating disorders, 294
  eclecticism, 272, 273
  efficacy of, evidence, 292, 294
  equivalency issues, 281, 282
  versus functional analytic
    psychotherapy, 290
Psychophysiological assessment, 47–49
Psychotherapists in Clinical Practice
  (Jacobson), 295
Psychotherapy
  of behavior therapists, 9
  commonalities, 272–290
  contextual approach, 286–288
  efficacy of, 290–292
  empirical approach, 283–286
  equivalency of, 280–282
  integration, 275–288
  meta analysis, 60–64
  nonspecific effects, 284, 285
  outcome issue, 280, 283–286, 290–292
  right of effective treatment, 290–292
Public Law *94-142*, 234, 235, 266, 267

Quality of life, 15
Quality of therapy, 109

Radical behaviorism
  consumer behavior application, 33, 34
  psychotherapy approach, 286–289
  trends, 2, 3
Rapid smoking, 207, 209
Rating scales, 45, 46

Rational–emotive therapy, 111–120
  negative emotions in, 113, 114
  outcome studies, 118
  scientific status, 112
  and theory of emotion, 114, 115
Recurrence, 69
Relapse rates
  anxiety disorders, 102
  methodology, 69
  prediction of, cognition, 105, 106
Relaxation training
  generalized anxiety disorder, 93, 94
  hypertension, 154–156
  panic disorder, 101, 102
Reliable change index, 65, 66
Research, and clinical practice, 295–298
Residential settings
  community resistance, 28
  and deinstitutionalization, 27–32
  staff training, 13
Respite care services, 237
Resting metabolic rate, 187
Right to effective treatment, 290–292
Roux-en-Y gastric bypass, 195, 196
Rule-governed behavior, 287

Satiation smoking, 207, 209
Schemas, and anxiety, 121
Schools, 254–270
  acceptance of behavioral technique, 254–257
  atypical children, 265–269
  delinquency prevention, 263–265
  versus home, oppositional behavior, 244
  and parent training, 236
  peer modeling, 260–263
  systems approach, 226, 227
  teacher ratings, 258–260
Scientist-practitioner model, 298, 299
Seclusion, 240
Selenium, 166
Self-Control Rating Scale, 129
Self-efficacy
  anxiety arousal role, 81–83

SUBJECT INDEX

anxiety model, 85, 86
and panic, 80-83
and sexual behavior, AIDS, 170
theory of, 78-80
Self-help groups, 29, 30
Self-management program
in doctoral training, 11
school settings, 260, 261
Self-regulation, 18
Self-statement modification, 64
Self-talk, 122
Separation anxiety, 123-125
Sex offenders, 48
Sexual abuse, children, 248-253
Sexual arousal, 48
Sexual behavior, and AIDS, 169, 170
Sibling training, 247, 248
Signal learning, 74n
Simple phobia, 48
Simulation training, 12
Skin conductance, 48, 49
Sleep learning, 174
Smoking (see Cigarette smoking)
Smoking Education Program, 156
Social cognitive theory, 80
Social Interaction Self-Statement Inventory, 56, 57
Social interactional perspective, 229
Social interactions, 40-42
Social isolation, 124, 125
Social phobia, 87-89
attribution specificity, 53, 54
fear reduction methods, 73-102
outcome research, 88
pharmacotherapy, 88, 89
Social problem solving, 135-137
Social skills training, 268
Social support
elderly well-being, 40, 41
and parent training, 243
systems theory, children, 226
Social workers, 300
Sociopolitical considerations, 30-32, 38, 39
Sodium restriction, 153, 154
SOM model, 58, 59

Special education, 266-269
Specific criteria, 65, 67
S-R Inventory of General Trait Anxiety, 51
Stanford Five City Project, 211
State-Trait Anxiety Inventory, 51, 52
"States of mind" model, 58, 59
Statistical criteria, 65
"Step-One Diet," 145, 148, 149
"Step-Two Diet," 145
Stereotypes, 18
Stimulus exposure (see Exposure technique)
Stress inoculation, 133-135
Stress reduction strategies
Army Research Institute evaluation, 175
hypertension, 154-156
Suicidal patients, 136, 137
Supervision model, 13
Supportive family treatment, 36, 37
Surgeon General's Report on Nutrition and Health, 180, 181, 184-186
Surgeon General's report on smoking, 202, 203
Surgery patients, 133
SyberVision, 174, 175
Symptom Checklist 90, 52
Systems theory
child abuse, 250
children, 225-228
evaluation, 6
family setting, 228-235

Task-irrelevant thinking, 122
Taylor Manifest Anxiety Scale, 51
Teacher-Child Interaction Project, 254
Teachers
acceptance of behavioral procedures, 254-257
behavioral training, 255
contingent verbal approval, 260
perception of handicapped, 267
Teachers' ratings
versus observational data, 258, 259

Teachers' ratings (*continued*)
  parent rating comparison, 259, 260
  research on, 46
Teaching-family model, 30
Technical eclecticism, 273-275
Technology, 7
Tenuate, 192
Test anxiety, 124
Therapeutic relationship
  and psychotherapy integration, 278
  in rational-emotive therapy, 115
  and training programs, 11
Therapists
  competence of, 109
  training effects, 130
Time-out
  acceptability to children, 240
  value of, 241
Tobacco use (*see* Cigarette smoking)
Token economy, 27, 28
Training programs, 298-300
  models of, 298-300
  paraprofessionals, 12-14
  personal therapy in, 10
  professionals, 9-12
  and therapist effectiveness, 130
Transference concept, 276, 277
Treatment acceptability, 238, 239
Treatment manuals, 107-109
Type A behavior, 158-162
  components, 161
  prospective studies, 159-161
  research trends, 161, 162

Uncontrollability, 85, 86

Vegetarian diets, 154
Verbal approval rates, 260
Verbal control, 287
Vermont home study, 30-32, 38
Vertical-banded gastroplasty, 195, 196
Very-low-calorie diets, 188-191
  Council on Scientific Affairs Report, 187
  and exercise, 190, 191
  maintenance of gains, 190, 191
  popularity of, 188
Vocational adjustment, 25, 26
Vulnerability, depression, 104-106

Weight reduction
  cancer control, 165, 166
  and hypertension, 153
  worksite programs, 171, 172
Western Collaborative Group Study, 159
Work productivity, 26
Worksite programs, 171-174
World Congress on Cognitive Therapy (1989), 104

Zung Self-Rating Anxiety Scale, 51, 52
Zung Self-Rating Depression Scale, 50